Texts and Studies in Ancient Judaism

Texte und Studien zum Antiken Judentum

Herausgegeben von / Edited by

Peter Schäfer (Princeton, NJ)
Annette Y. Reed (Philadelphia, PA)
Seth Schwartz (New York, NY)
Azzan Yadin (New Brunswick, NJ)

139

Holger Michael Zellentin

Rabbinic Parodies of Jewish and Christian Literature

Mohr Siebeck

HOLGER MICHAEL ZELLENTIN, born 1976; Studies of Religion in Strasbourg, Amsterdam, Jerusalem, Philadelphia and Princeton; taught Rabbinics and Late Antique Judaism in New Brunswick, New Jersey, and in Berkeley, California; beginning 2011 Lecturer in Religious Studies at the University of Nottingham, UK.

ISBN 978-3-16-150647-5
ISSN 0721-8753 (Texts and Studies in Ancient Judaism)

Die Deutsche Nationalbibliothek lists this publication in the Deutsche Nationalbiblio-graphie; detailed bibliographic data is available in the Internet at *http://dnb.d-nb.de*.

The book was typeset by Martin Fischer in Tübingen using Stempel Garamond and OdysseaU typeface, printed on non-aging paper and bound by Gulde-Druck in Tübingen.

Printed in Germany.

Acknowledgments

The present work is a complete revision of my 2007 PhD dissertation, *Late Antiquity Upside Down: Rabbinic Parodies of Jewish and Christian Literature*, written at the Department of Religion at Princeton University. Original work is always the product of many conversations; the present one is no exception. While it may be impossible to give due credit to all the voices that have inspired and supported me in this project, I will attempt to name some of the friends and scholars whose imprint on my thinking seems most prominent to me. At the same time, I want to ask forgiveness from those who have slipped my increasingly treacherous memory.

I want to name first my teacher, mentor, advisor, and true *Doktorvater*, Peter Schäfer. Seeking to specify how much energy he has invested over the past ten years in supporting my training and my scholarly work before, during, and even after my candidacy at Princeton would fill up many pages. Instead, I want to single out my gratitude for convincing me to tether my literary analyses of ancient texts more firmly to the socio-historical realities of their times. Peter's insistence on checking literary arguments for parody more thoroughly against the accessible historical background has profoundly shaped my dissertation and this book, as well as my approach to ancient Judaism in general.

Four scholars especially have made valuable suggestions for the book in its present form. Richard Kalmin and Burton Visotzky have read the entire manuscript and provided me with extensive feedback; their many suggestions helped sharpen my arguments and have reduced the number of faults in this book. Jeffrey Rubenstein and Joshua Levinson have likewise made valuable comments. The support of all four of them has proven essential at a time when it seemed easy losing my orientation in the maze of research and publishing. Joshua Levinson, moreover, taught me to read rabbinic texts as literature at the Hebrew University more than a decade ago, and has provided me with inspiration and guidance as I completed the present work.

Exhausted readers of this book will never know how much they are indebted to the untiring efforts of Noam Manor, who has rendered many of the most opaque of my thoughts into more intelligible language, and has ruthlessly exorcised the most blatant idiosyncrasies of my own penchant for literary playfulness. (For better or for worse, I have not heeded his suggestions at all times.) I also want to thank Jennifer Mann, Elisheva Sperber, Mira Wasserman, Naomi Seidman, Lisa Cerami, Daniel Boyarin, and Deborah Cohen for their editorial and scholarly suggestions.

Thinking about my scholarly identity in broader terms, I then want to express my gratitude to my teachers and fellow students at Princeton's Department of Religion, especially to the readers of my dissertation, Martha Himmelfarb and Annemarie Luijendijk, for their valuable advice and inspiring conversation. The same holds true for John Gager, Jeffrey Stout, Elaine Pagels, Cornell West, Annette Yoshiko Reed, Ra'anan Boustan, Moulie Vidas, and Eduard Iricinschi, whose scholarly companionship carried me through many dire straits, and who made it all seem worth it in those doubtful moments.

My colleagues at the Graduate Theological Union and at the University of California, Berkeley, have lent me invaluable assistance during the past three years. Many cups of coffee, water and wine, or bicycle rides with David Biale, Ronald Hendel, Arthur Holder, Erich Gruen, Christopher Ocker, Robert Alter, Inese Radzins, Munir Jiwa, and Emily Gottreich have made all the difference during my stay in Berkeley. Conversation, inspiration, encouragement and help provided over the years by Charlotte Elisheva Fonrobert, Israel Yuval, David Nirenberg, Averil Cameron, Carol Bakhos, Froma Zeitlin, Jan Joosten, David Kangas, Fred Astren, Daniel Stoekl-Ben Ezra, Irene Zwiep, Menahem Kister, Riki Ophir, Zehavit Stern, George Sutton, Anna Hoekstra, Victor Kal, and Howard Gold will likewise not be forgotten. Writing of the loving support and ironic gaze of those seven sharing my surname has fallen victim to censorship.

The institutional support I have received from the following organizations has made the writing of this work possible: The Graduate Theological Union; the Joint Doctoral Program in Jewish Studies and the Ancient History and Mediterranean Archeology Group at the University of California, Berkeley, and, at Princeton University, the Department of Religion, the Center for the Study of Religion, the Program in Jewish Studies, and the Program in the Ancient World. Last but not least I want to thank the editors of *Studies in Ancient Judaism* and the excellent staff of Mohr Siebeck, especially Henning Ziebritzki, for their support in the present and the previous publications.

Holger Zellentin   Berkeley, June 12, 2010

Table of Contents

"For Out of Babylon Shall Go Forth the Torah:"
A Few Notes on Parody and the Rabbis
(Yerushalmi *Nedarim* 6.13, 40a)

Parody is constituted by literary repetition of a text in a manner that introduces some variation; most succinctly put, it is repetition with a difference. The Late Antique Rabbis, however, habitually repeat tradition in new contexts, creating difference devoid of parody. How, then, do we recognize parodic difference? The following story from the Palestinian Talmud (henceforth: Yerushalmi) marks its repetition of Scripture as grotesquely different and thereby as charged with parody.

In the wake of the Bar Kokhba revolt, Rabbi Hananya migrates from Palestine to Babylonia and apparently lives in the town of Nahar Paqod.[1] There, he adds a month to that year's calendar in order to maintain the synchronicity of the Jewish lunar year with the natural solar year. Intercalation is a serious matter, normally governed exclusively by the rabbinic authorities in Palestine, and only when it is impossible for them do so is one allowed to intercalate in the Diaspora.[2] At the time of the story, however,

---

[1] In this book, "Palestine" denotes the Rabbis' "Land of Israel" according to common geographic usage without any intended comment on the current political situation. Likewise, "Babylonia" denotes the Rabbis' dwelling place in the Sasanian Empire in Mesopotamia, situated in modern day Iraq, again following common scholarly usage. On the Babylonian town Nahar Paqod, see, for example, *Betsa* 29a, *Ketubot* 27b, and *Hulin* 127a; see also Adolphe Neubauer, *La géographie du Talmud* (Paris: Michel Lévy frères, 1868), 363–365, and Aharon Oppenheimer, *Babylonia Judaica in the Talmudic Period* (Wiesbaden: Dr. Ludwig Reichert, 1983), 300–305. Oppenheimer persuasively argues that the story "does not seem to constitute proof that Hananiah's study house was in Nahar Paqod, and [the Palestinian Talmud, which relates the event] may have used the place name because it was known from the Prophets ... or for some other reason ... The name Paqod appears in Jeremiah as a synonym for Babylonia (Jer. 50:21, cf. Ezek. 23:23), Oppenheimer, ibid., 304.

[2] The exceptions to the rule that intercalation must occur in Palestine are discussed in the Palestinian Talmud, *Sanhedrin* 1,2/27 (19a) and *Nedarim* 6,13/11 (40a). See the extensive discussion in Isaiah M. Gafni, *Land, Center and Diaspora: Jewish Constructs in Late Antiquity* (Sheffield: Sheffield Academic Press, 1997), 102–11 as well as Sacha Stern, *Calendar and Community: A History of the Jewish Calendar, 2nd Century BCE–10th Century CE* (Oxford: Oxford University Press, 2001), 27–101; Aharon Oppenheimer, "The Attempt of Hananya, Son of Rabbi Joshua's Brother, to Intercalate the Year in Babylonia: A Comparison of the Traditions in the Jerusalem and Babylonian Talmuds," in: Peter

rabbinic authority had been reestablished in Palestine, and Rabbi Isaac and Rabbi Nathan are sent from Palestine to Babylonia to reprove Hananya for usurping a privilege reserved for the Palestinian Rabbis. They do so by repeating Scripture – with a difference:[3]

Rabbi Isaac stood up and read: "It is written in the Torah 'these are the appointed festivals of Hananya, the nephew of Rabbi Joshua.'"

[The Babylonian Rabbis] said: "These are the appointed festivals of G-d [the holy convocations, which you shall celebrate at the time appointed for them (Leviticus 23:4)]!"[4]

[Rabbi Isaac] said to them: In our place [גבן, i.e., in Israel, this is so, but here?]

Rabbi Nathan stood up and finished [the Scriptural citation]: "For out of Babylon shall go forth the Torah and the word of G-d from Nahar Paqod."

[The Babylonian Rabbis] said to him: "[No, it is written]: For out of Zion shall go forth Torah, and the word of G-d from Jerusalem" (Isaiah 2:3)!

He said to them: In our place [גבן, i.e. in Israel, this is so, but here?].[5]

As Dov Noy aptly noted over half a century ago, the passage is a clear instance of rabbinic parody.[6] Parody, according to Linda Hutcheon, is "a form of repetition with ironic critical distance, marking difference rather than similarity."[7] The Yerushalmi very clearly marks the differences between Scripture and its parodic repetition. In response to the parody, the Babylonian Rabbis in the Yerushalmi protest by repeating Scripture correctly, without parodic difference. Rabbi Isaac and Rabbi Nathan use this as an opportunity to point out that they imitate and distort Scripture in a way that emphasizes Hananya's impertinence. Their parodic version of the To-

---

Schäfer (ed.), *The Talmud Yerushalmi and Graeco-Roman Culture*, vol. II (Tübingen: Mohr Siebeck 2000), 255–63;" and Abraham Burstein, "לבעית עיבורי השנה בחוץ-לארץ," *Sinai* 19 (38) (1955), 32–46; esp. ibid., "עיבורי השנה בנהרדעא ובעסיא," *Sinai* 20 (41) 1957, 387–99.

[3] The Yerushalmi was redacted between the middle of the fourth and the middle of the fifth century. See Günther Stemberger, *Introduction to Talmud and Midrash* (Edinburgh: T&T Clark, 1996), 170–73 for further discussion and bibliography.

[4] The rabbis always abbreviate the Tetragrammaton and usually only cite the first two letters, *yud* and *heh*. Throughout this book, I follow this rabbinic practice by translating the Tetragrammaton as G-d and the term *elohim* as God.

[5] Yerushalmi *Nedarim* 6,13/13 (40a); see Peter Schäfer and Hans-Jürgen Becker (eds.), *Synopse zum Talmud Yerushalmi III* (Tübingen: Mohr Siebeck 1998), 256. All translations in this book, unless otherwise noted, are mine. Manuscript Leiden does not show any meaningful difference from the *Editio Princeps Venice*. The text also appears in the Palestinian Talmud, *Sanhedrin* 1,2/28–29 (19a), cited in ibid., *Synopse zum Talmud Yerushalmi IV* (Tübingen: Mohr Siebeck 1995), 160–61, with some distortions (for example, it is Rabban Gamliel who sends the two rabbis to Babylonia, not Rabbi Judah haNasi, and a verb is missing). The Babylonian Talmud retells this story in strikingly different ways, and without parody, in *Berakhot* 63a–b. For a comparison between the two stories, see Isaiah Gafni, *Land, Center and Diaspora*, 108–12.

[6] Dov Noy, "הפארודיה בספרות ישראל הקדומה," *Mahanayim* 54 (1961–62), 92–99.

[7] Linda Hutcheon, *A Theory of Parody: The Teachings of Twentieth-Century Art Forms* (Urbana and Chicago: University of Illinois Press, 2000), xii.

rah begins by citing the original, but they then state that the festivals are not God's but Hananya's and that Torah does not go forth from Zion but rather from Babylonia. The Palestinian Rabbis claim that if one were to allow the intercalation of months outside of Israel, one would, writes Noy, effectively "turn Zion into Babylonia and Jerusalem into Nahar Paqod."[8] Moreover, the story associates Hananya with the Tetragrammaton.[9] It thereby accuses Hananya of taking the place of the One whom the Rabbis perceive as the divine author of Scripture, an outrage rarely paralleled in rabbinic literature.[10] The format, finally, imitates the ancient synagogal presentation of the Torah: Rabbi Isaac reads from the Pentateuch, and Rabbi Nathan completes the reading, in the style of the *haftarah*, with a passage from the Prophets.[11] The seriousness of the format only heightens the tension with the absurdity of the content.

The text, however, does not wish to satirize Scripture or the Judaic tradition but to protect both against Hananya's alleged transgression. Linda Hutcheon writes that "parody ... is a form of imitation, but imitation characterized by ironic inversion, not always at the expense of the parodied texts."[12] In other words, the story seeks to expose the understanding of Scripture effectuated by Hananya's actions, an understanding that subverts Palestinian rabbinic authority over Babylonia.[13] The Yerushalmi uses parody in order to underline the discrepancy between Scripture and Hananya's actions. When the Babylonian Rabbis in turn rectify Isaac's and Nathan's citations, the two Palestinian sages respond: yes, in Israel this is how we would cite Scripture, but Babylonian Rabbis apparently hold a different po-

---

[8] My translation. Dov Noy, "הפארודיה בספרות ישראל הקדומה," 95.

[9] The parallel of the story in Yerushalmi *Sanhedrin* (see note 6 above) places the name of G-d next to that of Hananya, slightly softening the theological brazenness of the parody by avoiding the full substitution of G-d with a rabbi.

[10] See, e.g. Yevamot 105b. The only other instance in the Judaic tradition known to me in which the Tetragrammaton signifies someone other than the Jewish God occurs in the Hekhalot literature; see Peter Schäfer, *Synopse zur Hekhalot-Literatur* (Tübingen: Mohr Siebeck, 1981), § 15. Rabbinic familiarity with this literature is indicated by *Hagigah* 15a and *Sanhedrin* 38b. On rabbinic responses to Christian claims to G-d's name, see Peter Schäfer, *Jesus in the Talmud* (Princeton: Princeton University Press, 2007), 57–60.

[11] On the antiquity of the practice of Haftarah readings, see Charles Perrot, "The Reading of the Bible in the Ancient Synagogue," in Martin Jan Mulder (ed.), *Mikra: Text, Translation, Reading, and Interpretation of the Hebrew Bible in Ancient Judaism and Early Christianity* (Assen: Van Gorcum; Philadelphia: Fortress Press, 1988), 137–159, and Avigdor Shinan, "Sermons, Targums, and the Reading from Scriptures in the Ancient Synagogue," in Lee Levine (ed.), *The Synagogue in Late Antiquity* (Philadelphia: American Schools of Oriental Research, 1987), 97–110.

[12] Linda Hutcheon, *A Theory of Parody*, 6.

[13] Dov Noy suggests that "The Sages of Israel put the parody in the mouth of R. Hananya; he, as it were, is the parodist who ridicules the words of Scripture." (Dov Noy, "הפארודיה בספרות ישראל הקדומה," 95.) This formulation, while attractive in its pithiness, might take the conflation of the story's attribution of speech acts a little too far.

sition. As is often the case in rabbinic literature, the biblical punchline is not quoted in the text; rather, it is the continuation of the scriptural citation that the learned rabbinic audience is expected to grasp: all Jews must celebrate the festivals *at the time appointed for them* in Palestine and not according to Hananya's intercalation.[14] The Palestinian Rabbis eventually prevail.

Thus, the legal discourse in this passage from the Yerushalmi simultaneously uses and problematizes parody. It uses parody in order to expose Hananya's actions at the same time that it associates parody with transgression of rabbinic ritual law (henceforth halakha). The Yerushalmi does so in order to bolster its own authority over the Babylonian renegades. The parody is staged during a precise historical moment: Isaiah Gafni has described the halakhic and socio-political tension between the Rabbis of Palestine and Babylonia.[15] Accordingly, I argue that the amoraic rabbinic literature[16] of the fourth to the seventh centuries CE, the Palestinian Midrashim, the Yerushalmi, and the Babylonian Talmud (henceforth: Bavli) all addressed discursive tensions of their times by parodying literature and exegesis produced by Rabbis and by Greek and Syriac Christian authors. Such parodies appear, within narrowly defined limits, amidst the Rabbis' generally serious halakhic and midrashic discourse. These parodies, though not common, illuminate the Rabbis' practice of criticizing themselves and their opponents within and beyond their own groups and may lead us to reevaluate all instances of rabbinic repetition with a difference as expressions of possible critical distance.

---

[14] The Yerushalmi quotes the same scriptural citation, Leviticus 23:4, in a section that immediately precedes the parodic passage, using it as an exhortation to ensure the precision of calendrical calculations.

[15] On the story and its historical background, see Isaiah Gafni, *Land, Center and Diaspora*, 96–117, Jacob Neusner, *A History of the Jews of Babylonia* (Leiden: Brill, 1965), Volume I, 113–21, and Wilhelm Bacher, *Die Agada der Tannaiten* (Strasbourg: K.J. Trübner, 1890f.), 390 note 4. Rabbinic stories reflect specific moments in history yet rarely are those moments the ones described in the story. This, like most other rabbinic stories, likely postdates the events described therein by several generations. The adulthood of Rabbi Nathan and Rabbi Isaac (fourth generation Tannaim) may not have overlapped with that of Rabbi Hananya (a second generation Tanna, see the following note for the term).

[16] The term "amoraic literature" refers to texts redacted in the fourth through the seventh centuries CE that present the teachings and lives of the *amoraim*, the rabbis of the early third through the end of the fifth centuries CE and their predecessors, the *tannaim*. There is little sign of parody in the "tannaitic literature," the rabbinic literature redacted in the third and fourth centuries C.E, yet the issue does call for a thorough examination. For definitions of these terms, see Günther Stemberger, *Introduction to Talmud and Midrash* (Edinburgh: T&T Clark, 1996), 7. It should also be noted that the manuscripts of all rabbinic texts are from medieval times. I will consider the possibility of medieval emendations to the late ancient rabbinic sources where appropriate. For the importance of individual manuscripts, see Peter Schäfer's essay "Research into Rabbinic Literature: An Attempt to Define the *Status Quaestionis*," *Journal of Jewish Studies* 37 (1986), 139–152 and the ensuing debate in the same journal.

Blessed Are the Cheese Makers: Parody and Satire

The mishearing of "peacemakers" as "cheese makers" in Monty Python's Sermon on the Mount epitomizes timeless elements of parody as "a form of repetition with ironic critical distance, marking difference rather than similarity."[17] My definition of parody does not treat rabbinic parody as a "genre" but rather as a literary technique that is firmly embedded in the established rabbinic genres such as the talmudic *sugya*, the midrashic sermon, and midrashic exegesis. Instead of defining what parody *is*, I attempt to reach the most nuanced characterization that can serve as the basis for analyzing the largest possible number of rabbinic parodies. My approach follows Linda Hutcheon's well-known study (with some important historical strictures) as well as a little-noticed gem of literary theory, Patrick O'Neill's *The Comedy of Entropy*.[18]

Most contemporary theorists, Linda Hutcheon among them, seek to differentiate between a parody's nuanced way of relating to other texts on the one hand, and comical criticism, or satire, on the other.[19] Hutcheon asks:

[Parody's] repetition is always of another discursive text. The ethos of that act of repetition can vary, but its "target" is always intramural in this sense. How, then, does parody come to be confused with satire, which is extramural (social, moral) in its ameliorative aim to hold up to ridicule the vices and follies of mankind, with an eye to their correction?[20]

Hutcheon does not view satire, but rather textual markers of difference (i.e., irony) as the core of parody; at the same time, she grants the possibility, and even the frequent occurrence, of the interaction between parody and satire.[21] Others, like Margaret Rose, consider satire an integral part of parody.[22] Hutcheon's differentiation between parody and satire has rightly found wide acclaim in contemporary literary theory. Accordingly, all parodies in this book are *ironic parodies*. At the same time, however, I restrict my own discussion in the present book to parodies that also contain satirical elements: *satirical parodies*. While my focus on satirical parodies restricts the corpus of inquiry, each individual example can be assessed against the

---

[17] Linda Hutcheon, *A Theory of Parody*, xii.

[18] Patrick O'Neill, *The Comedy of Entropy: Humour, Narrative, Reading* (Toronto: University of Toronto Press, 1990). O'Neill's book is not concerned with Greco-Roman humorous discourse beyond Plato, Aristotle, and Aristophanes and, despite its merits, presents irony and parody as predominantly modern phenomena.

[19] Hutcheon, *A Theory of Parody*, 6, 20–21, 50–69.

[20] Hutcheon, *A Theory of Parody*, 43.

[21] Hutcheon, *A Theory of Parody*, 25, 30–49.

[22] Margaret Rose, *Parody//Metafiction: An Analysis of Parody as a Critical Mirror to the Writing and Reception of Fiction* (London: Croom Helm, 1979).

background of a broader basis of evidence, as becomes clear when considering the relationship of irony and satire.

I shall define irony as an implicit and allusive and satire as an explicit and demonstrative form of critical humor. According to this view, irony hints at the incongruity of several realities, without guiding the audience to appreciate these realities' actual collision within the text.[23] Satire, accordingly, marks the incongruity more clearly, and often implies or even offers a remedy; satirical parodies are therefore more evident than ironic ones. Restriction to satirical parodies for the purpose of this study will promote a better understanding of the literary function of rabbinic parodies. Investigation of rabbinic parodies in the context of their inner- and extra-textual targets as well as close attention to the historical circumstances in which these parodies were produced, yield additional evidence. Future discussions may consider ways in which rabbis ironize the texts they retell on a much broader scale; I regard this study as the first step in the reassessment of rabbinic modes of repetition.[24] For the same reason, I consider parodic

---

[23] See esp. Hutcheon's subtle outline of the relationship between irony and parody, *A Theory of Parody*, 50–68. In the words of O'Neill, irony "is a form of humor situation that is not necessarily or even usually actualized as comic experience" (*The Comedy of Entropy*, 79). The meaning of the term *eironeia*, originally denoting telling a lie, apparently shifted in the course of Plato's lifetime. In Plato, it means the stylistic telling of non-truths that the audience is meant to recognize, a line of thought more fully developed as *ironia* by Cicero and Quintilian. See Claire Colebrook, *Irony* (London: Routledge, 2004), 1–41; Melissa Lane, "The Evolution of Eironeia in Classical Greek Texts: Why Socratic Eironeia is not Socratic Irony", *Oxford Studies in Ancient Philosophy* 31 (2006), 49–83; Paul de Man, *Aesthetic Ideology* (Minneapolis: University of Minnesota Press, 1996); D.C. Muecke, *Irony and the Ironic* (London: Methuen, 1970); ibid., *Irony: The Critical Idiom* (Fakenham: Methuen, 1970); Northrop Frye, *Anatomy of Criticism: Four Essays* (New York: Athenaeum, 1957) and Linda Hutcheon's subtle outline of the relationship between irony and parody in *A Theory of Parody*, 50–68. Cf. also Daniel Boyarin's attempt to relate Socratic irony to the Bavli in *Socrates and the Fat Rabbis*.

[24] Hutcheon's differentiation between satire and parody is certainly helpful for the study of texts ancient and modern but it may be too subtle a differentiation for the present study of rabbinic texts in light of our far-reaching ignorance about them. Several recent studies pay very close attention to the use of irony in rabbinic literature, most importantly Joshua Levinson, who discusses many instances of ironic exegesis in *The Twice Told Tale: A Poetics of Exegtical Narrative in Rabbinic Midrash* (Jerusalem: The Hebrew University Magnes Press, 2005), see index, אירוניה [Hebrew]. Furthermore, see Peter Schäfer, "Rabbis and Priests, or: How to Do Away with the Glorious Past of the Sons of Aaron," in Gregg Gardner and Kevin Osterloh (eds.), *Antiquity in Antiquity: Jewish and Christian Pasts in the Greco-Roman World* (Tübingen: Mohr Siebeck, 2008), 155–172 and James A. Diamond, "King David of the Sages: Rabbinic Rehabilitation or Ironic Parody?," *Prooftexts* 27 (2007), 373–426. Despite the title, Diamond's persuasive study does not discuss the parodic ways in which the ironic texts he discusses relate to the biblical texts they repeat. See also Azzan Yadin, *Scripture as Logos: Rabbi Ishmael and the Origins of Midrash* (Pennsylvania: University of Pennsylvania Press, 2004), 188; pace Alexander Samely, "Scripture's Implicature: the Midrashic Assumptions of Relevance and Consistency," in *Journal of Semitic Studies* 37 (1992), 192. I suggest irony in the Tosefta's story of Rabbi

imitation and parodic allusion as contiguous modes of parody; I distinguish between them only in order to mark various degrees of intensity of textual imitation (as will become relevant especially in the case of parodies of non-rabbinic texts.

Collective Rabbinic Authorship

Investigation into rabbinic parody and satire requires grappling with the question of authorship. The precise historical identities of the authors of the rabbinic texts in general and their parodic intention in particular are largely unknowable. The texts themselves, however, do provide some information about their authors and audience. As the example from the Yerushalmi already makes clear, rabbinic literature is hyper-textual: it presupposes its audience's knowledge of the Hebrew Bible and previous rabbinic texts. To paraphrase David Kraemer's felicitous summary, the intended reader of the Babylonian Talmud is required to consider many texts simultaneously without losing track of their relationship to one another and their intrinsic hierarchy.[25] (This is true for Palestinian rabbinic literature as well.) Amending Kraemer's view, I would emphasize the oral performative nature of rabbinic texts, to which its authors and intended audience were finely attuned; I will thus refer to an "audience" rather than "readers."[26] The rabbis' orality

---

Eleazar ben Dama in Tosefta *Hulin* 2.22–23, see Chapter Five, note 121. See also note 72 below and Conclusion, notes 2 and 47.

[25] A member of the Bavli's intended audience, according to Kraemer, "lived and studied in … Babylonia … [H]e was a member of a schooled elite who understood Scripture in its original language, committed much of scripture to memory, and was able to apply certain specialized methods to its interpretation. He also commanded significant quantities of Mishna and related texts …[I]ts intended reader also required considerable ingenuity and intellectual prowess." David Kraemer, *Reading the Rabbis: The Talmud as Literature* (New York: Oxford University Press, 1996), 12.

[26] "The oralist approach to the rabbinic text," Martin Jaffee writes, "is a variant of the intertextualist approach to literary interpretation combined as well with a kind of 'audience-response' sensibility." Martin Jaffee, "What Difference Does the 'Orality' of Rabbinic Writing Make for the Interpretation of Rabbinic Writings?" in Matthew Kraus (ed.), *How Should Rabbinic Literature Be Read in the Modern World?* (Piscataway, NJ: Gorgias Press, 2006), 20. See also Martin Jaffee, *Torah in the Mouth: Writing and Oral Tradition in Palestinian Judaism, 200 BCE–400 CE* (New York: Oxford University Press, 2001). For the Bavli, see Yaakov Elman, "Orality and the Redaction of the Babylonian Talmud," *Oral Tradition* 14 (1999), 52–99 and Yaakov Sussman, כוחו של תורה שבעל פה' פשוטה כמשמעה: "קוצו של יו'ד," in: *Mehkere talmud: Kovets mehkarim be-talmud uvi-tehumim govlim* (Jerusalem, The Hebrew University Magnes Press, 2005), vol. III, 209–384. For the Mishna see Elizabeth Shanks Alexander, *Transmitting Mishnah: The Shaping Influence of Oral Tradition* (Cambridge: Cambridge University Press, 2006). For a summary discussion, see Martin Jaffee, "Oral Tradition and Rabbinic Studies," *Oral Tradition* 18 (2003), 37–39

must therefore guide our understanding of rabbinic literature as a literary remnant of a much broader oral tradition.

Balancing the textual evidence of parody with the social circumstances of its historical authors (i.e., with rabbinic cultures as such) adapts to the uncertainty regarding rabbinic authorship. This goes beyond the inclusion of satire in the study of parody. In the words of Hutcheon, we should consider "the parodic text's entire 'situation' in the world" – the time and the place, the ideological frame of reference, the personal as well as the social context – not only of the instigator of parody but also of its receiver."[27] Accordingly, I seek to integrate literary evidence into a historical study and historical evidence into literary analysis.[28] Parody is never an isolated literary exercise, and I will demonstrate that Palestinian rabbinic literature in particular relies on a plethora of cultural and literary prerequisites that are external to the text as we have it and can only be reconstructed by situating this literature in its late antique context. This applies to the Bavli as well, which on the whole extends more guidance to its audience.

I attempt to combine under the concept of *author* all evidence of the text's meaning – inscribed through literary means, checked against the plausible intention of its elusive historical producers, and including the oral-performative nature of the text.[29] A return to authorship and authorial intent does

---

and Martin Jaffee, "Oral Tradition in the Writings of Rabbinic Oral Torah: On Theorizing Rabbinic Orality," *Oral Tradition* 14 (1999), 3–32.

[27] Linda Hutcheon, *A Theory of Parody*, xiii.

[28] On the problems of relating a text to the world, see Dominick LaCapra, *Rethinking Intellectual History: Texts, Contexts, Language* (Ithaca: Cornell University Press, 1983), 23–71. We must not forget that we do not have unmediated access to any ancient society. Literature, however, is a social artifact, allowing us fruitfully to speculate on ancient societies *qua* societies. The linguistic and cultural efforts of recent scholarship to enhance the study of late ancient societies are illustrated, for example, in the work of Elizabeth Clark. See Elizabeth Clark, *History, Theory, Text: Historians and the Linguistic Turn* (Cambridge, MA: Harvard University Press, 2004.) See also a collection of essays responding to Clark, Dale B. Martin, and Patricia Cox Miller (eds.), *The Cultural Turn in Late Ancient Studies: Gender, Asceticism, and Historiography* (Durham, NC: Duke University Press, 2005).

[29] David Kraemer, citing Owen Fiss, writes: "Some critics continue to maintain that meaning is controlled by the text (this paradigm has surely dominated in talmudic studies). Others, in recent years, have argued that meaning is the construct of a reader ... [I]t seems ... reasonable, in practice, to locate the construction of meaning somewhere between these two extremes. The formulation of Owen Fiss suggests a practical balance: 'Interpretation, whether it be in the law or literary domains, is neither a wholly discretionary nor a wholly mechanical activity. It is a dynamic interaction between reader and text, and meaning the product of that interaction;" David Kraemer, *Reading the Rabbis: The Talmud as Literature*, 11, citing Owen Fiss, "Objectivity and Interpretation," in Sanford Levinson and Steven Mailloux (eds.), *Interpreting Law and Literature* (Evanston: Northwestern University Press, 1988 [1982]), 229. My approach is similar to Kraemer's; in addition, I seek to historicize both the text's author and his audience.

not need to ignore the valuable lessons derived in the process of overcoming these analytic conventions in the past decades.[30] Hence, I use the term author, in the singular, in order to determine the most likely historical intention of the man, or men, who shaped the rabbinic text in its fullest form.[31] For reasons of brevity, I occasionally speak of the text's intention, in which case I refer to the intention of its author(s).

The meaning of authorial intention, however, may differ from one rabbinic tradition to the other. To abbreviate a longstanding debate, I maintain that Palestinian rabbinic literature, in general, usually cannot be reduced to a single theme or idea.[32] Here, midrashic polysemy prevails by creating a composite and not necessarily consistent message; two opposing views often appear side by side. This composite style, however, still contains an identifiable hierarchy that one can relate to authorial intent, and parts of the text can have a parodic relationship to other parts of the same text or to previous texts. Moreover, even though this debate concerning Palestinian rabbinic literature is far from over, I suggest reading the Palestinian rabbinic parodies first and foremost as products of the temporally bound environment in which they were finally redacted. Hence, the concept of a midrashic author of a parody seems to be an effective tool of analysis (as I shall seek to show in Chapters Two and Five, and in the conclusion).

In the case of the Bavli, I maintain that the residual midrashic polysemy is subsumed under an even more distinct authorial voice. Recent scholarship has moved towards attributing the Bavli's extant text – and retrievable literary message – to the *stam*, its anonymous redactor, editor, or author, a

---

[30] Hutcheon rightly points out that "even in a theoretical age like our own that has cast deep suspicion on the concept of intentionality, the experience of interpreting parody *in practice* forces us to acknowledge at least an inference of intention and to theorize that inference." *A Theory of Parody*, xiii; see also 84–99. It is noteworthy that even a scholar so closely associated with modern literary theory as Daniel Boyarin has found his way back to accepting that authorial intent has some value in determining a text's meaning, see *Socrates and the Fat Rabbis* (Chicago: University of Chicago Press, 2009), 200–10.

[31] I assume that women had occasional access to rabbinic literature in late antiquity and certainly influenced its making, but I also hold that the authors of rabbinic texts and their intended audience are (defined as) predominantly male. For further discussion of the role of women in shaping talmudic discourse and scholarship on the matter, see Chapter Four.

[32] Among the many studies addressing the issue of midrashic polysemy (and its limits) are Joshua Levinson's, "אחת דיבר אלהים שתים זו שמעתי': קריאה דיאלוגית בסיפור הדרשני,", in ibid., Jacob Elbaum, and Galit Hasan-Rokem (eds.), *Higayon L'Yona: New Aspects in the Study of Midrash Aggadah and Piyut in Honor of Professor Yona Frenkel* (Jerusalem: The Hebrew University Magnes Press, 2006), 405–432; Daniel Boyarin, "De/re/constructing Midrash," in Carol Bakhos (ed.), *Current Trends in the Study of Midrash* (Leiden: Brill 2006), 299–322; ibid., *Intertextuality and the Reading of Midrash* (Bloomington: Indiana University Press, 1990); William Cutter, "Citing and Translating a Context: the Talmud in its 'Post Modern' Setting," *Judaism* 39 (1990), 104–111; David Stern, "Midrash and Indeterminacy," *Critical Inquiry* 5 (1988), 132–161; William Scott Green, "Romancing the Tome: Rabbinic Hermeneutics and the Theory of Literature," *Semeia* 40 (1987), 147–168.

turn that has been met with some resistance.[33] Such criticism of the over-emphasis of the *historical* role of the stam in the redaction of the Bavli may be justified. I have, however, pursued the present study in a way that may not be affected by the outcome of the debate. As long as the rabbinic texts I describe here were performed and reenacted in the final stages of their stammaitic redaction, it seems admissible to attribute authorial intention to those later performers whose discursive realm we can reconstruct based on the texts in our possession.[34] Moreover, the Babylonian parodies discussed in this book seem to presuppose some knowledge of other parts of the Bavli, again suggesting that they are from stammaitic times (as I shall show in Chapters One, Three, and Four).

---

[33] Current scholarship on the textual history of the Babylonian Talmud dates its final redaction, and thereby its current form, to between the fifth and the seventh centuries. A more precise dating is not essential for my purposes. See the useful, yet somewhat dated summary in Günther Stemberger, *Introduction to Talmud and Midrash*, 194–206 and especially Richard Kalmin, *The Redaction of the Babylonian Talmud: Amoraic or Saboraic?* (Cincinnati: Hebrew Union College Press, 1989). For a more recent overview and a recent argument for the completion of the Babylonian Talmud before the middle of the sixth century, see Yaakov Elman, "The World of the 'Sabboraim': Cultural Aspects of Post-Redactional Additions to the Bavli," inJeffrey Rubenstein (ed.), *Creation and Composition: The Contribution of the Bavli Redactors (Stammaim) to the Aggada* (Tübingen: Mohr Siebeck, 2005), 383–415. For a recent overview of scholarship on the role of the stam in the redaction of the Babylonian Talmud, see Jeffrey Rubenstein,"Introduction," in: ibid (ed.), *Creation and Composition*, 1–20; see also Joshua Levinson, *The Twice Told Tale*, 239–307. For a more reserved position vis-à-vis the importance of the stam, see Richard Kalmin, *Jewish Babylonian between Persia and Roman Palestine* (Oxford, New York: Oxford University Press, 2006), 11–12 and "The Function of the Stam and the Writing of History," in Aharon Shemesh and Aaron Amit (eds.), *Ma'aseh Hoshev: Studies in the Redaction and Development of Talmudic Literature* (Bar-Ilan University Press, forthcoming); Christine Elizabeth Hayes, *Between the Babylonian and Palestinian Talmuds: Accounting for Halakhic Difference in Selected Sugyot from Tractate Avodah Zarah* (New York: Oxford University Press, 1997); 3–30 and Robert Brody, "The Contribution of the *Yerushalmi* to the Dating of the Anonymous Material in the *Bavli*" in *Ma'aseh Hoshev*.

[34] The most important recent contribution emphasizing the essentially conciliatory halakhic endeavor of the Bavli is Barry Wimpfheimer's *Telling Tales out of Court: Literary Ambivalence in Talmudic Legal Narratives* (Philadelphia: University of Pennsylvania Press, forthcoming). Wimpfheimer's position is accepted by Daniel Boyarin (see *Socrates and the Fat Rabbis*, 142 f). I am currently writing an article in which I portray Palestinian Midrash and the Yerushalmi as more truly polysemic, in contrast to the more dominant presence in the Bavli of an authorial voice that seeks to establish less ambiguous meaning. I hold that the scholarship on midrashic polysemy most accurately describes Amoraic Palestinian literature but not so much the Bavli. I agree with Wimpfheimer's and Boyarin's attribution of striving towards univocality in the Bavli as we have it and seek to support their respective analyses by delineating the contrast between Palestine and Babylonia more clearly.

Humor in Antiquity

Most closely tied to the status of authorship is the question of how to understand intentional incongruity in assessing rabbinic parody. Parody simultaneously creates similarity and incongruity between itself and the text it repeats. The parody's message hence resides in an ancient sense of incongruity between two texts. Rabbinic parodies claim to know their adversaries' texts but proceed to portray them as incompatible with the way things are or ought to be according to the parodist's own world view.

To modern sensibilities, however, few ancient conventions seem natural; in fact, many seem odd. Speaking about rabbinic parody requires differentiating between accidental strangeness and intentional incongruity, between the blurred modern perception of the rabbis' opponents and these rabbis' willful distortion of them. This book attempts to use the concept of parody as a heuristic device for making the distinction between "strange to us" and "deliberately incongruous" in rabbinic literature. A closer look at humor as based on incongruence is therefore necessary for a study of parody.

Play is a core element of humor, and even a crude summary is helpful for the study of parody. Roger Caillois' classic definition of play states that it:

- is free, that is, it is not restricted by inherent necessities.
- is separate from ordinary life.
- is unproductive.
- is make-believe.
- if play is governed by rules (while fulfilling all of Caillois' other requirements), it becomes a game.[35]

Such a broad concept of play and game must be nuanced before it can be fruitfully used in the study of literature. Literature could itself be viewed as a game, being relatively free, unproductive, governed by rules, and make-believe; its purpose is to create a new (literary) reality. In order to avoid a concept that is too broad, I view make-believe and the creation of new realities as *additional* layers of the text: playful literature creates or evokes at least one new reality in addition to the one already present in a work's narrative reality.[36] For example, in the passage from the Yerushalmi, Hananya, in addition to fulfilling his literary role as a rabbi who migrates from Palestine

---

[35] Roger Caillois, *Man, Play, and Games* (New York: Free Press of Glencoe, 1961). Caillois' definition elaborates on Johan Huizinga's in his *Homo Ludens: a Study of the Play-Element in Culture* (London: Routledge & K. Paul, 1949). Huizinga's own definition of play seems too general for my purposes, for I could not find any aspect of life that is excluded from it.

[36] For a discussion of textual realities, see Roland Barthes, *The Pleasure of the Text* (New York: Hill and Wang, 1975), 45–56.

to Babylonia, takes on the role of the divine law-giver, a secondary reality within the text that the text itself marks as literarily "playful."

It has been remarked that one defining characteristic of rabbinic literature is its serious playfulness.[37] Whereas humor is necessarily playful, not all play is humorous, just as rabbinic literature is not humorous per se. I view humor as adding an element to play: incongruity between two (or more) literary realities. The mere presence of incongruity does not suffice to make a text humorous since it may simply be the result of accidental inconsistency. Especially in the case of the heavily redacted rabbinic literature, we must attempt not to assign meaning to something odd that may be the result of an error in the transmission or of our ignorance of ancient conventions. It is important, therefore, to point out that most existing theories of humor – ranging from sociological to linguistic and philosophical and traced from Aristotle to Rabelais, from the German Romantics to contemporary literary theorists – contain elements of the following notion: the condition for experiencing the comic lies in the audience's recognition of incongruity as *intentionally* playful.[38]

We may expect such intentional incongruity in literary works that express ideas differing from their own literary premises, if these works seem intact and logically sound otherwise. In other words, we have reasons to believe that the Yerushalmi cannot *really* mean that the Torah prefers Hananya's festivals to those of G-d. At the same time, establishing that the rabbis cannot have taken this or that scenario seriously must withstand historical scrutiny, an exceedingly difficult task. In rabbinic literature in general, the juxtaposition of legal realities or different scriptural interpretations must be viewed as congruent even when it may seem incongruent to us (as I shall discuss especially in Chapters One and Two).[39] Yet the rabbinic sensibilities

---

[37] According to Yitzhak Heineman, Midrash constitutes "serious play," a notion further developed by James Kugel and David Stern. See Yitzhak Heineman, דרכי האגדה (Jerusalem: The Hebrew University Press, 1954), 77; David Stern, "Midrash and the Language of Exegesis: a Study of Vayikra Rabbah Chapter 1," in Geoffrey H. Hartman and Sanford Budick (eds.), *Midrash and Literature*, (Evanston: Northwestern University Press, 1996), 105–124; and James L. Kugel, "Two Introductions to Midrash," in *Midrash and Literature*, 77–103. See also Howard Eilberg-Schwartz, "Who's Kidding Whom?: A Serious Reading of Rabbinic Word Plays," *Journal of the American Academy of Religion* 55 (2004), 765–88.

[38] See the history of the study of humor in O'Neill, *The Comedy of Entropy*, 24–53; Hutcheon similarly emphasizes authorial intentionality as a prerequisite to parody in *A Theory of Parody*, 84–99.

[39] Jeffrey Rubenstein elegantly summarizes the similar problem as it occurs in reading rabbinic exegesis: "[T]the notion of a "simple" meaning of which the rabbis must have been aware even as they proffered a "midrashic" interpretation to complement it has been problematized if not rejected by contemporary scholarship. Because the Sages held different assumptions concerning the biblical text (that no word or verse is superfluous, that there are no contradictions, etc.), their interpretations may seem *to us* to be forced or

concerning the limits of juxtaposed realities are far from arbitrary, and many of the scenarios in the examples in this book, such as Hananya as a divine law-giver, go far beyond these limits.

Humorous incongruity may be best conceptualized by situating irony as an intermediate step between the serious and the comic. To reiterate, irony hints at the incongruity of several realities without guiding the audience to appreciate these realities' actual collision in the text. All examples I discuss in this book contain elements of irony alongside elements of satire; at times, the distinction is minute. When Rabbi Isaac associates Hananya with God in his distorted citation, one could initially view his statement as ironic. As soon as the text's author leads the audience to perceive the collision of the two concepts of man and God, however, irony becomes realized as humor. The example from the Yerushalmi marks the transition from irony to humor by voicing the Babylonian audience's incredulous reaction to the text, thereby highlighting Hananya's usurpation of the role and name of the divine lawgiver.

Imitated Texts and Targeted Texts

When humor is employed critically, it becomes satire; the object of its criticism is the satire's target. This study concerns itself only with satirical parodies. I call the text a parody imitates the "imitated text." If the parody's target of satire is a text, I call it the "targeted text." The text imitated by parody is often not the target of the parody's satire. Parody itself, as Hutcheon puts it, "comes in a wide variety of tones and moods – from respectful to playful to scathingly critical," and it is upon the reader to decipher which modes are at play in any given moment.[40] The parodic and the satirical elements of any satirical parody relate to one another in a variety of ways, and so do the imitated text and the target text: the target can be the imitated text itself, an adaptation of it, or an entirely different text.

To reiterate this essential distinction for the textual relationship of a satirical parody, the target of satire and the parodied text are not necessarily one and the same. In all the parodies discussed in this book, however, the target of satire is closely associated with the imitated text – in effect, the target text is often a *reading* of the parodied text. The parody combines the imitation of the text with satirizing a previous reading of the same text, leading

---

imposed and not "simple," but for the rabbis they may have been the best they could do to make sense of the text" ("The Exegetical Narrative: New Directions," review of Joshua Levinson, *The Twice-Told Tale: A Poetics of the Exegetical Narrative in Rabbinic Midrash*, in *The Jewish Quarterly Review* 99 (2009), 88).

[40] Hutcheon, *A Theory of Parody*, xii.

to a triangular textual relationship. All parodies discussed in this book, in other words, contain elements of *exegetical parody*. Just as in the example from the Yerushalmi, the parodies imitate foundational texts – such as the Hebrew Bible, the Mishna, or the Christian Sermon on the Mount – in the context of what they consider their opponents' erroneous exegesis of these sources. Especially in cases when texts from within the rabbinic canon are imitated, the target of the parody's satire tends to be an opponent's alleged exegesis, more so, or rather than the underlying foundational text that the parody repeats, as is the case with the story of Hananya.

A parody may imitate a biblical passage in non-satirical ways and simultaneously satirize an objectionable exegesis of the passage; the targeted text in these cases is the exegesis, not the Bible. Conversely, rabbinic parodies of early Christian foundational texts tend to imitate Gospel passages that were of great importance to the Christian contemporaries of the parodies' authors, along with these texts' subsequent Christian exegesis as a secondary, sometimes more implicit target of satire. Yet even in such cases, we can see a residual respect for aspects of the Christian foundational text itself, especially in the case of the Bavli (as I shall argue in Chapters Four and Five and in the Conclusion).

A range of nuance is inscribed into the modern category of parody through its derivation from the Greek *par-hoidia*, a "counter-song" or a song sung "against" or "beside" another song.[41] When a rabbinic parody imitates an existing text in a way that satirizes the imitated text itself, the parody is a counter-song "against" the first song.[42] As Hutcheon points out, the meaning "beside" suggests "an accord or intimacy instead of a contrast. It is this second, neglected meaning of the prefix that broadens the pragmatic scope of parody."[43] Precisely in the rabbis' satire of Hananya's alleged exegesis we can discern accord or intimacy with the Bible, the text that the parody imitates. In this sense, the parody is sung "besides" the first song.

The critical gaze of the author of satirical parody focuses on the modes of discourse and the process of signification in the imitated text, and in the targeted text.[44] In Hutcheon's words, parody points to the "literariness" of

---

[41] For a useful summary of the development of the notion of "parody," see Marion Steudel, *Die Literaturparodie in Ovids Ars Amatoria* (Hildesheim: Olms-Weidmann, 1992), 11.

[42] Joseph Dane rightfully cautions against stating a definition of parody that is too limiting as such a definition is inevitably defied by literature. See *Parody: Critical Concepts Versus Literary Practice, Aristophanes to Sterne* (Norman: University of Oklahoma Press, 1988).

[43] Hutcheon, *A Theory of Parody*, 32.

[44] Jonathan Culler showed that "in so far as literature turns back on itself and examines, parodies, or treats ironically its own signifying procedures, it becomes the most complex account of signification we possess." See *The Pursuit of Signs: Semiotics, Literature, De-*

the imitated text.[45] Patrick O'Neill's writes that a literary parody "sharpens the reader's awareness of the literary medium itself, employing the devices of the [imitated] text while simultaneously ... laying them bare."[46] Accordingly, when a parody points to the text it imitates as a text, it has thereby already entered the realm of textual play and meta-criticism, another key quality of parody, according to Genette's classic essay.[47]

Following Genette, the parodies I discuss in this book all imitate extant texts or texts that we can reconstruct with some certainty along with some of their literary devices and their message. While I posit that most of these texts were created orally, I restrict myself to parodies that imitate texts that were eventually documented in writing. The satirical target of the parodies I present, however, does not need to be a demonstrably extant text. In the case, for example, of the Yerushalmi's parody of Hananya, we only have the imitated text, the Torah. The Torah, of course, is not subject to satire but represents the normative worldview, deviation from which the parody satirizes. We are, in effect, lacking an actually written targeted text of this parody's satire, such as a (putative) Babylonian story about Hananya's ac-

---

construction (Ithaca: Cornell University Press, 1981), 36. In my understanding, the alternate techniques of pastiche, travesty, and parody would fall on a sliding scale of imitative texts, with increasing levels of criticism and textual play. Pastiche is largely bound by the form and content of the imitated text; it is a retelling with room for irony. A travesty is free to invert aspects of the imitated text yet remains bound by aspects of that text's structure; irony and satire can be part of it. A parody, finally, has complete freedom in relation to the text it imitates as long as the audience recognizes the imitated text. In addition to engaging in a dialogue with the imitated text, parody has the most liberty to target other possible understandings of the imitated text and its underlying paradigms; it inverts and subverts freely. The most inclusive attempt to create formal boundaries between these genres was made by Genette. See Gérard Genette, *Palimpsestes. La littérature au second degré* (Paris: Seuil, Paris, 1982). See also Wolfgang Karrer, *Parodie, Travestie, Pastiche* (Munich: W. Fink, 1977); Winfried Freund, *Die Literarische Parodie* (Stuttgart: Metzler, 1981), 17–27; and Hutcheon, *A Theory of Parody*, 30–49. For a different definition, see, for example, Chris Baldick, who categorizes parody as a genre which performs "mockery" and pastiche as performing "flattery" of the respective imitated text. (Chris Baldick, "Pastiche," in: idem., *The Concise Oxford Dictionary of Literary Terms* (Oxford: Oxford University Press, 2001), 183–185). This distinction is of limited value if a text both mocks and flatters as the Yerushalmi does in the story of Hananya in the passage immediately preceding the parody.

[45] Hutcheon, *A Theory of Parody*, 31. Hutcheon relies on the work of Ziva Ben-Porat, who states that "[p]arodic representations expose the model's conventions and lay bare its device through the coexistence of the two codes in the same message" (Ziva Ben-Porat, "Method in *Madness*: Notes on the Structure of Parody, Based on the MAD TV Series," *Poetics Today* 1 (1979), 247, cited in Hutcheon, *A Theory of Parody*, 49).

[46] O'Neill (*The Comedy of Entropy,* 113) paraphrases Victor Shklovsky's "'Sterne's *Tristram Shandy*: Stylistic Commentary," in Lee T. Lemon and Marion Reis (eds.), *Russian Formalist Criticism: Four Essays,* (Lincoln: University of Nebraska Press, 1965), 30.

[47] See Gérard Genette, *Palimpsestes. La littérature au second degré*, 33–40. See also Genette's definition of parody as "hyper-textuality" (ibid., 49 and 182).

tions with which the authors of the Yerushalmi would have been familiar. The Yerushalmi's own report of Hananya's petulant actions in Babylonia scarcely suffices as a "text" containing any discernible literary features. Yet as I tried to illustrate, we do know enough about the relationship between the Palestinian and Babylonian rabbinic communitiesto be able to account for the target of satire as the impertinence of Babylonian rabbis. In Chapter Three, we will see that such parody was reciprocated.

Parody and Rabbinic Literature

The occurrence of satirical parody within rabbinic literature does not diminish this literature's serious nature. We should avoid a categorical distinction between "humorous" and "serious" when discussing late ancient rabbinic texts. This literature combines elements of humor with an utmost reverence that always underlies the discourse, even when it uses satirical parody to achieve it – the Yerushalmi quarrels with Hananya for nothing less than its own status and authority. Rabbinic literature combines the serious with the parodic and the satirical, recalling in some ways genres of Hellenistic literature, such as the late ancient philosophical narrative and the Greek novel.

These Hellenistic genres are instrumental for understanding rabbinic literature. In a recent publication, Daniel Boyarin makes a case for contextualizing the Bavli in what he calls the "serio-comic" discourse that prevailed in many late ancient Hellenistic texts: the *spoudogeloion*, which Boyarin develops in dialogue with the work of Mikhail Bakhtin.[48] Calling attention to authors from Roman Syria such as Lucian and his near-mythical predecessor Menippus, Boyarin redefines the term "Menippean Satire" as combining more than just poetry and prose and seeks to establish it as an important mode in the Bavli as well:

Menippean satire involves a kind of spoofing in which the heroes of an intellectual community are the spoofed heroes, at least in formal part via a yoking together of the serious and comical genres into single texts that observe no generic decorum, as was recognized already in antiquity. Since the force of this genre is to call into question the very seriousness and authority of the practice of the intellectuals themselves, this is also, I argue, an important avenue for understanding talmudic ideology. Signifi-

---

[48] Boyarin, *Socrates and the Fat Rabbis*, 14. Boyarin reexamines one of the roots of Hellenism, the culture of democratic Athens, in order to locate a type of serious discourse that employs the comic and comments on the qualities of its own genre. He argues that in Bakhtin's *spoudogeloion*, "the genre-name itself implies rather a yoking together of the seemingly incompatible, even antithetical, and that is precisely the circumstance that confronts us in both Plato and the Bavli, so this seems, *a priori*, a promising line of thought and research" (ibid). Boyarin then attempts to draw a line from classical Athens to the Bavli via the late ancient philosophical texts.

cantly, however, this calling into question or putting limits on the efficacy of intellectuals' practice does not involve an abandonment of the authority of those practices.[49]

Boyarin's central insight is of great value to my discussion of parody. For example, the "calling into question" of Hananya's authority by means of parody seems to be the main emphasis of the passage from the Yerushalmi. Yet the Yerushalmi's insistence on the proper intercalation of the year views itself as fully compatible with or even constitutive of talmudic discourse, of which Hananya is an important founding figure. The subversion of the authority of the targeted rabbis and their texts in the inner-rabbinic parodies discussed in this book is not the end goal of rabbinic parody. Ultimately, these texts reinforce the authority of the ancient heroes, such as Hananya, insofar as the heroes' authority is now vested in the parodies' authors as the true guardians of rabbinic tradition. In this sense, all the rabbinic parodies discussed in this book combine the serious with the comic; accordingly, Boyarin associates the serio-comic with parody.[50]

Boyarin argues that the genre of the serio-comic, including Menippean satire as well as motifs found in Lucian and Petronius, may have been "transmitted to the Babylonian Rabbis through the medium of oral transcultural transmission."[51] In order to argue for the plausibility of this suggestion, Boyarin relies on the ongoing "Hellenizing" of the Sasanian Empire through the migration of a Syriac Christian school from Edessa to Nisibis.[52] While I do share Boyarin's assessment of parts of the Bavli being serio-comic and of the importance of Hellenism for understanding its nature, I suggest that we should differentiate between Palestinian and Babylonian Hellenism, especially as a rabbinic phenomenon.

In Palestine, the rabbis had long been an integral part of the Hellenistic world, and their participation in Hellenistic parodic discourse is hardly surprising, far less than abstaining from parody would be. The rabbinic parodies share the same "serious" goals with the rest of rabbinic literature, even if they use non-serious means to overcome adversity. The prevalence

---

[49] Boyarin, *Socrates and the Fat Rabbis*, 26. For useful definitions of Menippean Satire, see Howard Weinbrot, *Menippean Satire Reconsidered: From Antiquity to the Eighteenth Century* (Baltimore: Johns Hopkins University Press, 2005), esp. 1–20 and Joel C. Relihan, *Ancient Menippean Satire* (Baltimore: Johns Hopkins University Press, 1993).

[50] One of the rabbinic texts Boyarin describes as Menippean Satire, *Avodah Zarah* 18a–b, is "close enough to set up the parodic allusion" to the Gospel narrative of Jesus on the cross (*Socrates and the Fat Rabbis*, 252–57), an important precedent for my own analysis in Chapter Four.

[51] Boyarin, *Socrates and the Fat Rabbis*, 138.

[52] Boyarin, *Socrates and the Fat Rabbis*, 138–40. Boyarin relies on the work of Isaiah Gafni, "Nestorian Literature as a Source for the History of the Babylonian *Yeshivot*," *Tarbiz* 51 (1981–82), 567–76 [Hebrew] and of Adam Becker, *Fear of God and the Beginnings of Wisdom: The School of Nisibis and the Development of Scholastic Culture in Late Antique Mesopotamia* (Philadelphia: University of Pennsylvania Press, 2006).

of humor, irony, and parody in Greek literature of the Classical[53] and late ancient periods has long been recognized,[54] including among Hellenistic Jews.[55] The occurrence of satire and parody in texts as interrelated with the literary and cultural pre-history of the rabbis as the Hebrew Bible[56] and, to

[53] Aristophanes' *Frogs* and Ovid's *Ars Amatoria* are the best known classical examples. F. J. Lelièvre ("The Basis of Ancient Parody," *Greece & Rome* 1 (1954), 81) already argued for the presence of parodies in Antiquity, despite the absence of a proper term for describing the technique. Noteworthy later studies include the work of Wolfram Ax, *Literaturparodie in Antike und Mittelalter* (Trier: Wissenschaftlicher Verlag, 1993); Simon Goldhill, *The Poet's Voice: Essays on Poetics and Greek Literature* (Cambridge: Cambridge University Press, 1991); Jean-Pierre Cèbe, *La Caricature et la parodie dans le monde romain antique des origines à Juvenal* (Paris: E. de Boccard, 1966); Marion Steudel, *Die Literaturparodie in Ovids Ars Amatoria*; Margaret A. Rose, *Parody: Ancient Modern, and Post-Modern*; eadem, *Parody / Meta-Fiction;* and Monique Trédé and Philippe Hoffmann (eds.), *Le Rire des Anciens: Actes du colloque international* (Paris: Presses de l'École Normale Supérieure: 1998). Note also the useful historical summary in Simon Dentith, *Parody: The New Critical Idiom* (London: Routledge, 2000), 39–54.

[54] On satire in the Greek novels, see especially Mikhail Bakhtin, *The Dialogic Imagination* (Austin: University of Texas Press, 1981); Alain Billaut, "Le comique d'Achille Tatius et les réalités de l'époque impériale," in Monique Trédé and Philippe Hoffmann (eds.), *Le Rire des Anciens: Actes du colloque international* (Presses de l'École Normale Supérieure: Paris, 1998), 143–160; and Kathryn Chew, "Achilles Tatius and Parody," *Classical Journal* 96 (2000), 57–70. For a brief discussion and of satire in late ancient philosophical discourse, see Boyarin, *Socrates and the Fat Rabbis*, 210–19.

[55] Erich Gruen reads many late ancient Greek Jewish narratives as humorous. See *Heritage and Hellenism: the Reinvention of Jewish Tradition* (Berkeley: University of California Press, 1998 and idem., *Diaspora: Jews amidst Greeks and Romans* (Cambridge: Harvard University Press, 2002). Gruen's view of humor has been described as too facile and lacking in evidence; see Gideon Bohak, "New Trends in the Study of Greco-Roman Jews," *Classical Journal*, 99 (2003), 195–202). Gruen, however, is well aware of the fact that many late ancient texts mix comical elements with serious ones and that the use of humor does not undermine serious messages. While Gruen may go too far at times, I agree with him on many of his detailed readings, as I have argued elsewhere concerning the case of Artapanus ("The End of Jewish Egypt: Artapanus and the Second Exodus," in Gregg Gardner and Kevin Osterloh (eds.), *Antiquity in Antiquity: Jewish and Christian Pasts in the Greco-Roman World* (Tübingen: Mohr Siebeck, 2008), 27–73.)

[56] Arguments asserting the presence of humor in the Hebrew Bible have been made by Yehuda T. Radday and Athalya Brenner in their collection *On Humour and the Comic in the Hebrew Bible* (Sheffield: The Almond Press, 1990). See also Nissan Ararat, "מעשה דור הפלגה כדרמה סאטירית," *Beyt Mikra* 39 (1994), 224–231; Eliezer Greenstein, "חכמים גם בלילה: הדו-שיח הבבלי בין האדון לעבדו וספר קהלת," *Beyt Mikra* 44 (1998), 97–106; Grace I. Emmerson, "The Song of Songs, Mystification, Ambiguity and Humour," in Stanley E. Porter et al. (eds.), *Crossing the Boundaries, Essays in Biblical Interpretation in Honour of Michael D. Goulder* (Leiden: Brill, 1994), 97–111; Donald Murray, "Humour in the Bible?," in Keith Cameron (ed.), *Humour and History* (Oxford: Intellect, 1993), 21–40; David Marcus, *From Balaam to Jonah: Anti-Prophetic Satire in the Hebrew Bible* (Atlanta: Scholars Press, 1995); and most recently Carolyn J. Sharp, *Irony and Meaning in the Hebrew Bible* (Bloomington: Indiana University Press, 2009). The rabbis may or may not have noticed biblical humor; in any case, its existence constitutes a meaningful continuity of humorous discourse from Israelite to Jewish literature.

a lesser degree, the New Testament should also be noted.[57] Furthermore, it has been established that post-talmudic rabbis engaged in parody and satire both in Palestine and Babylonia.[58]

At the same time, one must point out the marginal position of humor in some of the cultures surrounding the rabbis: humor is less prevalent in Greek and Syriac patristic sources, and I am not aware of comedy in contemporary Zoroastrian writings. Obviously, being part of the Hellenistic world does not automatically lead to participation in Hellenistic satire. It seems, for instance, that the church "fathers" of the East, and even more so of the West, distanced themselves from select aspects of Hellenistic Greek discourse (of which they very much remained a part), satire among them, as has been forcefully argued by Jean-Michel Poinsotte.[59] This does not mean that Christian literature is devoid of the comical, but it should give us pause when seeing Hellenism as

---

[57] See Paul Harle, "Un 'Private-Joke' de Paul dans le livre des Actes (26:28–29)," *New Testament Studies*, 24 (1978), 527–533; Jonsson Jakob, *Humour and Irony in the New Testament: Illuminated by Parallels in Talmud and Midrash* (Reykjavik: Bókaútgáfa Menningarsjóds, 1965); Lorenz Nieting, "Humor in the New Testament," *Dialog*, 22 (1983), 168–170; Tom Thatcher, "The Sabbath Trick: Unstable Irony in the Fourth Gospel," *Journal for the Study of the New Testament* 76 (1999), 53–77; David Elton Trueblood, *The Humor of Christ* (San Francisco: Harper, 1964); and Mark Nanos, *The Irony of Galatians: Paul's Letter in first-century Context* (Minneapolis: Fortress Press, 2002).

[58] For a discussion of satire in early Byzantine Piyut, see Ophir Münz-Manor, "Other Voices: Haman, Jesus, and the Representation of the Other in Purim Poems from Byzantine Palestine," in Yael Shapira, Omri Herzog and Tamar S. Hess (eds.) *Popular and Canonical: Literary Dialogues* (Tel Aviv: Resling, 2007), 69–79 and 211–217 [Hebrew]; and idem, "Carnivalesque Ambivalence and the Christian *Other* in Aramaic Poems from Byzantine Palestine," (forthcoming); for a discussion of satire in Babylonian post-talmudic writings, see David Stern, "'The Alphabet of Ben Sira' and the early History of Parody in Jewish Literature," in Hindy Najman and Judith H. Newman (eds.), *The Idea of Biblical Interpretation: Essays in Honor of James L. Kugel* (Leiden: Brill, 2004), 423 ff., and Dov Noy, הפארודיה בספרות ישראל הקדומה, 92–99. Even though the *Toldoth Yeshu* traditions still await analysis by contemporary scholars, the parodic nature of this text is widely acknowledged. See Philip S. Alexander, "Yeshu/Yeshua ben Yosef of Nazareth: Discerning the Jewish Face of Jesus," in George J. Brooke, *The Birth of Jesus: Biblical and Theological Reflections* (Edinburgh: T & T Clark, 2000), 9–21; Hillel I. Newman, "The Death of Jesus in the Toledot Yeshu Literature," *Journal of Theological Studies* 50 (1999), 59–79; Samuel Krauss, *Das Leben Jesu nach jüdischen Quellen* (Berlin: Calvary, 1902). This text is excluded from the present study partially because of the difficulty associated with its dating, cf. Willem Smelik, "The Aramaic Dialect(s) of the Cairo Geniza Toledot Yeshu Fragments" (forthcoming). Peter Schäfer is currently preparing a critical edition, translation, and commentary of this text.

[59] Jean-Michel Poinsotte, "Fin de l'Antiquité, mort du comique antique," in Monique Trédé and Philippe Hoffmann (eds.), *Le Rire des Anciens: Actes du colloque international* (Presses de l'École Normale Supérieure: Paris, 1998), 315–26. See also T. Koonammakkal, "Ephrem's Theology of Humour," *Studia Patristica* 41 (2006), 51–56 and W. Heffening,, "Die griechische Ephraem-Paraenesis gegen das Lachen in arabischer Übersetzung," *Oriens Christianus* III, 2 [21] (1927), 94–119. J. B. Segal states about Ephrem that "his work, it must be confessed, shows little profundity or originality of thought, and his metaphors are laboured. His poems are turgid, humourless, and repetitive." *Edessa, 'the Blessed*

a whole as the bridge that links the Babylonian rabbis to Greek modes of the serio-comic.[60] Likewise, the Christian anti-comical discourse should attune us to internal voices condemning parody in rabbinic texts as well, as I shall discuss in Chapter One. Nevertheless, it is my view that the serio-comic was one of the Palestinian rabbinic modes of discourse that the Bavli amplified, a view that provides both a literary prehistory to the Bavli's sense of the serio-comic as well as a possible *intra-rabbinic* mode of transmission of such discourse into rabbinic Babylonia. Such an intra-rabbinic transmission effectively allows us to discuss the rabbinic mode of the serio-comic separately from its transmission to Babylonia as part of the broader phenomenon of a continuing transfer of Hellenistic culture after the fourth century CE. Likewise, it emphasizes the importance of the Palestinian examples of rabbinic parody and satire for our understanding of the development of rabbinic literature, an issue I shall revisit in the Conclusion.

Given that parody was produced before, during, and after the classical rabbinic period, one would expect discussions about the existence of rabbinic parody to abound. For a number of possible reasons, however, the history of scholarship on rabbinic satire and parody is surprisingly fragmentary. The main impediment to a scholarly appreciation of rabbinic parody may be the challenge of determining its satirical targets.

On the one hand, there has been wide scholarly agreement that rabbis *knew* other rabbinical texts in detail and that the rabbis were *critical* of non-

---

City' (Oxford: Oxford University Press, 1970), 89. While Segal's vindictiveness seems unwarranted, it remains difficult to dismiss his assessment of Ephrem's sense of humor.

[60] For some examples of patristic humor, see Louis Leloir, "L'humeur au service d'un message spirituel: les Pères du Désert," in A. Theodoridis, P. Noster and J. Ries (eds), *Humeur, travail et science en Orient* (Louvain: Peeters, 1988), 83–91; in addition, the Syriac translation of the *Apophtegmata Patrum* rendered these playful texts accessible to a Syriac Christian audience; Georgios Tsananas, "Humor bei Basilius dem Grossen," in Anastasius Kallis, *Philoxenia: Festschrift B. Kötting* (Münster: Aschendorff, 1980), 259–279. Sergey Minov was kind enough to direct me to an instance of irony in the *Liber Graduum* 22.3; see Kitchen, R.A., and Parmentier, M.F.G. (trs.), *The Book of Steps: The Syriac Liber Graduum*, Cistercian Studies Series 196 (Kalamazoo, Michigan: Cistercian Publications, 2004), 254. The tradition of the Saint Symeon, the Holy Fool, contains many instances that fit Boyarin's description of the spoofed hero. Just like the rabbis, Saint Symeon does not shy away from starkly incongruent behavior; his hagiography contains many elements of what Boyarin calls *slum naturalism*. (See my Conclusion, pages 215 f., and Derek Krueger, *Symeon, the Holy Fool: Leontius' Life and the Late Antique City* (Berkeley: University of California Press, 1996), 2, 47–50, 126.) It is interesting to note that the "comic" enters Christian literature more dominantly in the early Middle Ages in works like the *Cena Cypriani*. See Lucie Dolezalova, "The Cena Cypriani, or the Game of Endless Possibilities," in Wilhelm Geerlings and Christian Schulze (eds.), *Der Kommentar in Antike und Mittelalter: Beiträge zu seiner Erforschung* (Leiden, Boston: Brill, 2002). See also the observation on role of humor in John of Ephesos as well as in post-Talmudic Zoroastrian polemics in Shai Secunda, "Reading the Bavli in Iran," *Jewish Quarterly Review* 100 (2010), 323 f.

rabbinic groups. Yet, on the other hand, few scholars considered how critical rabbis could be of their own tradition and few realized that the rabbis knew non-rabbinic texts (either written or orally transmitted) well enough to parody these texts. This book uses the concept of parody to combine a study of rabbinic criticism of existing literature, namely their own, with the study of rabbinic knowledge of non-rabbinic texts of which we can assume that they were critical. While the scope of this book does not allow for a more comprehensive evaluation of the Rabbis' knowledge of non-rabbinic texts – be it various forms of Greek, Samaritan, Zoroastrian, Manichean, or Mandean literatures – I will argue that rabbinic texts targeted at Christians are paramount for understanding rabbinic parody.

In short, a still widely held model of rabbinic culture views the Rabbis as (1) in conflict with gentiles, (2) ignorant of or uninterested in Christianity, and (3) submissive to rabbinic tradition. Rabbinic parodies may allow us invert this model and to view the Rabbis as (1) commensurate with surrounding gentile cultures (without blurring the prevailing cultural distinctions), (2) knowledgeable about and critical of Christian texts, and (3) in conflict with other rabbis and capable of self-criticism.

Rabbis and Others

In using parody as evidence of rabbinic self-reflection, I draw on new understandings of the ways in which rabbis relate to their own tradition. Rabbinic literature sees itself in constant dialogue with, and as heir to, previous rabbinic texts: the numerous redactions of all rabbinic literature attest to that. The analytical tools available to us for studying such redaction often include the problematic concept of the "influence" of rabbinic texts on subsequent texts in the same tradition and the later texts' "dependence" on the earlier ones.[61] My re-conceptualization of rabbinic redactors views them

---

[61] "Dependence" constructs the similarities between two texts as signs of the dominant influence of the earlier text on the later one. This allows primarily for mechanical adaptation of existing literature and effectively deprives later redactors of intellectual agency vis-à-vis their traditional sources. In contrast, I seek to further our understanding of rabbinic redactors as authors in their own right and rabbinic retellings of traditional stories as sites of critical recreation. The concept of influence and dependence have been challenged by many scholars; my own understanding builds on the work of Peter Schäfer, Richard Kalmin, and Jeffrey Rubenstein. Schäfer assails the concept of influence as fundamentally distorted and establishes the importance of the extant versions of rabbinic texts in place of previous putative ones. See Peter Schäfer's introduction in idem (ed.), *Talmud Yerushalmi and Graeco-Roman Culture* (Tübingen: Mohr Siebeck, 1998) 1–23. Kalmin emphasizes the sharp divergence within the rabbinic cultures of Palestine and Babylonia, hence creating room for Babylonian creativity. See Richard Kalmin, *Sages, Stories, Authors, and Editors in Rabbinic Babylonia* (Atlanta: Scholars Press, 1994) and the more recent *Jewish*

less as *receiving* earlier traditions and more as *choosing* from among them. In addition to recognizing the hermeneutic importance of differentiating between various adaptive strategies within rabbinic texts, I also emphasize the rifts within each rabbinic community and within each redacted text. The many tensions within the rabbinic movement turned the rabbinic corpus itself into the primary source of specific parodic targets, as I shall argue in Chapters One, Two, and Three.

Recent scholarship also offers insights into the Rabbis' familiarity with and participation in fundamental aspects of Greco-Roman[62] and Sasanian[63] culture and literature – the work of Richard Kalmin is especially exemplary in embracing simultaneously the Rabbis' citizenship in both the Roman and

---

Babylonian between Persia and Roman Palestine. Rubenstein, in line with Kalmin, uses the difference between earlier and later texts, and between texts from different locations, as a hermeneutical guide. For Rubenstein, the ideological emphases of a later text are most clearly visible precisely when that text changes details of an earlier source. See Jeffrey Rubenstein, *Talmudic Stories: Narrative Art, Composition, and Culture* (Baltimore: Johns Hopkins University Press, 1999). See also the splendid summary discussion by Michael L. Satlow, "Beyond Influence: Towards a New Historiographic Paradigm," in Anita Norich and Yaron Z. Eliav (eds.), *Jewish Literatures and Cultures: Context and Intertext* (Providence: Brown Judaic Studies, 2008), 37–53. All this, of course, is not to say that we can afford to ignore the fact that some later texts do, in effect, retell earlier or contemporary parallel materials in a way that limits the creative freedom at the same time as it enhances creativity within these limits. In my view, the intended audience was attuned to the "modular" nature of rabbinic texts and would relate these modules to each other, as I shall argue in some detail in Chapters One and Two. On this perennial issue, cf. for example, Shamma Friedman, "Uncovering Literary Dependencies in the Talmudic Corpus," in Shaye J.D. Cohen (ed.), *The Synoptic Problem in Rabbinic Literature* (Providence, RI: Brown Judaic Studies, 2000), 119–144.

[62] Much of the groundwork necessary for viewing the Rabbis as part of the Hellenistic world was laid by Saul Lieberman, *Hellenism in Jewish Palestine, Studies in the Literary Transmission, Beliefs and Manners of Palestine in The I Century B.C.E. – IV Century C.E.* (New York: Jewish Theological Seminary of America, 1950), and Henry A. Fischel, *Rabbinic Literature and Greco-Roman Philosophy: A Study of Epicurea and Rhetorica in Early Midrashic Writings* (Leiden: Brill, 1973). For a summary of the field, see Peter Schäfer's "Introduction" to idem (ed.), *The Talmud Yerushalmi and Graeco-Roman Culture* (Tübingen: Mohr Siebeck, 1998), vol. I, 1–17.

[63] See Jeffrey L. Rubenstein, *The Culture of the Babylonian Talmud* (Baltimore: Johns Hopkins University Press, 2003), and the work of Yaakov Elman, including "Marriage and Marital Property in Rabbinic and Sasanian Law," in Catherine Hezser (ed.), *Rabbinic Law in Its Roman and Near Eastern Context* (Tübingen: Mohr Siebeck, 2003), 227–276; idem, "Acculturation to Elite Persian Norms and Modes of Thought in the Babylonian Jewish Community of Late Antiquity," in Yaakov Elman, Ephraim Bezalel Halivni, and Zvi Arie Steinfeld (eds.), *Neti'ot Ledavid: Jubilee Volume for David Weiss Halivni* (Jerusalem: Orhot, 2004), 31–56; and most recently idem, "Who are the kings of East and West in Ber 7a? Roman Religion, Syrian Gods and Zoroastrianism in the Bavli," in Shaye J.D. Cohen and Joshua J. Schwartz (eds.), *Studies in Josephus and the Varieties of Ancient Judaism; Louis H. Feldman Jubilee Volume* (Leiden: Brill, 2007), 43–80.

the Sasanian worlds.[64] I argued above that we should understand rabbinic parody itself in light of this citizenship; the satirical targets of rabbinic parody are determined likewise by the Rabbis' lives under Roman and Sasanian rule. But whereas rabbinic parody of Greco-Roman literature is rare and I am not aware of rabbinic satirizing of Zoroastrians,[65] Christian literature may be the only non-rabbinic source that the Rabbis parody as emphatically as they do rabbinic texts, as I shall argue in Chapters Four and Five.

This book seeks to reassess the three studies of rabbinic parody known to me; it also adds four new examples. In 1876, Moritz Guedemann (of Vienna) was the first scholar to argue for the presence of literary satire in classical rabbinic literature, namely in a story of Imma Shalom in the Bavli.[66] Yet, Guedemann did not pay much attention to the literary and cultural implications of his findings. His suggestion that the story of Imma Shalom parodies the Sermon on the Mount is explored in Chapter Four of this book.[67] In

---

[64] See Richard Kalmin, *Jewish Babylonia between Persia and Roman Palestine* (Oxford: Oxford University Press, 2006); idem, *The Sage in Jewish Society of Late Antiquity* (New York: Routledge, 1999); idem, "'Manasseh Sawed Isaiah with a Saw of Wood:' An Ancient Legend in Jewish, Christian, Persian, and Arabic Sources," in Mark Geller (ed.), *Talmudic Archaeology* (Leiden: Brill, forthcoming); and idem "The Miracle of the Septuagint in the Babylonian Talmud," in Oded Irshai, Jodi Magness, Seth Schwartz, and Zeev Weiss (eds.), (Festschrift for Lee I. Levine (Winona Lake, IN: Eisenbraun's, forthcoming).

[65] Menahem Luz recognized the satirical nature of the rabbinic stories about a Greek philosopher; see Menahem Luz, "Oenomaus and Talmudic Anecdote," *Journal for the Study of Judaism*, 23 (1992), 42–80. One early attempt to read rabbinic texts as a parody of Greek philosophical texts was made by Henry A. Fischel, *Rabbinic Literature and Greco-Roman Philosophy* (Leiden: Brill, 1973); see "parody" in his index. While Fischel's Greco-Roman contextualization of rabbinic texts remains valid, his arguments too easily posited parody and did not find a receptive audience. See also Elimelekh Epshtain Halevi, שערי האגדה: על מהות האגדה, סוגיה, דרכיה, מטרותיה וזיקתה לתרבות זמנה (Tel Aviv: Levinsky, 1982) and idem, ערכי האגדה וההלכה לאור מקורות יוונים ולאטיניים (Tel Aviv: Devir, 1980). I shall revisit this issue in Chapter Five.

[66] The first systematic approach to ancient rabbinic humor can be traced to the same period, perhaps to the chapter "Raethsel und Witzesspiele" in Leopold Löw, *Die Lebensalter in der Jüdischen Literatur* (Szegdin: Sigmund Burger's Wwe, 1875), 346–351. More comprehensive research followed in 1886 with Alexander Kohut's "Wit, Humor and Anecdote in the Talmud and Midrash," *The American Hebrew* (May 7th–June 11th 1886), 2–3 (6 issues).

[67] Moritz Guedemann, *Religionsgeschichtliche Studien* (Leipzig: Oskar Leiner, 1876), 81–92. Guedemann uses the term "satire" in a way largely congruous with my own definition of parody. Israel Davidson, in his seminal study, *Parody in Jewish Literature*, published in 1907, seems unaware of Guedemann's claims and did not find parody in classical rabbinic literature. His insightful explanation for its absence, however, is telling: "In the few instances, where the rabbis travestied the subtleties of the schools, they did so at the risk of bringing reproach and ill-favor upon themselves" (York: AMS Press, 1966 [1907]), 2. Davidson sensed rabbinic humorous self-criticism, but the perception of rabbinic harmony, or *una vox rabbinica*, was perhaps still too strong at the time and did not allow him to explore the issue further. See also David Stern, "'The Alphabet of Ben Sira' and the Early History of Parody in Jewish Literature," 423 ff.

1951, Dov Noy published a brilliant, albeit brief, discussion of several short rabbinic parodies, most of which treat post-talmudic examples.[68] The piece from which I chose the earliest and perhaps most intriguing example above has not sparked much scholarly interest.

For reasons beyond the scope of this book – the Holocaust certainly affected views of talmudic comedy and ancient Jewish-Christian relations in a myriad of ways – it took more than a century before more research followed Guedemann's findings. It has only been in the past thirty years that scholarly discourse has intensified the long process of regarding rabbinic texts as literature.[69] By subjecting rabbinic texts to literary and historical inquiry, scholars began to notice and appreciate rabbinic satire as well.

The concept of parody as a subject worthy of reflection in light of contemporary literary theory was, to the best of my knowledge, first injected into the study of Palestinian rabbinic literature in 1993 by Joshua Levinson.[70] Levinson brought a pronounced Bakhtinian approach to his analysis and argued that a particular rabbinic text targets the Hebrew Bible itself. In Chapter Two, I develop Levinson's reading and attempt to show that this rabbinic parody imitates the Bible in order to reaffirm conservative rabbinic culture vis-à-vis the ascetic influence it satirically targets – reversing Levinson's argument that the parody challenges rabbinic norms. Despite the various studies that I have mentioned, the concept of parody has not yet

---

[68] Dov Noy, "הפארודיה בספרות ישראל הקדומה," *Mahanayim* 54 (1961–62), 92–99.

[69] This process may have begun with the work of Avraham Weiss. (For a summary of Weiss's work, see Aryeh Cohen, *Rereading Talmud: Gender, Law and the Poetics of Sugyot* (Atlanta: Scholars Press, 1998), 8–24.) One generation following the work of researchers such as Joseph Heineman, Arnold Goldberg, and Yonah Frenkel, scholars like Daniel Boyarin and David Stern began to realize the promise that literary theory holds for a more nuanced study of Midrash. For a history of the development of understanding rabbinic texts as literature, see Joshua Levinson, "Literary approaches to Midrash," in Carol Bakhos (ed.), *Current Trends in the Study of Midrash* (Leiden: Brill, 2006), 189–226. A few seminal studies are Joseph Heineman's אגדות ותולדותיהן: עיונים בהשתלשלותן של מסורות (Jerusalem: Keter, 1978); Arnold Goldberg's "Entwurf einer formanalytischen Methode für die Exegese der rabbinischen Traditionsliteratur," *Frankfurter Judaistische Beiträge*, 5 (1977), 1–41; Yonah Frenkel's דרכי האגדה והמדרש (Massada: Yad la-Talmud, 1991); Daniel Boyarin's *Intertextuality and the Reading of Midrash*; and David Stern's *Midrash and Theory: Ancient Jewish Exegesis and Contemporary Literary Studies* (Evanston: Northwestern University Press, 1996). Most recently, see Galit Hasan-Rokem, *Web of Life: Folklore and Midrash in Rabbinic Literature* (Stanford: Stanford University Press, 2000) and Dina Stein, מימרה מגיה מיתוס: פרקי דרבי אליעזר לאור מחקר הספרות העממית (Jerusalem: Magnes Press, 2004).

[70] Joshua Levinson, Levinson, "עולם הפוך ראיתי'-'עיון בסיפור השיכור ובניו," *Jerusalem Studies in Hebrew Literature*, XIV (1993), 7–23. See also Levinson's "'Tragedies Naturally Performed:' Fatal Charades, Parodia Sacra, and the Death of Titus," in Richard Kalmin and Seth Schwartz (eds.), *Jewish Culture and Society under the Christian Roman Empire* (Leuven: Peeters, 2003), 349–384, where he develops further the theory of the *parodia sacra*.

fully caught on in the world of rabbinic scholars. Recent scholarship, how-ever, has increasingly acknowledged the pertinence of humor and satire.[71] Interestingly, the work of scholars acknowledging parody also tends to be informed by the Christian cultural contexts of rabbinic literature.[72]

In this book, I argue that Rabbis criticized their own tradition and were familiar with non-rabbinic texts. I seek to examine Babylonian and Pales-tinian rabbinic parodies by alternately discussing examples emerging from the two centers of rabbinic culture. My analysis recognizes three modes of rabbinic parody:

– *Intra-rabbinic Parody*, as illustrated in Chapters One and Two, targets aspects of the same text in which the parody itself is found. In regards to both the Ba-bylonian and the Palestinian examples, I argue that the respective redactor of the rabbinic text inserts the parody in order to preserve and counter a segment of the polyvalent rabbinic tradition that he also retells. Such *redactional* parody indicates a combination of rabbinic self-reflection, self-criticism, and self-affirmation; the

---

[71] See David Lifshitz, "Humor as a Device for Solving Problems," *Justice* 15 (1997), 38–42 and "שמות וכינויים בתלמוד באספקלריה הומוריסטית," *Ve-Eleh Shemot* 3 (2002), 95–109; Rela Koslofsky, "'ר' יהושע בן לוי ומלאך-המות," *Mehqere Yerusha-layim befolklor yehudi*, 19/20 (1998), 329–344; Arkady Kovelman, "Farce in the Talmud," *Review of Rabbinic Judaism*, 5 (2002), 86–92; Eli Yassif, סיפורי הומור באגדה: טיפולוגיה," "נושא, משמעות, *Mehqere Talmud*, 3 (2005), 403–430; Marc Tanenbaum, "Humour in the Talmud" *Concilium* 5 (1974), 141–150; Benyamin Engelman, "הומור מוצהר, גלוי וסמוי בתלמוד הבבלי," in *Be-khol derakhekha da'ehu: ketav-et le-inyane Torah u-madah*, 8 (1990), 5–28; Daniel Boyarin, "Literary Fat Rabbis: On the Historical Origins of the Grotesque Body," in *Journal of the History of Sexuality*, 1 (1991), 551–584; and Samuel Egal Karff, "Laughter and Merriment in Rabbinic Literature," in Abraham J. Karp (ed.), *Threescore and Ten: Essays in Honor of Rabbi Seymour J. Cohen on the Occasion of his Seventieth Birthday* (Hoboken: Ktav, 1991), 75–85. On rabbinic irony, see also note 24 above.

[72] Israel Yuval, Daniel Boyarin, Burt Visotzky, Jeffrey Rubenstein, and Peter Schäfer have been particularity instrumental in rendering a scholarly discussion of rabbinic parody possible, as I shall argue in more depth in Chapters Four and Five. See Israel Yuval, *Two Nations in Your Womb: Perceptions of Jews and Christians in Late Antiquity and the Mid-dle Ages* (Tel Aviv: Am Oved, 2000) [Hebrew] and (Berkeley: University of California Press, 2006) [English]; Burton L. Visotzky, *Fathers of the World: Essays in Rabbinic and Patristic Literature* (Tübingen: Mohr Siebeck, 1995) and *Golden Bells and Pomegranates: Studies in Midrash Leviticus Rabbah* (Tübingen: Mohr Siebeck, 2003); Jeffrey Rubenstein, *Talmudic Stories: Narrative Art, Composition, and Culture* and *The Culture of the Baby-lonian Talmud* (Baltimore: Johns Hopkins University Press, 2003); Peter Schäfer, *Jesus in the Talmud* (Princeton, NJ and Oxford: Princeton University Press, 2007). For Boyarin, see below, Chapter Four, note 12. See also Daniel Stökl-Ben Ezra, "Parody and Polemics on Pentecost: Talmud Yerushalmi Pesahim on Acts 2?," in: Alberg Gerhards and Clemens Leonhard (eds.), *Jewish and Christian Liturgy and Worship: New Insights into its History and Interaction* (Leiden, Boston: Brill, 2007), 279–294 and Moshe Halbertal and Shlomo Naeh, "מעייני הישועה: סטירה פרשנית ותשובת המינים," in Joshua Levinson, Jacob Elbaum, and Galit Hasan-Rokem (eds.), *Higayon L'Yona: New Aspects in the Study of Midrash Ag-gadah, and Piyut in Honor of Professor Yona Frenkel* (Jerusalem: The Hebrew University Magnes Press, 2006), 179–98.

oral-performative nature of rabbinic literature is especially conducive to parodic retellings of received materials.
- *Inter-rabbinic Parody* targets rabbinic texts external to the author's own community: Palestinian Rabbis parodied Babylonian Rabbis, as illustrated above, and Babylonian Rabbis parodied Palestinian ones, as illustrated in Chapter Three. Inter-rabbinic parody combines rabbinic self-reflection, self-criticism, and self-affirmation regarding the author's own community with an emphasis on the difference between the two rabbinic communities in Babylonia and Palestine.
- *External Parody*, as illustrated in Chapters Four and Five, targets non-rabbinic texts and indicates the Babylonian and Palestinian Rabbis' familiarity with them; in the examples discussed in this book, this mode of parody always contains elements of rabbinic self-criticism as well.

This book is organized around these *modes* of parody, moving from intra-rabbinic to inter-rabbinic parody and finally to external parody. The rabbinic authors realized these modes of parody with the help of several *types* of parody, such as exegetical parody and redactional parody, which interact in various ways with the aforementioned modes of exegetical and redactional parody. Additional types are "voiced parody," a parody that occurs in the quoted locutions within a text (such as in the case of Rabbi Isaac and Rabbi Nathan) and "halakhic parody," the parody of any aspect of halakha (such as the parody of Hananya's calendrical calculations).

CHAPTER ONE

Of Mice and Men:
Rabbinic Parody and its Halakhic Limits
(Bava Metsiʿa 97a)

The *Shekhina* rests (on us)
not out of sadness and not out of laziness,
and not out of laughter (שחוק),
and not out of levity (קלות ראש),
and not out of conversation (שיחה),
and not out of idle talk (דברים בטלים),
but out of the joy of the commandment (שמחה של מצוה).
Shabbat 30a

The Bavli is the Rabbis' central literary achievement; its emphasis on halakha has shaped rabbinic Judaism to this day. This chapter discusses parody
in the Bavli and considers an excerpt from a *sugya* (a thematically arranged
segment of halakhic discourse in the Bavli) that as a whole treats property
law – specifically, liability for lost or damaged borrowed property. The
sugya first examines in detail the conditions under which a borrower is
responsible for restitution of the borrowed property. The very purpose of
a sugya is to harmonize tensions between different halakhic concepts. As a
whole, the sugya under discussion weighs various competing legal concepts
against each other, yet it generally does so in order to eliminate, not produce, meaningful incongruity.

However, one short passage in the sugya (found in *Bava Metsiʿa* 97a)
interrupts the smooth surface and threatens to undermine its discourse altogether – even if the sugya seems to disregard this disruption and continues
thereafter in regular manner. The sugya is in the midst of considering one of
several exemplary cases concerning liability for broken borrowed objects
when it introduces several rabbis, a lender, a borrower, mice, and a dead cat.

A man [גברא] borrowed a cat from his fellow [מחבריה].
The mice united [חבור] against it and killed it.
Now, R. Ashi sat and pondered thereon: "To what category does such a case belong?
  (Is it as though it had died from work, or not?")[1]

---

[1] This astute explanation of R. Ashi's question, a Hebrew phrase amidst otherwise
homogenous Aramaic, appears in the Vilna and Soncino prints and in Escorial G-I-3. It

R. Mordecai said to R. Ashi: "Thus said Abimi of Hagronia in Rava's name:
'[For] a man whom women killed – there is neither judgment nor judge [לא דינא ולא
דיינא]!'"
Others say: "[The cat] ate many mice, whereby it sickened and died."
R. Ashi sat and cogitated thereon: "To what category does such a case belong?"
Said R. Mordecai to R. Ashi: "Thus said Abimi of Hagronia in Rava's name:[2]
    '[For] a man whom women killed – there is neither judgment nor judge.'"

As part of the sugya's inquiry into liability for borrowed property, R. Ashi
seeks to reach a reasonable decision in this unusual case of a borrowed cat
killed by mice. In the same tone of serious halakhic inquiry that the sugya
maintains to this point, the rabbi asks whether the borrowed cat was "used
appropriately," which is the halakhic principle for determining liability for
borrowed objects. That the cat had contact with mice implies that it may
have died "from work," which means that it had been used as intended
and that the borrower is not liable. Why, then, does Rav Ashi continue to
wonder?

Richard Kalmin aptly points to the fact that if the cat died in the normal
course of its work, then the reasons for Rav Ashi's uncertainty are "not at
all apparent" since his "unwillingness to exempt the borrower seems totally
unwarranted."[3] The law clearly favors the borrower and exempts him from
any liability. Kalmin also notes that "the case of the cat killed by mice … is
outside the normal range of human experience … The borrower has no reason to anticipate such a danger to the animal, and, reasons Rav Ashi, might
not have accepted responsibility for such a bizarre turn of events when he
assumed the status of a borrower."[4]

I concur with Kalmin's sound reasoning on a halakhic level, but I hold
that the incident's bizarre nature, at the same time that it exempts the borrower, also indicates meaningful incongruence. The sugya's use of internal

---

seems to be an explanatory insertion; it is missing in Ms. Florence II-I-8, Ms. Munich 95,
and Ms. Vatican 115, and from the Cambridge Geniza Fragment T-S F2 (2) 14.

[2] The final attribution to Rava in the repetition of R. Mordecai's statement ("Thus did
Abimi of Hagronia, saying *in Rava's name*") is missing in the Soncino and the Vilna prints.
In all other textual witnesses I have consulted, however, it is included either in the form
of an explicit indication of the attribution to Rava (as in Ms. Escorial G-I-3, Ms. Florence
II-I-8, and Ms. Vatican 115) or indirectly in the form of textual witnesses that indicate a
full repetition of R. Mordecai's statement with the term "etc." (וכו' in Munich 95 and 'כול
in Cambridge Geniza Fragment T-S F2 (2) 14; the subsequent last line of the passage is
also implied by these two witnesses).

[3] Richard Kalmin, *The Redaction of the Babylonian Talmud: Amoraic or Saboraic?*
(Cincinnati: Hebrew Union College Press, 1989), 82.

[4] Kalmin, ibid.; see also Meiri and Tosafot *ad. loc.* Kalmin uses the case to differentiate
between an earlier, comparable incident (*Bava Metsi'a* 96b) in order to illustrate the difference between late Amoraic and stammaitic halakha, favoring the lender and the borrower respectively, an important observation that is not impinged upon by the present
considerations, which deal with the stammaitic text as we have it.

repetition, I argue, is a useful interpretive guide, highlighting the text's self-parody amidst a strikingly serious halakhic discourse. In my view, the sugya deconstructs and temporarily suspends its own legal and social categories, simultaneously engaging in halakhic discourse and meta-commentary on itself. The Bavli's tolerance of self-undermining, in the end, serves to refine and thereby reinforce the audience's handling of its legal categories and simultaneously allows it to explore and establish the limits of halakhic parody.

A closer look at the sugya reveals that Rav Mordecai simultaneously dismisses the case from the bench and the cat from its category as a legal entity by citing a comparable case, initially devoid of parody. His reasoning, as is so prevalent in the Talmud, remains implicit; it is the task of the audience to relate the cited reference to the case at hand. "[For] a man whom women killed – there is neither judgment nor judge," a statement authored by Rava, is cited by Rav Mordecai in the name of Abimi of Hagronia. The sugya expects its audience to understand two discursive levels implicit in Rava's statement. First, Rava is implying that the lack of masculinity of a man who had been killed – at the hands of physically weaker females – removes this parallel case from the homicide category.[5] The sugya implies that since the man failed to act as a man, he was not a "real" man by talmudic standards and therefore not a legal entity worthy of the court's deliberation.[6] Second, the audience is expected to understand the purpose of Rav Mordecai's quotation of Rava's statement in its present application. In accordance with it, the cat in the present sugya, having been killed by mice, failed to act like a

---

[5] In the Bavli, the exact phrase "there is neither judgment nor judge" means that the matter is self-evident and does not require a procedure for reaching a decision (see *Hulin* 59b and *Yoma* 72a). A looser parallel of this phrase is found in *Shabbat* 148b, לא בעינא דאיקום בדינא ודיינא, "I do not want to go to court and to bring a lawsuit" (Michael Sokoloff's translation, *A Dictionary of Jewish Babylonian Aramaic* (Ramat-Gan: Bar Ilan University Press, 2002), 319. In this case, דיינא is used as a verb, not as a noun). Intriguingly, in Palestinian Aramaic, the cognate phrase לית דין ולית דיין denotes exactly the same literal meaning as the verse in the present sugya, "there is neither judgment nor judge," but conveys a radically different message. In the Palestinian sources, the phrase is spoken by the impious, defending a position in which there is neither judgment nor judge, not just in a particular case, but categorically, asserting the absence of divine justice (see *Bereshit Rabbah* 26.6 and *Qohelet Rabbah* 1.4 and 11.8). If the Babylonian audience was to understand the sentence's older Palestinian meaning, the fate of the dead man, and of the dead cat, would cast a shadow of Ecclesiastical agnosticism over the entire debate. On Rava's familiarity with certain Palestinian traditions that make this reading more likely, see below, Chapter Three, note 29.

[6] Rashi aptly summarizes the case: "he should not have let himself be killed at their hands." (Rashi, *ad loc.*). Rabbenu Hananel, in his commentary *ad loc.* attempts to reconstruct a plausible scenario for the man's death; he does rely on details external to the text in a similar way in which the Bavli, in turn, fills in the biblical or rabbinic texts when confronted with irreconcilable divergences. The medieval imperative for coherence, in my view, exceeded that of Late Antiquity by far.

cat, and ought not to be considered a "real" cat by talmudic standards; the case, therefore, is unworthy of any further discussion, and the cat's owner is not entitled to restitution.

Even if parody is not present in the first part of the sugya, up to Rav Mordecai's first intervention, the audience already has to reconcile the sugya's conventional format and apparent sincerity with the incongruous posse of mice.[7] Mice are not known as animals that operate in groups or that initiate attacks on cats. It should be noted that for the Rabbis' Zoroastrian contemporaries, all cats, as well as mice, were considered among the *khrafstra* (noxious creatures), and killing them was a good deed.[8] Accordingly, some strands of talmudic thought view cats as problematic and promise impunity for those killing them or not returning them when found – especially if the cats are black.[9] Nevertheless, other appearances of cats in talmudic and Sasanian culture confirm the oddity of the sugya under discussion. Cats were common domestic animals in late ancient Mesopotamia and Persia, and some Sasanian[10] as well as talmudic narra-

---

[7] The sugya emphasizes the formality of the legal process by describing Rav Ashi as "sitting and pondering" (יתיב...וקמיבעיא) over the case. This description of Rav Ashi may be understood as a physical illustration of legal discussion. The portrayal of Rav Ashi's posture has several parallels in the Bavli; his image as a scholar often depicted in ceremonious deliberation resounds here. See, for example, *Yevamoth* 75b and especially *Bava Metsia* 77b, where we find the entire phrase and a possible source for the present sugya: "R. Ashi sat and cogitated thereon: "To what category does such a case belong? Does he buy it or not? R. Mordecai said to R. Ashi: Thus said Abimi of Hagronia in Rava's name: One is as many zuz, and he does not buy it." On the "recycling" of talmudic passages see Jeffrey Rubenstein, *Talmudic Stories: Narrative Art, Composition, and Culture* (Baltimore: Johns Hopkins University Press, 1999).

[8] See Mary Boyce, *A History of Zoroastrianism* (Leiden: Brill, 1989), 90–1. For examples, see Ervad Tahmuras Dinshalji Ankelsaria, ed., *Bûndahishn, being a facsimile of the TD manuscript no. 2 brought from Persia by Dastur Tîrandâz and now preserved in the late Ervad Tahmuras' library* (Byculla: British India Press, 1908), 147.15; translated in *Zand-Ākāsīh: Iranian or Greater Bundahišn / transliteration and translation in English by Behramgore Tehmuras Anklesaria* (Bombay: Dastur Framroze A. Bode, 1956), 189, 23.2; Edward William West, *Pahlavi Texts II*, Sacred Books of the East 18 (Oxford: Clarendon Press, 1882), 419.

[9] The *locus classicus* concerning cats is *Baba Qamma* 80a–b, where Rav states that "it is permissible to kill a cat, and it is in fact a sin to keep it, and the law of robbery does not apply to it [see Leviticus 19:13], neither does that of returning a lost object to its owner [see Deuteronomy 22:1–3]." As a counter-opinion, the response of R. Simeon b. Eleazar is: "It is permissible to breed village dogs, cats, apes, and porcupines, as these help to keep the house clean." The Talmud resolves the tension between the two statements by applying Rav's statements to black cats only and R. Simon's to white cats. On the behavior of mice, see, for example, the intriguing stories in *Pesahim* 10a–b, *Avodah Zarah* 68b–69a and *Hulin* 126b–127a.

[10] Mahmud Omidsalar writes that "a story in the Šāh-nāma (Moscow ed., IX, 192f. vv. 3082–3102) suggests that cats were common both as pets and mousers at the time of Khosrow II Parvēz (r. 590, 591–628). According to this story, Khosrow sent a wicked and ruthless man to Ray, the hometown of Bahrām Čōbīn … with the order to destroy it. The

tives[11] are based on sound observation of their behavior and recognition of their important role as mousers. Considering the sound status of mice and cats in these cultures renders the cat killed by mice more deliberately incongruous, even outright absurd – a literary motif for which we do have some precedent.

Such absurdity may convey a message. The antagonism between cats and mice was, indeed, a very popular motif in international folklore and art from ancient Egypt to Aesop's fables and far beyond.[12] Joshua Schwartz sees "some type of political satire" in the motif of warring cats and mice and has pointed to its occurrence in post-talmudic rabbinic literature, such as the *Alpha-Beta deBen Sira*.[13] In this parodic text, the animals invoke scriptural citations, but Schwartz does not explore the comical aspect of either the *Alpha-Beta* nor the present sugya.[14]

The concept of parody illuminates the literary function of the case of the cat in this sugya. The second part of the passage under discussion, introduced by the anonymous attribution "others say," proceeds to present a different version of the cat's fortune. The phrase "others say" suggesting alternate versions of a narrated fact, is very common in the Bavli and as such, inconspicuous – the Bavli considers all its versions of legal reality to

---

governor ordered all the house cats in the city killed, but this led to such an explosion in the mouse population that the inhabitants of the city were forced to abandon their houses. The city was saved when the queen brought a kitten to entertain the king, persuading him to remove the wicked governor from his post." See *Encyclopaedia Iranica*, ed. Ehsan Yar-Shater (London: Routledge, 1982), s.v. "cat." While Omidsalar quotes a tenth century source that may reflect later developments, its affirmation of using cats as mousers even in the face of governmental politics still indicates that the keeping of cats was at least a debated issue already in the Sasanian Empire.

[11] Cats and mice are often discussed in talmudic literature, and there are numerous halakhic passages that specify how to feed cats. Even intimate details, such as the independence of cats, draw the attention of talmudic authors. Based on the belief that eating food nibbled by mice leads to loss of memory, the Bavli observes that cats' consumption of mice explains why cats do not remember their masters (*Horayot* 13b). See the excellent discussion of Joshua Schwartz, "Cats in Ancient Jewish Society," *Journal of Jewish Studies* 52 (2001), 211–234.

[12] See Emma Brunner-Traut, "Der Katzenmäusekrieg im Alten und Neuen Orient," *Zeitschrift der Deutschen Morgenländischen Gesellschaft* 54 (1954), 347–51 as well as Stith Thompson, *Motif-Index of Folk-Literature: a Classification of Narrative Elements in Folktales, Ballads, Myths, Fables, Mediaeval Romances, Exempla, Fabliaux, Jest-Books, and Local Legends* (Bloomington and Indianapolis: Indiana University Press, 1955–1958), index, "cat," "mouse," and "mice."

[13] Schwartz, "Cats in Ancient Jewish Society," 229, n. 88

[14] Schwartz, "Cats in Ancient Jewish Society," 228, n. 79 and 230–32. See also Eli Yassif, *The Tales of Ben Sira in the Middle Ages: A Critical Text and Literary Studies* (Jerusalem: Magnes Press, 1984), 79–81, 241–42, and 298–300. On the parodic nature of the *Alpha Beta deBen Sira*, see note 58 in the Introduction.

be meaningful regardless of their apparent incompatibility.[15] This highlights the difficulty of detecting rabbinic parody: if the Bavli continually repeats similar halakhic precedents in order to emphasize a difference concerning some detail, how does it in turn mark such repetitions that expresss ironic or satiric critical distance? Moreover, the sugya now confronts its audience with the still uncommon yet more likely scenario of the cat dying of excessive work, that is, from overeating mice. This alternative at first appears to be a departure from the grotesqueness inherent in the first version, which describes a conspiracy of the mice against the cat.

The appearance of a return to straight halakhic discussion is treacherous. The sugya's author then reiterates R. Mordecai's remark from the first scenario, again citing Rava's statement that "[for] a man whom women killed – there is neither judgment nor judge." The repetition of R. Mordecai's statement once more relies on the audience's cooperation. The audience is called upon again to recognize that a man killed by women is not a man by talmudic standards, a principle applicable to the second case as well, yet with a variation in the method of killing. The audience is given to understand that a cat that dies as a result of mice, now from eating too many of them, is likewise not a cat. This first conclusion leads the audience to realize that Rava's statement about a man killed by women now similarly receives a new meaning. The man has died not from violence at the hand of females but from devouring too many of them: he died from too much sex, the metaphorical counterpart of devouring too many mice.[16]

This subtle shift from a lack of masculinity to the lack of virility as the cause of the man's death transfers the incongruence from the case under discussion to the parallel case, from a cat killed by mice to a man dying from too much sex. This shift is helpful to the sugya's expected task of resolving the question of who is required to pay for the dead cat. Yet it also invokes humans' excessive sexual activity in order to determine the halakhic category through which to perceive the behavior of domestic predators and their prey. The comparison between man and beast becomes a new, implied locus of discourse that nonetheless now usurps a central position in the sugya. Even if repeated verbatim, the meaning of the repeated statement is now even more, not less, grotesque than the first scenario.

---

[15] The Bavli uses the term "others say" to introduce juxtaposed realities that usually include attribution to different rabbis or the presentation of different scenarios. See, for example, Avraham Weiss, *The Talmud in its Development* (New York: Philipp Feldheim, 1954), 221–260 [Hebrew]; and Avraham Arzi, "איכא דאמרי," *Sinai* 89 (1981 f.), 151–56, who discusses three talmudic examples. The centrality of rabbinic discursive juxtaposition of varying and incompatible realities, in Palestine and Babylonia, has long been recognized; see note 32 in the Introduction.

[16] Rashi already understands the passage in this way, *ad loc.*

We may be able to detect parody in this repetition, since the repetition emphasizes ironic rather than halakhic difference. We need, of course, to modify the concept of parody according to talmudic literary conventions, since each repetition beginning with "others say" emphasizes a difference in the case at hand, usually to resolve a logical tension. The emphasized difference in this case, however, consists of the fact that the new case challenges the sugya's attempt to resolve halakhic tensions. The verbatim repetition of Rav Mordecai's words thereby becomes an ironic and comical imitation of the first scenario, reinforcing the sugya's play, in both scenarios of the cat's death, with double entendre, muddling distinctions between male and female, homicide and sex, humans and animals: incongruity writ large.

The sugya has thus deceived its audience, offering false relief from the grotesque by pretending to provide a more reasonable scenario in the guise of common halakhic discourse. Instead, it ironized the distinction between legal categories such as male and female, and man and beast, ultimately undermining the halakhic distinction between the case under discussion and the proffered parallel case that should have clarified, not ironized, the case at hand. By ironizing these legal categories, the sugya also ironizes the literary rules that govern its own production: Rava's first statement should have clarified the case of the cat, its repetition even more so. Instead, the repetition causes a momentary collapse of talmudic reasoning, short-circuiting any attempt to provide the type of halakhic clarification that constitutes talmudic discourse.

The imitation of Rava's statement in this sugya, under the common talmudic heading of "others say," is an ironic parody of a grotesque scenario. Moreover, since the Bavli here uses the common formulaic introduction "others say" in order to reduce the case to absurdity rather than to resolve it, we could conclude that the sugya seeks to imitate and possibly to ironize the countless similar instances of serious halakhic discourse in the Bavli that also employ this formula, intimating the possibility of parodying halakhic discourse as such or the cases of damaged borrowed property discussed earlier in the sugya. The question now becomes what the sugya wishes to accomplish with such a parody other than ironizing itself.

The introduction of satire alongside irony in our reading may answer this question. The target of satire here, in my view, is not halakhic discourse as such but Rava's discourse in the passage under discussion and in its immediate sequel, a story about Rava and his students. The passage has already parodied Rava's statement that "[for] a man whom women killed – there is neither judgment nor judge." Rava's implicit sexual politics presuppose a hypermasculine standard which Rava himself may fail to live up to, an insight that turns irony into satire. Satirizing Rava may seem counterintuitive given that he is an iconic symbol of talmudic discourse. A fourth century

Babylonian scholar and head of an academy in Mahoza, Rava is often cited as epitomizing the "dialectical" procedure of the Bavli.[17] Late ancient satire, however, tends to target one's own cultural heroes, as Daniel Boyarin recently emphasized.[18] He is, moreover, the character of another talmudic satire I discuss in Chapter Three. Hence, Rava being the target of satire in the case of the cat is a compelling possibility. In order to assess how this passage imitates the story about Rava in the sequel as well, I would like to point out the sugya's markers of incongruence in the rabbinic academy.

The unrealistic nature of the case and the repetition of Rava's statement create a sense of blatant halakhic discourse fraught with sexual tension concerning, if not transgression of, morality and gender roles. Still, before ascribing a humorous intention to the sugya's play with absurdity, it must be stressed that the Bavli contains many rhetorical structures that contemplate unlikely scenarios simply in order to determine the adaptability and bounds of halakhic categories. Cases that transcend the conceivable illustrate the Bavli's ostentatious celebration of exceeding precision in regards to halakhic matters without diminishing its own seriousness.[19] Yet in this sugya, both scenarios – mice killing a cat and a man dying from excessive sexual

---

[17] For a summary discussion of talmudic dialectics and further bibliography, see Jeffrey Rubenstein, "The Thematization of Dialectics in Bavli Aggada," *Journal of Jewish Studies* 54 (2003), 71–84; see also Barry Wimpfheimer, *Telling Tales out of Court: Literary Ambivalence in Talmudic Legal Narratives* (Philadelphia: University of Pennsylvania Press, forthcoming).

[18] See pages 16 f in the Introduction.

[19] One useful example of inconceivable scenarios, also involving sexuality and Rava, is the famous consideration of a man who falls off a roof, his penis accidentally penetrating (תקע) a woman's vagina (*Bava Qamma* 27a). Rava is fully aware of the realistic unlikelihood of such a scenario; elsewhere, for example, he ponders the necessity of erection in a case of unintentional heterosexual intercourse (*Yevamoth* 53b–54a). While the scenario is unlikely in real life, Rava remains serious, seeking to determine the legal implications of such a case. Elsewhere, the Bavli dismisses cases in which individuals transgress the fine line between sophistication and sophistry and excludes such rabbis from its discourse. In *Menahot* 37a–b, for example, Pelemo asks Rabbi on which head a man with two heads must first place his Tefilin. Rabbi, assuming the man seeks to ridicule him, asks him to leave or to accept a ban. Even if the case is eventually taken as a serious problem (a man reports having a child with two heads), Rabbi's reaction proves the Bavli's awareness of the susceptibility of its own halakhic discourse to parodic ridicule. A similar case involving the removal of a rabbi from the Beyt Midrash is that of Rabbi Jeremiah in *Bava Batra* 23b. The removal again indicates an attempt at parody. Although the precise halakhic transgression is too complex to be treated here, it suffices to note that elsewhere in the Bavli, Rabbi Jeremiah is explicitly accused of trying to make R. Zera laugh (לידי גיחוך), but the latter did not laugh (ולא גחיך, *Nidah* 23a). As Richard Kalmin aptly points out in his discussion on a statement concerning an elephant defecating a basket whole found both in *Bava Batra* 22a and *Menahot* 69a, the degree to which an absurd question reinforces or challenges proper rabbinic conduct is largely dependent on the context in which the question is asked (*Sages, Stories, Authors, and Editors in Rabbinic Babylonia* (Atlanta: Scholars Press, 1994), 5–7.

activity – are not ironic, or even coyly incongruous, but utterly absurd. I would be hesitant, however, to posit absurdity itself as an objective of any sugya whose function it is to harmonize, not ironize or even satirize, legal concepts. If absurdity in the sugya makes little sense in and of itself, it may serve a function that goes beyond the passage itself.

Indeed, this sugya employs several strategies to guide the audience towards perceiving the case of the cat killed by mice as a commentary on the relationship between rabbis and their insubordinate students, which is, in my view, the main concern of the entire passage under discussion. The vocabulary of the sugya reminds its audience of the danger emanating from one's "fellow," or rabbinic "colleague" (חבר) by repeating the same Aramaic root used in the description of the mice's "banding together" (חבור). This wordplay is especially astute in light of the discussion's rabbinic setting: the same Hebrew (and Aramaic) term "fellow" usually denotes a rabbinic colleague; it can likewise refer to a superior or inferior colleague or even be used as an honorary title for a learned rabbinical student.[20] Such students can band together and attack their master just like mice, as the audience will soon learn.

I shall confirm my reading of Rava's statement here and in the text's sequel as the target of the parody's satire by suggesting that the Bavli, in effect, uses the case of the cat as a parodic preface to the subsequent story of a student revolt against Rava. My reading of this text builds upon Barry Wimpfheimer's arguments in a recent pioneering analysis of the literary qualities of the conflict between Rava and his students.[21] In order to assess more fully the purpose of pairing this narrative with the case of the cat as a target text and a parody (Rava vs. students parodied by cat vs. mice), let us consider the following story about the academic demise of a talmudic master, which also contains a parody. (I repeat the case of the cat to illustrate the full effect of the juxtaposition of the two passages.)

A man [גברא] borrowed a cat from his fellow [מחבריה].
The mice united [חבור] against it and killed it.
Now, R. Ashi sat and pondered thereon: "To what category does such a case belong?
    (Is it as though it had died from work, or not?")
R. Mordecai said to R. Ashi: "Thus said Abimi of Hagronia in Rava's name:

---

[20] See Kalmin, *Sages, Stories, Authors, and Editors in Rabbinic Babylonia*, 208–09; the use of חבר in *Quiddushin* 33b is indicative of its hierarchical implications. The term equally designates a member of a religious group that is bound to close observance of the Levitical laws (see, for example, *Berakhot* 28b and *Bekhorot* 31a–b), but this association does not seem relevant here.

[21] Barry Wimpfheimer, "'But it is not so': Toward a Poetics of Legal Narrative in the Talmud," *Prooftexts* 24 (2004), 51–86; see also *Telling Tales out of Court: Literary Ambivalence in Talmudic Legal Narratives*.

'[For] a man whom women killed – there is neither judgment nor judge [לא דינא ולא
דיינא]!'"

Others say: "[The cat] ate many mice, whereby it sickened and died."

R. Ashi sat and cogitated thereon: "To what category does such a case belong?"

Said R. Mordecai to R. Ashi: "Thus said Abimi of Hagronia in Rava's name:
'[For] a man whom women killed – there is neither judgment nor judge.'"

Rava said: "If a man wishes to borrow something from another and be exempt [from
    liability for the item],

He should say to him, 'Give us a drink of water,' (so that it constitutes 'a loan [in the
    presence] of the owners [שאילה בבעלים]').[22]

But if he [the owner] is wise, he should answer, 'First borrow it, (and then I will give
    you a drink).'"[23]

Rava said: "A teacher of small [children, מקרי דרדקי], a gardener, a butcher, a circum-
    ciser, and a town barber – all [if they lend something] while at work, [do so under
    the laws of] the 'loan in [the presence of] the owner.'"

The rabbis said to Rava: "You are loaned to us, Master."

He became angry [אקפיד].

He said to them: "Do you want to deprive me of my monetary compensation [ממוני]?

On the contrary, you are loaned to me! For I can change you from one tractate to
    another while you cannot change [me]!"

But it is not so; he was lent to them during the *Kallah* days
while they were loaned to him during the rest of the year.

Rava is suggesting a sly way of obtaining a far-reaching waiver for a borrower's liability, exploiting the concept of a "loan in the presence of the
owner." This concept constitutes a peculiarity in rabbinic civil law; it was
derived from the notion of an "owner being with" a borrowed animal in
biblical property law. The halakhic details of this concept are essential for
understanding the sugya's parody of Rava.

In the Hebrew Bible, the "presence of the owner" simply refers to the
physical presence of the owner of a borrowed animal during its use for the
purpose of protecting it.[24] Given the possibility of the owner overseeing the
use of his animal, the biblical law exempts the borrower from liability for it.
The Mishna, the third-century halakhic corpus that constitutes the basis of

---

[22] Wimpfheimer points out that "this statement in parentheses, missing from the Florence II-I-8, Hamburg 165, and Cremona eb. T. IV 10 manuscripts, is an explanatory addition" ("But it is not so," 75 n6). It is also missing from the Cambridge Geniza Fragment
T-S F2 (2) 14).

[23] Wimpfheimer argues that "this statement [in parentheses], missing in Ms. Florence
II-I-8 and some geonic witnesses, is an explanatory addition ("But it is not so," 76 n8). I
do not share his confidence in this case that we can establish the "original" text of the
Bavli; an omission in this manuscript is equally possible. The statement appears in Ms.
Munich 95, Ms. Escorial G-I-3, Ms. Vatican 115, and in the Vilna and Soncino prints, yet
it is missing in the Cambridge Geniza Fragment T-S F2 (2) 14).

[24] Exodus 22:13–15 states that "when someone borrows [ישאל] an animal from another
and it is injured or dies, the owner [בעליו] not being present, full restitution shall be made.
If the owner was present, there shall be no restitution."

the talmudic commentary, applies the biblical law in order to rule in all cases of liability for loaned property, not just in the case of borrowed animals. The Mishna, emending Exodus, stipulates that in order to waive the borrower's liability, the owner himself must be hired, or "borrowed," along with his property.[25] This is logical from the point of view of the Mishna's authors because of two conflations in rabbinic thought. First, the Mishna, in its determination of the owner's responsibility, does not differentiate in this case between a paid and an unpaid engagement of the owner. Second, rabbinic Hebrew and Aramaic use the same word, שאל, for borrowing objects as well as engaging someone's services for free. The Mishna therefore translates the biblical "presence" of the owner into the owner's loaning himself along with is property. Reflecting this double conceptual conflation, I shall henceforth translate the "borrowing" of an owner as "engaging" him.[26]

Moreover, the Mishna specifies that the verbal contract governing the owner's services must be made *prior* to the request for the borrowed animal in order for the engagement to qualify as a "loan in the presence of the owner." If this condition is met, the owner is responsible for his property under all circumstances, regardless of his whereabouts and regardless of whether he receives payment for the services or not. In Wimpfheimer's words, the owner is "contractually present"[27] with the borrowed objects at all times since he has made a שאילה בבעלים, a "loan in the [presence of the] owner."

The talmudic sugya under discussion is, among other things, a legal commentary on the Mishna's halakha concerning borrowed property. Here, Rava presents an extreme case of the mishnaic rule in order to test and push the limits of a halakhic category, a "loan in the presence of the owner." For Rava, an owner's agreement to serve water to a prospective borrower (of an unspecified item) already constitutes a legally binding engagement of the owner along with the property he loans. Hence, a crafty borrower can exempt himself from liability for a borrowed item simply by requesting water from the owner *prior* to requesting to borrow his property. According to this logic, if the request for water is granted, it constitutes a contractual engagement and renders the subsequent loan liability-free; it will have been

---

[25] Mishna *Bava Metsi'a* 8.1 (Danby, modified): "If a man borrowed a cow together with the service of its owner, or hired its owner together with the cow, or if he borrowed the service of the owner or hired him, and afterward borrowed the cow, and the cow died, he is not liable, for it is written: *If the owner was present, there shall be no restitution*. But if he first borrowed the cow and afterward borrowed or hired the service of the owner, and the cow died, he is liable, for it is written: *The owner* [בעליו] *not being present, full restitution shall be made*."

[26] The Hebrew usage also governs the meaning of the term שאל in Aramaic; see Sokoloff, *A Dictionary of Jewish Babylonian Aramaic*, 1099.

[27] Barry Wimpfheimer, "'But it is not so,'" 52 f.

made "in the presence of the owner." One could hardly push the limit of the category any further than Rava does.

Rava's playful exploration of the limits of the halakha includes the appropriate response to such a contractual trap: "But if [the owner] is wise, he should answer him, 'First borrow it, and then I will give you a drink.'"[28] If the owner defers the contractual engagement by simply pouring the water *after* he loans his property, the borrower will be liable for it.[29]

Wimpfheimer suggests that Rava's "control of the legal material allows for law's metamorphosis into comedy," without specifying the nature or purpose of the comedic outcome.[30] While I agree with Wimpfheimer on the comical nature of the passage, it is not, in my view, Rava's initial procedure that is intended to appear comical. Rava is indeed ostentatiously playful, and perhaps his advice hints at the liberty he takes with the underlying biblical and mishnaic concept of "in the presence of the owner." Ultimately, however, Rava searches for an extreme case to which one can duly apply the mishnaic concept.[31] I doubt that the sugya in this respect intends to be more comical than any other talmudic sugya.

Still, Wimpfheimer's intuition does recognize an instance close to what I consider parody: the response of "the rabbis" to Rava's subsequent witty ruling. Rava's next statement declares that "A teacher of small [children], a gardener, a butcher, a circumciser, and a town barber – all [if they lend something] while at work, [do so under the laws of] the 'loan in [the presence of] the owner.'" In other words, since these professionals, in practice, are already engaged by the public, borrowers automatically become exempt from liability for items borrowed from the owners.[32]

---

[28] It is possible that this line ("but if he is wise …") is a Stammaitic comment. If this is the case, the stam, not Rava, provides the outlet for the owner. The source of the sentence does not affect my analysis in a significant manner.

[29] There is obvious tension between the Mishna's legal peculiarity and the meaning of biblical law. Rava, in the Bavli, heightens this tension by pushing the mishnaic concept as far as one can, but whether the Bavli is invested in drawing attention to this tension remains unclear. The incongruity between the Bible and rabbinic legislation may appear strange to a modern reader's sense of legal harmony whereas the Bavli exerts as much pressure as it can on any legal concept. This is the very nature of rabbinic legal discussion. The sugya may simply depict Rava as exploiting the ensuing legal loophole.

[30] Barry Wimpfheimer, "'But it is not so,'" 53.

[31] Barry Wimpfheimer, "But it is not so,'" 60. Wimpfheimer goes on to restrict the impact of such comedy by stating that talmudic debate cannot "constitute a deferral of meaning, because it is too closely connected to the realities of life."

[32] According to Wimpfheimer, Rava here characterizes public service as a new legal category of professional classification ("But it is not so," 54). Rava, however, also provides a similar list in *Bava Metsi'a* 109a–b and *Bava Batra* 31a–b where he also assumes a strict position towards the same public servants. Rava's negative perception of public servants increases the insult in his students' listing of Rava as a public servant himself. (See also *Sanhedrin* 17b for a slightly different list of public servants). Wimpfheimer addressed the

In response, the students repeat Rava's witty application of the law – with the difference that they use it against their teacher. Since he is their teacher, they declare that: "You are engaged by us, Master," implying that his ruling concerning public professionals would waive liability for any item they may borrow from him, too. If the property is damaged while in the students' possession, Rava would forfeit compensation since his prior engagement annuls their liability, hence his response, "do you want to deprive me of my monetary compensation?"[33] In effect, the students engage in parody, repeating Rava's jurisprudence with parodic irony and satirizing his halakha here and elsewhere.

Wimpfheimer notes that one of the professionals on Rava's list "is a 'teacher of children' – an unprestigious member of the secondary intelligentsia" (56). By describing Rava as a public professional, Wimpfheimer argues, the students not only threaten to damage him financially but also implicitly associate him with the "teacher of children" invoked by Rava himself.[34] "The Rabbis" quickly learn from their teacher, who had just drawn on the talmudic practice of testing categories and include the great Rava in the same category with a barber, a butcher, and even a teacher of small children. They expand the category of public service a little too much, undermining the rabbi's prestige by applying his very own logic and perception of public professionals.

The concept of literary parody illuminates the techniques and targets of the students' imitative criticism and extends Wimpfheimer's analysis of the passage.[35] Most importantly, the students' imitative technique mirrors the Mishna's terminology, and thereby Rava's use of the Mishna, satirizing his understanding of a "loan in the presence of the owner." The parody becomes evident upon noting that the students' statement precisely imitates the two components of the mishnaic term that Rava himself had exploited. The sentence "you are loaned to us, Master" corresponds to "a loan in the presence of the owner." A precise reading reveals the full extent of the pa-

---

parallel lists in a talk entitled "*Ashgera Delishna*: A Case Study in List Transmission" (paper presented at the annual meeting of the Association for Jewish Studies (AJS), Los Angeles, December 16, 2002), which he was kind enough to share with me. For a systematic study of conceptualization in the Bavli, see Leib Moscovitz, *Talmudic Reasoning: From Casuistics to Conceptualization* (Tübingen: Mohr Siebeck, 2002).

[33] The term ממון denotes money in general and monetary compensation for damages in particular. See Sokoloff, *A Dictionary of Jewish Babylonian Aramaic*, 682.

[34] According to Wimpfheimer, the students "in attendance translate [Rava's]... category of [public] employee ... into proximate reality by suggesting that Rava, their teacher, is in this category" ("But it is not so," 55). The audience, "offstage," may be just as surprised by the students' move as Rava is "onstage."

[35] The students' deflation of Rava entails their own deflation, for if he is the teacher, it follows that they are the children. There is a sense of comical self-deprecation here, which by no means diminishes the insult to Rava.

rodic repetition, since the student's customary address of Rava as "Master" is imbued with an additional parodic function. First, the mishnaic text refers to a "loan" (שאילה), and the students refer to Rava as "loaned" (i.e., engaged, שאיל לן). Second, the loan occurs in the presence of the "owner[s]" (בבעלים), so the students' customary address of Rava as "master" (מר, a partial synonym of בעל) now gains a parodic connotation.

The students to this point imitate the Mishna. Their statement, however, makes clear that the target of their satire is not the Mishna but Rava's interpretation of it, according to which the lenders are public professionals. Hence, the students satirize Rava's ruling at the expense of service professionals by imitating and manipulating his underlying mishnaic category and by including Rava in his own list of such professionals. They expose the weakness of Rava's maneuver by making him the subject of discourse.[36] The students' parody fuses imitation of the Mishna with an attack on Rava's exegesis, all, supposedly, in the context of the existing halakhic discussion. In other words, the students "simply" explore another extreme of Rava's category as he had done himself before, inverting authorship and the subject of halakhic discourse in the same way that the parodic repetition of Rava's statement usurped the center stage in the case of the cat.

This passage can be viewed as a miniature of *exegetical parody*, providing, along with the example from the Yerushalmi in the Introduction, another model for the primary type of parody discussed in this book. The students' imitation of the Mishna by no means seeks to satirize the mishnaic concept itself. Rather, the students' parody targets Rava's interpretation. By implicating Rava himself in the halakhic discussion, the students destabilize his authority.[37]

---

[36] Wimpfheimer writes, referring to a different case, that Rava is "contextualized – rendered part of the fabric of law that his students navigate their way around" ("But it is not so," 67).

[37] The implications of the students' parody go beyond the sugya under discussion and may target Rava as depicted elsewhere in the same tractate. Wimpfheimer, discussing other rulings of Rava in *Bava Metsiʿa*, indicates that Rava expresses "lenience toward the one watching" the goods or properties of another ("But it is not so," 64). The pro bono watchmen elsewhere in *Bava Metsʿia* correspond to the borrowers in our sugya: both are entrusted with the property of others, and in both cases, the sugya focuses on the question of liability for this property. Hence, it is quite possible that Rava's students target their teacher's lenient attitude towards the ones looking after the property of others as well. Wimpfheimer does not apply this crucial insight to the passage under discussion. Yet, he does portray Rava as an "activist judge," inclined towards the poor ("But it is not so," 68f). It is true that the sugya's author portrays Rava's legal tendency to benefit borrowers. It is difficult to apply the insight regarding the watchman to the case of the property borrower. Part of Rava's leniency towards borrowers originates already in the Mishna, and it is by no means clear that borrowers in a rural economy are structurally poorer than lenders; borrowers and lenders may trade roles on a daily basis, depending on the tools and animals

In addition to the imitation and satire of Rava's ruling, we find another aspect of parody in the students' exploitation of the ambiguity of the rabbinic term שאל, which denotes "borrowing" as well as "engaging." The surface meaning of the sugya suggests that Rava is the owner of property that can be borrowed, implying that Rava can be engaged along with it. The polysemy of the Hebrew word, however, leads the audience to perceive Rava himself as a borrowed item. Did the author of the sugya intend to objectify a talmudic master and equate him to damaged property?

One could argue that Rava becomes enraged, thereby deviating from talmudic behavioral norms and displaying characteristics of damaged property. In effect, losing self control and becoming angry may indicate ultimate defeat, as it did in the Hellenistic world.[38] Yet the sugya, at least for the time being, does not promote such a reevaluation. This passage alone does not give us any further hints that would allow us to determine Rava's status, simply as owner or as owner as well as borrowed and damaged property. The lexical ambiguity between "borrowed" and "engaged," as it plays out in the passage at large, however, constitutes a fulcrum that links the struggle between Rava and his students to the case of the cat to which I shall shortly return.

The students, however, have already parodied their teacher. A parody at the center of talmudic discourse, the pedagogic hothouse of the rabbinic academy, or *Beyt Midrash*, is not a trivial matter. Demoting a talmudic master undermines rabbinic culture per se.[39] At the same time, it is clear that the students are under the full control of the sugya's author. This author is using another type of rabbinic parody (in addition to exegetical parody) that I call *voiced parody*: the author uses the students' voices in order to express his own criticism of Rava, perhaps reflecting on the Bavli's potential

---

needed. The fact that the Mishna and the talmudic sugya do not distinguish between paid and unpaid engagement of the lender further complicates the matter.

[38] Rava's anger is the focus of Wimpfheimer's article ("But it is not so," 52–61). Self-control is the most central virtue of the Hellenistic world as may be best illustrated by the Greek novels (See, for example, B.P. Reardon (ed.), *Collected Ancient Greek Novels* (Berkeley: University of California Press, 2008), 48, 51, 69, 93, 180, 190, 271, 283, 287. For broader discussions on this topic in Greek and Roman culture, see, for example, Stuart E. Lawrence, "Self-Control in Homeric Deliberations," *Prudentia* 34 (2002), 1–15; Margaret deMaria Smith, "Enkrateia: Plutarch on Self-Control and the Politica of Excess," *Ploutarchos* 1 (2003–2004), 79–88; and Jean-Luc Gauville, "La conception du contrôle de soi dans le récit de l'«Épitomé des Césars»," *Cahiers des études anciennes* 37 (2001), 83–87. A study on the applicability of Hellenistic norms to rabbinic culture remains a desideratum. On rabbinic emotions, see Jeffrey Rubenstein, *The Culture of the Babylonian Talmud*, 54–79. On ascetic self-control, see also Chapter Two, pages 86–94, and Chapter Five, pages 187–89.

[39] For a summary of the hierarchical system of the rabbinic academy, see Jeffrey Rubenstein, *The Culture of the Babylonian Talmud*, 16–38 and Richard Kalmin, *Sages, Stories, Authors, and Editors in Rabbinic Babylonia*, 193–216.

vulnerability to parodic criticism.[40] Fending off, as it were, his own attack, the author of the sugya himself responds forcefully with three reactions to the students' halakhic parody. The first follows immediately: in the sequel, the sugya's author reports Rava's anger and his adamant insistence on controlling the curriculum: "For I can change you from one tractate to another, while you cannot change [me]!" Rava points out that the students are bound by his curriculum and are therefore engaged by him rather than the other way around. Rava responds, according to Wimpfheimer, "with a deliberate claim to authority and reminds the group of his authorizing presence."[41] The one who decides what "work" needs to be done is the master; those who follow his directions are the engaged workers. Liability for borrowed goods, therefore, remains with the borrowers, not the owner.

Rava's answer, even if fully cognizant of the students' challenge, seeks only to invert it, failing to raise the bar of talmudic debate as would be expected of a talmudic master. While Rava does not lack wit when turning the table on the students, he nevertheless depends on evoking the authority he momentarily lost and relies on force and status rather than responding to the students' sophisticated challenge with a worthy intellectual counter argument. Rava therefore breaches the contract of consensual talmudic study, just as the students crossed the fine line separating playful exploration of extreme halakhic cases from halakhic parody. Rava's defeat is accompanied, or perhaps even illustrated by anger and lack of self-control.

As is typical in the Bavli, the sugya itself assumes the ultimate responsibility for resolving the conflict between Rava and the students, constituting, in the wake of Rava's inept reaction, a second response to the students' halakhic challenge. The anonymous voice of the sugya's stammaitic author intervenes and announces that contrary to Rava's claim, "It is not so", reacting "strongly against Rava's claim to authority," as Wimpfheimer aptly puts it.[42] The stam concludes that in effect, Rava and his students are alternately engaged, taking turns in accordance with the traditional Babylonian rabbinic curriculum.

Rava, during the bulk of the year, is free to choose the mishnaic tractate for his teaching; the sugya views him as the master who engages the services of his students and is thus exempt from liability for property he may borrow from them. During the rabbinic months of intensive study, the *Kallah* months, the teacher is bound by the decision of the head of the previous Kallah, who decides which tractate will be studied during the subsequent

---

[40] This type of voiced parody also occurs in other examples of rabbinic parody, such as in the case of Rabbi Isaac's voicing of Hananya's parody discussed in the Introduction and in the voicing of gospel passages discussed in Chapter Four.

[41] "But it is not so," 58.

[42] "But it is not so," 58.

one. Since Rava cannot determine the curriculum during this period, the sugya argues, he is effectively engaged by the students, who in turn are free from liability for goods they may borrow from him.[43] The sugya transcends the conflict in the Beyt Midrash by finding an equitable solution, displaying its firm control over its voiced parody.

The sugya's resolution of the conflict clarifies that it does not endorse either side in the conflict; reading the story as a whole, the sugya seems to steer its audience away from the students' halakhic parody and from Rava's inadequate answer. It agrees, of course, with Rava's sense that the students' parody is unacceptable. Since Rava's answer to them is inadequate, however, the sugya offers a more erudite response to the students, thereby constituting a model for other teachers facing students' attempts to turn the tables, parodying the teacher as they incorporate him into the studied material. In its dismissal of the arguments of both sides, the stammaitic intervention ("it is not so") at the end of the episode seems to be aware of, and dismiss, halakhic parody, at least in this instance.

Without further ado, the sugya resumes halakhic discourse with yet another conflict, devoid of parody, between Rava and the rabbis about liability for borrowed property.[44] After ending the students' revolt with a binding halakhic decision about the liability for items borrowed by a teacher from his students and vice versa, the sugya leaves its audience without any further guidance for assessing the halakhic parodies it had just encountered. There is, however, a third, implicit response that the sugya offers to the students' halakhic parody, in addition to the ones already mentioned, and which is placed before the students' revolt: the case of the cat. This third response may reveal the sugya's awareness of the human element in the creation of halakha.[45] This parody is more immediately aligned with the sugya itself than the student revolt. The students' revolt, in other words, functioned as a powerful example of parody, from which the sugya ultimately distanced itself. The case of the cat, however, is part of the sugya's response to the

---

[43] The Kallah days are "the days in which Rava's prescription [of public service] enslaves its creator," as Wimpfheimer puts it ("But it is not so," 59). On the institution of the Kallah months, see Isaiah M. Gafni, *The Jews of Babylonia in the Talmudic Era* (Jerusalem: Merkaz Zalman Shazar, 1990) [Hebrew], 213 ff. On the possibly Christian provenance of the term "Kallah months," see idem "חיבורים נסטוריאניים כמקור לתולדות ישיבות בבל," *Tarbiz* 51 (1981), 572 f.

[44] The sugya accordingly continues its reflection on Rava's emotions. See Wimpfheimer, "But it is not so," 61–71.

[45] For a discussion concerning the Bavli's discourse on the human agenda at play in establishing law and history, see Moulie Vidas, "The Bavli's Discussion of Genealogy in *Qiddushin* IV," in: Gregg Gardner and Kevin Osterloh (eds.) *Antiquity in Antiquity: Jewish and Christian Pasts in the Greco-Roman World*, (Tübingen: Mohr Siebeck, 2008), 285–326.

students' attack in as far as it parodies the students' parody of their teacher. I suggest that the case of the cat structurally imitates the narrative of Rava and his students and that the sugya guides its audience towards a satirical understanding of the students' revolt just before relating it – an instance of what I identify as redactional parody. The author of a redactional parody controls both the imitated text and the parody. In this case, the parody preempts the audience from appreciating the student's attack of their teacher unchecked – the case of the cat precedes the students' revolt, and the parody thereby precedes the text it imitates. Rabbinic hyper-textuality accounts for this possibility of preemptive redactional parody (which we shall encounter again in Chapter Two). The two scenarios in the cat episode – the cat dying as a result of being attacked by mice or from eating too many mice – imitate and satirize the struggle between Rava and his students in a number of ways.

Most importantly, I suggest the following structural correspondence between the characters of the case of the cat and the students' revolt. Rava corresponds to the cat (a predator), his students to the mice, their united attack to killing; in short, Rava is compared parodically to the cat killed by mice. The two power struggles are structurally so similar that an audience expecting imitation and satire may immediately grasp the parody inherent to the case of the cat upon first reading the narrative of the student revolt. The first effect of recognizing the target of satire, of course, would be a ridicule of both sides to the conflict: Rava, the talmudic hero, at this point reveals himself as such a weak teacher that the image of a cat killed by mice seems appropriate. The students' insubordination in the face of their master, in turn, may have won the moment, but the parody is soon to depict them as mere mice.

The parody thus comments on the student revolt in accordance with the sugya's negative stance towards it. The basic structural correspondence between the two narratives undermines the student revolt as it is being told. Yet how can we be certain enough about the author's intentions? This parody works very differently from the previously suggested occurrence of parody in the student revolt. The parody's imitation of words from the Mishna and of Rava's jurisprudence that guided us there is missing here. The case of the cat, nevertheless, compensates for this absence by indicating its parodic treatment of Rava and his students in five ways that enhance the structural similarity.

First, the case of the cat, in and of itself, is an elaborate parodic commentary on the statement it cites in Rava's name ("[For] a man whom women killed – there is neither judgment nor judge."). I argued that the sugya satirizes Rava's statement concerning dead men. This can now be confirmed. By positing the case of the cat as a parody of the student revolt, the sugya's author turns Rava's own statement against him and refines the structural imitation of Rava as a cat. In the case of the cat, the statement was used to imply that a cat killed by mice is not a cat according to talmudic standards, and its owner therefore is not entitled to remuneration. Rereading the case of the cat as parody of Rava himself, we now understand that, in turn, a rabbi overcome by his students is also not a rabbi according to talmudic standards. The parody deploys Rava's very own logic against him, much like the students had done. The case of the cat parodies, but also illuminates, the case of the student revolt and at the same time is illuminated by it through a bidirectional reading in the best talmudic manner.[46]

Second, the sugya reinforces this basic parody by indicating that the cat is borrowed by a man's colleague (חבר). While "fellow" simply denotes another man, the same word can also refer to a rabbinic colleague, or student. The full potential of the wordplay between rabbinic "colleague" (חבר) and the united mice (חבור) now becomes evident in what is another bidirectional reading of the case of the cat as parody. The repetition of the Hebrew word guides the perceptive audience when it is trying to come to terms with a revolt of the rabbinic "fellows" against the rabbi in the rabbinic house of study. Once the audience perceives Rava as the cat and the students as the mice, it fully realizes the urgency of the sugya's play on the lexical ambiguity, showing that the rabbinic "colleagues" can indeed act as a mere posse.

Third, in a less pronounced, yet still palpable, structural parallel, the alternate scenario of the cat's death, from overeating, imitates Rava's forceful (if hardly spirited) response to his students. According to this scenario, the cat eats many mice and momentarily prevails, but the cat is not their true master: instead, it falls sick and dies. Similarly, Rava simply devours his students collectively by citing his authority over the tractates rather than by refuting them with more intellectual rigor. Rava's weak argument, even though it curtails the students' revolt, reveals acute signs social illness: anger and failure to respond in an appropriate manner.

Fourth, the sugya's parody has by now produced three frequently opposed pairs: man/women, cat/mice, and Rava/students. The two ways in which cats and men lethally interact with mice and women – murder or ravenous self-killing, that is, too much sex for the man or too much eating for the cat – hints towards the height of absurdity. Rava is either killed by the students, dies from too much sex with them, or perishes by devouring them all, an incongruent image indeed. When contextualizing this image in talmudic culture, however, the sugya's commentary on Rava's sexual politics in the case of the cat is now understood anew. Reconceptualized as a parody of

---

[46] The Bavli codifies such bidirectional readings by stating that a text "came to teach and found itself being taught about," בא ללמד ונמצא למד; see, for example, *Sanhedrin* 54a, *Hulin* 28a and *Arakhin* 34a.

the students' revolt, the sexual image becomes metaphorically precise. In the Bavli, sexual acts fall under the two opposing categories of "male-penetrating-conquering" and "female-penetrated-conquered."[47] In the first scenario evoked by the case of the cat, the students simply "kill" Rava through their own parody of his halakha. When Rava's statement in the case of the cat is quoted a second time, it implies that the dead man conquered and devoured the women sexually, leading to his demise, just as the cat ate too many mice. We are thereby given to understand that Rava, similarly, conquered and devoured his students in his response to their challenge. Rava wins the debate yet is eventually defeated in the second scenario as well, much like the cat, which dies from overeating, and the man who dies after having too much sex. Hence, the parody can be understood as commentary on Rava's pedagogic abuse of his students by insisting on his institutional authority rather than engaging them in rabbinic debate. Removing the barrier of consensual rabbinic study, in the ambivalent homoerotic environment of the Beyt Midrash, leads to Rava's demise as a figure of unchallenged authority.[48]

While the first four structural parallels are readily palpable, the fifth one would only be accessible to a rabbinic audience that accepts the parody's invitation to reexamine all the halakhic categories at play. For it now seems possible that the sugya parodically depicts Rava, like the cat, as damaged borrowed property, the topic of the entire sugya. A certain "damage" done to Rava indicated not only by his anger but also by the sugya's image of a teacher whose reputation is momentarily ruined by his students' attack. The sugya may exploit the ambiguity of the Hebrew and Aramaic word שאל in order to lead the audience to perceive this aspect of the parody. When the narrative of the student revolt is considered separately, Rava is clearly a "borrowed," (i.e., engaged) teacher, but it remains unclear to what extent the sugya exploits the lexical ambiguity and metaphorically portrays

---

[47] Michael L. Satlow, "'They Abused Him like a Woman': Homoeroticism, Gender Blurring, and the Rabbis in Late Antiquity," *Journal of the History of Sexuality* 5 (1994), 1–15. The most famous formulation of the ubiquitous late ancient paradigm that equated penetration with conquest, a formulation shared by the rabbis, may be Suetonius' report of the song sung during Caesar's triumph: "All the Gauls did Caesar vanquish, Nicomedes vanquished him; Lo! now Caesar rides in triumph, victor over all the Gauls, Nicomedes does not triumph, who subdued the conqueror (*De Vita Caesarum* II. XLIX).

[48] Daniel Boyarin reminds us that in the talmudic moral economy, homoeroticism must be transferred from a man to a woman, yet in this case, it is transferred from women to men. See *Carnal Israel: Reading Sex in Talmudic Culture* (Berkeley: University of California Press, 1995), 215–19. See also Boyarin's "Why is Rabbi Yohanan a Woman? Or, A Queer Marriage Gone Bad: 'Platonic Love' in the Talmud," in *Authorizing Marriage? Canon, Tradition, and Critique in the Blessing of Same-Sex Unions*, ed. Mark D. Jordan (Princeton: Princeton University Press, 2006), 52–67 and 178–184 and Charlotte Elisheva Fonrobert, "On *Carnal Israel* and the Consequences: Talmudic Studies since Foucault," *The Jewish Quarterly Review* 95 (2005), 462–269.

Rava as "borrowed" property as well. Once the audience, guided by the structural similarities and other markers (such as Rava's appearance in the two consecutive narratives), grasps that Rava is akin to the damaged cat, it understands the imitated texts anew. The cat, it turns out, fully imitates Rava in this regard as well. The cat is borrowed property just as "the rabbis" claim that Rava is "borrowed" (engaged); the cat is damaged (killed by mice), twice, just as Rava's failure contains two separate aspects: his failure to ensure discipline and once his authority is questioned, his failure properly to respond to the students' parody. Just as he became a "teacher of children" and a "public servant" in the students' voiced parody, he becomes borrowed damaged property in the sugya's redactional parody.

The various ways in which the case of the cat imitates the students' revolt, in my view, suggest that the sugya's redactor sought to parody and satirize Rava once more, this time along with his students. The recasting of the halakhic and narrative elements of the student revolt in the case of the cat satirizes both the weak teacher and the rebellious students. The image of Rava and his students as domestic animals ensures a satirical understanding of this parody.

This parody, however, is less clearly marked as such than the parodies generated by the repetition of Rava's statement in the case of the cat and by the students' imitation of Rava. It is, in fact, easy for an audience unaccustomed to bidirectional reading *and* unsuspecting of parody to miss it, for two interrelated reasons. The first is because it is a preemptive parody that presents the parody before the imitated text, just like in the example discussed in the Introduction, which cites the parody before the biblical verses it goes on to imitate. The second is because it is a redactional parody, a concept that we can now consider in more detail.

We do not know, of course, to what extent the author of this sugya relies on preexisting materials. The nature of the Bavli in general strongly suggests that such materials were used, and the completeness of both narratives (the case of the cat and the student revolt) suggests their preexistence as units as well.[49] If this is so, then the author of the sugya, as the redactor of such materials, fused the two textual units and thereby imbued them with a new meaning. An audience aware of the redactional quality of the sugya would have been attuned to the way in which the sugya's author arranged preexisting textual units still recognizable as such and to the textual relationship between them. Even if the original textual forms of these units remain

---

[49] The main proponents of a redactional archeology of the Bavli are David Halivni and Shamma Friedman. For a helpful summary and discussion of the work of Halivni and Friedman, see Aryeh Cohen, *Rereading Talmud: Gender, Law and the Poetics of Sugyot* (Atlanta: Scholars Press, 1998), 7–122. See also note 61 in the Introduction.

unrecoverable, it is likely that the sugya requires its intended audience to perceive the redactional units as such, and to relate them to each other as units. That such units were continuously retold in new contexts and with new nuance as part of their oral performances makes it even more likely that the Bavli's audience would perceive of such units as distinct entities that are relatable to each other.

Linking the textual units, in this case, would not have required the repetition of similar words in the second unit, other than the name "Rava;" the structural similarity and the conceptual proximity I established above would have been enough to prompt the audience to connect the dots. In this sense, the redactional nature of the Bavli lends support to my conjecture that the sugya's audience would have been attuned to meaning generated by the Bavli's pairing of textual units that remain recognizable as such. Likewise, if my reading of the unit is persuasive, one can conclude that the Bavli's audience was in effect attuned to rabbinic parody. The suggested case of redactional parody displays the sugya's self-reflection about the circumstances of its production.

Hence, the redactional parody in which one unit parodies another unit seems fully compatible with the overall purpose of the sugya. Whether the mice kill the cat and the students succeed or the cat dies from overeating and Rava prevails over his students at the expense of his reputation, the sugya's author always remains in complete control of the voices it permits into its discourse and solely defines the proper limits of halakhic discourse. Parody, in this reading, allows the Bavli to affirm his own version of the tradition as an epitome of talmudic Judaism.

The redactional nature of the parody also creates the framework for its preemptive nature. Despite his ideological distance from the actions of Rava and his students, the sugya's author may have left the imitated text more or less intact, and simply placed the parodying textual unit next to it, indeed even before it. This allowed the author to create a parody with minimal intervention in the text. In our case, the author uses the structural similarities of the two cases as a preemptive parody of the power struggle between Rava and his students. It is preemptive insofar as it denounces the students' revolt, and Rava's failure, even before these events occur in the text. The sugya shelters its audience from the inherent scandal that it would endure were it to hear the narration about an inverted hierarchy in the Beyt Midrash unchecked by its parody in the case of the cat. At the same time, the sugya preserves the (likely inherited) account of the student revolt. The technique of preemptive parody thereby honors the rabbinic literary tradition twice, first by including the imitated text in the canon in largely unmodified form and then by satirizing it subversive potential (a technique not unique to the Bavli as I shall argue in the next chapter).

When the score is settled between Rava and the students and between Rava, the students, and the stam, order returns; having safeguarded the limits of rabbinic discourse, parody fades. In the parody of Rava and his students, the author leads the audience to reflect on halakhic parody, especially on the parody of the power struggle in the Beyt Midrash. Such parody seems admissible, out of necessity. The students' revolt posed a threat to the desired learning process of the sugya's audience. The sugya has eliminated this threat, and cat and mice, men and women, teachers and students, all reassume their places in the established hierarchy, and the study of liability for borrowed animals resumes as planned.

CHAPTER TWO

The Grapes of Wrath:
A Palestinian Parody of a Temperance Sermon
(Wayiqra Rabbah 12.1)

First they done a lecture on temperance;
But they didn't make enough for them both to get drunk on.
– Mark Twain, *The Adventures of Huckleberry Finn*

Do not drink wine or strong drink.
– *Leviticus* 10.9

In the previous chapter, I argued that a stammaitic redactor of the Bavli parodies aspects of his own rabbinic tradition. The redactor of intra-rabbinic parodies has the authority to modify the parodied texts but instead chooses to leave the traditional sources intact and to imitate and to satirize them. An example from *Wayiqra Rabbah*, a Palestinian Midrash redacted between 400 and 500 CE, suggests that Palestinian rabbinic literature also includes instances of internal parody, that is, parodic satire emerging from the same rabbinic circles that had produced the imitated text itself.[1] This intra-rabbinic parody was probably also composed by a redactor of the text in which we find it, in this case a homily.

The "literary" nature of the homilies in *Wayiqra Rabbah* as such has long been recognized, as has the fact that the question of late ancient synagogal homiletics should not necessarily bear on a literary study (for brevity's sake, below I use the term "sermon" for the textual units of *Wayiqra Rabbah*).[2]

---

[1] On the dating of *Wayiqra Rabbah*, see Günther Stemberger, *Introduction to Talmud and Midrash* (Edinburgh: T&T Clark, 1996), 287.

[2] See Günther Stemberger, "The Derasha in Rabbinic Times," in: Alexander Deek, Walter Homolka, and Heinz-Günther Schöttler (eds.), *Preaching in Judaism and Christianity: Encounters and Developments from Biblical Times to Modernity* (Berlin, New York: Walter de Gruyter, 2008), 7–21 (Stemberger discusses traditional approaches on pages 7–10); Richard S. Sarason, "The Petihot in Leviticus Rabba: 'Oral Homilies' or Redactional Constructions?" *Journal of Jewish Studies* 33 (1982), 557–567; and most recently Burton L. Visotzky, "The Misnomers 'Petihah' and 'Homiletic Midrash' as Descriptions for Leviticus Rabbah and Pesikta DRav Kahana," *Jewish Studies Quarterly*, forthcoming; cf. Joseph Heineman, "The Art of the Sermon of Palestinian Amora'im: Analysis of two Proems," *HaSifrut/Literature*, 25 (1977) [Hebrew] 69–79. Visotzky here mounts a successful attack on the unspecified use of the term homily, yet does not offer a useful alternative; Stemberger's "Derasha" does not solve the problem either. Visotzky calls Heinemann's

Scholars, however, are still divided when it comes to describing the literary nature of the text. Polyphony and polysemy feature more prominently in *Wayiqra Rabbah* than in the Bavli; I recognize a development toward more unified authorial intention from the Palestinian texts to the Bavli. In Palestinian rabbinic literature, it is quite common for the text to make contradictory remarks, leading Burton Visotzky to regard Palestinian rabbinic Midrash, and especially *Wayiqra Rabbah*, as mere miscellany.[3] Others view the text as literarily coherent, a position applicable to the sermon under discussion in this chapter.[4] I prefer a middle ground between regarding the sermons in *Wayiqra Rabbah* as either coherent or incoherent, especially if one considers the possibility of polysemic oral retellings of complex literary rabbinic texts. The notion of polysemy, in the study of rabbinic parody, allows us to accept, within the same text, incompatibilities between the imitated text and its parody that are greater than the ones found in the Bavli. A complex message that highlights internal tensions can still bear a consistent message, as I shall soon seek to illustrate.

Joshua Levinson and Burton Visotzky have argued that *Wayiqra Rabbah* contains several parodies of Roman culture and especially of Christian Roman lore and literature; this chapter, therefore, is concerned less with the mere existence of parody in the collection than with the technique and precise target of one such intra-rabbinic redactional parody in the Midrash.[5]

---

term "literary homily" an "oxymoron," yet this proposition presupposes the existence of non-literary homilies or homilies devoid of literary qualities. Just as in the case of the Bavli, I see the production of *Wayiqra Rabbah* as intimately tied to the oral-performative culture of rabbinic discourse, yet there is no evidence that the synagogues were among the venues of rabbinic literary production. On the orality of rabbinic literature, see note 26 in the Introduction.

[3] Burton Visotzky rightly cautions that "we too readily superimpose our Western literary and philosophic structures upon ancient texts in the service of Scholarship" (*Golden Bells and Pomegranates: Studies in Midrash Leviticus Rabbah* (Tübingen: Mohr Siebeck, 2003), 16; see more generally ibid., 10–40). At the same time, the opposite problem persists, namely that we tend to read rabbinic texts not naturally as literature but as evidence of "rabbinic" Judaism. See note 69 in the Introduction.

[4] The most persuasive literary analysis of *Wayiqra Rabbah* may be David Stern, "Midrash and the Language of Exegesis: a Study of Vayikra Rabbah Chapter 1," in Geoffrey H. Hartman and Sanford Budick (eds.), *Midrash and Literature* (Evanston: Northwestern University Press, 1996), 105–124. Cf. also Jacob Neusner, *The Integrity of Leviticus Rabbah: The Problem of the Autonomy of a Rabbinic Document* (Chico: Scholars Press, 1985) and Visotzky's criticism of Neusner in Visotzky, *Golden Bells and Pomegranates*, 15 n. 24.

[5] For a discussion of Sermon 27 in *Wayiqra Rabbah*, see Burton Visotzky, "Anti-Christian Polemic in Leviticus Rabbah," *American Academy for Jewish Research Proceedings* 56 (1990), 94–100 reprinted in Visotzky's *Fathers of the World: Essays in Rabbinic and Patristic Literature* (Tübingen: Mohr Siebeck, 1995), 93–105]. Visotzky argues that the passage concerning the procreation of David parodies Christian Mariology. For Sermon 22 in *Wayiqra Rabbah*, see Israel Yuval, *Two Nations in Your Womb: Perceptions of Jews and Christians in Late Antiquity and the Middle Ages*, 53–65 and Joshua Levinson, "'Trag-

The twelfth sermon in *Wayiqra Rabbah* interprets the verse "יין ושכר אל תשת" (Leviticus 10:9), which appears in Leviticus after the death of Aaron's two eldest sons is recounted; for the rabbis, this verse means: "do not drink mixed wine and unmixed wine."[6] In its original context, this prohibits Aaron, and by implication all high priests, from consuming alcohol prior to officiating. The sermon in *Wayiqra Rabbah* expands the prohibition of wine in Leviticus to include grapes and, as Heineman has argued, to apply to virtually all Jews at all times: "one gains the impression that we are dealing with a general and unrestricted negative commandment."[7] I therefore call this sermon the *temperance sermon*.

Joshua Levinson has suggested that a short rabbinic story found in this temperance sermon parodies the biblical story of the death of Nadav and Avihu as well as its rabbinic interpretation in the sermon. Levinson's brilliant analysis remains the only study that focuses in depth on the literary technique of rabbinic parody in the amoraic period.[8] This chapter presents and discuses many of Levinson's suggestions in order to modify his claim. I agree that the parody imitates the biblical story of Nadav and Avihu and argue that its target is not the Bible but rather *only* the faulty interpretation of the story by the rabbinic author of the temperance sermon. Furthermore, in my view, the exegetical parody of the story targets not only this particular interpretation of the Bible but also the entire temperance sermon of which it is a part. I suggest that the temperance sermon displays non-rabbinic ascetic tendencies; the parody, in turn, undermines these tendencies and thereby reinforces rabbinic values. By considering the fourth- and fifth-century ascetic tendencies more broadly, as well as specifically a possible "Encratite" movement and Epiphanius' heresiological diatribe against these Encratites, I speculate on the cultural background of the temperance sermon. I argue that the sermon itself, and especially its extreme asceticism regarding wine, are troubling from a rabbinic standpoint. Finally, I hypothesize that the parodic story may have been added to the sermon at a relatively late stage of

---

edies Naturally Performed': Fatal Charades, Parodia Sacra, and the Death of Titus," in Richard Kalmin and Seth Schwartz (eds.), *Jewish Culture and Society under the Christian Roman Empire* (Leuven: Peters, 2003), 349–382. These studies focus more on the cultural context of these parodies than on their literary technique. I revisit them in more detail in Chapter Five, pages 170–71.

[6] The likely meaning in biblical Hebrew is "do not drink wine or strong drink." The semantic shift of the words from biblical to rabbinic Hebrew is reflected in *Sifre Bemidbar* 23: "Rabbi Eleazar HaQapar says: 'Wine' (יין) is mixed, 'strong drink' (שכר), is unmixed."

[7] "מתקבל הרושם כאילו מדובר ב'מצוות לא-תעשה' כללית ובלתי-מסויגת" (my translation of Joseph Heineman, "The Art of the Sermon of Palestinian Amora'im: 76).

[8] Joshua Levinson, "עולם הפוך ראיתי'-עיון בסיפור השיכור ובניו," *Jerusalem Studies in Hebrew Literature* 12 (1990), 7–29.

its redaction, allowing the parody to target much of the temperance sermon itself and to undermine its moralistic austerity vis-à-vis wine and exegesis.

Understanding the full parodic impact first requires a close reading of the story itself.[9]

The story of an old man who drank two pitchers [קיסטין] of wine every day.
One day he did not have [wine].
What did he do?
He sold a supporting beam from his house and drank.
He sold a supporting beam from his olive press and drank wine with [the proceeds.][10]
And his sons were defaming [מליזין] him.
And said: "Will this old father of ours [הדין סבא דאבונן] leave us [סבק] nothing after his death?
What shall we do?
Come, we shall take him and give him a drink of wine [ונשקה יתיה חמר],
And we shall make him drunk and say that he died,
And we shall go out and lay him in his grave [נשכבנה במשכביה]."
They did so unto him.
They took him and gave him to drink and made him drunk and said that he died,
And they went out and laid him down.

Wine merchants came by to enter that city.[11]
They heard that there was a seizure of goods.[12]
They said: "let us hide our wineskins in this graveyard and flee!"
They did this.
They hid their wineskins in the grave in which the old man was laid down.

After three days, he awoke from his sleep.
He saw that there was a wineskin for him.
He opened it and put it to his mouth.
He began to drink and to sing.

His sons said: "Shouldn't we go and see how our father is doing?
If he lives or if he is dead?"
They went and found him, and there was a wineskin put to his mouth, and he was drinking and singing.
They said: "Even here his creator has not forsaken [שבקיה] him.

---

[9] *Wayiqra Rabbah* according to Geniza Fragment T-S C2.162., cited according to Mordecai Margulies, *Midrash Wayyikra Rabbah* (New York: The Jewish Theological Seminary of America, 1993), 245 f. Joshua Levinson convincingly argued that this fragment reflects the oldest extant version of the story. See Levinson, "עולם הפוך ראיתי'–עיון בסיפור השיכור ובניו," 3f, n. 10. I discuss other manuscripts where appropriate.

[10] The story opens much more briefly in the manuscripts, simply stating that the man "sold all his household goods and drank wine from them [i.e., with the proceeds]." Only the Geniza fragment indicates how much the father drank.

[11] All the manuscripts describe the merchants passing by in a variety of ways, most adding that the merchants passed by the "door" (תרע) of the graveyard.

[12] דנגריא, from the Greek ἀγγαρεία; see Michael Sokoloff, *A Dictionary of Jewish Palestinian Aramaic* (Ramat-Gan: Bar Ilan University Press, 2002), 64.

What shall we do to him?[13]
Come, let us take him and make a statute [קטסטיס].[14]
One will give him drink on one day,
And [another] one will give him drink on one day."

This complete narrative, which I shall call the *story of the drunkard,* is written primarily in Aramaic with occasional Hebrew words. The father sells his household property and the physical foundation of his house and business, the olive press. "The sons," two or more, are concerned about their father's costly drinking habit and its potential impact on their inheritance.[15] They intoxicate him and place him in a grave. Even though the sons do not kill the father, they wait for three days before checking if he is still alive, which reveals their anticipation of his possible death.[16] Merchants, also driven by fears concerning financial loss, unintentionally provide the father with wine, and the sons find him alive, "drinking and singing." They conclude that they witnessed a divine intervention on their father's behalf, and vow to support their father and even to pay for his wine, supposedly solving the problem of his financial demise. I call their solemn declaration to provide for their father – a clear inversion of their original plan – the "statute of perpetual (moderate) drinking."

Rabbinic stories are morally prescriptive rather than historically descriptive. In other words, they tend to stipulate punishment for guilty individuals and mark their guilt through the punishment itself. That the sons punish themselves, even if in response to an epiphany they might have perceived mistakenly, raises questions concerning their guilt.[17] Hence, if the story's

---

[13] In most manuscripts: "Since heaven gave you, we don't know what we will do to you."

[14] From the Greek κατάστασις; see Sokoloff, *A Dictionary of Jewish Palestinian Aramaic,* 487.

[15] The cost of wine in fifth century Palestine is difficult to establish, but it was clearly not negligible. In comparison, *Bereshit Rabbah* 49.4 mentions that the price of a pitcher of wine, half of the amount that the father consumed in one day, was comparable to the price of a pound of meat or one loaf of bread (namely ten *follarion*). See also Levinson, 6. "'עולם הפוך ראיתי'–עיון בסיפור השיכור ובניו,".

[16] The macabre aspect of the story is stressed by Heineman, "The Art of the Sermon of Palestinian Amora'im," 78 and Levinson, "'עולם הפוך ראיתי'–עיון בסיפור השיכור ובניו,", 7. Levinson also places the story in the context of Roman patricide, certainly a helpful comparison for understanding the oppressive nature of the late ancient patriarchy. Cf. also Jacob Elbaum, who argues that the sons simply wanted to teach their father a lesson ("מעשים בשכור ומכוער באגדתנו ובאגדת יון," 124). Elbaum merely speculates on this point without explanation, perhaps having been influenced by his reading of a similar tale by Aesop, which I will discuss below.

[17] According to their normatively prescriptive framework, all cases of parody discussed in this book end with the victory of the rabbinic establishment: the rabbinic authorities of Palestine prevail in the Introduction; the rebellious students and the inept Rava are censored by the stam in Chapter One; Rava prevails in Chapter Three; Rabban Gamliel in Chapter Four; Rashbi in Chapter Five; and the rabbinic majority in the conclusion.

ending is indicative of the author's preference for how things should turn out, then the culprit is not the father but the sons who try to kill him. This does not mean that the story lauds the father's drinking habit, which displays unfitting weakness of body and mind. Still, as Joshua Levinson already noted, the drunkard's two pitchers of diluted wine a day is an elevated, but not excessive, quantity.[18] Elsewhere in the same sermon, real drunkards consume many times more than the father does.[19]

The story's repetition of Hebrew and Aramaic roots in different contexts constitutes its internal structure. This common rabbinic literary strategy generates meaning by fusing the respective contexts in which the roots appear. These repetitions constitute a self-referential framework that is our primary guide for accessing the meaning of any rabbinic narrative.[20] First,

---

For a discussion of the didactic nature of rabbinic stories, see Jeffrey Rubenstein, *Talmudic Stories: Narrative Art, Composition, and Culture* (Baltimore: The Johns Hopkins University Press, 1999), passim and especially 5–15 and Levinson, "עולם הפוך ראיתי'–עיון בסיפור השיכור ובניו," 7.

[18] For a comparison of quantity stipulations in Yerushalmi *Ta'anit* 4.6 (69c), see Levinson, "עולם הפוך ראיתי'–עיון בסיפור השיכור ובניו," 6 n. 25. The Aramaic קסיט stands for the Greek ξέστης, a pitcher, or the Greek measurement *xestes*. See Sokoloff, *A Dictionary of Jewish Palestinian Aramaic*, 498; concerning the *xestes* and its Latin cognate *sextarius* (one sixth of a *congius*), see H. G. Liddell and R. Scott, *Greek-English Lexicon: With a Revised Supplement* (Oxford, Clarendon Press, 1996), 1189f. The consumption of two pitchers each day, the equivalent of between a pint and a quart of wine, can hardly be understood as excessive, even if the alcohol content of wine may have been greater in Antiquity than it is now. That wine was mixed in rabbinic culture is undisputed (see Mishna *Pesahim* 10.1–9, Tosefta *Berakhot* 4.8, and *Sifre Bemidbar* 23), and we do know that the father drinks יין, i.e., mixed wine (see note 6 above). The rabbis never specify the exact mixing ratio, but we can assume that the rabbinic ratio corresponded to the commonly accepted Hellenistic standards. The consistent descriptions of Athanaeus and Plutarch indicate that the ratio would be either five parts of water to three parts of wine (yielding a beverage with 37.5 % wine), four parts of water to two parts of wine (yielding a beverage with 33 % wine), or three parts of water to one part of wine (yielding a beverage with 25 % wine; see Athanaeus 10.426d and Plutarch, *Quaestiones conviviales* 3.9. The daily quantity of alcohol consumed by the father was therefore at most half the amount contained in a standard bottle sold today.

[19] As Levinson notes, a drinker appearing in the sermon immediately following the present story consumes twelve pitchers per day; a third drinker consumes five pitchers and then is charged for ten. (Levinson, "עולם הפוך ראיתי'–עיון בסיפור השיכור ובניו," 6 and Margulies, *Midrash Wayyikra Rabbah*, 248–49). As noted above, in all other versions of *Wayiqra Rabbah* the exact quantity of wine is not mentioned, leading the audience to infer that the father drinks more than is indicated in the Geniza fragment. Since criticism of the father mitigates the sons' criminal acts, the manuscript versions diminish the tension between this story (protecting the father's right to drink) and the sermon in which it is found (categorically rebuking wine and grape consumption). The tension between the father's conduct and his eventual reward, in turn, is augmented in the manuscripts.

[20] The technique of generating meaning by repeating roots figures prominently in all of the amoraic of rabbinic literature; the best example of this technique included in this book is found in the Babylonian story of Bar Hedya discussed in Chapter Three. See

the story uses repetition to emphasize and endorse the sons' punishment according to the concept *measure for measure*, in the most literal sense.[21] Levinson notes that the sons' irreverent anger originates in the two קסטין ("pitchers") and ends up with a קטסטיס ("statute"), two similar sounding words.[22] The statute thereby sanctions moderate drinking, perhaps precisely of two pitchers a day. Linking the sons' "statute" to the father's "pitchers," the story clarifies that drinking should not be the subject of moralization in light of such severe transgressions as attempted patricide.

Levinson also points out the sons' fear that their father will not "leave" them anything and then realize that even in the graveyard, God did not "leave" their father, twice using the root שב'ק/סב'ק.[23] The repetition of the verb "to leave" in these two different contexts – leaving something to someone and leaving someone – juxtaposes the sons' transgression against God's commitment to the father.

The story's repetitive emphasis of the verb סבק simultaneously highlights the similar sounding, oft-repeated term סבא, "old man."[24] The "old man" is thereby characterized as the one who is supposed to do nothing more than "leaving behind" things and dying, which increases the contrast between the greedy sons and God's commitment to the father. While the homophony and thereby semantic effect is vague in this case, the story directly links the "old" (זקן) father with his "wineskin" (זיקה) through a full homophony, most notably in the formulation "their wineskins," זיקינן.

In these three instances, the story juxtaposes homophonic terms in order to fuse the sons' contempt for their old father with his need for wine. Thus, the story's internal structure, much like the narrative as a whole and its ending in particular, emphasizes the sons' guilt without entirely exculpating the father.

Still, rather than conveying his demise, the story condones perpetual drinking and provides financial security for the drinker, a striking outcome given the context of the rabbinic temperance sermon in which it appears.

Yonah Frenkel, דרכי האגדה והמדרש (Massada: Yad la-Talmud, 1991), 260–74 and his "שאלות הרמנוטיות בחקר סיפור האגדה," *Tarbiz* 47 (1977/78), 139–72 (reprinted in: idem, *The Aggadic Narrative: Harmony in Content and Form* (Tel Aviv: Hakibbutz Hameuchad Publishing House, 2001), 11–50. See also the collection of articles in John W. Welch (ed.), *Chiasmus in Antiquity: Structures, Analyses, Exegesis* (Hildesheim: Gerstenberg, 1981) on chiasmus in biblical, rabbinic, Christian, and Greco-Roman literatures.

[21] For a discussion of "measure for measure" punishments, see Aaron Shemesh, *Punishment and Sins from Scripture to the Rabbis* (Jerusalem: The Magnes Press, 2003) [Hebrew] and Martha Himmelfarb, *Tours of Hell: an Apocalyptic Form in Jewish and Christian Literature* (Philadelphia: University of Pennsylvania Press, 1983), 68–105.

[22] Levinson, "עולם הפוך ראיתי'–עיון בסיפור השיכור ובניו," 9.

[23] Levinson, "עולם הפוך ראיתי'–עיון בסיפור השיכור ובניו," ibid.

[24] I thank Daniel Boyarin for pointing this out.

The story's literary structure leads us to perceive the tension between the drinker's reward and the sermon's anti-drinking agenda. Such tension might be deliberate, as suggested by Levinson's discussion of halakhic satire in the story.

Halakhic Parody?

The story of the drunkard is blatantly humorous, as scholars have long recognized, and contains examples of non-parodic satire, allowing us clearly to differentiate between its satirical and parodic elements.[25] Levinson argues that the sons' support of their father's drinking habit satirizes Palestinian halakha, particularly *Tosefta Qiddushin* 1.11:

These are the obligations of the son towards the father: to feed him and to give him drink (משקה) and to clothe him and to cover him.

The sons' decision to provide their father with drink (משקי) imitates and inverts this halakha. While "drink" in the Tosefta may well include wine, the halakhic intention was most likely not to support parental alcoholism. Yet, perpetual wine drinking is the outcome of the story, a result of the sons' statute, which they understand as divinely sanctioned!

In Levinson's view, the Tosefta's halakha in the story of the drunkard "is fully fulfilled, even if ironically, thereby providing another hint of the existence of *parody* [of the halakhic text]."[26] Levinson rightfully limits his claim to a "hint" of parody. In effect, it is hardly a parody at all. In my view, the story of the drunkard inverts the application of the halakha without imitating it as a text and without satirizing its premises. On the contrary, only the presupposition of the halakha's validity allows for perceiving the ridiculous nature of the sons' self-imposed punishment of providing their father with wine. Hence, the target of the satire is not the Tosefta; if fact, it does not target an extant text at all; instead, the sons' ironic application of the halakha satirizes filial revolt in general.[27]

---

[25] Jacob Elbaum attributes to the story "מעשים בשכור ומכוער באגדתנו ובאגדת יון", "הומור עדין" 125); Heineman calls it "entertaining" ("The Art of the Sermon of Palestinian Amora'im: Analysis of two Proems," vii) and a סיפור הומוריסטי (ibid., 77). According to Levinson, it is a parody of the Nadav and Avihu incident (Levinson, "עולם הפוך ראיתי'–עיון בסיפור השיכור ובניו, 17) and a Bakhtinian "parodia sacra" (ibid.), as I shall shortly discuss in detail.

[26] My translation and emphasis, "והצו הזה מקוים כאן בצורה מלאה אם גם אירונית (ובכך ניתן עוד 9. "עולם הפוך ראיתי'–עיון בסיפור השיכור ובניו, רמז לקיום פרודיה של טקסט הלכתי)", Levinson, ",

[27] Levinson notes another case of an ironic fulfillment of the halakha in the sons' actions. He writes that the post-mishnaic tractate *Evel Rabbati* (or: *Semahot*) 8.1 stipulates that "one goes out to the graveyard and visits (ופוקדין) the dead until three days [after their death], and one does not suspect at all the ways of the Amorites [in doing so]. A story of one whom they visited [and found alive], and he lived for twenty five years and

Levinson's analysis, however, still draws our attention to a central aspect of the story of the drunkard. By satirically fulfilling the Tosefta's halakha, the story highlights the sons' provision of wine as its prominent literary device. Convincingly, Levinson bases on the provision the claim that the story imitates the biblical narrative concerning Nadav and Avihu *along with its rabbinic interpretation*. I agree only with the latter part of Levinson's view. The statute of perpetual drinking, indeed, features as the story's main device of exegetical parody of the erroneous rabbinic reading of Nadav and Avihu in the temperance sermon.

A Parody of Nadav and Avihu

One way to locate the satirized target of the story of the drunkard is to recognize the tension it creates by making the audience privy to information not known to its characters. Whereas the sons consider the wine found in the grave to be the result of divine intervention, the audience knows that the wine was hidden there by merchants trying to avoid its confiscation. The sons' mistaken perception of a haphazard situation as divine intervention is a source of dramatic irony that marks a rift between the story's protagonists and the audience as well as between the protagonists themselves. As Levinson observes, "the sons are not aware of the actions of the wine merchants,

---

thereafter he died." This rabbinic halakha allows for, and even prescribes, a visit to the dead to ensure that the person is not merely *scheintot*. It explicitly dispels any suspicion that this practice is magical or idolatrous, indicating that the typical formula of the "ways of the Amorites" is non-applicable. (On the "ways of the Amorites," see Guiseppe Veltri, *Magie und Halakha: Ansätze zu einem empirischen Wissenschaftsbegriff im spätantiken und frühmittelalterlichen Judentum* (Tübingen: Mohr Siebeck, 1997), 93–220.) The sons in the story of the drunkard fulfill this prescription disingenuously; they set out, "not to see whether their father lives, but to assure themselves that 'that old man' is really dead," as Levinson puts it (Levinson, "עיון בסיפור השיכור ובניו,"-'עולם הפוך ראיתי' " 8). Levinson calls this an "ironization" of halakha, yet here he stops short of calling the sons' behavior parody, and rightfully so. The story seems to imitate and pervert this halakha as well in a comical way. The sons are portrayed as fulfilling the halakha in a false, macabre, and absurdly precise manner: after the proscribed period of three days, they ask themselves not whether their father may be alive, but "whether he lives or whether he is dead," perverting the original intention of the halakha. Indeed, the father remains alive after his burial, much like the anonymous man in *Evel Rabbati*, who lived "for twenty five years" after having been placed in a graveyard alive. Reading the story of the drunkard against the background of the halakha emphasizes the story's irony since the financial burden of the sons' self-imposed statute grows with the father's possible longevity. The story's comical effects depend on upholding the halakha: its satirical target is not the imitated halakha itself but the criminal behavior of unruly sons. Its satire is conservative, ridiculing the criminal digression from the halakha's proper application. Note that the final redaction of the imitated text, tractate *Semahot*, is likely earlier, but possibly also later, than *Wayiqra Rabbah* (See Stemberger, *Introduction to Talmud and Midrash*, 248).

the father is not aware of the actions of either the sons or the merchants. We, the readers, privy to it all, know that their interpretation of reality is erroneous. It was not God who helped the father miraculously, but the wine merchants, who themselves sought to flee from the authorities."[28] Levinson recognizes the important role of misunderstanding and misinterpretation in the story, a near-Shakespearean amalgamation of mistaken causal relationships.[29]

Did the sons witness a miracle or just an amusing coincidence? In order to support Levinson's view of the sons' error, one could point to the sons' patricidal tendencies. In late ancient literature, moral failure often coincides with or leads to hermeneutical failure, and evil sons are likely to err.[30] I still wonder, however, why the story of the drunkard would construct a discrepancy between human action and divine authorship. Levinson's reading implies that the sons would have acted not only outside the bounds of morality but also outside the reach of divine authority. Alternatively, the merchants can be viewed as God's agents or messengers, a common perception in other rabbinic narratives.[31]

---

[28] My translation, "הבנים אינם מודעים לפעילות הסחרים, האב אינו מודע לפעילות בניו והסחרים גם יחד. אנו, הקוראים, העדים לכל, יודעים שפירושם למציאות מוטעה. לא האל עזר לאב בנס, אלא הסוחרים, שגם הם ניסו לברוח מן הסמכות." Levinson, "עיון בסיפור השיכור ובניו,'-'עולם הפוך ראיתי'" 12. Levinson also emphasizes the parallel in the story between the earthly authorities from which the merchants are fleeing and the divine authority that the sons perceive as responsible for the miracle. I do not see this as central to the story since the earthly authority, at the time of the composition of *Wayiqra Rabbah*, is a Christianizing Roman government. This government is not comparable to the rabbis' divine authority; it is far from evident that the rabbis would recognize this authority at all as I shall seek to illustrate in Chapter Five. Even if the story were to construct the authorities as gentile Roman, I would still hesitate to accept this aspect of Levinson's analysis.

[29] Levinson supports this reading by pointing out that the story of the drunkard may have set the framework for questioning faulty and perverted interpretations more generally. He notes that at the beginning of the story, the sons themselves "defame" their father as a drunkard, hoping that his death "would be interpreted as a punishment for his exaggerated drinking during his lifetime, as measure for measure," Levinson, "'עולם הפוך ראיתי'-עיון בסיפור השיכור ובניו," 7. Levinson points out that the *hiphil* verbal pattern of לו"ז generally denotes public accusations that are false and socially subversive, an ingenious yet fragile reading. The verb's general meaning, in my view, does not bear the weight that Levinson's interpretation ascribes to it. In other words, if the story's author wished to emphasize the public aspect of the sons' defamation campaign, he could have done so more effectively.

[30] I discuss this point in detail in Chapter Five. See also John Winkler, "The Mendacity of Kalasiris and the Narrative Strategy of Heliodoros' Aithiopika," *Yale Classical Studies* 27 (1982), 93–158. In addition, I discuss below the reasoning of Epiphanius' heresiology, which describes his heretical opponents as vicious and at the same time hermeneutically misguided.

[31] For example, in *Wayiqra Rabbah* 22.3, God manipulates the fate of individuals by sending an animal to take someone's life. In general, the Palestinian rabbis combine a notion of individual agency *with* divine involvement in earthly matters, as I will discuss at length in Chapter Five.

We ought to avoid any facile explanation of the origin of the wine as either haphazard or divinely orchestrated. The story's ambiguity in this regard may be viewed as a hermeneutical question about the attribution of divine intervention to earthly events, one of the main concerns of Greek literature at the time.[32] Moreover, the ambiguity surrounding the wine's appearance reinforces the story's central question about the permissibility of drinking. Here, too, the story remains ambiguous. Although the sons misconstrue the situation, their misconstrual ultimately saves the father (along with his habit) on the one hand and leads to their punishment on the other. The story ends with a moral and hermeneutical conundrum concerning the permissibility of drinking that frustrates any attempt to understand the story without considering its broader context. This conundrum, in my view, is part of the point of the story: life is complicated, and so is interpreting the Bible. Simple readings, like the one performed by the sons, and a simple moralistic dismissal of wine, like the one advanced by the temperance sermon, already constitute a hermeneutical and moral failure.

Levinson similarly states that a "normative" reading of the text in the context of the sermon fails, and he seeks to address the tension between the various points of view in the story by turning to its narrative context, the temperance sermon in *Wayiqra Rabbah*.[33] To reiterate, the sermon is structured as a long commentary on Leviticus 10:9, the prohibition of wine following the story of Nadav and Avihu, the text that the story of the drunkard repeats – with a difference.

In the Bible, Nadav and Avihu, the two eldest sons of Aaron, are burnt to death in front of the altar on the occasion of the consecration of the Tabernacle, immediately after heavenly fire consumes the first offering.[34] Leviticus 10 recounts the death of Nadav and Avihu:

1 Now Aaron's sons, Nadav and Avihu, each took his censer, put fire in it and laid incense on it; and they offered strange fire [אש זרה] before G-d, such as he had not commanded them.[35] 2 And fire came out from the presence of G-d and consumed

---

[32] This is another theme discussed by Winkler in "The Mendacity of Kalasiris" and a prominent issue in the Greek novels. See note 30 above and Chapter Five for a longer discussion of this matter.

[33] Levinson, "עולם הפוך ראיתי'–עיון בסיפור השיכור ובניו," 13, constructs the failure to read the text in a normative way based on the conflict between the audience's expectation of punishment for the drinker and the statute of perpetual drinking.

[34] The Bible previously mentions the two men as Aaron's eldest sons (Exodus 6:23; see also I Chronicles 6:2 and 24:1–2). The audience later learns that they had officiated with Moses, Aaron, and the seventy elders at Sinai (Exodus 24:1 and 9) and that Nadav and Avihu did not have sons (Numbers 3:2–4 and 26:60–61). Leviticus 16, in the course of enumerating the prescriptions for the Day of Atonement, recalls the importance of the orderly performance of the worship in the context of the death of Aaron's sons.

[35] The rabbis always abbreviate the Tetragrammaton, and usually only cite the first two

them, and they died before G-d. 3 Then Moses said to Aaron, "This is what G-d
meant when he said 'Through those who are near me, I will show myself holy [בקרבי
אקדש], and before all the people I will be glorified." And Aaron was silent. 4 Moses
summoned [Aaron's cousins] and said to them, "Come forward, and carry your kins-
men away from the front of the sanctuary to a place outside the camp …[After the
deed is done, Aaron and his sons are told that they may not mourn.]…8 And G-d
spoke to Aaron: 9 Do not drink wine or strong drink [יין ושכר], neither you nor your
sons, when you enter the tent of meeting, that you may not die; it is a statute forever
throughout your generations. 10 You are to distinguish between the holy and the
profane and between the unclean and the clean.

In Leviticus, the death of Nadav and Avihu may come as a surprise, and the
precise nature of their transgression is not entirely clear. A straightforward
reading of the passage suggests that Nadav and Avihu's unsolicited approach
to the altar with "strange" fire is the immediate cause of their death and that
the subsequent passage in Leviticus, which prohibits officiants from drinking wine, is not part of the same narrative.[36] For some of the Jewish exegetes
of Late Antiquity, however, the appearance of this prohibition – and the
capital punishment that its violation carries – immediately following the
death of Aaron's sons suggested a different explanation for the nature of
Nadav and Avihu's sin: they performed the ceremony while intoxicated.
Among these exegetes was the author of the temperance sermon in *Wayiqra
Rabbah*, in which the story of the drunkard is found.

Levinson argues that the story parodies the rabbinic interpretation of the
death of Nadav and Avihu, featuring wine as its cause. He emphasizes that we
need to consider the story of the drunkard against the background of the entire temperance sermon in which it is found,[37] mentioning in passing that the
temperance sermon, not the Bible, blames the death of Aaron's sons on wine.[38]

---

letters *yud* and *heh*. To reiterate, throughout this book, I render this rabbinic practice by
translating the Tetragrammaton as G-d and the term *elohim* as God.

[36] Biblical scholarship suggests that the narrative of the death of Nadav and Avihu
might be related to a polemic against the first king of northern Israel, Jeroboam (9th century BCE), and his sons Nadav and Avijah. This historical context, however, was long
forgotten by the time of the oldest commentators on Leviticus. See, for example, Edward
Greenstein, "An Inner-Biblical Midrash of the Nadab and Abihu Episode," in *Proceedings of the Eleventh World Congress of Jewish Studies* (Jerusalem: World Union of Jewish
Studies, 1994), A *71–*78 [Hebrew]; Bryan D. Bibb, "Nadab and Abihu Attempt to Fill a
Gap: Law and Narrative in Leviticus 10.1–7," *Journal for the Study of the Old Testament*,
96 (2001), 83–99; Walter J. Houston, "Tragedy in the Courts of the Lord: a Socio-Literary
Reading of the Death of Nadab and Abihu," *Journal for the Study of the Old Testament*,
90 (2000), 31–39; and Martin A. Greenberg, "The True Sin of Nadab and Abihu," *Jewish
Bible Quarterly*, 26 (1998), 263–267.

[37] Levinson wishes, "להרחיב את מעגל ההקשרים האפשריים ולראות את הספור על רקע הפתיחתא כולה,"
Levinson, "עולם הפוך ראיתי'-עיון בסיפור השיכור ובניו," 15. I will consider the temperance sermon in its entirety, not just its *petichta* as Levinson does.

[38] Levinson, ibid.

In concurrence with my view, Levinson sees the story as targeting "essentially" the biblical narrative, albeit it only in its interpretation in the temperance sermon.[39] The story of the drunkard, he shows, imitates and inverts five central aspects of the story of Aaron's sons – according to the rabbinic temperance sermon's understanding that wine was the reason of their death:[40]

- Drinking results in the death of Aaron's sons, while his sons' apparent death results in the drunken father's return to drinking.
- Aaron's sons drink and die and are burried by their father, whereas the drunken father's drinking habit leads to his "temporary" burial.
- In the biblical story, the sin is drinking and the punishment is death, whereas in the story of the drunkard, attempted murder is the sin, and financial support of the father's continued drinking is the punishment.
- Aaron's sons enter drunk into the purest of all places, the tabernacle, and subsequently die, whereas the drunken father is brought drunk to the most impure of all places, the graveyard, in anticipation of his death,[41] but leaves alive and just as drunk.
- The result is a statute that prohibits Aaron's drinking (Leviticus 10:9), whereas the drunken father's sons institute a statute that enables his continued drinking.

Levinson's analysis of the story of the drunkard, in my view, provides conclusive evidence for the imitation and inversion of the story of Nadav and Avihu (as understood by the temperance sermon). The story is modeled very closely on the rabbinic view of the biblical narrative that considers wine to be the cause of the sons' death, inverting the narrative and its interpretation at the same time. In Levinson's view, the story of the drunkard parodies the Bible as parodia sacra; for him, we are dealing with a Bakhtinian carnival that contrasts "an elitist-normative text of the Beyt Midrash with a lowly folktale, macabre and funny."[42]

Indeed, the rabbis would have reason to take issue with aspects of the Nadav and Avihu narrative. Joseph Heineman already argued that the story of the drunkard may respond to a vexing aspect of the biblical narrative, the unpredictable death of Nadav and Avihu: "God, far from cruelly punishing the drunk[en father], does not forsake him, and even provides for him; hence the death of the drunken sons of Aaron can not possibly be ascribed to an outburst of anger on the part of the Deity."[43] Levinson accepts Heineman's point that our story comments on God's demonic role in the biblical

---

[39] "הסיפור אינו היפוך סמלי רק של פסוק היעד של הפתיחתא אלא גם, וזה העיקר, של סיפור נדב ואביהו," Levinson, ibid., 16.

[40] Levinson, ibid., 17.

[41] As an addendum to Levinson's observations, Aaron's sons are taken out of the pure and holy camp after their death (Leviticus 10:5) whereas the drunken father is taken out of the impure place.

[42] Levinson, ibid., 17 and 19. On the "folk" aspect of the story of the drunkard, see note 72 below.

[43] Heineman, "The Art of the Sermon of Palestinian Amora'im," vii.

story of Nadav and Avihu, a God who "bursts forth without warning and punishes in the twinkling of an eye."[44] It may seem, at first, that the author of the story of the drunkard parodies the biblical narrative and God's actions.

The story of the drunkard, moreover, also imitates another biblical narrative concerning intoxication, the story of Lot's daughters in Genesis (19:32–37). The author of the story of the drunkard must have expected his audience easily to recognize the imitation of this text as well since the temperance sermon repeats verbatim the Genesis 19 story about Lot's daughters:[45]

Come, let us make our father drink wine [לכה נשקה את אבינו יין] and we will lie [נשכבה] with him so that we may preserve offspring through our father. So they made their father drink wine that night; and the firstborn went in, and lay with her father; he did not know when she lay down or when she rose. On the next day, the firstborn said to the younger, "Look, I lay last night with my father; let us make him drink wine tonight also; then you go in and lie with him so that we may preserve offspring through our father. So they made their father drink wine that night also; the younger rose and lay with him; and he did not know when she lay down or when she rose. Thus, both daughters of Lot became pregnant by their father.

The biblical narrative of Lot's daughters shares many aspects with the story of the drunkard. The story of the drunkard, which inverts the narrative of Nadav and Avihu, imitates the Genesis narrative of Lot's daughters in a mostly "straight" manner:

- Lot's daughters mention that their father is "old" (אבינו זקן). The story of the drunkard introduces the "old man" (זקן אחד), and his sons disrespectfully call him, "this old father of ours" (סבא דאבונן).
- Lot's older daughter expresses her concern that she will never bear children and procure heirs to Lot in anticipation of their father's death: "there is not a man on earth to come in to us, in accordance with the world's custom (Genesis 19:31)." In the story of the drunkard, the sons explicitly raise a similar concern about their father's imminent death and a related concern about inheritance – namely that their own inheritance is shrinking.
- Lot's older daughter proposes a morally questionable solution, using an exhortative verb of motion: "come" (לכה). The story of the drunkard imitates this, using the Aramaic "let's go" (אתון). In addition to this rather common exhortative verb, the story continuously imitates the opening sentence of the Genesis narrative.

---

[44] "עולם הפוך" Levinson, "מתגלה בו צד דמוני של האל, המתפרץ ללא אזהרה ומעניש כהרף עין," "ראיתי'-עיון בסיפור השיכור ובניו," 19. Similarly, Shinan calls the punishment "disproportionate" ("The Sins of Nadav and Avihu in Rabbinic Aggadah," 202). Heineman goes as far as to call their burning "the cruel and arbitrary act of a demonic deity" ("The Art of the Sermon of Palestinian Amora'im," vii.). He argues that both in *Sifra* and in Sermon 20 in *Wayiqra Rabbah* … "מובאים הסברים מהסברים שונים למותם של נדב ואביהו. המינוון הרב של הסיבות או של החטאים" "מוכיח עד כמה היתה פרשה זו מוקשית בעיני החכמים והטרידה אותם," ibid., 77.

[45] Margulies, *Midrash Wayyikra Rabbah*, 253 f.

The sons' utterances are precise imitation of those of Lot's daughters in both style and content: just as the daughters state "let's make our father drink wine" (נשקה את אבינו יין), so do the sons (ונשקה יתיה חמר). The daughters wish to lay with their father (נשכבה), and the sons lay their father in his "laying place" (נשכבנה במשכביה), his grave.

- Lot's daughters immediately execute their plan. The Bible, quoted in full in the temperance sermon, repeats the words that describe the daughters' plan when relating its execution: "Come, let us make our father drink wine and we will lie with him … So they made their father drink wine … And the firstborn went in, and lay with her father." The story of the drunkard therefore also repeats the words that describe the sons' plan: "Come, we'll take him and give him wine to drink … and we'll go out and lay him in his grave. They did this to him, they took him and gave him to drink and made him drunk … and they went out and laid him down."
- The drunken father, much like Lot, is neither aware of the plot nor conscious of it when it is carried out, unlike the audiences of both texts, who are fully aware of the plots.

The story of the drunkard imitates the story of Lot's daughters structurally, lexically, and thematically. It creates an imitative framework that explicitly juxtaposes the two stories. The imitation leads the audience to compare the characters' respective crimes: laying with one's father and laying one's father in a grave. Murder and incest are both capital crimes in rabbinic culture, at least in halakhic theory, and both are considered together in the Mishna and the Yerushalmi.[46] In both stories, the characters use wine in order to gain access to their fathers' treasures, financial inheritance in one case and semen in the other.

The fact that the imitation of the biblical narrative leads to its inversion becomes apparent only when the audience of the story of the drunkard begins to ponder the logical conclusion of the parallels between the two stories, as its author likely intended them to do. In this sense, casting the sons in the role of Lot's daughters inverts gender roles. The inverted imitation of Lot's narrative allows the parodic author to insinuate the unspeakable: the sons' "laying" down of their father now invokes the actions of Lot's daughters: rape, at least metaphorically speaking.[47]

With this starkly incongruent image, the story of the drunkard derails the initial process of a straightforward imitation of the biblical narrative and leads the audience to the recognition of the diametrically opposing outcomes of the crimes. Whereas the daughters gain offspring, along with the contempt of subsequent generations, for their deeds, the sons end up

---

[46] See Mishna *Sanhedrin* 9.1 and Yerushalmi *Sanhedrin* 9:1 (26c). The Mishna addresses incest committed by a man, which does not impinge on the present irony. It should be noted that incest, the daughter's crime, is punishable by burning, perhaps another ironic reference to the death of Nadav and Avihu.

[47] On the metaphorical use of rape, penetration, and violent conquest in rabbinic literature, see note 47 in Chapter One, where I argue that the Bavli employs a similar motif.

paying dearly for their actions, vowing to support the father's drinking habit. Once more, imitation and inversion of the biblical narrative seem to be the organizing principle of the story of the drunkard: it retells the narrative of Lot's daughters in a playful and grotesque way. The imitation and partial inversion of the narrative substantiates the ambiguous status of the sons vis-à-vis the story of Lot's daughters.

Yet what would be the point of all this madness? There is one simple way to resolve this ambiguity, which results from the way in which the story of the drunkard imitates the two biblical accounts (the stories of Lot's daughters and Aaron's sons). I suggest modifying Heineman's and to a degree, Levinson's readings of the story of the drunkard as responding to the biblical narrative of Nadav and Avihu. While the Bible is indisputably the imitated text, I hold that the story of the drunkard satirically targets the text that interprets these biblical narratives as being exclusively caused by wine drinking: the temperance sermon in *Wayiqra Rabbah*. The story of the drunkard, in my view, imitates the Bible in order to satirize the exegesis found in the temperance sermon.

A Parody of the Temperance Sermon

The tensions between the outcome of the story of the drunkard and the message of the temperance sermon in which it is found has long been recognized. Heineman already realized that the story does not serve "to reinforce the … admonition against drunkenness" that the sermon promotes.[48] Levinson's reading similarly emphasizes the incompatibility of the story and the sermon. To reiterate, he acknowledges that the temperance sermon, not the Bible, blames the death of Aaron's sons on wine.[49] We should expect, however, that the rabbis had sufficient distance from their own hermeneutics to differentiate between a biblical narrative and its rabbinic interpretation, especially a seemingly odd interpretation such as the sermon's understanding of the story of Nadav and Avihu; my discussion below of the many divergent interpretations of Nadav and Avihu's death amply accounts for this.

To summarize, the temperance sermon in *Wayiqra Rabbah* is radically opposed to the consumption of wine and even grapes. The sermon supports this attitude by broadening the applicability of Leviticus 10:9 ("do not drink mixed wine and unmixed wine").[50] This verse is the centerpiece of the sermon's diatribe against drunkenness, wine, and the consumption of grapes. It disregards the specific cultic context of the biblical prohibition,

---

[48] Heineman, "The Art of the Sermon of Palestinian Amora'im," vii.
[49] Levinson, "עולם הפוך ראיתי'–עיון בסיפור השיכור ובניו", 13.
[50] See note 6 above.

which pertains only to the officiating high priest.[51] As, Levinson has shown, the story of the drunkard satirizes above all the sermon's generalization of Leviticus 10:9. The sons' institution of the statute of perpetual drinking imitates and satirizes the sermon's central argument that Leviticus 10:9 is an ordinance of perpetual temperance.

With this in mind, I would like to suggest that the sermon itself is the story's target of satire. In order to illustrate the sermon's radical nature and contextualize it among fifth-century ascetic movements, my discussion will at times go beyond presenting the targeted elements alone. The temperance sermon, while innovative, seems not to have been written by an outsider but rather by a member of the rabbinic elite, a gifted and highly trained rabbi who advances a clear and consistent argument.[52]

Despite the tensions with rabbinic views on wine, the structure of the temperance sermon is entirely integrated into the highly defined, standard format of *Wayiqra Rabbah*, whose literary and "constructed" nature was discussed above.[53] Each of the thirty-seven homilies in this collection of sermons is based on an individual verse from Leviticus. Each opens with a *petichta* ("proem," "opening") in which the writer scrutinizes the verse from Leviticus and relates it to another biblical verse, typically from *ketuvim* ("Writings," such as Psalms and Proverbs). The petichta is followed by the *gufa* or "main" part of the sermon (which is occasionally considerably shorter than the petichta); a very short eschatological *hatima* ("closure") concludes each sermon.[54] The temperance sermon's petichta cites Leviticus

---

[51] Heineman ("The Art of the Sermon of Palestinian Amora'im," 77) pointed out that the sermons in *Wayiqra Rabbah* often disregard the biblical context of the words on which they expound; indeed, this is a common option in rabbinic exegesis. This, however, does not really apply in this case. Rather than simply ignoring the cultic specification in Leviticus, the sermon generalizes its advocacy of temperance to the extent that it also covers the case of Aaron's sons and subsequently rereads Leviticus in light of its own norms. As noted earlier, Heineman states that "מתקבל הרושם כאילו מדובר ב'מצוות לא-תעשה' כללית ובלתי-מסויגת," ibid., 76.

[52] I do not share Visotzky's view that *all* of *Wayiqra Rabbah*, and particularly sermon 12, is a "rabbinic miscellany." Nonetheless, Visotzky's strictures require a reassessment of the relationship between polysemy and coherence in *Wayiqra Rabbah* and perhaps in all Palestinian Midrash. See note 3 above and Introduction, pages 8–10. See also Heineman, who stresses the independence of the sermon's author: "אף-על-פי ש[הדרשן] מקבל אפוא בפתיחתא זו כמה תפיסות מסורתיות שהגיעו אליו מדורות קודמים, אין בכך כדי לטשטש את גישתו המקורית לחלוטין ואת עיצובה העצמאי של דרשתו," "The Art of the Sermon of Palestinian Amora'im," 76.

[53] See note 2 above.

[54] The structure of the homilies is the same in all available textual witnesses of *Wayiqra Rabbah*, yet neither the verb *patah* nor the term *gufa* appear in all of them. Just as in the case of calling *Wayiqra Rabbah* "homiletic," we must consider Visotzky's well-founded strictures against naively equating the text's opening with actual sermons delivered in the ancient synagogues. (See note 4 above, and Burton Visotzky, *Golden Bells and Pomegranates*, 23–30). Likewise, I chose to retain the traditional term "sermon" for the sake of convenience. See also Pinhas Mandel, "על 'פתח' ועל פתיחתה: עיון חדש," in Joshua Levinson,

10:9 and interprets it in relation to Proverbs 23, a scriptural passage from the wisdom tradition.[55] The petichta rearranges verses from Proverbs 23 to illustrate the damage caused by the consumption of any amount of wine.[56]

The story of the drunkard parodies both particular elements of the sermon as well as its themes more globally. Moreover, the story of the drunkard can be viewed a stumbling stone within the sermon that divides the sermon in two parts, one before and one after the story, relating to each of the two parts individually. I first present the sermon's opening, up to the story of the drunkard; I then continue with the ways in which the story parodies the first part of the sermon, and finally, I discuss the second part of the sermon along with the story's preemptive parody thereof.

The sermon opens by focusing on Proverbs 23:31–32: "Do not look at wine when it is red, when it sparkles in the cup and goes down smoothly.[57] In the end it bites like a serpent and stings like an adder." The temperance sermon responds to the verses by describing the four types of ill fate awaiting wine drinkers "in the end":[58]

– In the interpretation of "do not look at wine when it is *red*," the sermon associates the redness of wine with the redness of menstrual blood. It infers that a wine drinker would in the end (-ש סוף) not abstain from having intercourse with his wife even if she warns him that she is ritually impure.[59] The implication is that wine leads to sexual misconduct.

Jacob Elbaum, and Galit Hasan-Rokem (eds.), *Higayon L'Yona: New Aspects in the Study of Midrash Aggadah, and Piyut in Honor of Professor Yona Frenkel* (Jerusalem: The Hebrew University Magnes Press, 2006), 49–82; Richard S. Sarason, "The Petihot in Leviticus Rabba: "Oral Homilies" or Redactional Constructions?," *Journal of Jewish Studies* 33 (1982), 557–567; Heineman, "The Art of the Sermon of Palestinian Amora'im," 69–79; David Künstlinger, *Die Petichot des Midrasch rabba zu Leviticus* (Krakow: Verlag des Verfassers, 1913); Abraham Goldberg, "The Term *gufa* in Midrash Leviticus Rabba," *Leshonenu* 38 (1968–69), 163–69 [Hebrew]; and ibid, ויקרא של העריכה מעקרונות כמה על" ",רבה, in Joshua Levinson, Jacob Elbaum, and Galit Hasan-Rokem (eds.), *Higayon L'Yona* (Jerusalem: Magnes Press, 2007), 333–344.

[55] Proverbs 23: 29 "Who has woe? Who has sorrow? Who has strife? Who has complaining? Who has wounds without cause? Who has redness of eye? 30 The ones who linger late over wine, the ones who keep trying mixed wines. 31 Do not look at wine when it is red [כי יתאדם, literally: when it turns red], when it sparkles in the cup [כי יתן בכוס עינו, according to *Wayiqra Rabbah*. The Leningrad Manuscript of the Bible has בכיס] and goes down smoothly [ויתהלך במישרים, literally: when it walks as if on a plain]. 32 At the last it bites like a serpent and stings like an adder. 33 Your eyes will see strange things, and your mind utter perverse things. 34 You will be like one who lies down in the midst of the sea, like one who lies on the top of a mast. 35 'They struck me,' you will say, 'but I was not hurt; they beat me, but I did not feel it. When shall I awake? I will seek another drink.'"

[56] The order of explicit citations from Proverbs 23 is first verse 31, then verses 34–35 and 29–30, followed by a long passage on verse 32.

[57] See above, note 55.

[58] Margulies, *Midrash Wayyikra Rabbah*, 243–247.

[59] Wine as a symbol of menstrual blood, or blood in general, is very widespread in rabbinic literature and is found elsewhere in *Wayiqra Rabbah* (see 11.2, 19.4, and 33.6).

- If a rabbinic scholar drinks wine, he is bound in the end (סוף ש-) to "declare the clean unclean and the unclean clean" (שמטמא את הטהור ומטהר את הטמא). Although this is a common phrase in rabbinic literature, its inclusion here constitutes an elegant return to the language of Leviticus 8:10, the scriptural passage immediately preceding the Nadav and Avihu story ("You are to distinguish between … the unclean (הטמא) and the clean (הטהור)"). From the outset, the temperance sermon emphasizes the fate of Nadav and Avihu.
- In the interpretation of "when it sparkles in the *cup*," the sermon plays with the homonymy of the words *kos*, "cup" and "purse" *kis*. According to the sermon, while the drinker sets his eyes on the glass, the storekeeper sets his eyes on the drinker's purse, taking advantage of his intoxication.
- In the interpretation of "and goes down *smoothly*," the sermon insists not only that wine goes down smoothly as if it "walked on a plain" but that the drunkard walks in a plain (bare) house since "in the end (סוף ש-) he will sell his household items and drink wine with [the proceeds]." Following this interpretation comes the story of the drunkard.

The audience, of course, expects the story to corroborate the sermon, yet the former ends up countering the latter.[60] The phrase "in the end" (סוף ש-) is used in three of the four descriptions of ill fate in the first part of the sermon. The repetition of the phrase here and in the sermon's gufa emphasizes the catastrophic long-term effects of wine as the petichta's central message; this is the conclusion that one would expect to find in the story of the drunkard as well. In these four cases, the sermon does not distinguish between moderate and heavy consumption of alcohol. According to the sermon's position, drinking even the slightest quantity is considered a transgression of boundaries severe enough to destroy wealth and social status.

The story of the drunkard shifts the audience's attention to violations far more dangerous than drinking a little wine. The story's satire of the sermon suggests that drinking wine by no means entails a necessary deterioration of moral character. Rather than resorting to wine to explain the evil motivations of the patricidal sons, the story lets their poor moral character speak for itself. Most notably, the satire counters the sermon's emphasis on the outcome of drinking by proposing a very different result: "in the end," the sons decide to support and enable their father's habitual drinking, a satire of the sermon's moralizing tendency.

As part of its satire of the general premises of the sermon and the vilification of wine, the story of the drunkard also imitates and satirizes particular claims made in the sermon. In each case, the evil nature of the drunkard's sons undermines the sermon's attempt to blame wine for various matters that the story parodies.

---

60 Levinson, "עיון בסיפור השיכור ובניו, 'עולם הפוך ראיתי'", 14.

- The sermon asserts that wine leads to impure sex. The story of the drunkard, in turn, uses sexual imagery from the biblical story of Lot's daughters to depict the sons' attempted patricide. The imitation of elements of the narrative of Lot's daughters leads the audience to associate patricide with incest and to dissociate poor moral character from drinking.
- The sermon warns that wine leads scholars to confound purity and impurity, invoking the discourse of purity and impurity in the biblical story of Nadav and Avihu. As the result of the sons' greed, the father is sent to the impure graveyard alive – a theme fully developed in the story's imitation of the Nadav and Avihu story.
- Whereas the sermon cautions against the financial exploitation of drinkers, the story of the drunkard ends with the financial exploitation of the sons. More precisely, while the sermon asserts that a drinker will eventually sell his property to buy wine, the story parodies this statement by concluding with the statute of perpetual drinking.

In short, immediately following the sermon's description of the pitfalls awaiting drinkers, based on its interpretation of Proverbs 23, the story of the drunkard imitates and satirizes different aspects of the sermon's predictions.

In a manner typical of redactional parodies, like the one discussed in the Chapter One, the story of the drunkard does not imitate specific words but leads the audience by presenting inverted scenarios in close proximity to the target text. The extent to which the story of the drunkard and its statute of perpetual drinking disrupt the flow of the sermon cannot be over-emphasized. The story is the second longest episode in the sermon and features prominently in its opening.[61] It is therefore impossible for the sermon's audience to miss the story and its conspicuous satire of the sermon's agenda up to this point. The sermon then continues as if the story did not interrupt its vilification of wine. (The strong tension between the sermon and the story could be viewed as one indicator that the story is a later addition.)

In turn, the story's parody of the sermon is more focused on the part of the sermon that begins after the story; here, the imitation of words from the target text is frequent. In other words, the audience does not have the opportunity to consider the sermon apart from the parody; the implications of the preemptive parody are present almost from the outset. Following the story of the drunkard, the petichta continues by interpreting Proverbs 23:33–35.[62] For example, the sermon uses Proverbs 23:35 ("When shall I

---

[61] The story of the drunkard is second in length only to the sermon's interpretation of the death of Nadav and Avihu. The sermon contains approximately fifteen hundred words, the story of the drunkard approximately one hundred; the story begins in the first tenth of the sermon.

[62] Margulies, *Midrash Wayyikra Rabbah*, 248–49. In Proverbs, the passage constitutes a vivid account of nausea from drunkenness; the sermon first dramatizes the effect and then understands the verse as "they deceived me (טלמין ליה), but I did not feel it" and lists several financial and personal disasters that befell heavy daily drinkers. One drinker is financially exploited, having consumed two and a half quarts while being charged for five, or having

awake? I will seek another drink") to maintain that even the next morning, the drinker does not refrain from drinking, despite his misery, but rather seeks more wine. In parodic contrast, the story of the drunkard enacts the sermon's prediction of seeking more wine as divinely approved: God himself, the sons reason, provides more wine for the awakening drinker!

The sermon then continues with Proverbs 23:29–30 ("Who has woe? Who has sorrow? Who has strife? Who has complaining? Who has wounds without cause? Who has redness of eye? The ones who linger late over wine, the ones who keep trying mixed wines") in a straightforward way, rebuking the behavior of wine drinkers in often amusing ways.[63] The last verse cited in the sermon's petichta is Proverbs 23:32 ("at the last, it bites like a serpent and stings like an adder").[64] The very specific term "פרש" means "to sting" or "to secrete poison" in biblical Hebrew but also denotes "to separate" in mishnaic Hebrew. Accordingly, the temperance sermon interprets the verse from Proverbs as saying that "just as this adder separates between life and death, so does wine." The sermon's central image equates wine with a serpent's venom; the sermon blames wine or drunkenness for the mishaps of four biblical characters: Adam and Eve, Noah, Aaron's sons, and Lot. All four examples are relevant in gauging the sermon's radical nature vis-à-vis other rabbinic texts; the story of the drunkard specifically parodies the sermon's interpretation of the stories of Lot and Aaron's sons.

---

drunk five while being charged for ten. The amount of alcohol consumed is the equivalent of over half a gallon in today's terms, probably producing severe effects even the next day; see note 18 above for a discussion of alcohol content.

[63] Margulies, *Midrash Wayyikra Rabbah*, 249–52. Following an interpretation of Proverbs 23:29 ("who has wounds without cause?"), we learn that yet another drinker regularly consumes twelve pitchers. Having drunk only ten pitchers one day, he cannot fall asleep. During his nocturnal excursion to the bar to finish his daily dose after curfew, he is mistaken for a thief and beaten. Thus, he is the one that has "wounds without cause." Despite the sermon's severity, such an image does not lack elements of slapstick and the grotesque: deception, the drinker's lack of sense and perception, and macabre comedy. The temperance sermon uses its comical illustrations of Proverbs to strengthen its portrayal of the pitiful nature of drinkers.

[64] Margulies, *Midrash Wayyikra Rabbah*, 252–54. The three Oxford manuscripts (147, 2335, 2634/8 in A. Neubauer, *Catalogue of the Hebrew Manuscripts in the Bodleian Library* (Oxford: Clarendon Press, 1886 [repr. 1994]), ב, א and ק in Margulies' version) blame wine also for the exile of the ten tribes; for the separations between Judah and Benjamin, between King Ahasuerus and Queen Vashti, and between Lot and Aaron; and for King Belshazzar's death. The majority of important manuscripts agree with the shorter version. I believe that the text of the Oxford manuscripts contains additions, partially inspired by Sifra *Ha'azinu* 13.6 or *Bereshit Rabbah* 36.4, that do not concern the present inquiry. Note that the list in all the other manuscripts, which contain only the stories of Noah, Lot, and Aaron, discuss a father and his children three consecutive times, which makes it very probable that the majority of manuscripts represent an earlier, complete, literary unit, to which further examples were appended in the text found in the three Oxford manuscripts.

[1] "*Wine separated Adam and Eve in regards to death.*" The sermon reports that the forbidden fruit tasted by Adam was a grape, causing Adam's separation from the Garden of Eden. The temperance sermon identifies one single fruit. In contrast, *Bereshit Rabbah* (a roughly contemporary rabbinic commentary on Genesis) provides a long list of possible fruits, illustrating the sermon's quest for secure and simple interpretations in response to rabbinic indeterminacy.[65] The sermon then infers from Adam's case that "in this way, grapes brought bitterness into this world." Not Adam's disobedience but the grape itself is considered to be the reason for human mortality, shifting agency from the human to the fruit, a point of view unparalleled in rabbinic thought, as far as I know. (The story of the drunkard does not parody this passage.)

[2] "*Wine separated Noah and his sons in regards to slavery.*" The sermon's author considers Noah's intoxication to be the reason for Ham's servitude, which separated Noah's sons. While Noah's drunkenness is part of the biblical narrative and the rabbinic tradition, the temperance sermon places the blame for Noah's nakedness on the consumption of an unspecified amount of wine. In contrast, *Bereshit Rabbah* emphasizes that Noah drank excessively, making this interpretation of the temperance sermon once more unique in its disregard for the amount of alcohol consumed.[66] (Again, the story of the drunkard does not parody this passage.)

---

[65] The temperance sermon proves its point by citing Deuteronomy 32:32: "Their grapes are grapes of poison, their clusters are bitter, their wine is the poison of serpents, the cruel venom of asps." The connection between wine and snakes in Deuteronomy 32 leads the reader back to the same link in Proverbs 23:32 ("at the last it bites like a serpent and stings like an adder"), which the sermon cites here, constituting another elegant exegetical circle. *Bereshit Rabbah* also uses Deuteronomy 32:32 as its proof (*Bereshit Rabbah* 15.7; see also *Pesiqta de Rav Kahana* 20 and *Sanhedrin* 70a). Yet, we should note that whereas *Bereshit Rabbah* suggests many kinds of fruit and understands the "snakes" in Deuteronomy symbolically, the temperance sermon in *Wayiqra Rabbah* focuses on one fruit exclusively and leaves open the possibility of interpreting wine as a "serpent" literally.

[66] In Genesis 9:18–29, Noah, in the wake of the flood, planted a vineyard, became intoxicated, and uncovered himself (ויתגל) in the tent. The incident led to the servitude of Ham. *Bereshit Rabbah* notes that the grammatical form of the verb employed in the Bible to express that Noah "uncovered" himself, גל'ה, is very rare (the *Hitpa'el* indeed occurs only here and in Proverbs 18:2) and thus proposes to understand the verb according to another meaning of the same Hebrew root: "to exile oneself." *Bereshit Rabbah* picks up on the tradition from *Sifre Devarim* and claims that wine caused Noah's exile (גלות), as well as that of the ten tribes (36.4). *Bereshit Rabbah* makes it clear that Noah consumed too much wine (שתה שלא במדה), and that the excessive amount, not the wine itself, was the problem. The same text also states that one must not be "passionate" (להוט, literally "glowing") for wine, thus again permitting its consumption but warning against exaggeration, all in stark contrast to the categorical prohibition we find in the temperance sermon.

[3] *"Wine separated Lot and his daughters in regards to bastardy."* As mentioned above, the temperance sermon reimagines the story of Lot and his daughters. It stays faithful to the source from Genesis cited above. However, while other rabbinic texts simply wonder about technical details like the provenance and nature of the wine used by the daughters, the temperance sermon shifts the emphasis to the moral implications of using wine.[67] In the Bible, wine is an accessory to the daughters' plot to steal semen from their father. In the sermon, wine becomes the main culprit, a dangerous poison without which the daughters' plot could never have been carried out. The story of the drunkard carefully imitates the sermon's reading of the biblical narrative of Lot's daughters as I sought to illustrate in detail above. The story then parodies the sermon's reading by contrasting its claim that wine is the source of all evil with the agency and criminal intent of the drunkard's sons.

[4] *"Wine separated between Aaron and his sons in regards to death."* In its final example of "separation," the temperance sermon places the blame for the death of Aaron's sons, their "separation from life," on their consumption of wine prior to entering the tabernacle. The Bible, as noted above, does not report their drinking. While drinking wine is one of the many possibilities suggested by other rabbinical texts as the true sin of Nadav and Avihu, only the temperance sermon names wine as their *only* sin.[68] In the absence of a scriptural prooftext, the sermon presents a parable to show that the sons died as a punishment for intoxication, even though the Bible stipulates it as a sin punishable by death only several verses after reporting their death:

Rabbi Ishmael expounded: "the two sons of Aaron died only because they entered drunk from wine [שתויי יין]." Rabbi Phinehas in the name of Rabbi Levi reflected on [the statement of] Rabbi Ishmael: "The matter is like a king that has a trustworthy personal attendant [בן בית נאמן] and bodyguard. [The attendant] stood at the entrance of the tavern [החנות]. [The king] severed his head without saying a word and appointed somebody else as his attendant. And we do not know why he killed the first one other than based on what he ordered the second [attendant]: 'Do not approach the tavern.' We [now] know that this is why he killed the first [attendant]. So it is written: 'And the fire went out from G-d and consumed them and they died before G-d.' We do not know why they died other than that the Holy one, Blessed be He, commended Aaron, saying: 'Do not drink wine or strong drink.' We [now] know that they died only because of the wine."

---

[67] Instead of blaming wine for the incest, *Sifre Devarim Ekev*, for example, wonders about the source of the wine. This question is answered with a reference to Joel 4:18: "On that day, the mountains shall drip sweet wine." (*Mekhilta Shira* 2 states the same.) *Bereshit Rabbah* repeats the same tradition and places the story in an eschatological context: this wine was a taste of the world to come (51:8). Concerning the use of Joel 4:18, see notes 71 and 98 below.

[68] See pages 79–86 below.

In a blatantly open recognition of the King's (i.e. God's) unpredictable behavior, Rabbi Ishmael's version of the story of Aaron's sons rationalizes the death of God's trustworthy attendants Nadav and Avihu by fusing the episode with the subsequent biblical commandment not to drink wine. He concludes that the servant must have died because he drank wine at the tavern despite the fact that the servant, or the audience, could not have known about the prohibition against approaching the tavern. The parable broadens the applicability of the prohibition of alcohol to include even physical proximity to a tavern. At the same time, it admits and sharpens, rather than mitigates, the problematic nature of its understanding of the biblical narrative. God killed two seemingly innocent, righteous people. The servant is called "trustworthy," and this certainly also refers to Aaron's sons. The temperance sermon entirely ignores the nature of the fire as well as all other possible sins listed elsewhere in rabbinic literature. Instead, it once more advocates one single interpretation in place of multiple rabbinic options: wine is evil.

This last biblical interpretation in the temperance sermon is the central target of the story of the drunkard's parody. We are now in a position to attempt a more nuanced reading of the parody. The sons' misinterpretation of the wine in the graveyard as a miracle may be the author's way of imitating and targeting the sermon's reading of the Nadav and Avihu story. The sermon, by way of Rabbi Phinehas's explanation of Rabbi Ishmael's statement, takes the punishment, and the subsequent statute against wine in Leviticus, as an illustration of the sin committed by the servant and by Nadav and Avihu. It understands the divine manifestation and God's subsequent prohibition as proof of the transgression. The sons, likewise, proclaim an ordinance in response to a perceived divine manifestation, an ordinance that attempts to correct their transgression; the ordinance, however, is based on a mistaken interpretation of reality and enables perpetual drinking. Hence, the sons' misperception of the wine as a miracle exposes the folly associated with the sermon's making such inductive leaps.

Perhaps in its most central challenge of the sermon, the story points out that one cannot take accidents, tragic or joyful, as proof or disproof of divine intention, neither in the case of wine in the graveyard nor in the case of Aaron's sons. Hence, the drunkard's sons' institution of the statute of perpetual drinking based on their misperception counters once more the sermon's generalization of the priestly decree against wine in Leviticus 10:9 as well as its underlying reading of the cause of Nadav's and Avihu's death. This exegetical parody does not disprove the possibility that Nadav and Avihu were intoxicated. But it parodies the sermon's straightforward, monocausal, and utterly un-rabbinic interpretation of Nadav and Avihu as having died *only* and *certainly* because of wine. The story of the drunkard does not satirize the biblical narrative at all, and it does not endorse alcohol-

ism, but it satirizes the sermon's ethical and hermeneutical pitfalls in reading
the Bible: a lack of tolerance toward moderate wine consumption and, as it
were, a lack of midrashic disposition.

The story of the drunkard parodies many details in the sermon's petichta.
However, it does not focus to the same extent on the gufa, the main body
of the sermon, which is substantially shorter than the opening. The gufa,
at the same time, carries on and reinforces the same themes that appear in
the petichta. We should also note that the gufa is as radical, or even more
radical, in its preaching against wine than the petichta. It first singles out
grapes as a fruit with multiple names, undetermined status in sacrifice and
tithing, and due to its difficult digestion.[69] The gufa's polemics mingle
consumption of unfermented grapes, moderate consumption of wine, and
heavy drinking. By association, all of these "in the end" cause vomiting.
Grapes in every form and wine in any amount eventually lead the drinker
to forget about the existence of his own limbs and to be despised. The
sermon uses the term "in the end" (סוף) three times, neatly paralleling its
use in the petichta and emphasizing the effects of wine. The story of the
drunkard imitates and satirizes this aspect of the sermon's petichta and gufa
by presenting a very different result of drinking: the statute of perpetual
drinking. Hence, I see the entire temperance sermon, not just its petichta,
as the parody's target text.

Notably, the sermon blames even the destruction of the Temple on the
consumption of wine. We learn that Solomon does not drink wine for seven
years during the construction of the Temple. When the construction is
completed, he celebrates his marriage and drinks an unspecified amount of
wine; the following morning he oversleeps, the key to the Temple under his
pillow, thus delaying the morning sacrifice and causing God to contemplate
for the first time the destruction of Jerusalem. Solomon's mother, in another
instance in the sermon of the grotesque, strikes the King of Israel with her
shoe as she finds him asleep.[70]

The Sermon concludes with God's complaint over losing His "house"
(i.e., the Temple) and two "princes," Nadav and Avihu, due to wine consumption. The sermon's return to the theme of Aaron's sons emphasizes the
centrality of their case in the sermon's argument; the story of the drunkard,
likewise, focuses on this interpretation as its most central target of satire.

The sermon's *hatima*, in contrast, provides a typical eschatological outlook, predicting that even if wine causes many disasters in this world, it will
bring joy in the world to come. Only here and in the story of the drunkard
the sermon is aligned with the rabbinic tradition; the consumption of wine

---

[69] Margulies, *Midrash Wayyikra Rabbah*, 259–262.
[70] Margulies, *Midrash Wayyikra Rabbah*, 262–265.

in the world to come is commonplace in rabbinic literature.[71] The story of
the drunkard, accordingly, does not respond to the sermon's hatima.

The story of the drunkard thus imitates and satirizes the themes and
particular features of the temperance sermon, especially the petichta. It
ridicules the sermon's generalization of Leviticus 10:9 and its allegation
that alcohol leads to financial demise and exploitation, the fusion of purity
and impurity, and sexual misconduct. By fulfilling the drunkard's request
for more wine as a result of a mistakenly perceived miracle, it satirically
reaffirms the sermon's claim that drinkers "in the end" demand more and
more wine. Most importantly, it parodies the sermon's interpretation of the
death of Aaron's sons and the crime of Lot's daughters as caused by wine
and contrasts the sermon's ascetic tendencies with its own focus on fundamental moral issues – incest and murder – and the concrete reality of strive
between fathers and sons.

Such scathing satire and intimate parodic relationship between the sermon and the story suggests that the story was composed by a different
author, and that it is a later addition to the sermon. The story was likely incorporated into the sermon by one of its redactors; it is another example of
redactional parody. The uniform compositional nature of the individual sermons and of *Wayiqra Rabbah* as a whole further supports this suggestion.

Redaction and Adaptation: Between Aesop and Wayiqra Rabbah

Although there is no textual evidence that supports this claim, the story of
the drunkard in my view was incorporated into the sermon after its original
composition and thus constitutes a redactional parody. Two more observations substantiate this reading: the folkloristic context of the sermon and the
fifth-century debates on asceticism.

Elbaum, Levinson, and others have noted that the story itself, and its burlesque aspects, evoke a folkloristic atmosphere.[72] Jacob Elbaum illustrated

---

[71] The hatima uses Joel 4:18 as a prooftext, also in an eschatological context, for example, in *Sifre Devarim Ekev, Bereshit Rabbah* 51.8 and 70.6, and sermon 11 in *Wayiqra
Rabbah* (see note 67 above and note 98 below). The eschatological banquet includes the
consumption of wine since the times of Isaiah; see Isaiah 25:6–8 and 1QS28a 2:11–22; see
also Mark 14:23–25 and Dennis E. Smith, *From Symposium to Eucharist* (Minneapolis:
Fortress Press, 2003).

[72] Jacob Elbaum ("מבוא באגדת יין," 122f) follows Dov Noy, מבוא
לספרות האגדה (Jerusalem: The Hebrew University of Jerusalem, 1966), 12–14. Heineman,
following Elbaum, calls the story an "international folk tale" ("The Art of the Sermon
of Palestinian Amora'im," 78), and according to Joshua Levinson, there is no doubt that
the story of the drunkard existed independently and was integrated into *Wayiqra Rabbah*
(Levinson, "עולם הפוך ראיתי'–עיון בסיפור השיכור ובניו," 11).

this claim by considering Aesop's "Story of a Woman and a Drunkard Husband," which circulated widely during the time of the redaction of *Wayiqra Rabbah*. In this story, a woman tries to terrify her husband by placing him in a graveyard in order to solve his drinking problem. The husband proves immune to the cure. Much to the audience's surprise and likely amusement, he demands drink rather than food. The story explicitly states that excessive consumption of alcohol corrupts a person to the point that even in the face of death he demands more wine.[73] Elbaum notes that the literary affinity between the story of the drunkard and Aesop's tale is self evident, and Heineman asserts that the two stories differ only "a little."[74] And indeed, the two stories include:

– A drunken paterfamilias admonished for his behavior by a family member.
– Passing out from excessive consumption of wine, he is carried to and placed in a graveyard.
– The person/s that bring him to the graveyard return/s, finding him wanting more wine and realizing that the plot had failed.
– As a result, the drunkard's dependence on wine continues.

The clear similarities between Aesop's tale and the story of the drunkard confirm the folkloristic aspects suggested by Elbaum, Heineman, and Levinson. This holds true even though there are noteworthy differences between the tale and the story in *Wayiqra Rabbah*. Most importantly, the sons' mistaken perception of divine approval of their father's drinking habit as well as their subsequent vow stand in perverse relationship to the moral of Aesop's tale.[75] The differences between the two texts, in my view, all pre-

---

[73] "A woman had a husband who was a drunkard (μέθυσον). In order to deliver him from his vice, she planned something: She watched him closely until he was asleep from drinking, and in a manner of a dead person was insensible. She heaved him over her shoulders, carried him to the cemetery, put him down and left. The moment she suspected him to have sobered up, she went knocking on the door of the cemetery. He said: 'Who is knocking on the door?' The woman answered: 'I came to bring food for the dead.' He: 'Don't bring me food, good man, but rather drink, since you do me pain by talking about eating but not about drinking!' She, beating her breast, said: 'How miserable I am. My plan did not have any effect since you, husband, not only did you not grow up, but you also have become worse; your vice has become your second nature.' The story makes clear that one must not become accustomed to a bad practice since there is a moment that the habit rests on you even involuntarily." My translation, text according to A. Hausrath and H. Hunger, *Corpus Fabularum Aesopicarum* (Leipzig: Teubner, 1970), no. 278. On the circulation of Aesop, see Émile Chamgry, *Ésope, Fables* (Paris: Les Belles Lettres, 2002), XXI–XLI.

[74] See Jacob Elbaum, "מעשים בשכור ומכוער באגדתנו ובאגדת יון," 125 and Heineman, "The Art of the Sermon of Palestinian Amora'im," 78.

[75] I see four additional main differences. 1) In contrast with Aesop's tale, the story of the drunkard is not concerned with alcoholism itself but with the financial implications of the father's drinking habit and its impact on his sons' inheritance; 2) The wife in Aesop's tale attempts to deliver the drunkard from sin and thereby save his life whereas the sons

cisely correspond to the ways in which the rabbinic story of the drunkard imitates and satirizes the temperance sermon. The falsely perceived miracle, for example, emphasizes the story of the drunkard's parody of the temperance sermon's reading of Leviticus 10:9 as an ordinance against drinking.[76]

Hence, the author of the story of the drunkard may have adapted a folkloristic model in the service of literary parody.[77] While the story of the drunkard repeats this model with a difference, it seems clear that the differences between the rabbinic story and Aesop's tale emphasize the story's parody of the sermon, not of the folkloric model. Parody, in other words, easily coexists with other forms of intertextuality and with other forms of textual repetition. The suggested textual relationship between the sermon, the story, and the folkloristic model provides a possible scenario for my presentation of a redactional parody. Just like in the Bavli, the redactor of the temperance sermon may have sensed the parodic potential in juxtaposing the sermon with a story like Aesop's. He may have modified it to suit his particular exegetical needs, and placed it at the beginning of the sermon. And just as with the Bavli, we should consider the possibility that the in-

---

in the story of the drunkard seek to protect their inheritance at the expense of the drunkard's life; 3) The marital relationship in Aesop's tale is replaced by a paternal relationship in the story of the drunkard in which the sons serve as "undertakers;" and 4) The wife in Aesop's tale intends to feed the drunkard whereas the father is ironically "nourished" by the merchants' inadvertent gift.

[76] In correspondence with the previous note: 1) The temperance sermon's exegesis of Proverbs 23:31 ("and goes down *smoothly* [ויתהלך במישרים, literally, when it walks as if on a plain]") claims that a drunkard will live in an empty house as a result of consuming alcohol. The story of the drunkard pretends to illustrate this allegation but eventually perverts it. This highlights the story's parody of the sermon's reading of Proverbs. The drinker will be fine, the story tells us, since God, vis-à-vis the sons, will provide for him and even support his habit; 2) The temperance sermon claims that wine in the story of Lot led to incest. This emphasizes the story of the drunkard's parody of the sermon's exegesis. According to the story of the drunkard, wine is not to blame but rather humans are held responsible for their actions at all times; 3) The two sons in the story of the drunkard recall the temperance sermon's exegesis of the story of Aaron's sons, claiming that God killed them because they were drunk. According to the story of the drunkard, their death might have been a tragic accident, and good rabbis read the Bible in more than one way; and 4) This parodies the sermon's reading of Proverbs 23:35, which anticipates such a demand for more drink.

[77] For a discussion of the relationship of folklore and Midrash, see Galit Hasan-Rokem, *Web of Life: Folklore and Midrash in Rabbinic Literature* (Stanford: Stanford University Press, 2000) with Dan Ben-Amos' review, "Lamentations Rabbah: Trauma, Dreams, and Riddles," *Prooftexts* 21 (2001), 399–409. More recent definitions of folklore seek to diminish the divide between "low" folklore and "high" rabbinic literature; see Dina Stein, מימרה מגיה מיתוס: פרקי דרבי אליעזר לאור מחקר הספרות העממית (Jerusalem: Magnes Press, 2004) and Eli Yassif, "Jewish Folk Literature in Late Antiquity," in: W.D. Davies and Louis Finkelstein (eds.), *The Cambridge History of Judaism* IV, (Cambridge, UK: Cambridge University Press, 2006), 721–748. Yassif discusses another fable from Aesop that has a parallel in the Bavli; see ibid., 738.

tended audience would be attuned to the redactor's technique of juxtaposing various preexisting compositional units, most often to enhance a message, sometimes to undermine it.

The redaction history proposed above demonstrates the plausibility of my reading of the story of the drunkard as a redactional parody. I shall now consider the historical context of the temperance sermon, suggesting that the tensions between the sermon and the story of the drunkard reflect discussions about wine in the fourth- and fifth-century Roman East. Here, we find social polarization concerning the question of alcohol consumption, contextualizing both the sermon's advocacy of temperance and its inversion in the story of the drunkard.

Aaron's Sons and Wine in Wayiqra Rabbah

The literary analysis of the temperance sermon and the story of the drunkard reveals their radical contrast and their status as a target text and a satirical parody, respectively. The question then arises: why would a redactor of the temperance sermon seek to satirize the sermon itself? Indeed, if my understanding that the sermon radically opposes the consumption of wine is correct, a far more vexing question ensues: how did the temperance sermon come into being and why was it included in *Wayiqra Rabbah* in the first place?

These two questions help us recognize that the story of the drunkard and *Wayiqra Rabbah* share an ideological stance on wine and that the temperance sermon is the exception. Investigation into prevalent rabbinic attitudes towards the consumption of wine and temperance in the time of *Wayiqra Rabbah* may allow us to corroborate this suggestion. The story of the drunkard's attitude towards wine is fully in line with the balanced rabbinic approach of its time, especially as expressed in other parts of *Wayiqra Rabbah*. This is true also of the ambiguous exegetical stance towards Nadav and Avihu, which the story of the drunkard generates through parody. The temperance sermon, in turn, shows essential affinity with contemporaneous ascetic movements. This reconfirms my suggestion that the parody is a late addition to the sermon from yet another angle.

The reason for the death of Nadav and Avihu had been the subject of rabbinic and patristic discussion for hundreds of years before the redaction of *Wayiqra Rabbah*.[78] The early Palestinian Midrash *Sifra* introduces a long

---

[78] See Avigdor Shinan, "The Sins of Nadav and Avihu in Rabbinic Aggadah," *Tarbiz*, 48 (1979), 201–214 [Hebrew]; Jacob Elbaum, "מעשים בשכור ומכער באגדתנו ובאגדת יון," *Mahanayim*, 112 (1967), 122–129; Heineman, "The Art of the Sermon of Palestinian Amora'im," 69 [Hebrew]; Robert Kirschner, "The Rabbinic and Philonic Exegeses of the

list of possible reasons for their death. For *Sifra*, the two sons may have been burned because of a cultic accident: they simply used the wrong kind of fire by mistake[79] or mistimed their entrance to the Tabernacle.[80] Sifra also suggests that the brothers might have lacked the proper disposition of priests; that is, they were disrespectful[81] or perhaps overly zealous.[82] A final option proposed in *Sifra* is that Nadav and Avihu were sacrificed.[83]

In the time of the redaction of *Wayiqra Rabbah*, rabbinic opinions regarding the sins of Nadav and Avihu became more focused. For example, another sermon in *Wayiqra Rabbah* (sermon 20, concerning the verse "After the death of the two sons of Aaron") indeed includes many of *Sifra's* statements about Nadav and Avihu[84] and some of its underlying arguments

---

Nadab and Abihu Incident (Lev 10:1–6)," *Jewish Quarterly Review* 73 (1983), 375–393. Cf. also Scott A. Swanson, *Fifth Century Patristic and Rabbinic Ethical Interpretation of Cult and Ritual in Leviticus* (PhD diss., Hebrew Union College, 2004).

[79] For example, they may have taken the fire from a stove, *Sifra Shmini Mekhilta deMiluim*, 32.

[80] Ibid., *Ah're Mot* 1.1.

[81] In particular, they did not honor their father (*Sifra, Shmini Mekhilta deMiluim*, 32). Other suggestions include not accepting advice from each other, or from Moses, and not following his commands. According to one opinion, they even pronounced rules in Moses's presence (*Sifra, Shmini Mekhilta deMiluim*, 32; see also *Sifra, Ah're Mot* 1.1. Pronouncing rules in the presence of one's master is a sin nominally punishable by death in rabbinic culture; see *Sifra, Shmini Mekhilta deMiluim*, 32 and *Eruvin* 63a). The following version is noteworthy: Nadav, the elder, said to Avihu: "Soon the two old ones (זקנים, i.e., Moses and Aaron) will die and we shall lead the community." Thereupon, God, perhaps with a dose of sarcasm, is reported to say to Himself: "We will see who buries whom" (ibid. *Sifra Shmini Mekhilta deMiluim*, 21).

[82] Nadav proposed to his brother to add fire when seeing that God's presence, the *Shekhina*, did not descend despite the Israelites' sacrifices (an addition to the biblical story). In response, God, again with possible sarcasm, explains the broken symmetry inherent in their punishment: "I will honor you more than you honored me. You brought impure fire (אש טמאה) in front of me, I will burn you with pure fire" (באש טהורה, ibid., 22). Another reading suggests that as they finally saw "new fire" (אש חדשה) coming down from the sky (according to Leviticus 9:24), they joyfully "were about to add love to love" (עמדו להוסיף אהבה על אהבה, ibid, 32). The passage does not indicate that the fire they saw was the one that subsequently burned them nor does it attempt to resolve the extreme tension it creates by contrasting their piety with their unforeseeable death. It thus stands as a silent accusation, perhaps against God's injustice in light of the tragic outcome.

[83] In order to console his brother, Moses is portrayed as claiming, without exonerating their sin, that Nadav and Avihu were superior to him and Aaron (ibid., 23). He reinterprets the death of Aaron's sons twice, regarding their death first as a consecration of the tent of meeting (בהם הבית נתקדש, *Sifra Shmini Mekhilta deMiluim*, 23), and second as a sanctification of God's name (קדושת שמו, ibid, 36). See also *Sifra, Ah're Mot*, 1.13 where it is made clear that their death is a punishment.

[84] The entire discussion in *Wayiqra Rabbah* 20 is paralleled in the *Pesiqta de-Rav Kahana, Aharei Mot* 5–9. There is no scholarly agreement as to which of the two texts is earlier (see Stemberger, *Introduction to Talmud and Midrash*, 314f) and the question has to be bracketed for the present inquiry. See also *Esther Rabbah* I.22.

that question the appropriateness of their punishment.[85] Sermon 20, however, goes much beyond *Sifra* and comes close to accusing God of injustice
for punishing them too harshly.[86] It provides eight possible reasons, including wine, for the death of Nadav and Avihu: approaching the altar, the
nature of their sacrifice, bringing strange fire, not accepting advice from
one another,[87] recent consumption of wine, wearing improper priestly garments, not having purified themselves by washing their hands and feet, and
not having sons.[88] Sermon 20 in *Wayiqra Rabbah* has a twofold strategy: it
exceedingly portrays the sins as "priestly related," and it makes them appear
as accidental, hence more tragic. This strategy may respond to patristic anti-
Jewish polemics that used the story of Nadav and Avihu, a possibility that
does not directly concern the present discussion.[89]

---

[85] Heineman writes that the homilies in *Wayiqra Rabbah* "skillfully integrate many
different materials and shape them anew according to the purpose in the preacher's mind."
("The Art of the Sermon of Palestinian Amora'im," vi).

[86] Sermon 20 comes close to accusing God of injustice. The sermon wonders how it can
be that the emperor Titus was allowed to desecrate the Temple and remain alive whereas
the two sons of Aaron died instantly during sacrifice (*Wayiqra Rabbah* 20.5). After a short
digression, the sermon uses Proverbs 17:26 in order to express an explicit complaint about
the injustice done to Aaron's sons: "To impose a fine on the innocent is not right, or to
flog the noble for their integrity."

[87] *Wayiqra Rabbah* 20.8 and Margulies, 361 f. In its adaptation of the charges against
Aaron's sons found in *Sifra*, Sermon 20 alters the deeds and lessens the severity of their
sins even more. In the sermon, the audience is reminded that Nadav and Avihu wished to
replace the "two old people" though it does not recall God's sarcastic response and even
denies that they voiced their intention aloud (ibid., 10) as in the *Sifra* narrative. Most of all,
it omits the serious charge that they did not honor their father. Sermon 20 then mentions
that Aaron's sons approached the altar in an unfit manner, but it transforms their act into
an encounter with God and a mystical experience (ibid., 10).

[88] *Wayiqra Rabbah* 20.9 and Margulies, 362–64.

[89] Avigdor Shinan realizes that Sermon 20 contains a "polemical thread" ("The Sins of
Nadav and Avihu in Rabbinic Aggadah," 203) though he does not specify the nature of
this polemic. The church fathers' replacement theology welcomed a biblical narrative in
which priests die. The fate of Nadav and Avihu figures prominently in the work of the
Cappadocians Gregory of Nazianzus, Basil of Caesarea, and Gregory of Nyssa. Also,
Theodoret, Bishop of Cyrrhus in Syria, stresses the symmetry between the sin that Nadav and Avihu must have committed and their punishment (*Questiones in Octateuchum*
162.19). Intriguingly, the principle of measure for measure is also a central feature in the
story of the drunkard. Theodoret states explicitly that he thinks of the Jews when talking
about the sons of Aaron, and he specifies that Nadav's fire was too "legalistic," a standard
patristic criticism of Judaism. Unlike the Jews, who brought a "fire of law" (νομικὸν πῦρ),
the church brings "new fire" (καινὸν πῦρ) to the altar, which God accepts (*Explanatio in
Canticum Canticorum* 188.9–14). Theodoret (~393–~457) wrote this commentary in the
midst of the dyophysite controversy, probably after 420, though before the Council of
Ephesus in 431 and the anti-Origenist debate; he may well have written during the period
during which *Wayiqra Rabbah* was redacted. See Jean-Noël Guinot, "La Christologie
de Théodoret de Cyr," *Vigilae Christianae* 39 (1985), 256; Marcel Richard, "Notes sur
l'évolution doctrinale de Théodoret de Cyr," *RSPT* 25 (1936), 459–481; and, idem.,
"L'activité littéraire de Théodoret avant le concil d'Éphèse," in: *RSPT* 24 (1935), 82–106.

In contrast with Sermon 20, the temperance sermon is concerned only with drinking and does away with all the other possible reasons for the death of Nadav and Avihu. Ignoring the eight possible causes of death mentioned above, the temperance sermon presents only one reason for their death; their *only* sin is the consumption of wine, probably an unintentional transgression. The temperance sermon's position is tenuous given that the prohibition postdates the offense. Like Sermon 20, the temperance sermon emphasizes the brothers' righteousness. However, as we have seen, the temperance sermon uses Aaron's sons as an important example in its attempt to vilify the consumption of wine and other grape products, considered by the sermon to be the real portents of evil.

The temperance sermon is not only the sole rabbinic text of its time that blames Lot's fate on the consumption of wine rather than on the actions of his daughters, but it also provides drinking wine as the *only* possible sin of Nadav and Avihu, again conflating rabbinic polysemy and yielding an ascetic and monocausal reading.[90] The argument of the temperance sermon is hardly compatible with the long rabbinic tradition, and its extreme asceticism is unique as well. Intriguingly, nowhere else in earlier or contemporaneous rabbinic literature do we find such a sustained stance against the consumption of wine, and some of the later rabbinic sermons that express this view rely on the sermon under discussion.[91] We have, therefore, good evidence for the incompatibility of the temperance sermon and a palpable aspect of rabbinic "orthodoxy," an incompatibility that begins to explain the story of the drunkard's wish to parody the sermon.

In Jewish culture, wine and grapes are an integral part of worship.[92] The Bible of course offers many passages that warn against the dangers of over-

---

[90] Two later possible texts that accept wine as the only reason for the death of Nadav and Avihu are *Shir haShirim Rabbah* 5:1 and *Bemidbar Rabbah* 13.2.

[91] Even though Heineman recognizes that the sermon creates the impression that it amounts to a general prohibition of alcohol (see note 7 above), in the English summary of his article, he calls it "a rather conventional sermon against drunkenness" ("The Art of the Sermon of Palestinian Amora'im," vii, cf. ibid., 76). Heineman's examples of such conventional homilies, however, are taken from much later texts, such as *Tanhuma, Shmini* 5.11 (Buber Tanhuma Shmini 7); via Elbaum, ("יין, מעשים בשכור ומכוער באגדתנו ובאגדת" 122 n. 4) from *Ester Rabbah* 5.1 (a parallel of the temperance sermon); *Midrash Mishle Rabbah* 23.29 (ed. Buber 48.1); and *Midrash haGadol Leviticus, Shmini* 9 (ed. Rabinowitz 198). See also *Bemidbar Rabbah* 10.2; cf. also *Sanhedrin* 70a. I could not find any rabbinic examples from before or contemporary with *Wayiqra Rabbah* that condemn wine in such categorical and relentless terms.

[92] See, for example, Numbers 28:14. The Babylonian exemption from the requirement for wine in worship, which permits the use of beer instead of wine in the *Kiddush* ritual, is a later development; see *Pesahim* 107a. Concerning the requirement for wine in Kiddush and *Havdalah*, see the tractates *Berakhot* of the Mishna and the Talmudim.

consumption,[93] just as Greek texts from the early Common Era reveal an awareness of the dangers associated with intoxication.[94] Still, we must not forget that rabbinic, Hellenistic, and "orthodox" Christian traditions all laud wine explicitly and that it plays an important role in many of their rituals.[95] At times, the wine-affirming exegesis of early rabbis and church fathers is intriguingly similar.[96] Particularly, *Wayiqra Rabbah* often permits[97]

---

[93] For wine's ill effects, see Isaiah 5:11f, 28:7, 51:21; Jeremiah 23:9; Hosea 4:11 and 7:5; Joel 1:5; Habakkuk 2:15; Proverbs 23:29–35, 21:17, and 4:17. For a praise of wine in the Bible, see Psalms 104:15; Ecclesiastes 9:7 and 10:19; Amos 9:14; and Zechariah 10:7.

[94] See, among the plethora of literature, Lucian, *Symposion* 17.43–48; Plutarch, *Quaestiones Conviviales*, passim; and Pliny the Elder, *Naturalis Historia* 14.28.

[95] Most late ancient Christian writers on the subject highlight New Testament evidence for the liturgical uses of wine. Rabbinic writings take the liturgical use of wine for granted and discuss its proper use. Heineman noted the idiosyncrasy of the temperance sermon's attempt to push wine out of rabbinic culture, without trying to dissolve it. See Heineman, "The Art of the Sermon of Palestinian Amora'im," 76: "דרשה על נושא היין מן הראוי שתדבר בגנות השכרות...וזאת על אף ההערכה החיובית של היין הנמצאת במקרא...ולעתים אף היין הנמצאת במקרא...ולעתים אף בדברי חז״ל...ועל אף חובת שתיית היין המעוגנת בהלכה." For a collection of sources, see Smith, *From Symposium to Eucharist*. For a discussion of the wine industry in Late Antiquity, see, for example, Joshua Schwartz, "Treading the Grapes of Wrath: The Wine Press in Ancient Jewish and Christian Tradition," *Theologische Zeitschrift*, 49 (1993), 215–228 and 311–324; Shlomo M. Paul, "Classifications of Wine in Mesopotamian and Rabbinic Sources," *Israel Exploration Journal* 25 (1975), 42–44; Daniel Sperber, "On Pubs and Policemen in Roman Palestine," *Zeitschrift der Deutschen Morgenländischen Gesellschaft* 120 (1970), 257–263; and Erwin R. Goodenough, *Jewish Symbols in the Greco-Roman Period*, v 5–6: Bread, Fish, and Wine (New York: Pantheon Books, 1956).

[96] As a general example, Clement of Alexandria wrote in his *Paedagogus*, at the turn of the third century, two consecutive chapters on eating and drinking. In the second chapter, he uses Amos 6:6 in order to warn against "luxurious decadence" (τρυφὴν) that comes with drinking wine (2.30.3), "Alas for those who lie on beds of ivory ... who drink wine from bowls ...[Therefore they shall be the first to go into exile]." Similarly, the third century Palestinian Midrash *Sifre Devarim* uses the same scriptural verse in its attack on dining, wining, and idleness and places the blame for the exile of the ten tribes on precisely these activities (*Ha'azinu* 13.6). The ten tribes are one of a series of examples of groups that rebelled against God; *Sifre* explicitly views their behavior as a result of "dining, wining, and idleness" (מתוך מאכל ומשתה ומתוך שלוה). These groups include the generation of the flood, the people of Sodom, the people of the tower (of Babel), the generation of the wilderness, the children of Job, the ten tribes, and last but not least, the people of the Days of the Messiah (13.13; see also *Sifre Devarim*, *Ki Tetseh* 10). Both the Christian and the rabbinic interpretations stay close to the biblical verse and do not prohibit drinking but only excessive consumption of alcohol. It should also be noted that the alleged innocence of Lot and his daughters is a broader topic in Christian discourse; see Irenaeus, *Adversus Heraeses* 4.31 and Augustine, *Contra Faust.* xxii, 44.

[97] *Wayiqra Rabbah* includes positive images of wine in the context of worship (1.2f. and 11.1–4). It uses wine as a symbol of proselytes (1.2) and the vineyard of Israel (11.7 and 36.2). Wine is associated with the Day of Atonement (29.8), the Torah (30.1), and with a blessing (36.3). Likewise, wine is said to be comforting (34.13). Furthermore, the Midrash recounts a story in which the Palestinian Rabban Gamliel, after having drunk wine, "a fourth according to the Italian measure," makes sure to sober up before annulling somebody's oath and states that doing so is a general rule (37.3). This indicates that rabbis, according to *Wayiqra Rabbah*, did indeed drink wine regularly and had specific rules

and regulates[98] the consumption of wine, and complete abstinence is clearly rejected from Tannaitic to Amoraic times, even in response to the destruction of the Temple.[99] The only biblical traditions that promote abstinence from wine and grapes are the Rechabites and the *Nazir*, as described in Numbers 6:1–21.[100] However, there is evidence that the concept of the Nazir was, at least partially, put into practice by Christians from the first- to the fifth-century.[101] The rabbis, in contrast, regulated but also resisted the practice of becoming a Nazir, certainly because the destruction of the Temple complicated the matter yet conceivably also in response to its emphases in Christianity.[102] *Wayiqra Rabbah*, for example, recounts a humorous episode

concerning its handling. (On the amount of wine consumption and the alcohol content, see note 18 above.)

[98] Sermon 11 in *Wayiqra Rabbah* similarly understands the description in Joel 4:18 as portraying an eschatological event, thus establishing wine for the world to come (11.7); see notes 67 and 71 above. Sermon 5 interprets "wine from bowls" in Amos 6 to indicate "wine that opens the body" (i.e., to lust) and wine that enticed the ten tribes (5.3). Thus, this sermon, although condemning one type of wine, limits the condemnation to wine coming from a certain region and does not prohibit it altogether.

[99] For a discussion of temporary abstinence, see Mishna and Tosefta *Ta'anit*, passim. For the rejection of abstinence in response to the Temple's destruction, see Tosefta *Sotah* 15.11, repeated in *Bava Batra* 60b. See also page 88.

[100] See Jeremiah 36 and 2 Kings 10:15. Eliezer Diamond has convincingly argued that this biblical tradition is best understood as a way of self-offering; see "An Israelite self-Offering in the Priestly Code; a new Perspective on the Nazirite," *Jewish Quarterly Review* 88 (1997), 1–18. This concept was certainly put into practice in biblical times and throughout the Second Temple period. The most famous Nazirites were Samson and the prophet Samuel. See also Antonio Cacciari, "Philo and the Nazirite," in Francesca Calabi (ed.), *Italian Studies on Philo of Alexandria* (Leiden: Brill, 2003), 147–166.

[101] According to New Testament texts, Jesus acted as a Nazirite by renouncing wine for a certain period; see Matthew 26:29, Mark 14:25, Luke 22:20, and Acts 21:23. The title "Nazorean" in Matthew 2:23 probably alluded to the same idea, though this is disputed; see Ernst Zuckschwerd, "Nazōraîos in Matth 2, 23," *Theologische Zeitschrift*, 31 (1975), 65–77. The idea of the Nazir was mostly treated historically or exegetically by Christian authors. For example, the second "Letter on Virginity" attributed to Clement of Rome, mentions Samson as a Nazirite (9). Origen pays a lot of attention to the Nazirites throughout his exegetical works. Eusebius reports that according to Hegesippus, James, Jesus' brother, was a Nazirite (*Ecclesiastical History* 2.23); see Ernst Zuckschwerd, "Das Naziräat des Herrenbruders Jakobus nach Hegesipp (Euseb, H E II 23:5–6)," *Zeitschrift für die Neutestamentliche Wissenschaft und die Kunde der älteren Kirche*, 68 (1977), 276–287. The ideal of the Nazir was part of the monastic tradition. Gregory of Nazianzus argues at one point that Nazirites, thus probably monks as well, should elect a bishop (*Funeral Oration to his Father* (Oration 18), 35.1032.18–22). Elsewhere, he regrets that they opposed the election of his friend Basil of Caesarea as bishop (unsuccessfully, *Funeral Oration for Basil the Great* (Oration 43), 28.3.3–4).

[102] It is not clear whether Jewish Nazirites remained after the destruction of the Temple, when sin-offering, practiced at the conclusion of the period of abstinence, could no longer be administered. The mishnaic tractate *Nazir* and *Sifre Bemidbar Naso* suggest that the concept of the Nazir had perpetrated deeply into the daily life of many lay Jews. It is possible that these early rabbinic texts invoke the practice critically. The rabbinic evidence, however, does not allow us to draw historical conclusions. Later rabbinic evidence is

at the expense of drunkards and Nazirites alike, marking its own inclination towards moderate consumption.[103] The temperance sermon, in turn, does not mention Nazirites – an understandable strategy given the contentious nature of the issue, yet also an intriguing silence in light of its own insistence on temperance.[104] In short, wine is an integral part of rabbinic culture in general, and the temperance sermon is an anomaly in *Wayiqra Rabbah* specifically. Most centrally, its treatment of the story of Nadav and Avihu focuses on one aspect of the rabbinic tradition while ignoring most others, and its vilification of wine and grapes is utterly non-rabbinic.

Hence, we see that the approach to alcohol and to the story of Nadav and Avihu in the story of the drunkard is fully in line with the conventions of *Wayiqra Rabbah* and contemporary rabbinic texts. The presence of the story of the drunkard within *Wayiqra Rabbah*, therefore, does not result

---

clearly aware of the problem that one could not conclude the rite without the prescribed sacrifice even in the times of the Second Temple. *Bereshit Rabbah* recounts the story of three hundred Nazirites who came to Jerusalem in need of nine hundred sacrifices in the days of Shimon ben Shetach, a Palestinian sage prior to the destruction of the Temple (91.3, see also Yerushalmi *Berakhot* 7:2 11b). According to the legend, Shimon ben Shetach absolved half of the group from their Naziriteship on technical grounds after finding a basis for doing so (מצא להם פתח). For the other half, he had the sacrifices procured by the king. Even if the large number of people in the story seems to be motivated by rabbinic literary convention, the author of the story took for granted the presence of Nazirites before the Temple's destruction. Based on the mishnaic material, Weiss-Halivni has argued convincingly that the rabbinic contempt for Nazirites stemmed from the unseriousness with which the concept was used in everyday life (David Halivni Weiss, "On the Supposed Anti-Asceticism or Anti-Nazritism of Simon the Just," in *JQR* 58 (1967–69), 243–252). See also the tractates *Bekhorot*, *Nedarim*, and *Nazir* (passim) in the Talmud Yerushalmi. The very interesting, but later, Babylonian evidence concerning Nazirites has to be disregarded for a proper assessment of the Palestinian situation. The Bavli disapproves of Naziritism and seems to believe that it became very widespread after the destruction of the Temple; see *Nedarim* 10a and 77b; *Nazir* 19a; *Ta'anit* 11a; and *Bava Bathra* 60b. See also Maas Boertien, *Nazir* (Berlin: Walter de Gruyter, 1971) and H. Salmanowitsch, *Das Nazirāat nach Bibel und Talmud* (PhD diss., Giessen University, 1931).

[103] In *Wayiqra Rabbah* 24.8 a king who has a wine cellar stations guards in it, some of them Nazirites and some drunkards (שכורין). At evening time, he comes to give them their compensation, and gives the drunkards twice as much as he gives the Nazirites. When the Nazirites complain about the unfair treatment, the king explains to them that it is much harder for the drunkards to resist the temptation of drinking the king's wine and that they therefore deserve a higher compensation. This comic treatment mocks Nazirites and drunkards alike; it gains a parodic edge when placed in the context of the Christian emphasis on the concept of the Nazirite, the Encratite tendencies during the time of the redaction of *Wayiqra Rabbah*, and the New Testament's parables about kings, vineyards, and workers' compensation (see, for example, Matthew 20:1–15).

[104] Most notably, the temperance sermon does not exploit the opportunity to comment on a term that appears both in Leviticus 10:9, its base verse, and the biblical text instituting Naziritism. Numbers 6:3 states that Nazirites "shall separate themselves from wine and strong drink (מיין ושכר)," that is, mixed and unmixed wine according to the rabbinic lexicon, using the same terminology that appears in Leviticus 10:9. The temperance sermon, here, is suspiciously silent on the topic of Naziritism.

in any ideological tension. The temperance sermon's radical dismissal of wine and grapes, by contrast, is a unique episode in the rabbinic Judaism of its time. To reiterate, the tension between the sermon and *Wayiqra Rabbah* is, to a certain degree, mitigated by the presence of the parody. This short narrative challenges the sermon's polemic; if the audience realizes its parodic potential, the sermon's ascetic radicalism is neutralized. Hence, the consideration of rabbinic attitudes toward alcohol partially accounts for the inclusion of the parody in the temperance sermon and the inclusion of the sermon in *Wayiqra Rabbah*. In order to grasp the cultural context of the sermon, I turn now to non-rabbinic sources.

Encratites and the Temperance Sermon

Much of the temperance sermon's argument and mono-causal exegesis can be explained by its comparison with the tenets of the Encratite movement. The term "Encratite," meaning "self-mastery" or "continence," is prevalent in late ancient Greek literature.[105] From the second century onwards, however, "Encratites" is a term used by Christian orthodox authors to describe a group of extreme ascetic "heretics." The heresiological "evidence" stretches from the time of Irenaeus's polemics against the Encratites to the official prohibition of Encratism in the decree of Theodosius II in 428 CE and beyond, and is thus contemporaneous with the redaction period of *Wayiqra Rabbah*.[106] In Peter Brown's words,

---

[105] See H. Chadwick, "Enkrateia," in Theodor Klauser, *Reallexikon für Antike und Christentum, Sachwörterbuch zur Auseinandersetzung des Christentums mit der antiken Welt* (Stuttgart: Hiersemann, 1950), vol. V, 343–365. For the common use of the term, see, for example, page 188.

[106] Encratites are first mentioned by Irenaeus of Lyons (*Adversus Haereses* 1.26). We learn for the first time from Hippolytus of Rome that these extreme ascetics renounced not only marriage and the consumption of meat but also drinking wine: they were "drinkers of water" (ὑδροποτοῦντες, *Refutatio Omnium Haeresium* 8.20). They were also mentioned by Clement of Alexandria in his *Pedagogus* 2.2.33 and in *Stromata* 3.49.1–6, 3.79.1–86.1, and 7.17.108f; by Eusebius in the *Ecclesiastical History* 4.28.2; and by Jerome in *Adversus Joviaianum*, 1.3, 1.23. Intriguingly, the *Theodosian Code* (16.5.7.3, see also 16.5.9.1 and 16.5.11) also accuses "Manicheans" of calling themselves "Encratites" in order to avoid charges. On the early "Encratites," see Yves Tissot, "L'Encratisme des Actes de Thomas," in Hildegard Temporini et al. (eds.), *Aufstieg und Niedergang der römischen Welt: Geschichte und Kultur Roms im Spiegel der neueren Forschung* (Berlin: Walter de Gruyter, 1988) II vol. 25 no. 6, 4415–4430. Kathy L. Gaca (in "Driving Aphrodite from the World: Tatian's Encratite Principles of Sexual Renunciation," *Journal of Theological Studies*, 53 (2002), 28–52) explores the Greek mythological background of Tatian's teachings. Also, cf. Jean Daniélou, *The Theology of Jewish Christianity* (London: Darton, 1964), 375 (absent in the French original, Daniélou makes the Encratites Jewish Christians in the English version). See also Robert McWilson, "Alimentary and Sexual Encratism in the

Contemporaries assigned to the views of Tatian, and of the many groups loosely associated with him, the general term of "Encratite" – from *enkrateia*, continence. The Encratites declared that the Christian church had to consist of men and women who were "continent" in the strict sense: they had "contained" the urge to have sexual intercourse with each other. To this basic continence, the Encratites added dietary restraints, abstention from meat and from drinking of wine.[107]

The groups loosely associated with Tatian, Brown argues, were distinct enough from "orthodox" Christians in their theological profile that contemporaries recognized their teachings as Encratite. Similarly, Richard Slater considers the Encratites to be a sizable Christian ascetic movement.[108] Based on the literary and epigraphic evidence, he suggests that the Encratites were very active in Asia Minor until the fifth century CE.[109]

Given the protean nature of the term "Encratite" and of heresiological evidence in general, it is difficult to assess the social and theological reality of *the* Encratites as a clearly identifiable group; undoubtedly, some of the writings that have been deemed Encratite by ancient and modern scholars might not belong in that category.[110] Despite the prevalence of the term in Greek thought in general and in Christianity in particular, it is entirely unclear whether the term refers to a school, a sect, a movement, or even a line of argument within Christian circles. Moreover, as part of the vibrant development of asceticism throughout Late Antiquity, many groups prac-

---

Nag Hammadi Texts," in Ugo Bianchi (ed.), *La tradizione dell'enkrateia: motivazioni ontologiche e protologiche* (Rome: Edizioni dell'Ateneo, 1985), 317–322.

[107] Peter Brown, *The Body and Society: Men, Women, and Sexual Renunciation in Early Christianity* (New York: Columbia University Press, 1988), 92 f.

[108] Richard N. Slater, "An Inquiry into the Relationship between Community and Text: The Apocryphical Acts of Philip 1 and the Encratites of Asia Minor," in: F. Bovon, A. Brock, and C. Matthews (eds.), *The Apocryphal Acts of the Apostles: Harvard Divinity School Studies* (Cambridge: Harvard University Center for the Study of World Religions, 1999), 281–306. Based on a careful analysis of two manuscripts of the *Acts of Philip*, Slater tries to show that the Theodosian decrees caused a spurt of literary activity of an increasingly marginalized group (ibid., 304f).

[109] In two letters written between 374–75 (number 188 and 199), Basil of Caesarea in Cappadocia calls for a gathering of bishops to coordinate actions against the Encratites. This leads Slater to conclude that "the sect had become so widespread and influential as to be worrisome to the bishops" and that Basil "assumes the existence of an Encratite hierarchy with bishops, clergy, and lay leadership" ("An Inquiry into the Relationship between Community and Text," 29).

[110] The *Acts of Philip*, for example, denounce only excessive consumption of wine (see 1.11), never wine itself, and thus may well fall outside the (heresiological) category of Encratite. Other texts that have been considered to be of Encratite origin include the *Acts of Thomas* (see especially 121 on water for the Eucharist), the *Acts of Paul* (Hamburg Codex), and the *Acts of Peter* (see especially 2 on water). See also Eric Junod and Jean Daniel Kaestli, "L'histoire des Actes Apocryphes des Apôtres du 3e au 9e siècle: le cas des Actes de Jean," *Cahiers de la Revue de Théologie et de Philosophie* 7 (1982), 1–152.

ticed various forms of asceticism that partially overlapped with those of the Encratites, particularly abstinence from wine.[111]

Regardless, there is sufficient evidence in patristic discourse that indicates that groups of extreme ascetics entirely denounced any use of wine in the time of the redaction of *Wayiqra Rabbah*. The evidence from Asia Minor is of primary relevance to Palestine as well.[112] The widespread ascetic rejection of wine at the time of the redaction of *Wayiqra Rabbah* already provides the general context for the temperance sermon and the story of the drunkard: one rabbi could have been inspired by the rejection of wine in contemporary ascetic movements and composed the sermon while another rabbi forcefully opposed such "heresy" and incorporated the story.

In light of the Encratites' importance in Christian discourse, and perhaps in daily life as well, it is possible that the rabbis were aware of this ascetic movement and its teachings. Peter Brown suggests that the rabbis of Palestine rejected the Encratites' polemics against sexual intercourse. For instance, the Encratites "asserted that Eve had met the serpent, who represented the animal world, and that the serpent had taught Eve to do what animals do–to have intercourse."[113] In Brown's opinion, which I consider plausible, *Bereshit Rabbah* (22.2) "tacitly combated" such views, insisting that for the rabbis, inversely, "it was Adam and Eve who taught the animals how to have intercourse by initiating the act."[114] The familiarity of Palestin-

---

[111] Asceticism as a broader phenomenon obviously predates the age of Constantine; see Peter Brown, *The Body and Society*, 33–198. Avoidance of wine, more particularly, has been an issue in many late ancient cultures as well. On the Christian and Jewish Nazirites, see pages 84–85 above. The aforementioned stoic avoidance of wine also obviously predates the age of Constantine; see Peter Brown, *The Body and Society*, 33–198 and Epictetus (*Dissertationes ab Arriano digestae* 3.13.21). The abstinence from wine among monks was widespread, especially in the Syriac tradition; see Sebastian Brock, "Sobria Ebrietas according to some Syriac Texts," *Aram*, 17 (2005), 185–191 and Shafiq Abouzayd, "The Prohibition and the use of Alcohol in the Syrian Ascetic Tradition and its Biblical and Spiritual Origins," *Aram*, 17 (2005), 135–156. Moreover, the use of water during the Eucharist (or similar practices) might have been common among other Christian groups even though Epiphanius describes it as a peculiar Encratite practice. Concerning a similar practice of the equally protean "Ebionites," see Irenaeus, *Adversus Haeresis* 5.1.3 and Epiphanius, *Panarion* 30.16.1, and for a similar practice in the West, see Cyprian of Carthage (Epistle 63).

[112] See Burton L. Visotzky, "Jots and Tittles: On Scriptural Interpretation in Rabbinic and Patristic Literatures," *Prooftexts* 8 (1988), 257–270; reprinted in *Fathers of the World*, 28–40, and pages 187–89.

[113] Peter Brown, *The Body and Society*, 94.

[114] Peter Brown, *The Body and Society*, 94. The Bavli's strictures against Encratites are even more developed. According to Brown, the Encratite "exegesis presented sexuality itself, as such, as the abiding sign of an unnatural kinship with the animal world that the serpent had forced upon Adam and Eve." (ibid.). Brown contrasts this view with the teachings of the Bavli (*Avodah Zarah* 22b), which suggest that the serpent, who "came over" Eve (עַל...שְׁבָא, i.e., had intercourse with her) had incited in Eve, and therefore in

ian rabbis with such particular Encratite teachings against sex indicates that the rabbis could have been aware of the Encratite position against wine as well.

This is the cultural context of the temperance sermon. The most specific evidence of the Encratites, in Epiphanius' *Panarion*, indeed shares important characteristics with the sermon, and the heresiological context of this evidence, in turn, is aligned with the story of the drunkard. In the late fourth century, the heresiologist Epiphanius of Salamis (Cyprus), a native and long-term resident of Judea, noted that the Encratites were active in places ranging from Rome to Asia Minor and Antioch (2.215.1).[115] Epiphanius is the only external source that provides explicit details concerning the Encratites' disavowal of wine. Well known for his liberal construction of heresiological taxonomy, Epiphanius reports the existence of three related groups of extreme ascetics, all sharing the denunciation of marriage and wine: the "Severians," the "Tatianists," and the "Encratites."[116] The Encratites' scriptural arguments are intriguingly comparable to the teachings of the temperance sermon:

Encratites ... celebrate mysteries with water. They do not drink wine at all and claim that it is of the devil and that those who drink and use it are malefactors and sinners ... And they hunt for texts against wine-drinkers to suit their taste and support their fiction, seize on them, and say that anything like wine [τὸ τοιοῦτον εἶδος] is from the devil. "Noah drank wine," they say, "and was stripped naked. Lot got drunk [μεθυσθεὶς] and unknowingly lay with his own daughters. The calf was made during a drinking bout [μέθης]. And the Scripture says, 'Who hath confusion? Who hath contention? Who hath resentments and gossip? Who hath afflictions without

---

humanity, desire for bestiality (ibid.; see also *Yevamoth* 103b and *Shabbat* 146a, Elaine Pagels, *Adam, Eve, and the Serpent* (New York: Random House, 1988), and A. Orbe, "El pecado original y el matrimonio en la teologia del s. II," *Gregorianum* 45 (1964), 449–50). Most intriguingly, *Bava Batra* 60b argues against a Jewish group that renounces wine, meat, and marriage as a result of the Temple's destruction, fulfilling all three main categories against Encratite asceticism.

[115] Epiphanius was born in Palestine, more precisely in *Besanduk* near *Eleutheropolis* (today's *Beyt Guvrin*), which is in Judea, after the year 310. After living as a monk in Egypt, he returned to Judea, where he founded a monastery in 333. In 367, he became Bishop of Salamis and wrote his *Panarion* between 374 and 377. See Andrew Louth, "Palestine: Cyril of Jerusalem and Epiphanius," *Cambridge History of Early Christian Literature* (Cambridge: Cambridge University Press, 2004), 283–288.

[116] Epiphanius often divides heretical groups in his attempt to match the number of heresies with the eighty concubines in Song of Songs 6:8–9; we should therefore be cautious about the three separate subgroups that he delineates. See Proem I 1.3 (in Frank Williams, *The Panarion of Epiphanius of Salamis, Book I* (Leiden: Brill, 1994), 3). Epiphanius treats Severus and the Severians, Tatian, and the Encratites in three consecutive chapters in his *Panarion*, parts 45–46 in section II and 47 in section III (sections II and III are continuous; see Williams, *The Panarion of Epiphanius of Salamis*, 346–52 and *The Panarion of Epiphanius of Salamis, Books II and III* (Leiden: Brill 1994), 3–6). Epiphanius explicitly states that "certain persons whom we call Encratites are Tatian's successors," (ibid, 3).

cause? Whose eyes are inflamed? Is it not they that tarry long at wine, that seek out the place where drinking is?' [Proverbs 23:29–30]. And they track down other texts of this kind and make a collection of them for their credibility's sake, without realizing that all immoderation is in every way grievous and declared to be outside of the prescribed bounds.[117]

Insofar as Epiphanius's account in this instance is reliable, the Encratites assembled a collection of biblical sources from which they inferred the evils of wine: the stories of Noah, Lot, the golden calf, and Proverbs 23. The temperance sermon's choice of biblical prooftexts largely overlaps with the Encratite list. Both cite the stories of Noah and Lot as well as the same passage from Proverbs 23; most importantly, both texts "track down other texts of this kind and make a collection of them for their credibility's sake," at the expense of the rabbinic tradition in the case of the sermon.[118]

The similarity between Epiphanius's evidence and the temperance sermon goes even beyond the general dismissal of wine and the shared biblical prooftexts. Epiphanius conveys additional Encratite teachings, which recall the "Gnostic" myths of the time while at the same time resembling the views of the rabbinic temperance sermon. Epiphanius alleges that Severus

"claims that the devil is the son of the chief archon ... After descending in the form of a serpent, he went wild and lay with the earth as with a woman, and as he ejaculated the seed of its generation, the vine was begotten by him. Hence ...[he] represent[s] the roundness of the vine as its likeness to a snake, and he says that the vine is like a snake because it is rough. And the white vine is like a snake, but the black one is like a dragon. And the vine's grapes are also like drops or flecks of poison because of the globular or tapered and entirely different shape of each grape's curvature. And for this reason it is wine that confuses men's minds and sometimes makes

---

[117] *Panarion* 2.216–217, translation based on Frank Williams's (*The Panarion of Epiphanius of Salamis, Books II and III* (Leiden: Brill 1994), 4 f.).

[118] The temperance sermon uses Proverbs 23:29 f. to illustrate the fate of various wine drinkers, see pages 71–73 above. As remarkable as the similar choice of biblical texts may seem, it should be noted that the list of applicable biblical references explicitly related to wine and disaster is limited and that Noah and Lot feature prominently in Genesis – they are the most obvious examples of the abuse of alcohol in the Bible. Moreover, the overlap is incomplete in two instances: the story of Aaron's sons does not appear in the Encratite version whereas the golden calf is absent from the rabbinic sermon. Given the Encratites' overall "Gnostic" approach, however, the absence of the story of Aaron's sons, representatives of the temple cult, no less, is not surprising, a fact corroborated by the Christian attacks on Nadav and Avihu mentioned earlier. In turn, the omission of the golden calf in the temperance sermon dovetails with the generally coy reading of this incident elsewhere in *Wayiqra Rabbah*. (Sermon 27 in *Wayiqra Rabbah* blames the making of the calf on the non-Jews who came from Egypt, and Burton Visotzky has argued convincingly that it does so in response to the Christian accusations of Jewish idolatry. See *Wayiqra Rabbah* 27.8 and parallels and Visotzky, "Anti-Christian Polemic in Wayiqra Rabbah," 89–92.) The similarities between the Encratite teachings and the temperance sermon thus remain far-reaching, while the small differences can be understood more clearly in light of the texts' respective cultural contexts.

them amorous, sometimes drives them wild; or again, renders them angry since the body grows dim-witted from the power of the wine and the poison of this dragon. Persons of this persuasion therefore abstain from wine altogether.[119]

In Severus' view, as represented by Epiphanius, the grapevine itself is an offspring of the devil; it is similar to a snake; the grapes correspond to drops of poison; it confuses men and makes them wild and amorous. Some of Severus's claims about wine were commonplace from biblical times to Late Antiquity. This accounts for some of the incidental similarities between the temperance sermon and Epiphanius's description. For example, the both narratives use the image of wine as a serpent's poison. While the image seems to be uniquely rabbinic in the time of *Wayiqra Rabbah*, both the rabbinic sermon and Severus could have borrowed it, for example, from Proverbs 23:32.

Some of the similarities between the temperance sermon and the Encratites' position, however, are more specific. Consideration of these similarities *alongside* the remaining differences in detail highlights the shared ideology against wine as well as the specific theological nature of the Encratite stance and the largely rabbinic orientation of the temperance sermon in many of its non non-oelological details. First, both the Encratites and the temperance sermon allege that wine leads to confusion, violence, and inappropriate sexual arousal – a commonplace assertion about wine. Both texts, for example, agree that wine leads to illicit sex. In stark contrast to the celibate tendency of the Severians and Encratites, the rabbinic sermon imagines illicit *matrimonial* intercourse, indicating that wine leads to cohabitation during menstruation. The similar teachings in both texts part ways precisely in relation to fundamental principles other than wine.

In two additional instances, however, the Encratites and the temperance sermon exhibit intriguing similarities in their views of wine that were by no means conventional in Late Antiquity. Severus describes the multiple shapes of the grapevine. The sermon, in turn, singles grapes out as having many names and because of their undetermined status in sacrifice and tithing. Both texts, hence, object to the multifarious nature of grapes and grapevines, an objection that the sermon translates into its halakhic taxonomy. This objection, as far as I know, is unique in rabbinic literature of the period and is intimately reminiscent of Encratite discourse.

Most importantly, the temperance sermon denounces the consumption not only of wine but also of unfermented grapes. It relates grapes to the original sin, blaming the fruit, and not the actions of Adam and Eve, for introducing sin into the world, and complains about its unclear cultic status.

---

[119] Panarion 3.45.1. Translation based on Frank Williams's (*The Panarion of Epiphanius of Salamis, Book I* (Leiden: Brill, 1994), 346).

This sounds to me like a rabbinic version of Severus's "Gnostic" teachings, which personify grapes as the offspring of the devil.[120] At the same time, regardless of how detrimental grapes and wine had been for mankind and the Jews, it is impossible for the temperance sermon explicitly to prohibit wine, much like advocating Kiddush with water instead of wine would be. The temperance sermon remains rabbinic, even if marginally so, and seems inspired by Encratite teachings, a plausible scenario given the movement's prevalence during the time of the redaction of *Wayiqra Rabbah*.

The similarity between the sermon and the Encratite view in regards to the multiformity of wine and its role in the genesis of evil provides a plausible cultural context for the temperance sermon. Both the sermon and the Encratites rely on the same biblical prooftexts (the stories of Noah and Lot's daughters, Proverbs 23, and, to a degree, the story of Adam and Eve) in the same geographic region during the same century. The Encratites and the temperance sermon have a similar strategy for reading biblical texts. Both shift agency, and moral responsibility, from the biblical figures to wine, and both generalize warnings about wine that in the Bible are limited to its over-consumption. A dialogue, direct or indirect, between the sermon's author and "the" Encratites, seems likely. While a healthy suspicion toward Epiphanius's account of "the" Encratites suggests that we do not necessarily with a well defined group, we can surmise that his description of Encratite teachings to a degree reflects real teachings of his time. Epiphanius thereby provides strong evidence for a plausible context for the temperance sermon.

Perhaps the sermon's author was a rabbi who came into contact with Encratite teachings akin to those conveyed in Epiphanius' account, and perhaps upon learning that all evil stems from the grape, Jewish history from the destruction of the first Temple to his own days suddenly began to make sense to him. He did what any rabbi would have done and integrated new insight into his rabbinic perspective. The homogenous teachings of the sermon, its smooth literary surface, its rabbinic acumen, and full internalization of the literary standards of *Wayiqra Rabbah* strongly suggest that the sermon is one unified and internally coherent composition – excluding the story of the drunkard.

Epiphanius rebuts the Encratites by accusing them of misreading the biblical texts that prohibit excessive drinking: the Encratites do not realize,

---

[120] It should also be noted that Adam and Eve learning about intercourse from the serpent was a central aspect in the imagery of Encratite sexual renunciation, to which, according to Peter Brown, the rabbis objected; see pages 86–88 above. In Epiphanius's account, the devil's intercourse with the earth produced wine. The temperance sermon's accusation that grapes are the origin of sin sides with the Encratite view of wine as the cause of all evil. At the same time, the sermon remains within the realm of rabbinic "orthodoxy" by stopping short of associating wine with satanic progeny even though the audience is led to just this conclusion.

he writes, that "all immoderation is in every way grievous." This reproach constitutes an intriguing parallel with the rabbinic view of wine in *Wayiqra Rabbah* in general and with the story of the drunkard's parodic response to the sermon in particular. Epiphanius's endorsement of moderate consumption of wine is in line with other church fathers, as I argued above. Similarly, the Palestinian rabbis promoted moderate consumption of wine, as is evident in *Wayiqra Rabbah* and elsewhere. The rabbinic and Christian "orthodoxies" are therefore aligned, highlighting the heresy associated with the Encratites and the temperance sermon.

Epiphanius's account, therefore, provides two plausible cultural contexts for the temperance sermon. First, the Encratites, broadly conceived, held beliefs about wine similar to those found in the sermon, associating wine with social and sexual misconduct in the Bible and in contemporary times and even blaming wine for being the origin of evil. Second, Epiphanius's attempt to refute the Encratites constitutes a precedent for the story of the drunkard: just as Epiphanius insists that only excessive consumption of wine is harmful, the parody of the temperance sermon redirects the audience from the vices of drinking to the much more profound vice of filial impertinence, slander, and attempted patricide, and concludes with the statute of perpetual moderate drinking. The story of the drunkard thus refutes the sermon's ordinance against the consumption of wine by parodying its (rabbinic) heresy; it is thus a heresiological parody cognate in its social function with Epiphanius's *Panarion*. The historical and the literary contexts both seem conducive to viewing the story of the drunkard as a response to the sermon.

If we agree that the story of the drunkard effectively neutralizes, or at least moderates, the sermon's extreme position, we can now view the sermon as a whole – including its own parody, and only in light of the parody – as forming a rabbinic testimony to the dangers of excessive drinking and as a valuable exegesis of Leviticus 10:9 that fifth-century rabbinic circles would deem acceptable. In other words, the temperance sermon never actually crosses the line of rabbinic "orthodoxy" and never prohibits wine explicitly. The story of the drunkard, understood as part and parcel of the sermon by later readers and redactors, may have been enough to cloak and to mitigate the sermon's already veiled radical nature. In this way, the parodic and moderating effects of the story of the drunkard may have allowed the redactor to include the neutralized sermon in *Wayiqra Rabbah* in the first place. I suggested that the temperance sermon makes a coherent and structured moralist argument and radically narrows the breadth of the rabbinic stance concerning a number of exegetical and ethical topics. Only its parody makes it palatable to the polysemic and morally complex world of the rabbis. This is at least one plausible explanation of the literary tensions in the temperance sermon and in *Wayiqra Rabbah* in general. While the precise redaction history is irretrievable, I submit that we find intra-rabbinic parody in Palestine as well and that this particular parody is a redactional and partially preemptive parody, akin to the case of the cat in *Bava Metsi'a*.

Chapter Three

The Interpretation of Dreams:
A Parody of the Yerushalmi's Dream Book
(Berakhot 56a–b)

כאשר פתר לנו כן היה
As he interpreted for us, so it was
– *Genesis* 41:13

שאין החלום הולך אלא אחר פתרונו
Since a dream fulfills itself
according to its interpretation
– Yerushalmi *Ma'aser Sheni*, 4,9.14 (55c)

The examples of redactional parody in the Bavli and in *Wayiqra Rabbah* illustrate that Babylonian and Palestinian rabbis parodied texts that emerged from their own communities; I call this mode of parody intra-rabbinic. This chapter explores a satirical parody of a text that originated in another rabbinic community; I call this mode inter-rabbinic parody. In light of the ambiguous relationship between the rabbinic communities of Roman Palestine and Sasanian Mesopotamia discussed in the Introduction, we may expect to find examples of Palestinian rabbis parodying Babylonian rabbinic texts and Babylonian rabbis parodying the work of their Palestinian counterparts. To reiterate, the Palestinian rabbis dwelled in the ancient Holy Land and composed the Mishna and much of its interpretation, which later became the foundation of all Babylonian rabbinic literary activity. Hence, as Daniel Sperber describes in a seminal study[1], the Palestinian rabbis seem to have

---

[1] Many recent studies claim that the Bavli's attitude toward the academies of Palestine is a combination of reverence and revisionist elitism, but we still lack fundamental insights into this complex issue. The most suggestive discussion of this topic is Daniel Sperber's "On the Unfortunate Adventures of Rav Kahana," in Shaul Shaked (ed.), *Irano-Judaica: Studies Relating to Jewish Contacts with Persian Culture throughout the Ages* (Jerusalem: Ben-Zvi Institute for the Study of Jewish Communities in the East, 1982), 88–100. Sperber discusses a Palestinian rabbinic composition that depicts the community of Palestinian rabbis as superior and satirizes Kahana, a young and inept Babylonian rabbi. He suggests that the Babylonian rabbis retold the story, inverting the hierarchy and making Rav Kahana its sophisticated hero. See also Isaiah Gafni, "א"ע קיז ק ב סוגיית לאור הבבלית הישיבה", *Tarbiz* 49 (1980), 292–301; Shamma Friedmann, "The Further Adventures of Rav Kahana: Between Babylonian and Palestine," in: Peter Schäfer (ed.), *The Talmud Yerushalmi and Graeco-Roman Culture*, vol. III (Tübingen: Mohr Siebeck 2002), 247–71; and Geoffry

felt contempt for at least some of their Babylonian colleagues, viewing them as parvenus; the Babylonian rabbis, in turn, considered themselves more sophisticated and learned than the rabbis of Palestine.

These tensions between the two rabbinic communities set the stage for their parodic criticism of one another. Analyzing Palestinian parody of Babylonian rabbis is complicated by the fact that all extant Babylonian rabbinic texts postdate the classical Palestinian Midrashim and the Yerushalmi by more than a century. It may therefore be impossible to trace the Babylonian sources imitated by such parodies. Nevertheless, the example of Rabbi Hananya discussed in the Introduction does illustrate that Palestinian rabbis indeed used parody as a satirical tool against Babylonian rabbis. Consideration of Palestinian rabbinic parodies of particular Babylonian rabbinic texts will have to await the discovery or definitive identification of fifth-century, or earlier, Babylonian rabbinic literature. We can, however, examine the Bavli's parody of Palestinian rabbinic texts.

Rava, the Fool

In Chapter One, I described Rava as the target of the Bavli's intra-rabbinic satirical parody. The example below combines Babylonian intra-rabbinic satire with inter-rabbinic parody of a Palestinian text. In this Babylonian parody of the Yerushalmi, Rava features once more as both an iconic figure as well as a vehicle for, and subject of, satire. In *Berakhot* 56a–b, two rabbis, Rava and Abaye, seek the services of Bar Hedya, a professional dream interpreter. The two rabbis repeatedly tell Bar Hedya their respective dreams, which always happen to be identical. Bar Hedya, however, offers strikingly different interpretations of these dreams: favorable interpretations for Abaye, who pays for Bar Hedya's services, and unfavorable ones for Rava, who does not pay the fee. All of Bar Hedya's predictions seem to come true. When Rava finally realizes that Bar Hedya's interpretations and predictions depend on monetary compensation, and thereby his own fate on the whim of the interpreter, he curses Bar Hedya, who shortly thereafter is executed in Rome.

The *Bava Metsi'a* parody discussed in Chapter One portrays Rava ambiguously and satirizes his incompetent handling of his students' attack.

Hermann, "The Story of Rav Kahana (BT Baba Qamma 117a–b) in Light of Armeno-Persian Sources," in Shaul Shaked and Amnon Netzer (eds.) *Irano-Judaica VI* (Jerusalem: Makhon Ben Zvi, 2008), 53–86. For more recent discussions, see Richard Kalmin, *Jewish Babylonia between Persia and Roman Palestine* (Oxford: Oxford University Press, 2006) and Moulie Vidas, "The Bavli's Discussion of Genealogy in *Qiddushin* IV," in Gregg Gardner and Kevin Osterloh (eds.), *Antiquity in Antiquity: Jewish and Christian Pasts in the Greco-Roman World* (Tübingen: Mohr Siebeck, 2008), 285–326.

Rava, or more precisely, his views concerning the potency of dreams, are targeted by the satire in the present case as well. The satire does not target Rava alone, however, but also his Jewish adversary, Bar Hedya, the professional dream interpreter. Richard Kalmin, in a short and astute study, notes that the story of Bar Hedya polemicizes against professional dream interpreters, but he does not proceed to discuss its parodic aspects and its textual relationship to the Yerushalmi.[2] I argue that this Bavli story is a satirical parody that models Bar Hedya's behavior on the second century Palestinian Rabbi Ishmael, also a professional dream interpreter, as described in a passage often called the Yerushalmi's "dream book."[3] The Bavli repeats much of the Yerushalmi's dream book with ironic distance, especially elements there attributed to Rabbi Ishmael, to Rabbi Eliezer, and to Rabbi Aqiva. Particularly, Bar Hedya reenacts Rabbi Ishmael's practice of offering different interpretations of the same dream image, his insistence on receiving payment for his services, his hermeneutical virtuosity in the interpretation of dreams, and his cruel punishment of a anyone who refuses to pay. Bar Hedya's ability to avert or bring about the death of the dreamer's spouse and children also imitates Rabbi Eliezer. And finally, Bar Hedya's capacity for offering reassuring and positive interpretations of frightening dreams repeats a story about Rabbi Aqiva.

Isaac Afik has already labeled the Bar Hedya story in the Bavli a "Menippean satire," which a useful point of departure for the present study.[4] Afik takes the Palestinian characteristics of the story, such as the use of Palestinian forms of Aramaic, as proof of the putative Palestinian origin of the entire story.[5] I agree with Afik that the story is satirical and that the Palestinian context is crucial for understanding it. However, instead of examining the Palestinian "origin" of the story as a whole in terms of the literary influence of Palestinian rabbis on Babylonian ones, I focus on how the story displays

---

[2] Kalmin states that the "story ... involves (Babylonian) Amoraim and polemicizes against a professional dream interpreter. It is unclear, however, whether the story polemicizes against professional dream interpreters in general, or only against especially corrupt individuals who cynically use their power for personal gain" (*Sages, Stories, Authors and Editors in Rabbinic Babylonia*, 69). I shall discuss Kalmin's suggestion in detail on page 136 below.

[3] *Ma'aser Sheni* 4:9 55b–c; see note 76 below.

[4] Isaac Afik (Abecassis), *Hazal's Perception of the Dream* (PhD diss., Bar Ilan University, 1991 [Hebrew]), 370–385. As outlined in the Introduction, I view Menippean Satire as one of the literary contexts of rabbinic parody; see page 16f. I discuss several of Afik's contributions throughout this chapter.

[5] For Afik, the story was originally a Palestinian satire transmitted from Palestine to Babylonia and in the process it became far removed from its original Palestinian satirical target, which, Afik believes, was the competing Palestinian rabbinic schools of dream interpretation. Afik focuses on tracing the story to its original Palestinian setting. I find no evidence for these competing schools in Palestine, as I seek to make clear in my discussion of the key passage in Bavli *Berakhot* 56a (see p. 133f.).

its Babylonian author's literary creativity. I understand him as carefully imitating a central Yerushalmi text, or an approximate retelling thereof with which he was familiar, in order to emphasize *difference*, not similarity. If we believe that this author had the autonomy to scrutinize tensions between different aspects of Palestinian dream interpretation – while maintaining the traditional authority of the Yerushalmi – then we should also hold this author capable of assuming the critical distance prerequisite for ironizing and parodying the Yerushalmi as well.[6]

Most importantly, the Bar Hedya story grapples with the Palestinian notion that "a dream follows its interpretation." The Bavli presents this view in the passage immediately preceding the Bar Hedya story (*Berakhot* 56a):

R. Bizna bar Zabda said ...
"Twenty four dream interpreters were in Jerusalem,
And once I dreamed a dream and went to all of them,
And what this one interpreted for me was not what that one interpreted for me,
And [still] it all came true for me,
to prove that which is said [שנאמר]: 'All dreams follow the mouth' [כל החלומות הולכים אחר הפה]."

The Bavli imagines the practice of dream interpretation as flourishing in Jerusalem.[7] It explains the astonishing fact that all the different interpretations of the same dream came true by citing a *Baraita*, an extra-mishnaic early rabbinic statement: "All dreams follow the mouth" (כל החלומות הולכים אחר הפה), that is, the mouth of the interpreter. The dream symbol itself is meaningless independent of interpretation. Nearly an identical view concerning the power of interpretation is explicitly expressed in the climax of the Yerushalmi's dream book.[8] According to these Babylonian and Palestin-

---

[6] Afik himself realized that "the irony in the story is generated by the use of unexpected meanings connoted by slang, dialects and pron[]unciation deriving from different areas." Isaac Afik, *Hazal's Perception of Dreams*, VIIIf; see also 219–263. If the story indeed makes a conscious use of dialects, one might wonder how dialects simultaneously help Afik distinguish between the story's Palestinian "origin" and its present Babylonian form.

[7] Cf. Isaac Afik, *Hazal's Perception of Dreams*, 65–74. The passage is reported in the name of Palestinian rabbis yet does not have a parallel in Palestinian midrashic literature. For an extensive bibliography on the topic of rabbinic dream interpretation, see Philip Alexander, "*Bavli Berakhot* 55a–57b; The Talmudic Dreambook in Context," *JJS*, 46 (1995), 230. See also Haim Weiss's recent dissertation, היבטים ל-"חז בספרות החלום של ותפקידו מעמדו, (PhD diss. תרבותיים: קריאה ספרותית ב'מסכת החלומות' שבתלמוד הבבלי (מסכת ברכות, נ"ה ע"א-נ"ז ע"ב), The Hebrew University of Jerusalem, 2006).

[8] While the Bavli states that "all dreams follow the mouth," the Yerushalmi indicates that "a dream fulfills itself according to its interpretation (שאין החלום הולך אלא אחר פתרונו, *Yerushalmi, Ma'aser Sheni* 4:9.14 (55c)). The story and the doctrine cited there also appear in *Bereshit Rabbah* 89.8 and *Ekha Rabbah* 1.14–18. The Palestinian version emphasizes the act of interpretation (פתרונו) rather than the "mouth" of the dream interpreter, who therefore is portrayed in the Bavli as capable of assuming an even more significant role than in the Yerushalmi – an issue thematized in the Bar Hedya story.

ian sources, the rabbinic dream interpreters of Palestine believed that the outcome of a mantic dream was determined less by the dream symbol and more by its creative interpretation based on rabbinic hermeneutical guidelines. I therefore call it the "Palestinian doctrine." The Bar Hedya story in the Bavli confirms and confounds this Palestinian doctrine in its parody of the Yerushalmi's dream book.

The story in the Bavli carefully models Bar Hedya on the dream interpreters in the Yerushalmi in order to illustrate what happens if a professional dream interpreter, who according to the Palestinian doctrine fully controls the fate of the dreamer, happens to be corrupt. The story explicitly cites and reaffirms the effectiveness of the Palestinian doctrine; at the same time, it satirizes its susceptibility to abuse. It is another exegetical parody of traditional rabbinic sources, this time of the Yerushalmi.

The Bar Hedya Story

The following text is based on the *textus receptus* of the Vilna edition of the Bavli, with references to various manuscript traditions.[9] To aid the discussion, given the story's imposing length, I divide the story into the following subsections that the narrative creates, after (I) a short exposition, by alternating the following details of the narrative: (II&III) the dream symbol; (IV) the characters; (V) the favorable/unfavorable nature of the dream interpretations; and (VI&VII) the geographical setting of the story.

I   Bar Hedya was an interpreter of dreams.
      To the one who gave him compensation [אגרא], he interpreted [the dream]
          favorably,
          and to the one who did not give compensation, he interpreted unfavorably.
      Abaye and Rava had dream visions.
      Abaye gave [Bar Hedya] a *zuz*, and Rava did not give him [a zuz].

---

[9] See *Berakhot* 56a–b. The manuscripts vary in spelling, order of the dreams, and sometimes even in imagery. An eclectic edition, such as the one provided in Chapter One (*Bava Metsi'a* 97a), or grouping two textual traditions, such as the example in Chapter Four (*Shabbat* 116a–b), seems impracticable here. My analysis is based on the Vilna print, and I discuss the most important variations in the following manuscripts: Ms. Munich 95, Ms. Oxford 366 (fol. Add. 23), Ms. Paris 671, Ms. Florence II-I-7, some Geniza fragments, and the Soncino print (*editio princeps*). For a brief characterization of these manuscripts and further bibliography, see Michael Krupp, "Manuscripts of the Babylonian Talmud," in Shmuel Safrai (ed.), *The Literature of the Sages, First Part: Oral Tora, Halakha, Mishna, Tosefta, Talmud, External Tractates* (Assen: Van Gorcum 1987), 346–66. For a synoptic edition based on the Vilna prints, several manuscripts, and Geniza fragments, see Isaac Afik, *Hazal's Perception of Dreams*, 179–218. Afik's extensive source-criticism (ibid., 219–263), however, does not allow for an adequate analysis of the story since his critical method is marred by his presupposition that the story originated in Palestine.

II.1   [Rava and Abaye] said to [Bar Hedya]: "We were made to recite [אקרינן, i.e., a
        Scriptural verse] in our dreams,[10] 'Your ox shall be butchered before your
        eyes [but you shall not eat of it' (Deuteronomy 28:31)]."
        To Rava, [Bar Hedya] said:[11] "Your business will fail [פסיד], and it will not do
        you good to eat because of your heart's sadness."
        To Abaye, he said:[12] "Your business will prosper [מרווח], and it will not do you
        good to eat because of your heart's joy [מחדוא]."

II.2   They said to him: "We were made to recite: 'You shall have sons and daughters
        [but they shall not remain yours, for they shall go into captivity' (Deuter-
        onomy 28:41)]."
        To Rava, he said: "In its bad sense [כבישותיה]."
        To Abaye, he said: "Your sons and daughters will abound [נפישין],
        and your children will marry everywhere,
        and it will seem to you as if they went into captivity."

II.3   "We were made to recite: 'Your sons and daughters shall be given to another
        people [while you look on; you will strain your eyes looking for them all day
        but be powerless to do anything' (Deuteronomy 28:32)]."
        To Abaye, he said: "Your sons and daughters will abound [נפישין].
        You will tell [your wife to marry them] to your relatives,
        and she will tell [you to marry them] to her relatives,
        and she will force [ואכפה] you and give them to her relatives,
        and it will be like a different people."
        To Rava, he said: "Your wife will die,
        and your sons and daughters will go to a different woman,
        as Rava said in the name of Rabbi Jeremiah Bar Aba in the name of Rav:[13]
        'What does Scripture mean by "Your sons and daughters shall be given to
        another people?" That is a stepmother.'

II.4   "We were made to recite: 'Go, eat your bread with enjoyment [and drink your
        wine with a merry heart; for God has long ago approved what you do'
        (Ecclesiastes 9:7)]."[14]
        To Abaye, he said: "Your business will prosper [מרווח],
        and you will eat and drink and read [Scripture] because of your heart's joy
        [מחדוא]."

---

[10] Concerning the translation of "we were made to recite," see Sokoloff, *A Dictionary
of Jewish Babylonian Aramaic*, 1041. The manuscripts offer a variety of alternatives, such
as "we read" and "they read to us."

[11] Some manuscripts explicitly add here that Bar Hedya interprets the verse unfavorable
for Rava (Ms. Oxford 366 (fol. Add. 23) and Ms. Paris 671: בבישתא, Ms. Florence II-I-7
בבישתיה, and Ms. Munich 95: כבישתא). Ms. Munich 95 also here point that he interprets
dreams favorably for Abaye (בטיבותיה).

[12] Some manuscripts add here that Bar Hedya interprets the verse favorable for Abaye
(see Ms. Oxford 366 (fol. Add. 23) בטבא, Ms. Paris 671 לטבא, Ms. Florence II-I-7 בטיבותיך,
and the previous note for Ms. Munich 95).

[13] Ms. Munich 95 and the Soncino print quote the saying only in the name of Rava
himself.

[14] Ecclesiastes 9:9 continues: "Enjoy life with the wife whom you love, all the days of
your vain life that are given to you under the sun." As it so often does, the Bavli empha-

To Rava, he said: "Your business will fail [פסיד],
    you will butcher but not eat [טבחת ולא אכלת],
    and you will drink and read [Scripture] to quell [לפכוחי] your fear."

II.5 "We were made to recite: 'You shall carry much seed into the field [but gather little in, for the locust shall consume it' (Deuteronomy 28:38)]."
    To Abaye, he said [i.e., interpreted the dream] based on the former [half of the verse].
    To Rava, he said [i.e., interpreted the dream] from the latter [half of the verse].

II.6 "We were made to recite: 'You shall have olive trees [זיתים] throughout all your territory [but you shall not anoint yourself with the oil (ושמן), for the olives shall drop (Deuteronomy 28:40)]."
    To Abaye, he said [i.e., interpreted the dream] from the former [half of the verse].
    To Rava, he said [i.e., interpreted the dream] from the latter [half of the verse].

II.7 "We were made to recite: 'All the peoples of the earth shall see that you are called by the name of G-d, and they shall be afraid of you' [Deuteronomy 28:10]."
    To Abaye, he said: "You will become reputable since you will be the head of the academy; fear of your person will be prevalent [literally "fall," נפלת] everywhere."
    To Rava, he said: "The provision house of the king will be broken into,
    and you will be arrested [ומתפסת] for theft,
    and everybody will draw *qal vahomer* from your case."[15]
    The next day the provision house of the king was broken into, and they came and arrested Rava.

III.1 They said to him: "We saw [in our dream] lettuce [חסא][16] on the mouth of a jar."
    To Abaye, he said: "Your business will double like lettuce."
    To Rava, he said: "Your business will be bitter like lettuce."[17]

III.2 They said to him: "We saw meat on the mouth of a jar."
    To Abaye, he said: "Your wine will become sweet [בסים],[18] and everybody will come and buy meat and wine from you."

---

sizes the part of the scriptural passage that it does not quote. Through this omission, the story alludes to the two rabbis' wives, mentioned in the preceding dream interpretation.

[15] The Bavli here seems to imply the following: if even the great Rava could not escape denouncement and arrest, this would be more so for common people; hence, they are "afraid of" him as predicted in Deuteronomy. See note 43 below for a discussion of the implications and the manuscript variants.

[16] Ms. Munich 95 adds דקדחא, Ms. Paris 671, דקדח: "sprouted" lettuce, which is indeed bitter.

[17] The story seems to imply what Ms. Munich 95 and Ms. Paris 671 explicate already in the dream (see the previous note): that the lettuce is bitter because it already sprouted.

[18] In Babylonian Aramaic, the term בסים means "sweet" (see Sokoloff, *A Dictionary of Jewish Babylonian Aramaic*, 224). Interestingly, in Palestinian Aramaic, the word also denotes "sweet," but it can denote "vinegar" as well (see Sokoloff, *A Dictionary of Jew-*

To Rava, he said: "Your wine will ferment, and everybody will buy meat to eat with it."

III.3 They said to him: "We saw a vat hanging from a palm tree."
    To Abaye, he said: "Your business will be uplifted like a palm tree."
    To Rava, he said: "Your business deals will be sweet as dates [i.e., for the customers]."[19]

III.4 They said to him: "We saw a pomegranate sprouting from the mouth of a jar."
    To Abaye, he said: "Your business goods will be as expensive as pomegranates."
    To Rava he, said: "Your business goods will be as tart [קאוי][20] as pomegranates."

III.5 They said to him: "We saw a vat that fell into a well [לבירא]."
    To Abaye, he said: "Your business goods will be in demand, as they say 'the bread[21] fell into the well and is found no more.'"
    To Rava, he said: "Your business goods will spoil [פסיד] and will be thrown into a well.

III.6 They said to him: "We saw a donkey standing on our pillow [אאיסדן] and braying."
    To Abaye he said: "You will be king [of the academy], and an *amora* will stand next to you."
    To Rava he said: "[The phrase] 'the first born of a donkey [פטר חמור, Exodus 13:13]' is erased from your *Tefilin*."
    He [Rava] said to him [Bar Hedya]: "I looked at them and they were there!"
    He [Bar Hedya] said to him [Rava]: "The *vav* from [the phrase] 'the first born of a donkey [פטר חמור], is erased from your Tefilin."

IV.1 Finally, Rava went to him alone.
    He said to him: "I saw that the outer doorway fell [דשא ברייתא דנפל]."
    He said to him: "Your wife will die."

IV.2 He said to him: "I saw that I lost [נתור] my molars and teeth."
    He said to him: "Your sons and daughters will die."

IV.3 He said to him: "I saw two doves flying away from me."
    He said to him: "You will divorce two women."

---

ish Palestinian Aramaic, 106). Cf. Isaac Afik, *Hazal's Perception of Dreams*, 236, and see page 122 f.

[19] The Bavli seems to imply that the business deals will be "sweet" for the costumers, thus disadvantageous for Rava, the vendor.

[20] See Sokoloff, *A Dictionary of Jewish Babylonian Aramaic*, 990. The more common spelling, "קוויה," appears in Ms. Florence II-I-7 and Ms. Oxford 366 (fol. Add. 23).

[21] The Vilna print is the only source that specifies what fell into the proverbial well. Ms. Munich 95 has "הני מידי," "those things fell in the well," Ms. Paris 671 "הא", "this fell in the well," Ms. Oxford 366 (fol. Add. 23) "האי", "these fell in the well," and it is missing from Ms. Florence II-I-7, "[it] fell in the well." The phrase seems to have been a Babylonian proverb known to the intended audience, although I could not find it elsewhere in rabbinic literature. Its meaning, in any case, is clear enough: the well signifies a place in which lost objects cannot be found.

IV.4 He said to him: "I saw two turnip tops [גרגלידי דלפתא]."
He said to him: "You will receive two blows [קולפי]."
Rava went on that day to sit the whole day in the study house.
He saw two blind men [lit. "full of light," סגי נהורי] fighting each other.
Rava went to separate them, and they struck [ומחוהו] him twice.
They wanted to strike once more.
He [Rava] said: "I have had enough [מסתיי]! I saw two."[22]

V.1 Finally, Rava went and gave him compensation.
He said to him: "I saw a wall breaking [דאיתבר]."
He said to him: "You will acquire property without limits [מצרים]."

V.2 He said to him: "I saw the mansion of Abaye fall and its dust covered me."
He said to him: "Abaye will die and his academy will go to you."

V.3 He said to him: "I saw my mansion fall, and everybody came and took the bricks."
He said to him: "Your teachings will be dispersed everywhere."

V.4 He said to him: "I saw that my head was split [דאבקע], and I lost [נתר] my brain."
He said to him: "The flock [אודרא, i.e., the stuffing][23] of [your] pillow [בי סדיא] has fallen out."

V.5 He said to him: "I was made to read the Egyptian *Hallel* [הללא מצראה][24] in my dream."
He said to him: "A miracle [ניסא] will happen to you."

VI [Bar Hedya] was once about to enter a boat [בארבא] with this one [Rava].
[Bar Hedya] said: "This man to whom a miracle will happen, why [would] I [travel with him]?"
As he went out, a book fell from him [i.e., he dropped it].
Rava found it and saw that it was written in it: "All dreams follow the mouth."
He said: "Wicked man, because of you it was fulfilled [קיימא], and all this pain!
I forgive you for everything except for the daughter of Rav Hisda [i.e., the death of Rava's wife].
May it be [God's] will that this man be delivered to a kingdom without mercy on him."
He [Bar Hedya] said: "What shall I do? It has been taught that even an unwarranted curse of a wise man comes [true],
so much more Rava's, which denounced me justly [דבדינא]."

---

[22] As Richard Kalmin pointed out, one of the Geniza fragments lacks the two final lines of IV.4 (Kalmin, *Sages, Stories, Authors, and Editors in Rabbinic Babylonia*, 68 n. 19). See the discussion concerning this matter in note 55 below.

[23] See Sokoloff, *A Dictionary of Jewish Babylonian Aramaic*, 85. On the spelling and the manuscript variants, see note 55 below.

[24] The *Hallel* is a recitation of Psalms 113–118, part of the morning liturgy and of some holiday prayers in most traditions. The "Egyptian *Hallel*," according to Rashi, is a shorter version of the *Hallel* recited during the latter days of Passover.

He said: "I will depart [איקום] and exile myself,
as Mar has taught: 'Exile atones for guilt.'"[25]

VII He arose [קם] and exiled himself to Rome.
He went and sat [אזל יתיב] at the entrance of [the house of] the king's chief of
the embroiderers.
The chief embroiderer had a dream vision.
[The embroiderer] said to [Bar Hedya]: "I saw in my dream that a needle
pierced my finger [מחטא עייל באצבעתי]."
[Bar Hedya] said to him: "Give me a zuz."
And he did not give it to him, and he did not tell him anything.
He said to him: "I saw in my dream that decay fell on two of my fingers."
He said to him: "Give me a zuz."
And he did not give it to him, and he did not tell him [the dream's interpreta-
tion].
He said to him: "I saw that decay fell on my entire hand."
He said to him: "Decay fell on all of the silk garments [שיראי]."
The royal household heard [about the issue] and brought the chief embroiderer
in order to kill him.
[The embroiderer] said to them: "Why me? Bring the one who knew and did
not say it."
They brought Bar Hedya.
They said to him: "On account of your zuz, the silken garments of the king
have been destroyed."[26]
They tied [כפיתו] two cedars [ארזי] with a rope [בחבלא].
They bound one foot to one [חד] cedar and one to another cedar,
and released [ושרו] the rope so that his head was split [דאצטליק] in one and one
[חד וחד],
and he fell in two [parts].

Bar Hedya possesses a book on dream interpretation, which contains the
Palestinian doctrine that "all dreams follow the mouth." In the broadest
sense, the Bar Hedya story confirms and parodies this doctrine by staging
its possible results. The result, however, is not a satire of the doctrine per se
but rather of its misuse and abuse. In order to prepare my discussion of how
the Bar Hedya story parodies the Yerushalmi's narratives about rabbinic
dream interpreters (such as Rabbi Ishmael and his colleagues), I first present
the story as a satire of Bar Hedya's abuse of the Palestinian doctrine and of
Rava's naïveté.

The story leads its audience through the long episode by repeating many
of its themes in order to emphasize important narrative turns. The story, for

---

[25] Ms. Munich 95 and Ms. Paris 671 add: "half of the guilt [חצי עון];" see notes 62 and
63 below.

[26] Ms. Munich 95, Ms. Oxford 366 (fol. Add. 23), Ms. Paris 671, and the Soncino print
add here: "Rava said: 'I will not forgive him until his head is split in two.'" They thereby
explicitly link Bar Hedya's subsequent death to Rava's curse.

example, anticipates Bar Hedya's death several times. The rabbinic audience, of course, is well attuned to this kind of repetition, but only toward the end of the story does it become clear that Bar Hedya's denouement was present from the outset, thereby creating a sense of (divine) justice as Bar Hedya meets his just desserts.[27] The repetition thus generates a secondary layer of narrative structure. The two inscribed hermeneutical guides, the story's sub-sections and its method of overlapping anticipation and fulfillment, never conflict with one another but rather jointly emphasize the outcome of the story. I will argue that the story's parody of the Yerushalmi dream book builds on the narrative created by these two overlaying structural devices.

(I) Bar Hedya is a Hawk

The opening introduces the three protagonists: Bar Hedya, a professional dream interpreter, and Rava and Abaye, the dreamers. Rava is the iconic figure who is the object of halakhic parody and satire in the *Bava Metsi'a* story discussed in the Introduction; Abaye is equally well-known in the Bavli. The two were contemporary heads of academy: Rava in Mahoza, a suburb of the Persian capital, Ctesiphon, and Abaye in Pumpedita, west of Ctesiphon. The Bavli often depicts "Rava and Abaye" as polemical interlocutors.[28] Consequently, the two are a perfect pair for the purposes of our story: their often conflicting modes of interpreting halakha leads the audience to recognize Bar Hedya's conflicting interpretations of the rabbis' dreams. The Bavli, moreover, often associates Rava with Palestinian rabbinic learning.[29]

---

[27] On narrative frames, see Yonah Frenkel, דרכי האגדה והמדרש (Massada: Yad la-Talmud, 1991), 260–74; on thematic repetition, see note 20 in Chapter Two. On foreshadowing in Greco-Roman literature, see Tomas Hägg, *Narrative Technique in Ancient Greek Romances: Studies of Chariton, Xenophon, Ephesius, and Achilles Tatius* (Stockholm: Svenska institutet i Athen, 1971).

[28] Richard Kalmin considers the possibility that Abaye's interlocutor is not Rava, the fourth-generation amora from Mahoza but rather Rabbah, the third generation amora from Pumpedita, Abaye's teacher; see *Sages, Stories, Authors and Editors in Rabbinic Babylonia*, 176–192. The spelling of the two names is indeed a fickle guide, as Shamma Friedman has long shown, "כתיב השמות "רבה" ו"רבא" בתלמוד הבבלי," *Sinai* 110 (1992), 140–64. Since the story relates Abaye's death and Rava's becoming head of the academy, we can be certain that the present story has Rava, not Rabbah, in mind; see also notes 39 and 101 below. For one of the many studies on the dialectics of Rava and Abaye, see, for example, D. Hanschke, "Abbaye and Rava: Two Approaches to the Mishna of the Tannaim," *Tarbiz* 49 (1979f), 187–193 [Hebrew]. Cf. also Afik's claim that the two heroes in the story represent the opinions of the two academies that they once headed concerning dream interpretation, transferring a purported Palestinian struggle to Babylonia; see Afik, *Hazal's Perception of Dreams*, 386–406.

[29] See Zvi Moshe Dor, תורת ארץ-ישראל בבבל (Tel Aviv: Devir, 1971) and Richard Kalmin, *Jewish Babylonia between Persia and Roman Palestine*, 173–86.

With unmitigated bluntness, the story's opening line introduces Bar Hedya's corruption and his impact on future events. The Palestinian doctrine is confirmed. Rava, however, does not suspect that Bar Hedya is involved with Rava's own misfortunes. The story portrays Rava as obstinate, and as naïve in failing to notice the relationship between paying or not paying Bar Hedya's fee. Hence, Bar Hedya's respective interpretations allow the audience to enjoy the comical aspects of Rava's tragic demise while also empathizing with the founding father of Babylonian rabbinic culture – a central element of the story's humorous mischief.

The story portrays the perpetrator of the crimes, Bar Hedya, as a contemporary of the two renowned rabbis. Yet unlike them, he is a secondary character in the Bavli; he is, most importantly, portrayed as a frequent visitor to Palestine.[30] Richard Kalmin convincingly argues that the Bar Hedya portrayed in the text must be regarded as a rabbi himself, noting that "we find Bar Hedya engaging in standard rabbinic activity in three other contexts in the Talmud."[31] The fact that Bar Hedya is never addressed or referred to as rabbi does not in itself suffice to determine his status, but it should be noted that there is some ambiguity in the Bavli concerning his position. His name means "hawk" in Babylonian Aramaic, and he shares it with an ominous angelic figure in the Bavli.[32] Bar Hedya is mentioned five times in the Bavli; in one place, the Bavli contradicts the Palestinian legal testimony he provides. Elsewhere, we learn that a practice for whose halakhic admissibleness Bar Hedya testified might not have received rabbinic approval, as suggested, tellingly, by Abaye.[33] His place on the minority side of controversial questions should not be overinterpreted, however, as contradictions and differences of opinion constitute the nature of the Bavli, and Bar Hedya makes

---

[30] Kalmin seems to accept the historical existence of a Bar Hedya and, based on his interpretation of talmudic references to this figure, remarks: "To judge from these sources, Bar Hedya is most likely a fourth-generation amora, that is, a contemporary of Abaye and Rava who spent time in Palestine." Richard Kalmin, *Sages, Stories, Authors and Editors in Rabbinic Babylonia*, 69.

[31] Kalmin, *Sages, Stories, Authors and Editors in Rabbinic Babylonia*, 69.

[32] On the name Bar Hedya as meaning "hawk," spotting its prey from a distance, see *Hulin* 63b and *Wayiqra Rabbah* 5.2 (see also Margulies *ad loc* on a spurious Rabbi Yohanan *Bar Shahina*, perhaps from the Arabic *shahin*, a white falcon). Concerning Bar Hedya as an angelic figure holding back the south winds, see *Bava Batra* 25a and *Gittin* 31a. Cf. also Afik, *Hazal's Perception of Dreams*, 219–21 and Aaron Hyman, *Toldot Tannaim ve-Amoraim* (Jerusalem: Makhon Pri ha'Aretz, 1981), 285 [Hebrew].

[33] We read in *Sukkah* 43b that "all those who go down to Palestine" contradict Bar Hedya's testimony from Palestine. In *Mo'ed Qatan* 18b, Abaye dismisses Bar Hedya's Palestinian testimony, arguing that what Bar Hedya reports as being a local custom might not have had rabbinic approval. Philip Alexander understands Bar Hedya to stand for the non-rabbinic side in a conflict between rabbis and dream-interpreters, but he does not support this view with further evidence (Philip Alexander, "Bavli Berakhot 55a–57b: The Talmudic Dreambook in Context," 247).

three other, less problematic, appearances in the Bavli.[34] Hence, we are on the safest ground if we read the story as employing Bar Hedya as a rabbinic figure whose reliability had neither been established nor refuted, and most importantly, as a figure associated with Palestinian traditions. Rava perhaps should have exercised more caution when seeking his services, just as the Bavli always scrutinizes Bar Hedya's Palestinian testimony.

(II) Rava is a Thief

Subsection II consists of contradictory dream interpretations and features recurrent themes. In this subsection, Abaye and Rava are "made to recite" in their dreams seven scriptural passages, mostly from the Deuteronomic curse of Israelites who did not follow the biblical commandments.[35] These "scriptural" dreams anticipate, for the first time, Bar Hedya's eventual downfall. The story moves from scriptural passages to the interpretation of palpable dream symbols in subsection III and then returns to a scriptural passage, the story's last dream symbol, in subsection V. The recurrence of a "scriptural" dream in subsection V highlights the story's climax; this scriptural dream results in Bar Hedya's losing his dream book and eventually in his downfall. Also, the scriptural curse theme anticipates Bar Hedya's execution following the curse cast upon him by Rava in subsection VI. These carefully crafted structural devices highlight the story's satirical as well as its parodic elements, as we shall see.

The biblical curses, which have the function of dream symbols, moreover, are not easily reconcilable with Rava's and Abaye's well-known piety. It is likely that the Bavli seeks to create tension between the pious dreamers and the presupposition of impiety derived from their scriptural dream symbols. The thematic repetition of predictions involving family, business, and academic affairs substantiates Abaye's gain and Rava's loss from their engagement with Bar Hedya. In addition, these repetitions also organize the internal structure of each subsection, often in the typical rabbinic style of chiastic repetition of themes and words.[36]

---

[34] In *Gittin* 5b, Bar Hedya wishes to carry a divorce certificate to Palestine but receives contradictory instructions. In *Avodah Zarah* 30a, he provides an example, which is declared unsuitable (because it involves danger of life and thus belongs to another category of argumentation). His claims are accepted only once, in *Hulin* 6b.

[35] For the curse of the Israelites, see Deuteronomy 28:15–68. It is preceded by a short blessing (28:1–14), one verse from which is cited in II.7.

[36] For example, in II.1 and II.4, Bar Hedya interprets the scriptural verses as signifying good business deals for Abaye and bad ones for Rava (in both interpretations, Bar Hedya uses the words "fail" (פסיד), "prosper" (מרווח), and "joy" (מחדוא). The "business" motif in II.1 and II.4 creates a frame that encloses II.2 and II.3. The latter pair also forms a unit created by the "children" motif: an abundance of children for Abaye and for Rava, the

The primary narrative technique in this subsection is repeatedly to surprise the audience with Bar Hedya's ingenious ability to provide antithetical
interpretations for each scriptural verse, which, as we shall see, is modeled
on the Yerushalmi's depiction of Rabbi Ishmael. The playful nature of these
surprises sets the stage for and interacts with the story's more overtly comical elements in the sequel. One example suffices to illustrate the resulting
combination of twisted categories and frustrated expectations:

II.3 "We were made to recite: 'Your sons and daughters shall be given to another
people [while you look on; you will strain your eyes looking for them all day
but be powerless to do anything (Deuteronomy 28:32)].'"
To Abaye, he said: "Your sons and daughters will abound [נפישין].
You will tell [your wife to marry them] to your relatives,
and she will tell [you to marry them] to her relatives,
and she will force [ואכפה] you and give them to her relatives,
and it will be like a different people."
To Rava, he said: "Your wife will die,
and your sons and daughters will go to a different woman,"
as Rava said in the name of Rabbi Jeremiah Bar Aba in the name of Rav:[37]
"What does Scripture mean by 'Your sons and daughters shall be given to
another people?' That is a stepmother."

It is typical in rabbinic literature that the un-cited continuation of a biblical prooftext (provided above in square brackets) is at least as important
as the cited portion. Bar Hedya interprets the powerlessness of the cursed
Israelites in Deuteronomy 28:32 as Abaye's powerlessness in the face of his
wife's intentions to marry off their children, amusingly turning national
warfare into a family drama apparently all too familiar to the story's rabbinic audience.

In response to Rava's dream, however, Bar Hedya does not simply let
the biblical curse speak for itself as he does with the preceding dream[38] and
as the audience therefore now expects. Instead, Bar Hedya seeks to display
his rabbinic acumen by using Rava's own reasoning against Rava himself;
if "another people" refers to a stepmother,[39] Bar Hedya grimly deduces,

---

loss of children to captivity and the death of his wife. The order of speakers superimposes
another structural parallelism on the same segments: Bar Hedya speaks first to Rava, then
to Abaye in II.1 and II.2 whereas II.3 and II.4 invert this order. On chiastic structures, see
Chapter Two, note 20.

[37] Ms. Munich 95 and the Soncino quote the saying only in the name of Rava himself.

[38] II.2.

[39] This line of reasoning is cited one other time in the Bavli, in *Yevamot* 63b. There is
great variation among the manuscripts about its attribution, but Rava is never given as
its author. The rabbi who interprets Deuteronomy 28:32 exactly like Rava, according to
Bar Hedya, is referred to as Rav Hanan bar Rava in the name of Rav (Vilna and Pesaro
prints), Rabbi Jeremiah bar Abba (Ms. Moscow Guenzburg 594 and Ms. Vatican 111),
and Rabbi Jeremiah bar Abba in the name of Rav (Ms. Munich 141; Ms. Munich 95; Ms.

Rava's wife will die and he will remarry. While Bar Hedya's attribution of this line of reasoning to Rava cannot be confirmed, the prediction nevertheless comes true. Causing the death of Rava's spouse is Bar Hedya's unforgivable capital sin and for a third time anticipates his subsequent death. In subsection VI, Rava curses Bar Hedya precisely for having caused her death. The "death of the spouse" along with Bar Hedya's execution constitute the story's pivotal themes (the death of a spouse is also the pivotal image in the imitation of the Yerushalmi story about Rabbi Eliezer).

Both the favorable and unfavorable interpretations of the biblical verse mark Bar Hedya's whimsical genius and oracular manipulation. By now, the audience understands that the narrative enacts Rava's stupefaction in the face of the Palestinian doctrine, that is, Bar Hedya's control of Rava's fate. The numerous examples of Bar Hedya's abuse of power expose the moral consequences of professional rabbinic dream interpretation and the mortal danger associated with the services of a corrupt interpreter, as Richard Kalmin has pointed out.[40]

The scriptural dream symbol concluding this subsection contains an unexpected narrative twist; likewise, dramatic closure is the structural device used to conclude all of the story's subsequent subsections. By now, the audience is accustomed to the following pattern: the pious rabbis dream about Deuteronomic curses, and Bar Hedya ingeniously provides contradictory interpretations of them, nullifying or exacerbating them respectively. The story deviates from this pattern only once, citing a blessing from Ecclesiastes that Bar Hedya interprets as a curse for Rava.[41] Two additional scriptural curses are followed by a blessing:

II.7 "We were made to recite: 'All the peoples of the earth shall see that you are called by the name of G-d, and they shall be afraid of you' [Deuteronomy 28:10]."
   To Abaye, he said: "You will become reputable since you will be the head of the academy; fear of your person will be prevalent [literally "fall," נפלת] everywhere."
   To Rava, he said: "The provision house of the king will be broken into, and you will be arrested [ומתפסת] for theft, and everybody will draw *qal vahomer* from your case."
   The next day the provision house of the king was broken into, and they came and arrested Rava.

_____

Oxford 248 (367); and fragment Cambridge F-S F1 (1) 1); Ms. Moscow Guenzburg 1017 attaches the saying to a different verse altogether. Bar Hedya's quotation of "Rava's" reasoning, moreover, could also be "Rabbah's;" see note 28 above. Even if it was Rabbah's, the audience might still have appreciated the use of a line of reasoning associated with Rava through homophony.

[40] Kalmin, *Sages, Stories, Authors and Editors in Rabbinic Babylonia*, 67–69.
[41] II.4, citing Ecclesiastes 9:7.

The blessing from Deuteronomy immediately precedes the long curse in Deuteronomy 28, which is the basis for Abaye's success and Rava's misfortunes, attesting to the story's careful composition and intimate dialogue with Scripture.[42] The audience is therefore eager to learn how Bar Hedya will manage once more to turn the dream's blessing into a curse, and Bar Hedya lives up to the audience's expectations. In Deuteronomy 28:10, the nation fears God's powerful name, "and they shall be afraid of you," that is, of the Israelites protected by God's name. Based on the Palestinian hermeneutical doctrine of *qal vahomer*, concluding from the lesser to the greater, Bar Hedya recklessly interprets the fear as people's "fear" of Rava's good name – a fear based on Rava's impending fall. The Bavli here seems to imply the following: if even the great Rava could not escape denouncement and arrest, much more so common people; hence they are "afraid of" him as predicted in Deuteronomy.[43] Since Rava is about to be arrested for theft, his impeccable reputation and fame are now threatened. The image of the rabbinic leader as an alleged thief borders on slapstick comedy.

Rava's eventual arrest confirms that Bar Hedya's arbitrary, even capricious, interpretations come true – Bar Hedya may be morally unreliable, but he is still in control of the future, which confirms and confounds the Palestinian doctrine. Tacitly, the story presupposes that Rava is acquitted and released given his role in the sequel of the narrative. Rava's incarceration is an implicit interruption of the narrative, which indicates the transition to the next subsection of the story. The break itself emphasizes the story's structure, and Bar Hedya's interpretation, unbeknownst to him, anticipates his own death once more.[44] Rava is arrested and is accused by the king of the Sasanian Empire of damaging (stealing) the king's property, and Bar Hedya is ultimately arrested and then accused and sentenced to death by the king

---

[42] II.7, Deuteronomy 28:10.

[43] The Vilna and Soncino prints simply name the *qal vahomer* (*a minori ad majus*) rule and leave the reasoning implicit as does Ms. Florence II-I-7 on the margin. Several of the manuscripts, such as Ms. Oxford 366 (fol. Add. 23) and Paris 671, have the people reason על אחת כמה וכמה (Ms. Munich 95 has the logically similar לא כ"ש). On the "Seven *Middot*" of Rabbi Hillel or the "Thirteen *Middot*" of Rabbi Ishmael ben Elisha, already attested in Tannaitic times, see Stemberger, *Introduction to Talmud and Midrash*, 16–22. To the best of my knowledge, no other dream interpreter, in the Yerushalmi or in the Bavli, cites such a hermeneutical rule in order to reach a conclusion, emphasizing the odd nature of the present case.

[44] Afik states that the story is not interested in such details as chronology and the smoothness of the plot since Rava's arrest does not impede the flow of the narrative (Isaac Afik, *Hazal's Perception of Dreams*, 352f.). I would suggest the opposite. The story, in my view, does not smooth out the interruption of the narrative. Instead, it consciously and carefully crafts a break in the plot, marking the transition to the next set of dream interpretations.

of the Roman Empire for damaging his property (leading to its decay).[45] Only in hindsight does the audience understand how the abuse of the great Rava at the hands of the corrupt dream interpreter neatly corresponds to the latter's death.

(III) Amoraim are Asses

The subsection following Rava's dramatic arrest presents dream symbols of a different kind. Rather than reciting scriptural verses in their dreams, Abaye and Rava now report dreaming about physical, everyday-life objects. Rava's and Abaye's respective business dealings, that is Abaye's profits and Rava's losses, continue to be the primary theme. The final dreams in this subsection, much like in subsection II, also mark a climactic closure, exemplary of the literary style of the section as a whole as well as anticipating the circumstances of Bar Hedya's death in ever more detail:

III.5 They said to him: "We saw a vat that fell into a well [לבירא]."
> To Abaye, he said: "Your business goods will be in demand, as they say 'the bread fell into the well and is found no more.'"
> To Rava, he said: "Your business goods will spoil [פסיד] and will be thrown into a well.

III.6 They said to him: "We saw a donkey standing on our pillow [אאיסדן] and braying."
> To Abaye he said: "You will be king [of the academy], and an *amora* will stand next to you."
> To Rava he said: "[The phrase] 'the first born of a donkey [פטר חמור, Exodus 13:13]' is erased from your *Tefilin*."
> He [Rava] said to him [Bar Hedya]: "I looked at them and they were there!"
> He [Bar Hedya] said to him [Rava]: "The *vav* from [the phrase] 'the first born of a donkey [פטר חמור], is erased from your Tefilin."

Rava's business goods will "spoil" (פסיד), anticipating the "decay" (תכלא) of the king's garments at the end of the story, the immediate cause of Bar Hedya's execution.[46] Then, both rabbis see "a donkey standing on [their] pillow and braying."[47] Bar Hedya predicts that Abaye will become head of an academy, with an amora standing next to him as his assistant.[48]

---

[45] Moreover, as mentioned before, the rabbis' dream symbols switch from scriptural verses to palpable symbols after this dream, highlighting Bar Hedya's downfall in subsection V as being triggered by this switch.

[46] III.5.

[47] III.6.

[48] The amora had the important role in rabbinic academies of reciting verses, a task requiring a loud voice but not necessarily a trained analytical mind. The term amora is not to be confused with the same word used to describe a rabbi of the amoraic period;, see note 16 in the Introduction.

Bar Hedya's interpretation relies on the homophonic association, according to Babylonian pronunciation, of donkey, *hamra* (חמרא), and amora (אמורא), a comically disrespectful reference to *amoraim*, as Afik accurately points out.[49] At the same time, the theme of "becoming head of a rabbinic academy" anticipates how Rava learns, in subsection V, about Abaye's imminent death and his inheritance of Abaye's academy.

Bar Hedya then interprets Rava's dream about a braying donkey as signifying that the scriptural verse "first born of a donkey" will be erased from his Tefilin,[50] a serious matter in light of the magical potency ascribed to Tefilin.[51] Rava proves the interpretation wrong, marking Bar Hedya's first mistake (after possibly misquoting Rava in subsection II). The narrative leads the audience to recognize the limits of Bar Hedya's mantic powers, contrasting rabbinic authority with his usurpation of power.

Bar Hedya, nevertheless, manages to redeem himself by limiting the alleged erasure to one letter, a *vav* in the word חמור, "donkey," one of the words in Exodus 13:13, the biblical passage written on the Tefilin. Even if Bar Hedya's quick-minded conciliation of contradictory realities in exemplary talmudic fashion wins the day, the matter remains as humorous as the association of amoraim and asses. In any case, the *vav* was most likely missing from kosher Tefilin, and Bar Hedya's claim that it "fell" from Rava's Tefilin would preposterously render the kosher form the exception, a ridiculously contrived way of extricating himself from the situation.[52]

---

[49] Afik, *Hazal's Perception of Dreams*, 242 and 377. Note the different, and even more suggestive, spelling of "donkey" in the Parma print, *hamara*, חמארא.

[50] Phylacteries, a leather object used for morning prayers and containing scriptural verses, including Exodus 13:13.

[51] See Yehudah Cohn, *Tangled up in Text: Tefillin and the Ancient World* (Providence, R.I.: Brown Judaic Studies, 2008).

[52] No Tefilin from rabbinic times were preserved, but Exodus 13:13 was spelled without a vav before and after the rabbinic period, indicating the possibility of such a spelling on rabbinic Tefilin as well. Yehudah Cohn informed me that Exodus 13:13 is spelled without a *vav* in the medieval masoretic text of the Bible and on medieval Tefilin as well as on all legible Tefilin found in the Judean Desert. See M. Morgenstern and M. Segal, "XHev/SePhylactery," *Discoveries in the Judaean Desert* 38 (Oxford: Oxford University Press, 2000), 183–91 and Yonathan Adler, "Identifying Sectarian Characteristics in the Phylacteries from Qumran," *Revue de Qumran* 23 (2007), 79–92. Since rabbinic texts often include biblical *vavim* that Qumran and Medieval manuscripts do not, this holds true despite the fact that all Palestinian and Babylonian rabbinic citations of the phrase "first born of a donkey" indeed include the *vav* (see, for example, the numerous examples in *Bekhorot* 5b–12b in the Bavli; *Qiddushin* 1.6.2–10 (60d–61a) and *Qiddushin* 2.9.2–7 (63a) in the Yerushalmi; and Exodus 34:20, the masoretic parallel text of Exodus 13:13).

(IV) Two Blows for Rava

Bar Hedya's authority still prevails but continues to deteriorate in subsection IV. The narrative tension increases as the somber predictions become more severe now that Rava meets Bar Hedya alone but still refuses to pay his fee. Bar Hedya repeats and escalates the disasters he inflicts upon Rava in subsection II, where he predicts the captivity of Rava's children and the death of his wife.[53] Bar Hedya now predicts the death of Rava's children as well; the prediction is confirmed as accurate later in the story.[54] The repetition of the "death of the spouse" theme marks its significance to the narrative, (highlighting the story's parody of the respective Yerushalmi story about Rabbi Ishmael as well).

The last dream in this subsection, at the same time, provides some comic relief with a most literal application of the Palestinian doctrine, which once again exemplifies the way in which this section plays with the dream symbols:

IV.4 He said to him: "I saw two turnip tops [גרגלידי דלפתא]."
He said to him: "You will receive two blows [קולפי]."
Rava went on that day to sit the whole day in the study house.
He saw two blind men [lit. "full of light," סגי נהורי] fighting each other.
Rava went to separate them, and they struck [ומחוהו] him twice.
They wanted to strike once more.
He [Rava] said: "I have had enough [מסתיי]! I saw two."[55]

Rava's unwitting attackers are literally blind, especially to Rava's status. The slapstick-like image of two blind men (who cannot recognize Rava) dealing blows to the head of a rabbinic academy furthers the story's ridicule of Rava's esteemed public image. After being humiliated by his continuous inability to recognize Bar Hedya's corruption, by his association with the scriptural curses of sacrilegious Israelites, by the accusation of theft, and by

---

[53] II.2–3.

[54] IV.1–2.

[55] IV.4, based on the Vilna and Soncino prints, Ms. Munich 95, and Ms. Florence II-I-7. Ms. Oxford 366 (fol. Add. 23) and Ms. Paris 671 read: "'I saw two in my dream.' And they left him." As Kalmin points out, the last two lines of this segment (along with the satirical climax) are missing from one Geniza fragment of the Leningrad library (Abraham Katsh, *Ginzei Talmud Bavli: The Antonin Genizah in the Saltykov-Schedrin Public Library in Leningrad* (Jerusalem: Rubin Mass, 1979), vol. I 16); it is also missing from the fragment Cambridge F-S F1 (1) 41, which indicates an unspecified number of beatings (Kalmin, *Sages, Stories, Authors and Editors in Rabbinic Babylonia*, 68). I do not think, however, that this fact suggests that the dream was added to the reading of the majority of manuscripts. In all the manuscripts, the segment's position fits perfectly in the structural pattern I sought to demonstrate, that is, each last segment of each part containing both a satirical and a narrative climax. Furthermore, the outright satirical character of this scene might have tempted a copyist to omit the slapstick elements if he wished to soften the satirical aspects of the story. Adding the two last lines seems less likely than deleting them.

his "faulty" Tefilin, Rava is now beaten up by members of his own community.

Bar Hedya predicts that Rava will be struck twice; Rava protests prior to receiving the third blow, invoking the image of only two blows in his dream. The victim of the dream interpretation takes control of his destiny and assumes the very mantic powers of the interpreter. Bar Hedya is correct about the number of blows only because Rava believed in the interpreter's ability to predict the future, indeed a self-fulfilling prophecy and a reduction to absurdity of the Palestinian doctrine – the intervention of the dreamer is hardly predicted here. Yet despite the ironic distance from the Palestinian doctrine, self-fulfilling prophecies are fulfilled prophecies nonetheless, and Bar Hedya once more prevails. Rava's intervention, at the same time, anticipates another self-fulfilling prophecy, preparing the audience for Bar Hedya's ultimately bringing about his own downfall when aids the fulfillment of Rava's curse in subsection VI.

(V) Rava Loses his Brains

In subsection V, after an inexplicable delay, Rava finally pays the interpreter's fee, and Bar Hedya's predictions change dramatically. The blessings Rava now receives stand in sharp contrast to the disasters he experiences prior to paying, but he still does not seem to recognize the cause of his previous hardships or his change of fortune:

V.1   Finally, Rava went and gave him compensation.
      He said to him: "I saw a wall breaking [דאיתבר]."
      He said to him: "You will acquire property without limits [מצרים]."

V.2   He said to him: "I saw the mansion of Abaye fall and its dust covered me."
      He said to him: "Abaye will die and his academy will go to you."

V.3   He said to him: "I saw my mansion fall, and everybody came and took the bricks."
      He said to him: "Your teachings will be dispersed everywhere."

V.4   He said to him: "I saw that my head was split [דאבקע], and I lost [נתר] my brain."
      He said to him: "The flock [אודרא, i.e., the stuffing][56] of [your] pillow [בי סדיא] has fallen out."

The negative images in Rava's dreams – a breaking wall, two falling houses, a splitting head – strengthen the tension between the dream symbols and

---

[56] See Sokoloff, *A Dictionary of Jewish Babylonian Aramaic*, 85. The spelling in the Vilna print is also found Ms. Florence II-I-7 (אודרי). The copyists must have had difficulties with this word: Ms. Oxford 366 (fol. Add. 23) has אודרא and Ms. Munich 95 אורדא, probably influenced by the full cognate עדרא. Ms. Paris 671 has איסטא, the meaning of which is uncertain. On the importance of the word's Palestinian cognate, see pages 124f. below.

reality even further; these symbols are also reminiscent of the Yerushalmi story about Rabbi Eliezer. With considerable ease, Bar Hedya turns these somber images into signs of prosperity. Rava's simpleminded insistence on returning to Bar Hedya might cause the audience to empathize with him or to enjoy its superior vantage point and Rava's misery, or both.

Bar Hedya now predicts Rava's commercial and educational prosperity as well as Abaye's death.[57] The pace of the narrative quickens. The audience learns about Rava's becoming the head of Abaye's academy as Bar Hedya's diametrically opposed predictions manage to manipulate the image of their falling mansions. Abaye attains leadership of his academy in subsection II; the story's perceptive audience understands that losing it constitutes an important turning point anticipated earlier in the story.[58] The story emphasizes the anticipation and fulfillment of Rava's ascent to the position of "head of the academy" by simultaneously repeating an adjacent image. In subsection II, Abaye's dream that allows him to become the head of an academy involves a pillow (אאיסדן). Now, a pillow, spelled slightly differently (בי סדיא), reappears as part of Bar Hedya's interpretation of Rava's dream, immediately after the prediction that Rava would become head of the academy (the word denoting a pillow also evokes a passage in the Yerushalmi's story about Rabbi Ishmael).

Similarly, Rava's dream image itself – his head splitting and his brain falling out – once more anticipates Bar Hedya's own demise.[59] The audience is soon to learn that it is not Rava's head but Bar Hedya himself that will be split, seemingly the true consequence of Rava's gory dream. The narrative here switches from dream images to Rava's recitation of one more scriptural verse. The return to one last scriptural dream symbol indicates the approaching closure. The dream symbols shift from scriptural verses (in subsection II), to symbols taken from everyday life (in subsections III and IV), and finally back to one final scriptural verse. Bar Hedya understands this verse, the "Egyptian *Hallel*", to signify that Rava will be the subject of a miracle. Since this *Hallel* is cited on Passover, the festival celebrating the miraculous release of the Israelites from bondage, the reference to a liberating miracle would have been obvious to the text'saudience.[60] The miracle is the downfall that Bar Hedya brings upon himself.

---

[57] The report that Abaye died before Rava is consistent with other passages in the Bavli (see *Ketubbot* 65a and 106a and *Gittin* 60b.)

[58] II.7.

[59] V.4. Together with Bar Hedya's interpretation of the *vav* erased from Rava's Tefilin in III.6, this interpretation of the split pillow illuminates the past rather than predicts the future, another internal repetition. The story also plays on juxtaposing illumination of the past with prediction of the future in Bar Hedya's last dream interpretation in subsection VII.

[60] See note 24 above.

(VI) Rava needs a Miracle

In subsection VI, Bar Hedya, fearing the very miracle he had predicted, disembarks the boat on which he and Rava are about to travel.[61]

VI   [Bar Hedya] was once about to enter a boat [באראב] with this one [Rava].
       [Bar Hedya] said: "This man to whom a miracle will happen, why [would] I [travel with him]?"
       As he went out, a book fell from him [i.e., he dropped it].
       Rava found it and saw that it was written in it: "All dreams follow the mouth."
       He said: "Wicked man, because of you it was fulfilled [קיימא], and all this pain!
           I forgive you for everything except for the daughter of Rav Hisda [i.e., the death of Rava's wife].
           May it be [God's] will that this man be delivered to a kingdom without mercy on him."
       He [Bar Hedya] said: "What shall I do? It has been taught that even an unwarranted curse of a wise man comes [true],
           so much more Rava's, which denounced me justly [דבדינא]."
       He said: "I will depart [איקום] and exile myself,
           as Mar has taught: 'Exile atones for guilt.'"

The narrative implies that Bar Hedya thinks that Rava will be saved miraculously from a shipwreck while all the other passengers will drown. His fear of his own prediction ironically triggers its fulfillment through the loss of his dream book, seemingly the true miracle he unwittingly participated in bringing about. In subsection IV, Rava actively enables the fulfillment of his dream about the two blows. The "self-fulfilled prophecy" theme now causes Bar Hedya's downfall. Rava finds the book that Bar Hedya loses. To his great surprise and exasperation, Rava finally learns that the Palestinian doctrine, and hence Bar Hedya himself, are the cause of his misfortunes. Impervious to the lessons of experience, the wise fool Rava learns from a book what should have been clear to him all along.

Rava curses Bar Hedya only on account of his wife's death, graciously forgiving his other crimes. This ironically forgives the death of Abaye, Rava's stock opponent and predecessor as head of the academy. Rava's curse, singling out the death of his wife as its only cause, is anticipated by the scriptural curses and prediction of her death in subsection II. The story already emphasized the centrality of the "death of the spouse" theme for its self-referential (and ultimately parodic) structure by repeating the prediction of her death in subsection IV.

Bar Hedya accepts Rava's verdict, participating in causing a prophecy, Rava's curse, to fulfill itself. He cites, again imprecisely, a statement in the name of an anonymous rabbinic master: "exile atones for guilt." The one ex-

---

[61] Traveling by boat was a necessity near Rava's home town of Mehoza. See, for example, *Berakhot* 59b and *Shabbat* 124b, 133b, and 147b.

tant talmudic source containing this statement indicates that its author was Yehuda bar Hiya and that exile atones only for *half* (מחצה) of the guilt.[62] Bar Hedya might not remember the name of Yehuda bar Hiya and claims that exile atones for *all* his guilt – an opinion ascribed in the Bavli to the Palestinian Rabbi Yohanan. Bar Hedya's error is his final one, anticipating his death quite accurately. He omits the "half," and is, in turn, himself cut in half.[63]

(VII) Bar Hedya Cut in Half

The last subsection includes the story's anticipated climactic finale:

VII He arose [קם] and exiled himself to Rome.
He went and sat [אזל יתיב] at the entrance of [the house of] the king's chief of the embroiderers.
The chief embroiderer had a dream vision.
[The embroiderer] said to [Bar Hedya]: "I saw in my dream that a needle pierced my finger [מחטא עייל באצבעתי]."
[Bar Hedya] said to him: "Give me a zuz."
And he did not give it to him, and he did not tell him anything.
He said to him: "I saw in my dream that decay fell on two of my fingers."
He said to him: "Give me a zuz."
And he did not give it to him, and he did not tell him [the dream's interpretation].
He said to him: "I saw that decay fell on my entire hand."
He said to him: "Decay fell on all of the silk garments [שיראי]."
The royal household heard [about the issue] and brought the chief embroiderer in order to kill him.
[The embroiderer] said to them: "Why me? Bring the one who knew and did not say it."
They brought Bar Hedya.

---

[62] *Sanhedrin* 37b.

[63] Some of the manuscripts assimilate Bar Hedya's mistaken quotation into the "correct" version, perhaps "correcting" what seems to be an intentional error. Ms. Munich 95 and Ms. Paris 671 have Bar Hedya quote it "correctly," as in *Sanhedrin* 37b, effectively dissimulating his mistake (see note 25). The Vilna print, preserving Bar Hedya's mistake, follows Ms. Oxford 366 (fol. Add. 23), Ms. Florence II-I-7, the Soncino print, and the Cambridge Geniza fragment T-S F1 (1) 41. This makes it more difficult to analyze the story's anticipation of this aspect of Bar Hedya's punishment, the fact that he will be cut in half, but it is still likely enough that the text'saudience was able to recognize it. We should note an interesting parallel in the story. Bar Hedya's suggestion in subsection III concerning the amended spelling of Rava's faulty Tefilin is not reliable; he thereby anticipates his error here, which leads to his exile. When audiences first hear subsection III, it is impossible for it to understand fully Bar Hedya's mistake concerning Rava's Tefilin (given the lack of historical data about Tefilin from rabbinic Babylonia). This same difficulty about the story's attribution of error to Bar Hedya, rendered blurry for historical reasons there, occurs here for reasons of textual redaction and copyists' variations.

They said to him: "On account of your zuz, the silken garments of the king have been destroyed."[64]

They tied [כפיתו] two cedars [ארז] with a rope [בחבלא].

They bound one foot to one [חד] cedar and one to another cedar,

and released [ושרו] the rope so that his head was split [דאצטליק] in one and one [חד וחד],

and he fell in two [parts].

Bar Hedya chooses to be exiled to "Rome," beyond the reach of rabbinic authority. Whether the reference is to Rome or to "New Rome," Constantinople, makes little difference in this passage.[65] "Rome," signified the seat of the imperial authority presiding over Palestine and the capital of the rival of the Sasanian Empire, the home of the Babylonian rabbis. It was, moreover, a city in which dream interpretation was a dangerous profession: the Christianizing Roman Empire exercised strict control over the orthodoxy of dream interpretation and continued the policy of the Roman Empire to curtail popular dream interpreters.[66]

In Rome, Bar Hedya immediately resumes his dubious business. Perhaps slightly repentant for his past faults and failures, he does not, at first, interpret the dream of the chief embroider unfavorably even though he refuses to pay and instead does not interpret it all. Nevertheless, after the dreamer refuses to pay a third time, the king's garments decay and the embroiderer informs the king that Bar Hedya is to blame.

The audience now realizes how closely the final dreams in three of the subsections and their respective interpretations anticipate Bar Hedya's death. In subsection II, Bar Hedya predicts the decay of Rava's property; in the final subsection, the king's garments decay. At the end of subsection II, Bar Hedya predicts that the king will arrest Rava and blame him for his lost property; now Bar Hedya himself is arrested and blamed for the king's ruined property. At the end of subsection V, Rava dreams about his head splitting; here Bar Hedya's entire body is split.[67] At the end of subsec-

---

[64] Rava has a more active role in the execution in Ms. Munich 95, Ms. Oxford 366 (fol. Add. 23), Ms. Paris 671, and the Soncino print: "Rava said: 'I will not forgive him until his head is split in two.'"

[65] See Sokoloff, *A Dictionary of Jewish Babylonian Aramaic*, 1065. The term "New Rome" (Νέα Ῥώμη or *Nova Roma*) was first used during the First Council of Constantinople in 381, likely long before the composition of this story, and the capital of Byzantium seems like the most probable location of Bar Hedya's death.

[66] See note 89 below.

[67] The fact that Bar Hedya is split in two not only recalls Rava's dream but also inverts a scene in Daniel in which the Persian king threatens his dream interpreters that if they are not be able to interpret his dream, he will "make them into pieces" (Daniel 2.5). While these interpreters are threatened with dismemberment for not being able to interpret a dream, Bar Hedya is dismembered for being greedy and interpreting a dream unfavorably. It is not clear, however, whether the Bavli actually invokes these parallels.

tion VI, Bar Hedya seeks to avert Rava's curse by enacting it himself and leaving for Rome.

The story wittily intertwines dream interpretation and fulfillment with an elaborate system of anticipation. This structure leads the audience through horror and comic relief and highlights the extent of Bar Hedya's corruption, his lack of sympathy for his victims, and the justice brought about by his execution. The apparent targets of the story's satire are the wicked Bar Hedya and the foolish Rava. In my view, the satirical treatment of Bar Hedya and Rava, along with the story's structure, help the audience recognize the story's imitation (with a difference) of the dream book in the Yerushalmi. Bar Hedya and Rava represent different aspects of the Palestinian doctrine, as expressed in the Yerushalmi's dream book, and the Bar Hedya story parodies the Yerushalmi in order to satirize the doctrines' abuser and his victim.

Rabbi Ishmael between the Yerushalmi and the Bavli

The Yerushalmi contains a sequence of dreams and dream interpretations that represents broadly the Palestinian rabbinic attitude toward these matters. Scholars have come to refer to this text, along with its close parallel in another Palestinian rabbinic compilation, as the Yerushalmi's "dream book."[68] There are similar and much more elaborate compilations in Greek,[69]

---

[68] *Ma'aser Sheni* 4:9 (55b–c). The Yerushalmi is generally thought to have been edited between the middle of the fourth and the middle of the fifth centuries CE; see Stemberger, *Introduction to Midrash and Talmud*, 187. Concerning the Yerushalmi dream book, see Isaac Afik, *Hazal's Perception of Dreams*, 21 ff.; Rivka Ulmer, "The Semiotics of the Dream Sequence in Talmud Yerushalmi Ma'aser Sheni," *Henoch* 23 (2001), 305–323; and Pinhas Mandel, מדרש איכה רבתי: מבוא, ומהדורה ביקורתית לפרשה השלישית, (PhD diss. The Hebrew University of Jerusalem, 1997). The sequence in the Yerushalmi has a very close parallel in *Ekha Rabbah*, a Palestinian Midrash edited in the fifth century (1.14–18; see Stemberger, ibid., 307). Brigitte Stemberger suggests that the parallel material in *Ekha Rabbah* (1.14–18) is a reworking of the passage from the Yerushalmi dream book (Brigitte Stemberger, "Der Traum in der Rabbinischen Literatur," *Kairos, Zeitschrift für Religionswissenschaft und Theologie* 18 (1976), 9, n. 47). The later Babylonian parody seems to imitate a text slightly closer to the version in the Yerushalmi than in *Ekha Rabbah;* I will focus on the Yerushalmi and mention the parallels in *Ekha Rabbah* only where they affect the present analysis. My arguments remain valid for the dream book in *Ekha Rabbah* as well.

[69] On the relevance of Artemidorus' *Oneirocritica* to rabbinic dream interpretation, see Philip Alexander, "Quid Athenis et Hierosolymis? Rabbinic Midrash and Hermeneutics in the Graeco-Roman World," 117f. and "Bavli Berakhot 55a–57b: The Talmudic Dreambook in Context," 241–244; Saul Lieberman, *Hellenism in Jewish Palestine: Studies in the Literary Transmission Beliefs and Manners of Palestine in the I Century B.C.E – IV Century C.E.* (New York: The Jewish Theological Seminary of America, 1950), 71–5; Brigitte Stemberger "Der Traum in der Rabbinischen Literatur," 23; and Haim Weiss, מעמדו ותפקידו של החלום בספרות חז"ל. Indeed, many of the dream symbols and even a few respective interpretations in the respecitve interpretations in the Bar Hedya story as

Syriac, and other literatures.[70] In the Bavli story, Bar Hedya possesses a book on dream interpretation, which he ends up losing. This book, intriguingly, contains a paraphrase of the Palestinian doctrine, which originates in the Yerushalmi's dream book. Bar Hedya's possession of this book, and the inclusion of the Palestinian doctrine in it, indicate the story's association of Bar Hedya, the Babylonian visitor to Palestine, with the Palestinian rabbinic dream culture in general and the Yerushalmi's dream book and the Palestinian doctrine in particular.[71] I seek to illustrate that the author of the Bar Hedya story models his narrative almost entirely on passages from the Yerushalmi's dream book – but with a difference.

Bar Hedya and Rabbi Ishmael: Dreams of Destruction

Most importantly, both the last subsection of the Bar Hedya story and the following story about Rabbi Ishmael in the Yerushalmi's dream book share a common structure and include the same dream symbols and interpretations:[72]

Somebody came to Rabbi Ishmael Bar Yose and said to him: "I saw in my dream that I was told, 'in this way your finger [אצבעתך] fell down.'"

---

well as in the Yerushalmi's dream book have parallels in Artemidorus and in Byzantine, Syriac, and Arabic dream books, a topic that requires further investigation. Concerning other Greek manuals of dream interpretation, see Steven M. Oberhelman, *Dreambooks in Byzantium: Six Oneirocritica in Translation, with Commentary and Introduction* (Surrey: Ashgate, 2008); and Steven F. Kruger, *Dreaming in the Middle Ages* (Cambridge; New York: Cambridge University Press, 1992), and note 89 below.

[70] See G. Furlani, "Une clef des songes en syriaque," *Revue de l'Orient Chrétien* 21 (1918–19), 119–44 and 224–248; Steven M. Oberhelman, *The Oneirocriticon of Achmet: A Medieval Greek and Arabic Treatise on the Interpretation of Dreams* (Lubbock: Texas Tech University Press, 1991); John Lamoreaux, *The Early Muslim Tradition of Dream Interpretation* (Stony Brook: SUNY Press, 2002); idem., "The Sources of Ibn Bahlul's Chapter on Dream Divination," *Studia Patristica* 33 (1997), 553–557; Franz Drexl, "Achmet und das syrische Traumbuch des cod. syr. or. 4434 des Brit. Mus.," *Byzantinische Zeitschrift* 30 (1929–30), 110–113; and Maria Mavroudi, *A Byzantine Book on Dream Interpretation: The Oneirocriticon of Achmet and Its Arabic Sources* (Leiden: Brill, 2002), 237–255.

[71] Given the circulation of dream books in the Greco-Roman world, the audience of the Bar Hedya story was probably not surprised by the existence of a self-contained Palestinian rabbinic "dream book" separate from the Yerushalmi (or its parallel). However, in light of the general familiarity of the authors of the Bavli with Palestinian rabbinic materials, and possibly with Greco-Roman dream books, there is no need to speculate about whether Bar Hedya's book actually existed. Moreover, we should note the unique character of the Yerushalmi dream book. Unlike its Greco-Roman counterparts, and unlike the Bavli, it does not contain a simple guide to dream interpretation in the typical style of "symbol x means y." Instead, it addresses only hermeneutically trained rabbis. It seems therefore just as likely that the Yerushalmi's dream book could have been brought to Babylonia as part of a larger written or oral composition. See Lieberman, *Hellenism in Jewish Palestine*, 71–5.

[72] Talmud Yerushalmi *Ma'aser Sheni*, Ms. Leiden, 4:9.12 (55c), cited in Peter Schäfer, *Synopse zum Talmud Yerushalmi I/6–11* (Tübingen: Mohr Siebeck 2001), 276–77.

He said to him: "Give me compensation [אגרי], and I will tell you."
He said to him: "I saw in my dream that I was told, 'in this way there will be a swelling in your mouth [בפומך].'"
He said to him: "Give me compensation, and I will tell you."
He said to him: "I saw in my dream, 'in this way your finger rose.'"[73]
He said to him: "Didn't I tell you, 'give me compensation, and I will tell you'? As
   you were told, 'in this way [your finger fell downward],' rain fell on your [stored]
   wheat. As you were told, 'in this way [there will be a swelling in your mouth],'
   it swelled. And as you were told, 'in this way [your finger rose],' it sprouted."

The Yerushalmi's dream book recounts Rabbi Ishmael bar Yose's ingenious
reading of the dream symbol as well as his demand for payment. It also
emphasizes the damage the rabbi allowed for the dreamer to suffer, despite
the fact that his only shortcoming lies in refusing to compensate Rabbi
Ishmael.[74] Rabbi Ishmael's insistence on receiving payment even after the
catastrophes had already occurred highlights the fact that they could have
been avoided had Rabbi Ishmael interpreted the dreams in the first place.
The *Yerushalmi's* dream book seems to side with the rabbi, who acts like
a professional dream interpreter; it describes rabbinic dream interpreters
"without a hint of criticism," Kalmin aptly notes.[75] The Yerushalmi gives no
indication that compensation for dream interpretation is reproachable and
does not object to the fact that Rabbi Ishmael might have been responsible
for the dreamer's loss, as the Palestinian doctrine would suggest.

In my view, the Yerushalmi's acquiescence to Rabbi Ishmael is questioned
in the Bavli. The Bavli imitates the narrative about Rabbi Ishmael and
considers the potential implications of his actions. The last subsection of
the Bar Hedya story, recounting his death in Rome, indicates that the Bar
Hedya character is a parodic rendition of Rabbi Ishmael of the Yerushalmi's
dream book:

– The officer responsible for the king's garments in the Bar Hedya story has a dream
  that unfolds in three consecutive parts, just like the dream that Rabbi Ishmael
  interprets.
– In both cases, the rabbinic dream interpreter asks for compensation and twice
  refuses to interpret the dream before receiving it. Both texts use the term "אגרי /
  אגרא."
– The symbol in the first and third dreams is a finger. A finger likewise appears in
  the first and second dreams that Bar Hedya at first refuses to interpret. Both texts
  use the word "אצבע."
– In both stories, the consequence of not paying the interpreter is the destruction by
  "natural" causes of property looked after by the unfortunate dreamer.

---

[73] Or "is erected" (זקיף). See Sokoloff, *A Dictionary of Jewish Palestinian Aramaic*, 181.
[74] Sprouted wheat cannot be stored as seedlings or used for baking.
[75] Kalmin, *Sages, Stories, Authors and Editors in Rabbinic Babylonia*, 66. Kalmin refers
to the closely parallel material in *Ekha Rabbah*.

– Most importantly, in both cases, the events "predicted" by dreams seem to un-
fold throughout the narrative: the damage from the first two dreams was limited
in both dreams, while the man's dreams kept recurring. The interpreter delivers
the devastating news only after everything is lost. The damage could have been
prevented had the dream interpreter revealed the meaning of the dreams earlier.

The structural and contextual similarities between the two Talmudim, along
with the starkly different outcomes, are the first indicators of a parodic
relationship between the two stories, especially given the likelihood that
the Bar Hedya story presupposes its audience' familiarity with the story
about Rabbi Ishmael. The author of the Bar Hedya story indicates that
Rabbi Ishmael's demand for compensation, while acceptable in general,
can be dangerous when exercised by a corrupt dream interpreter. Whereas
the Yerushalmi's dream book accepts the dangers associated with professional rabbinic dream interpretation, the Bavli from the outset considers
Bar Hedya's conduct a crime punishable by death.

The Bar Hedya story points to a central ambiguity in the Yerushalmi's
dream book. Even though the Yerushalmi explicitly cites and explains the
Palestinian doctrine, it never questions its applicability in the case of Rabbi
Ishmael's unfavorable dream interpretations. The audience cannot determine whether the Rabbi *causes* the destruction of the wheat, in accordance
with the doctrine, or simply allows it to happen, as the story itself suggests.
The Bavli, after generations of methodical reflection on the Palestinian rabbinic tradition, seems to systematize the logic at work in the Yerushalmi's
dream book.

Accordingly, the Bar Hedya story implies that dream interpreters must be
held accountable for the consequences of their interpretations, just as Rava
does. The Bar Hedya story focuses on the Yerushalmi's ambiguity, exposing the injustice done by a corrupt parodic double of Rabbi Ishmael and
presenting Bar Hedya as a symbolic Palestinian perpetrator. The dreamer
in the *Yerushalmi's* dream book loses his grain, and the chief embroiderer
loses his clothing, but ultimately, it is Bar Hedya, the dream interpreter,
who loses his life in the Babylonian response to the cynical professionalism
acceptable to the Yerushalmi.

The Bavli ironically imitates the Yerushalmi story about Rabbi Ishmael
in other ways as well. The following passage from the Yerushalmi's dream
book illustrates Rabbi Ishmael's exegetical virtuosity:[76]

Somebody came to Rabbi Ishmael Bar Yose and said to him: "I saw in my dream that
my vineyard brought forth lettuce [חסין]."

---

[76] Yerushalmi *Maʿaser Sheni*, Ms. Leiden, 4:9.11 (55b–c), cited in Schäfer, *Synopse*,
276–77. On this and the following story, see Rivka Ulmer, "The Semiotics of the Dream
Sequence in Talmud Yerushalmi Maʿaser Sheni," 316f.

He said to him: "Your wine [חמריה] has turned sour [בסים], and you will take lettuce and dip it in vinegar [בסין]."

Rabbi Ishmael creatively links the bitterness of lettuce with the grapevine, predicting the wine's spoilage. The Bar Hedya story imitates this passage as well, integrating it into its structure of contradictory interpretations and suggesting once more that the interpreter is to blame for unfavorable consequences of dreams. The imitation includes the Yerushalmi's dream symbol in one dream and the Yerushalmi's interpretation of it, with a lexical twist, in the subsequent one.

The Bavli adopts the Yerushalmi's "lettuce" as a dream symbol in subsection III, in which the two rabbis dream about seeing lettuce on the mouth of a jar. (Both the Yerushalmi and the Bavli use the word "חסא."[77]) Immediately thereafter, Bar Hedya interprets another dream symbol (meat) that is seen on the mouth of a jar; the similar symbol prompts the audience to ponder the two consecutive dreams at once.[78] Bar Hedya understands the meat to mean that Rava's wine will ferment, paralleling the wine in Rabbi Ishmael's interpretation, which turns into vinegar. The word for sour wine in the Yerushalmi is "בסים." In Palestinian Aramaic, this word means "sweet" as well as "sour," the quality of the wine in the dream book. In Babylonian Aramaic, however, the word only means sweet.[79] Seemingly exploiting the lexical difference, Bar Hedya causes Abaye's wine to become "sweet," adopting the Yerushalmi's word for "sour" but invoking instead its Babylonian meaning.

Bar Hedya's characterization in the Bavli emphasizes Ishmael's capriciousness. It adopts the dream symbol from the Yerushalmi, lettuce, its interpretation as signifying (sour) wine, and a lexical ambiguity between Palestinian and Babylonian Aramaic. It then provides numerous examples of Bar Hedya's using these elements from the Yerushalmi in order to reward Abaye and punish Rava. Bar Hedya's repetition of contradictory interpretations is in line with the rabbinic penchant for hermeneutical play, even as

---

[77] III.1.

[78] III.2.

[79] See note 18 above. Afik already realized that the Bavli uses the word "בסים" in a similar context but with a radically different outcome. Afik, however, flattens any potential literary meaning of this difference and instead uses it as evidence that the "source of this narrative [Bar Hedya's] is Palestinian and has undergone several Babylonian reworkings" (Isaac Afik, *Hazal's Perception of Dreams*, 236, my translation). I agree with Afik in regards to the importance of the Palestinian meaning of some of the terms used in Bar Hedya story. In my view, however, the Palestinian "source" of the Bar Hedya story did not travel to Babylonia in a series of oral permutations (as other stories of course may have). Rather, I propose that the story deliberately plays with the differences between Western and Eastern rabbinic Aramaic in order to emphasize its cultural distance from the Yerushalmi's dream book and its conventions.

he perverts it viciously. The story uses the linguistic variation to distinguish itself from the Palestinian text that it imitates.

The link between Bar Hedya and Rabbi Ishmael implicates the latter and accuses him of damaging the wine, which is akin to Bar Hedya's offenses in the Bavli.[80] The Bar Hedya story's exploitation of the polysemy of Palestinian Aramaic draws our attention to Rabbi Ishmael's exploitation of the polysemy of dreams in the Yerushalmi and to his ability freely to shape the future of the dreamers. Rabbi Ishmael's responsibility for the loss of the wheat is the logical conclusion in accordance with the Palestinian doctrine. The Bar Hedya story ironizes the premises of the Palestinian doctrine by exposing the conundrum engendered by a corrupt dream interpreter.

Bar Hedya and Rabbi Ishmael: Dreams of Disease

The Bar Hedya story exploits the differences between Palestinian and Babylonian Aramaic yet again. In another passage from the Yerushalmi's dream book, Rabbi Ishmael rebukes a prankster for inventing a dream in order to ridicule the rabbi. The false dream contains several dream symbols, including "cedars" (ארזין) and a "barn" (אדרא).[81] Rabbi Ishmael condemns the prankster to perpetual agony, being "neither living nor dead," by interpreting the dream as representing the prankster's future sickbed: the "cedars" stand for the sides of the bed and the "barn" for a mattress made of straw.[82] This harsh prediction, the Yerushalmi hastens to add, indeed comes true. The Yerushalmi insists on the validity of the Palestinian doctrine even in the extreme case of a fake dream.

In the Bavli, Bar Hedya (mis)interprets Rava's dream about his head splitting open as signifying the "stuffing" (אודרא) of his pillow, presumably made of straw.[83] The dream, as argued above, anticipates Bar Hedya's own execu-

---

[80] III.2.

[81] See Sokoloff, *A Dictionary of Jewish Palestinian Aramaic*, 36.

[82] Talmud Yerushalmi *Ma'aser Sheni*, Ms. Leiden, 4:9.13 (55c), cited in Peter Schäfer, *Synopse*, 276–77. The Yerushalmi, immediately after allowing the loss of wheat, recounts the following story: Rabbi Ishmael encounters a Samaritan who mischievously invents a dream in order to trick the rabbi. The fabricated dream features several items, including four cedars and a barn, on which the dreamer sits . Rabbi Ishmael realizes that the dream is contrived but still interprets it in order for the Samaritan "not to get nothing out of it." Ishmael interprets the dream symbols as referring to parts of a bed. He "foresees" the Samaritan agonizing in a sickbed. The prediction comes true even though the dream never occurred. The rabbi is once again victorious, and the Yerushalmi justifies the punishment of the prankster, *inter alia*, proving the validity of the Palestinian doctrine. Concerning this story, see Rivka Ulmer, "The Semiotics of the Dream Sequence in Talmud Yerushalmi Ma'aser Sheni," 316–18.

[83] V.4. Concerning the meaning of this word, see note 56 above.

tion, aided by "cedars" (ארזי). The Bar Hedya story uses the words "ארזי"
and "אודרא" in order to indicate that it deliberately alludes to the Rabbi
Ishmael story in this case as well, once more playing with the lexical ambiguity between Palestinian and Babylonian Aramaic. The use of identical
words, first with similar and then with quite different meanings, helps the
audience recognize the relationship between the two stories. Rabbi Ishmael
invokes cedars in his brutal punishment of the prankster who invents the
dream; the Bavli, in turn, also invokes cedars in punishing Bar Hedya for
inventing "true" dream interpretations. (Both the Yerushalmi and the Bavli
use the word "ארז.") Additionally, in Babylonian Aramaic, "אודרא" means
not barn but "stuffing," and hence, when Bar Hedya (mis)interprets Rava's
dream about his brain as signifying his pillow's "stuffing" the audience is
reminded of the Yerushalmi's punishment of the prankster.

While this is a case of parodic allusion more so than of full-fledged
parody, it seems that the Bavli punishes Bar Hedya partially because he
represents yet another aspect of Rabbi Ishmael's heritage,the punishment of
the prankster. By exploiting the lexical differences between Babylonian and
Palestinian Aramaic, the story anticipates Bar Hedya's political exile from
Babylonia with a kind of linguistic exile of Palestinian Aramaic, thereby
once more pointing to the Palestinian tradition that it ironizes by presenting
Babylonian culture as normative. The Bavli's characterization of Bar Hedya
through the imitation of and allusion to Palestinian rabbinic dream interpreters is similarly visible in the following parodic imitation, the last and
most important example from the Yerushalmi's dream book I shall discuss.

Bar Hedya and Rabbi Eliezer: Dreams of Death

To reiterate, the Bar Hedya story ironizes the Yerushalmi's dream book
by combining elements of the Palestinian doctrine with the interpreter's
demand for monetary compensation. The doctrine itself might have originated among Palestinian rabbinic exegetes of the Book of Genesis. The
Yerushalmi celebrates this doctrine towards the end of the dream book in a
story about Rabbi Eliezer, a story that the Bar Hedya story imitates as well:[84]

A woman came before Rabbi Eliezer.
She said to him: "I saw in my dream the beam in my house [ביתא] break [מיתברא]."
He said to her: "You will have a male son."
She went and had a male son.
After some time, she went and demanded to see him [Rabbi Eliezer].

---

[84] Talmud Yerushalmi *Ma'aser Sheni*, Ms. Leiden, 4:9.14 (55c), cited in Schäfer, *Synopse*,
276–79.

His students said to her: "He is not here."
They said to her: "What do you want from him?"
She said to them: "I saw in my dream the beam in my house break."
They said to her: "Your husband will die."
As Rabbi Eliezer returned, they told him what happened.
He said to them: "You killed a man."
Why? Because a dream fulfills itself according to its interpretation [שאין החלום הולך אלא אחר פתרונו],
As it is said: "And as [כאשר] he interpreted for us, so it was [Genesis 41:13]."

The Yerushalmi's dream book describes the case of a woman who dreams twice that the beam in her house breaks. Having seen this image for the first time, the woman relates it to Eliezer, a learned Palestinian tannaitic rabbi who himself becomes the vehicle for satire elsewhere in the Yerushalmi, as I suggest in the Conclusion to this book. Eliezer accurately predicts the birth of a son. Then, seeing the same image in a second dream, she returns, obviously expecting a similar interpretation. The rabbi tragically is absent, and she relates the dream to his incompetent students. They predict the death of the dreamer's husband.[85] Upon the return of Eliezer, he blames his students for effectively having killed the husband since "every dream follows its interpretation," citing a verse from the biblical story about Joseph's dream interpretation as a prooftext. The students learn that they could, and should, have interpreted it differently, but the damage cannot be undone.

The Palestinian doctrine's emphasis on the decisive role of the dream interpreter, only minimally constrained by the dream symbol, is unparalleled in other traditions; the dream book derives the doctrine from the Bible with the help of midrashic reasoning. In Genesis, Joseph interprets the dreams of two Egyptian officials. Their dreams are comparable; both include objects relating to their respective trades. Joseph interprets the dreams as signifying upward movement. The upward movement in the case of the first dreamer refers to the elevation of his social status whereas the upward movement of the second dreamer signifies that he will be decapitated and hanged from a tree.[86] The prosperous official later recalls Joseph's accurate interpretations, stating, in the common translation: "*as* he interpreted for us, so it was" (כאשר פתר לנו כן היה). The Yerushalmi, however, understands the biblical word "כאשר" to mean "since," indicating that what transpired occurred *because* of Joseph's interpretation. It views Joseph not as a seer but as the

---

[85] In the Yerushalmi manuscripts Leiden and Vatican and the Amsterdam and Venice prints, the students predict that the woman will give birth to a son *and* that her husband will die. Ms. Moscow and London, as well as the parallels in *Bereshit Rabbah* and *Ekha Rabbah* (in all the manuscripts), however, include only the former.

[86] Genesis 40. Concerning dreams in the Bible, see, for example, Jean-Marie Husser, *Dreams and Dream Narratives in the Biblical World* (Sheffield: Sheffield Academic Press, 1999).

orchestrator of future events, thereby establishing the Palestinian doctrine.[87] Further contextualization of the Palestinian doctrine, beyond its biblical origin, would carry us too far from the Bar Hedya story.[88] Tentatively, the Palestinian doctrine could be understood as a reaction against imperial Roman decrees, which viewed dream interpretation unfavorably, as Kalmin emphasizes.[89] Yet the precise history of the Palestinian doctrine is ultimately irrelevant to the Bavli's ironization of it.

Intriguingly, the Yerushalmi already problematizes the dangers inherent to its own doctrine: the story of Rabbi Eliezer holds the dream interpreter accountable, as Galit Hasan-Rokem explains:

---

[87] Genesis 41:13. Concerning the ancient Near Eastern context of the roots פשר and פתר, see A. Leo Oppenheimer, *The Interpretation of Dreams in the Ancient Near East* (Philadelphia: American Philosophical Society, 1956), 177–353; for the biblical context, see Maren Niehoff, "A Dream which is not Interpreted is like a Letter which is not Read," *Journal of Jewish Studies*, 43 (1992), 73.

[88] For a wider discussion of the Hellenistic context of rabbinic dream interpretation, see Philip Alexander, "Quid Athenis et Hierosolymis? Rabbinic Midrash and Hermeneutics in the Graeco-Roman World," in Philip Davies and Richard White (eds.), *A Tribute to Géza Vermès: Essays on Jewish and Christian Literature and History* (Sheffield: Sheffield Academic Press, 1990), 117; Sandor Lorand, "L'interprétation des rêves selon le Talmud," *Revue d'histoire de la médecine hébraïque*, 9 (1957), 70; Richard Kalmin, *Sages, Stories, Authors and Editors in Rabbinic Babylonia*, 73 f. Concerning dreams among "Hellenistic" Jews, see also Frances Flannery-Dailey, *Dreamers, Scribes, and Priests: Jewish Dreams in the Hellenistic and Roman Eras* (Leiden: Brill, 2004). An interesting cultural comparison could be made with early Christian approaches to dreams; see, for example, Bart J. Koet, *Dreams and Scripture in Luke-Acts: Collected Essays* (Leuven: Peeters, 2006).

[89] Kalmin points to the Christian Roman government's condemnation of divination through dreams shortly after the Edict of Milan (*Sages, Stories, Authors and Editors in Rabbinic Babylonia*, 78). He tentatively suggests that while the earlier Palestinian rabbis had a positive attitude towards professional dream interpreters, the later Palestinian rabbis developed a negative stance, possibly reflecting the change in Christian attitude. Afik also recognizes the influence of "the Roman authorities' attitude towards dreams" on the story (*Hazal's Perception of Dreams*, IX). My reading of the Yerushalmi dream book indeed hints at some Roman influence on the rabbis, as Kalmin and Afik suggest, but with different implications. While a discussion of the evidence is not possible here, it is clear that the tannaim had an overwhelmingly negative attitude toward dream interpretation, which might very well have been influenced by Roman attempts to suppress the practice. The Palestinian rabbis in the fourth and fifth centuries, however, emphatically *confirmed* the role of the professional dream interpreter. The Christian church's and Christianizing Roman government's new and vigorous attacks on private professional dream interpreters may have inspired the Yerushalmi dream book's *support* of this rabbinic practice. On the other hand, clandestine as well as strictly regulated "orthodox" dream interpretation flourished in the Byzantine Empire. Thus, a more nuanced contextualization of the rabbinic attitudes remains a desideratum. Concerning the Christian prohibition and the flourishing of dream interpretation in the Byzantine Empire despite the governmental efforts, see Mark Holowchak, *Ancient Science and Dreams: Oneirology in Greco-Roman Antiquity* (Lanham: University Press of America, 2002), Steven M. Oberhelman, *Dreambooks in Byzantium*, 50; and Steven F. Kruger, *Dreaming in the Middle Ages*, 7–13. See also notes 69 and 70 above.

"[The Rabbi's] maturity and his interpretive skills enable him not only to interpret the dream image in more sophisticated terms ... but also to extract from the seemingly catastrophic image the growth latent in destruction ... The students are incapable of this, and hence their tragic mistake."[90]

The rabbinic students, even if they do not realize it, have mantic powers, and their interpretation bears consequences. Like the sorcerer's apprentice, they seem not yet fully aware of their own power; in any case, they cannot wield it properly. They interpret the dream unfavorably instead of following in the footsteps of their rabbi. Hence, the story encourages the rabbinic dream interpreter to predict, and thus bring about, a beneficial future, and the Yerushalmi shows keen awareness of the potentially destructive result of inept dream interpretation.

Although the Bar Hedya story imitates most aspects of the Rabbi Eliezer story, it portrays Bar Hedya as ignoring the Yerushalmi's implicit instructions to protect the dreamer. Moreover, the interpretations that Bar Hedya offers Abaye and Rava recall the ones that Rabbi Eliezer *and* his students, respectively, offer the woman. The Bavli ironically conflates into one person the precise contrasting juxtaposition the Yerushalmi engenders by contrasting the actions of the rabbi to those of the students. In subsection II, Bar Hedya predicts that Abaye will have numerous children, tantamount to Rabbi Eliezer's prediction of the birth of a son.[91] Bar Hedya then predicts the death of Rava's "house" (using the Hebrew synonym "ביתהו" for wife), recalling the students' prediction of the death of the dreamer's spouse while the death of Rava's children constitutes an inversion of Rabbi Eliezer's prediction of the birth of a son.[92] The Bar Hedya story assigns one of the woman's dreams and its interpretation to Abaye and the other set to Rava, heightening the tension between the opposing outcomes even more than in the Yerushalmi. At the same time, the story emphasizes the death of Rava's wife as its central structural element and as the primary reason for Bar Hedya's execution.

In addition to the predictions of Rabbi Eliezer and his students, the Bar Hedya story also imitates the woman's dream. First, Rava dreams that his "outer doorway" falls, recalling the falling of the beam (also an architectural feature) in the woman's dream.[93] In subsection V, the Bar Hedya story imitates and expands the image of the breaking beam in three consecutive

---

[90] Hasan-Rokem, *Web of Life: Folklore and Midrash in Rabbinic Literature* (Stanford: Stanford University Press 2000), 104 f., discussing the Yerushalmi's parallel in *Ekha Rabbah* (Buber) 1.1 (=1.18).

[91] II.2 and II.3.

[92] II.3 and IV.2.

[93] IV.1, "דשא ברייתא דנפל," "דשא ברייתא" according to the Vilna print. Bar Hedya, like the students in the Yerushalmi dream book, explains that the collapse of a built structure indicates the death of the dreamer's spouse. Some of the manuscripts include the Yerushalmi's image of

dream images relating to the destruction of buildings:[94] a breaking wall, the falling of Abaye's house, and the collapse of Rava's mansion. (The Bavli uses the Yerushalmi's verb, "תבר", and transposes the meaning of "בית," "house," from the woman's dream image to the victim of the interpretation of Rava's dream, his wife.) The fact that Rava now occupies the place of the powerless woman seems by no means accidental. Reminiscent of his fate in *Bava Metsi'a* 97a, Rava is called upon to assert the Bavli's view of his "masculine" role. He does so by cursing Bar Hedya precisely for causing the death of his wife, recalling the mistake committed by Eliezer's students.[95]

The imitation of Rabbi Eliezer and his students serves the purposes of the Bar Hedya story. Just as in the case of Rabbi Ishmael, Bar Hedya ironizes the Yerushalmi story about Rabbi Eliezer and his students. Rabbi Eliezer himself fares well from the perspective of the Bar Hedya story: he does not demand money, and he reproaches his students for the death of the dreamer's spouse. His death is deemed accidental, and the students' ignorance stands in stark contrast to Bar Hedya's premeditated brutality, which is enabled by his rabbinic knowledge, not the lack thereof. Presenting Bar Hedya as a perverted imitation of Rabbi Eliezer and his students allows the story to highlight Bar Hedya's wickedness satirically. At the same time, the story's precise imitation of Rabbi Ishmael and Rabbi Eliezer and his students leaves little room for doubt that the text the Bavli repeats with a difference is the Yerushalmi's dream book.

In a similar way, the Bar Hedya story imitates other aspects of the Yerushalmi's dream book. For instance, Bar Hedya's favorable interpretation of Rava's three consecutive dream images recalls Rabbi Aqiva, who similarly provides favorable interpretations of three seemingly disastrous dream images. (Both the Yerushalmi and the Bavli use the word "ניסין / ניסא," playing on its double meaning of "miracle" and "Nisan."[96]) Rabbi

---

a beam "breaking" (מיתברא) in a "house" (ביתא). Oxford 366 (fol. Add. 23) reads "א'ל חזאי דביתא דנפל ואיתבר," and Ms. Paris 671,"א'ל חזאי דשא דביתא דנפל ואיתבר דביתא דאיתבר ונפל,".

[94] V.1–3.

[95] The differences in gender relations between the stories in the Yerushalmi and the Bavli points to another possible underlying cultural distinction between the two rabbinic communities. In the Yerushalmi's dream book, the dreaming woman is portrayed as constantly being under male domination: she is the bearer of a son and the spouse of a husband, and she is completely dependent upon males, the rabbi and his students. The Bar Hedya story replaces the woman with Rava, whose position is even more passive and subordinate toward Bar Hedya. In the Bavli, Rava regains agency the moment he recognizes the effects of the Palestinian doctrine and finally avenges the death of his wife. The Bavli, even if in the end it remains within the bounds of traditional gender roles, can apparently play with them more freely than the Yerushalmi.

[96] Talmud Yerushalmi *Ma'aser Sheni*, Ms. Leiden, 4:9.16 (55c), cited in Schäfer, *Synopse*, 278–79. Rabbi Aqiva's student dreams that he will die during the month of Adar, not see the month of Nisan, and not reap what he had sown (זרע). Rabbi Aqiva reinterprets the names of the months; he suggests that the word Adar is similar to the word "בהדרא," that

Aqiva, of course, does not demand payment whereas Bar Hedya's favorable interpretations are the result of Rava's eventual payment. While Bar Hedya's actions seem partially modeled after Aqiva, the Bar Hedya story does not criticize the Rabbi Aqiva passage. Instead, Rabbi Aqiva's moral integrity only highlights Bar Hedya's corruption.

Furthermore, Rabbi Ishmael's father, Rabbi Yose ben Halafta, offers different interpretations to two dreamers reporting the same dream: one will prosper while the other will receive lashes.[97] Even though the dreams seemed identical to the dreamers, Rabbi Yose finds a subtle difference. The Rabbi Yose story invokes the interpretations of Yose's biblical namesake, Joseph, and the biblical evidence for the validity of the Palestinian doctrine.[98] This narrative in the Yerushalmi provides the model for subsections I, II, and III of the Bar Hedya story, in which identical dreams receive antithetical interpretations.[99] The imitation, once more, exposes Bar Hedya's perversion: Yose identifies a subtle difference between the dreams whereas Bar Hedya arbitrarily provides antithetical contradictory interpretations of identical dreams.

The Bar Hedya story imitates almost the entirety of the Yerushalmi's dream book, in the process satirizing the excess associated with professional dream interpretation. This excess, according to the Bavli, results from the combination between the liberties granted by the Palestinian doctrine (evident in the imitation of Rabbi Eliezer) and professional dream interpreters' demand for compensation (evident in the imitation of Rabbi Ishmael). The Yerushalmi's dream book begins to scrutinize the implications of its own doctrine by considering ignorant dream interpreters, such as Rabbi Eliezer's students, but it never considers the doctrine in conjunction with remunera-

---

is, the "splendor" of the student's future Torah book, understands Nisan as the miracles (ניסין) that the student will not require, and explains that the student will "sow" children but not "reap" them because they will live longer than he will. Rava's three dreams about collapsing buildings are structurally similar to this narrative: both turn disastrous images into splendid outcomes, proving that Bar Hedya is capable of turning the disastrous into the beneficial. Also, Rabbi Aqiva's logic in reinterpreting the word Nisan indicates that the need for a miracle is a sign of a preexisting danger, precisely the same logic that leads Bar Hedya to conclude that Rava will require a miracle in subsection V. Rava recites the Egyptian Hallel, which is read during Passover, that is, during the month of Nisan.

[97] Talmud Yerushalmi, *Ma'aser Sheni*, Ms. Leiden, 4:9.8 (55b), cited in Schäfer, *Synopse*, 276–77.

[98] The two officials in the Joseph story also have similar dreams about items held above one's head, like the crown of olives in the dream interpreted by Rabbi Yose. Additionally, both of them are "elevated," one becoming prosperous while the other is hanged on a tree.

[99] More specifically, Yose's interpretation may be the model for Abaye's "elevation" to the position of head of academy and for the blind men striking Rava, but these interpretations are not derived from the same dream. (Abaye becomes the head of the academy in II.7, where us the blind men strike Rava in IV.4.) The two stories also share the image of the olives (both the Yerushalmi and the Bavli, in II.6, use the word "זיתים").

tion, nor does it address the possibility of the existence of villains like Bar Hedya, who would have destabilized the Yerushalmi's ideals.

As is the case with all the parodies discussed in this book, the focus of the parody's satire lies not in the distant past (in this case, in Palestine) but in Babylonian rabbinic circles. It should be noted that the dream book deserves to be parodied especially, and perhaps solely, since it informs aspects of the Babylonian rabbinic dream culture, the conduct of Babylonian dream interpreters, and most importantly, Rava's views concerning the Palestinian doctrine. I conclude this chapter with a discussion of the Babylonian context of the Bar Hedya story which will lead us to the interface between the parody and its satirical aspects.

Bar Hedya and the Bavli's Dream Book

The Babylonian "dream book" is in fact a passage included in a sugya in tractate *Berakhot* (55a–57b). Much like the Yerushalmi's dream book, but significantly longer, this passage is a detailed deliberation on the nature and meaning of dreams.[100] The Bar Hedya story is included in this dream book, which thus serves as the story's literary context. The Bavli's dream book discusses the Palestinian doctrine on one other occasion. In a sequence immediately preceding the Bar Hedya story, partially cited earlier, the rabbi who struggles most with the doctrine is none other than Rava (*Berakhot* 55b). The passage reveals Rava as a satirical target of the Bar Hedya story.[101] It begins with a general statement about the mantic power of dreams:

Shmuel, when he saw a bad [בישא] dream [image], said "'Dreams speak in vain [השוא]'" [Zechariah 10:2].
When he had a good [טבא] dream [image], he said [interpreting the same verse as a question]: "'do dreams really [כי] speak in vain?',
for it is written, 'in a dream, I will speak to him'" [Numbers 12:6].

---

[100] Concerning the Bavli's dream book, see Kalmin, *Sages, Stories, Authors and Editors in Rabbinic Babylonia*, 61–80; Alexander, "Bavli Berakhot 55a–57b: The Talmudic Dreambook in Context;" Afik, *Hazal's Perception of Dreams*, and Weiss, מעמדו ותפקידו של החלום בספרות חז״ל.

[101] As Kalmin convincingly argues, the text does not allow us to decide whether this Rava is Abaye's teacher "Rava" (commonly transcribed as "Rabbah") or "Rava," Rav Hisda's son-in-law, the main character in the Bar Hedya story (see note 28 above). Yet, this is an ambiguity that the author of the Bar Hedya story might have faced as well. Because of the proximity between the subsequent passage and the Bar Hedya story, I am inclined to believe that the author of the story, or at least the dream book's final redactor, understood the passages about "Rava" to be referring to the protagonist of our story, Bar Hisda's son-in-law.

Rava raised a difficulty: "It is written 'in a dream I will speak to him,' and it is written 'dreams speak in vain.'"
This is not a paradox: here, through an angel, and there, through a demon.

Shmuel uses the Bible to theorize dreams in general. He makes deliberately playful use of the polysemy of the Bible and cites an ambivalent prooftext for both the acceptance of a good dream and the dismissal of a bad one. He seems to believe in the mantic power of dreams. Bad dreams ought to be regarded as vain in order avoid their realization. In the case of a good dream, however, Shmuel provides a different interpretation for the same verse from Zechariah. Shmuel now suggests that the word "כי" should not be understood according to the original context in Zechariah but rather as a question that anticipates a negative answer: no, dreams do not speak in vain. He also introduces a second, seemingly less ambiguous prooftext (Numbers 12:6) for the validity of favorable dreams, stating explicitly that God speaks to His prophets in their dreams.[102] Since rabbis must be able to harmonize scriptural passages, the verse from Zechariah needs to be read as a question. The passage illustrates the inclination of the Bavli's dream book, as already noted by Kalmin, to favor favorable interpretations, and it allows the dreamer to choose an appropriate biblical verse.[103]

But Rava does not accept this solution. He points out that the tension between the two prooftexts persists. The author of the sugya resolves Rava's objection with a reference to the duality of dreams, arguing that they can be either angelic or demonic – powers very familiar to the audience of the Bavli. This solution implies that all bad dreams originate in demons, all good ones in angels, and that one should disregard all bad dreams and embrace positive ones, or at least interpret bad dreams favorably – the attitude that characterizes the Bavli's dream book in general.

---

[102] The scriptural context of Numbers 12:6 reveals that God speaks to Moses directly but to other prophets *only* through dreams; hence, the Bavli indicates that dreams are both true and a secondary level of revelation.

[103] Kalmin states that "according to the Bavli, Amoraim (both Palestinian and Babylonian), are distinguishable from Tannaim in that Amoraim tend to minimize the force of negative dream interpretations found in earlier sources, and Amoraim tend more than Tannaim to interpret dreams positively. These differences are very likely motivated by the forces which led to differing rabbinic attitudes toward professional dream interpreters, and which also motivated Amoraim to equip individuals to handle dreams on their own" (*Sages, Stories, Authors and Editors in Rabbinic Babylonia*, 73). Kalmin summarizes the Bavli's attitude correctly, but the Bavli's depiction of the Palestinian reality raises some questions. Despite a tendency in amoraic Palestinian dream culture to favor favorable dream interpretations, we saw that the Yerushalmi's dream book, an amoraic text, emphatically endorses professional dream interpreters who provide unfavorable interpretations when appropriate. Yet I agree with Kalmin that Babylonian Amoraim indeed tend to minimize the implications of unfavorable dream interpretation, to reject professional dream interpreters, and to ensure that individuals are able to interpret their own dreams favorably; see esp. Bavli *Berakhot* 56b.

Hence, the dream book describes Rava as being at odds with Shmuel's selective approach to dreams, a fact that might help illuminate the irony of his role in the Bar Hedya story. In the literary reality of the story, Rava accepts neither Shmuel's solution nor the sugya's response to his own challenge. Had Rava only known that he had the liberty to accept positive dreams and dismiss negative ones with a scriptural citation, he would not have consulted a dream interpreter at all and would have been able to avoid much suffering.

At the same time, Rava's emphasis on the mantic powers of dreams – essentially limiting the role of the interpreter – might explain more precisely the Bar Hedya story's motivation for satirizing him. Rava's possibly misguided insistence on the mantic powers of dreams might necessitate his harsh treatment at the hands of Bar Hedya, who becomes the story's tool in reforming Rava's unnecessary acceptance of unfavorable dream interpretation. Given the general tendency of the Bavli's dream book to favor positive interpretations, it becomes clear that the Bar Hedya story is not only an inter-rabbinic parody, imitating and ironizing Rabbi Ishmael and the Palestinian dream book, but also an intra-rabbinic satire of Rava.

The immediate sequel to Rava's response to Shmuel's position allows for an even more precise contextualization of Rava's satirical function in the Bar Hedya story. Rava here explicitly seeks to qualify the Palestinian doctrine:

[Hebrew] R. Bizna bar Zabda said
reporting R. [ר'א] Aqiva
reporting of R. Panda
reporting of R. Nahum
reporting of R. Biryam
in the name of [משום] a certain elder (and who was this? R. Bana'ah):
"Twenty four dream interpreters were in Jerusalem,
and once I dreamed a dream and went to all of them,
and what this one interpreted for me was not what that one interpreted for me,
and [still] it all came true for me,
to prove that which is said [שנאמר]: 'All dreams follow the mouth' [כל החלומות הולכים אחר הפה]."
[Aramaic] Is 'All dreams follow the mouth' scriptural?
Yes, as Rabbi Eleazar said, for Rabbi Eleazar said: "Whence do we know that all dreams follow the mouth?
As it is said: '*since* he interpreted for us, so it was' (Genesis 41:13)."
Rava said: "This refers to a case where he interprets for him the essence of his dream [מעין חלמיה],[104]
As it is said: 'He gave an interpretation to each according to his dream' [איש כחלמו פתר, Genesis 41:12]!"

To reiterate, the passage associates the Palestinian doctrine with professional Palestinian dream interpreters, referring to them hyperbolically as twenty-

---

[104] Translation based on Sokoloff, *A Dictionary of Jewish Babylonian Aramaic*, 857.

four different interpretations. Reading the Bar Hedya story as a parody of the Yerushalmi's dream book and as a satire of Rava, R. Bizna's report now becomes apposite. The imposing length of the list of authorities cited by R. Bizna is remarkable. Even though it is not the only such list in the Bavli, it is surprising that the report is eventually attributed to an anonymous source, a *reductio ad absurdum* indeed.[105] Moreover, three of the listing six rabbis are mentioned nowhere else while one of the three bears the name of a demon.[106] The odd name, much like Bar Hedya's avian name, suggests that the character might be less than sacrosanct.

The Bavli, however, discredits neither this report nor the Palestinian doctrine. On the contrary, it elevates the doctrine and introduces it with the solemn formulaic expression "as it is said," usually reserved for scriptural citations, but here used for a Baraita.[107] Again, such a blatant "error" does not seem accidental. Switching to Aramaic, the stam wonders whether the doctrine is indeed scriptural as the introductory formula suggests. His answer to his own question cites Rabbi Eleazar's formulation of the doctrine based on the Joseph story in Genesis 40. The Bavli might be implying that even though the statement itself is not a verbatim repetition of Scripture, its message certainly is.[108] In the Yerushalmi dream book, Rabbi Eliezer

---

[105] Anonymous reports as such are very common in the Bavli. Citations that attribute a saying to "a certain elder," however, usually contain only one other authority, not a long list (see, e.g., *Gittin* 72b and 73b, *Baba Qamma* 71a and 72a, and *Hulin* 50a). In contrast, a similar long list that ends with a "certain [anonymous] elder" appears, to the best of my knowledge, only once in the entire Bavli (*Hulin* 50a). Intriguingly, this list of six tradents also includes R. Nahum and a certain R. Birayim (בריים), whose name recalls R. Biryam (בירים). The citation in *Hulin*, moreover, is discredited, thereby raising doubts over R. Bizna's story here as well. Such lists, also known as *isnad*, become crucial in early Muslim culture. It is noteworthy telling that some of the tradents of Jewish traditions (*isra'iliyat*) were defamed by a few Muslim commentators as a "chain of falsehood" (*silsalat al-kadhib*, see Ignaz Goldziher, *Muslim Studies* (Oxford: Oxford University Press, 1971), 228 note 2 and Gordon Darnell Newby, "Tafsir Isra'iliyyat," in: Alford T. Welch (ed.), *Studies in Qur'an and Tafsir* (*Journal of the American Academy of Religion Thematic Studies* 57 no 4, 1979), 688f). Similarly, it is quite possible that the Bavli here at least ironizes its own chain of tradition.

[106] The figure of Rabbi Panda appears only here while a demon by the name of *Panda* appears in *Shabbat* 67a. This is the only appearance of the figure of R. Bizna as well while several rabbis bear the name of "son of Bizna (ביזנא)"; see for example *Berakhot* 3b and 7a, *Bava Metsi'a* 59a; Yerushalmi *Sheqalim* 8:4.4 (51b (only in Ms. London and the Amsterdam print; all others read (ביסן/ביסנא); *Bava Qamma* 5:9.3 (5a); and *Bereshit Rabbah* 56.7. R. Biriyam appears only here; on a rabbi with a similar name, see the previous note.

[107] See Bacher, *Die exegetische Terminologie der jüdischen Traditionsliteratur: Teil 1, Die Bibelexegetische Terminologie der Tannaiten* (Leipzig: J.C. Hinrichs, 1899), 6.

[108] Kalmin's conjecture that the formula is intended to refer to a dream manual rather than to the Bible is pertinent only to an earlier layer of the Talmud. In its present form, the formula seems to be an explicit reference to the biblical source of the doctrine, not to a dream manual. See Richard Kalmin, *Sages, Stories, Authors and Editors in Rabbinic Babylonia*, 70.

derives the Palestinian doctrine from Genesis 40; in the Bavli, Rabbi Eleazar invokes the same verse. The confusion between Eliezer and Eleazar is
common in rabbinic literature. Moreover, in the parallel of the Yerushalmi
dream book in *Ekha Rabbah*, Rabbi Eleazar is the protagonist.

The Bavli, hence, explicitly repeats the Yerushalmi's Palestinian doctrine
immediately before the Bar Hedya story. While the Yerushalmi states that "a
dream fulfills itself according to its interpretation" (שאין החלום הולך אלא אחר
פתרונו), the Bavli states that "all dreams follow the mouth" (כל החלומות הולכים
אחר הפה). The shift from "interpretation" to "mouth," in light of the Bar
Hedya story and the odd list of cited authorities, suggests a further ironization of the Palestinian doctrine. The "mouth" is not constrained by exegetical practices in the way that "interpretation" is. The Babylonian tradition
presents the doctrine as giving even more freedom to the interpreter than
the Palestinian tradition, setting the stage for the hyperbolic enactment of
the dangers associated with the Palestinian doctrine in the Bar Hedya story.

The Bavli's audience, hence, is familiar with the doctrine and with its
Palestinian provenance. Furthermore, the passage's preceding report about
the dream interpreters in Jerusalem suggests that the Babylonian rabbis associated this doctrine with Palestinian professional dream interpreters – as
does the Bar Hedya story, in which a visitor to Palestine is the professional
dream interpreter.

The Bar Hedya story satirizes Rava's dream theory, as becomes clear from
Rava's objection to the sequel of the passage just discussed:

Rava said: "This refers to a case where he interprets for him the essence of his dream
[מעין חלמיה],
As it is said: 'He gave an interpretation for each according to his dream' [איש כחלמו
פתר, Genesis 41:12]!"

Rava limits the Palestinian doctrine and its reliance on Joseph's interpretation to specific aspects of a dream, thereby protesting against granting
dream interpreters complete freedom. Rava points out that Joseph's interpretations followed the dream closely, literarily, that it was "similar to" the
dream, seemingly implying that this made the interpretations come true.
Hence, the Bavli's dream book links Joseph's dream interpretations not only
to the Palestinian doctrine but also to Rava's view on dreams.

Rava revisits the Palestinian interpretation of Genesis 41 and states that
the dream is the source of its mantic power while the interpretation merely
reveals it. Rava does not contradict the Palestinian doctrine explicitly. Yet
according to the Bavli dream book, Rava repeatedly diminishes the doctrine's implications and affirms the independent power of the dream images
themselves. The dream book's author seems to find Rava's stance problematic. The Palestinian doctrine, the author seems to argue throughout the

Bar Hedya story, could be true, a fact that should make dreamers wary of unfavorable dream interpretations in general and professional dream interpreters in particular. The Bar Hedya story satirizes those who do not heed its warnings.

Rava takes issue with the Palestinian doctrine, and his portrayal in the Bar Hedya story satirizes his views. The story, for its own purposes, disregards the fact that Rava seems to be aware of the doctrine and satirizes his emphasis on the power of dreams. Rava, who should know better, is made an exemplary victim. When Rava brings about the death of the dream interpreter, Bar Hedya's corruption and Rava's naïveté cancel one another out in Rava's late insight and Bar Hedya's death, and the dream book continues its explanation of rabbinic dream interpretation as if nothing, or almost nothing, had happened. This inter-rabbinic parody of Palestinian rabbinic Judaism simultaneously satirizes intra-rabbinic affairs in Babylonia.

While Rava is an obvious target of the story's satire, it is impossible to know whether contemporary dream interpreters were also targets. Richard Kalmin raises the question concerning the intended target:

We can be reasonably certain that the story's message is not: Go to a dream interpreter, but make sure to pay the fee. I reject this understanding because no one emerges from their encounter with Bar Hedya unscathed, including Abaye, who pays the fee at the outset ... The story ... involves (Babylonian) Amoraim and polemicizes against a professional dream interpreter. It is unclear, however, whether the story polemicizes against professional dream interpreters in general, or only against especially corrupt individuals who cynically use their power for personal gain.[109]

In light of my reading of the Bar Hedya story as a parody of the Yerushalmi dream book, the Bar Hedya story shows that professional rabbinic dream interpreters operating within the framework of the Palestinian doctrine are always prone to misuse their power cynically and become corrupt. The abusers of power as well as their victims are the targets of the story's satirical elements. Whether they existed and the extent of their activity and influence, of course, will probably remain a mystery, but in any case, the story in the Bavli renders them entirely unnecessary for any wise rabbi seeking to engage in the dream interpretation.

---

[109] Kalmin, *Sages, Stories, Authors and Editors in Rabbinic Babylonia*, 69.

CHAPTER FOUR

Margin of Error:
A Babylonian Parody of the Sermon on the Mount
(Shabbat 116a–b)*

> I did not come to reduce (למיפחת) the Torah of Moses
> and not to add (לאוספי) to the Torah of Moses did I come
> – *Shabbat* 116a

> The horse-leech has two daughters:
> "Give, give" (Proverbs 30.15)
> What is "Give, give"?
> Rav Hisda said in the name of Mar 'Ukba:
> It is the voice of two daughters who shout
> from Gehenom to this world: "Bring, bring."
> Who are they? Heresy and the government.
> – *Avodah Zarah* 17a

The previous chapters focused on intra-rabbinic parody (imitating and satirizing Rava and his students and the temperance sermon) and a Babylonian
inter-rabbinic parody (imitating the Yerushalmi dream book in order to satirize Rava). In the final two chapters and in the conclusion, I discuss external parodies: Babylonian and Palestinian rabbinic parodies of non-rabbinic
texts. Given their temporal and cultural proximity to the rabbis, the Christian foundational texts and their patristic Greek and Syriac interpretations
are the most obvious external targets of rabbinic satire. Christian supersessionism, the belief that Christianity and the "New Testament" took the place
of Judaism and the "Old Testament," may have sufficiently troubled the
rabbis and led them towards parody and satire of Christian texts. Rabbinic
authors were familiar enough with Christian scriptural reasoning to be able
to parody Christian exegesis as well.[1] I argue that rabbinic exegetical paro-

---

* A preliminary version of this chapter was published as "Margin of Error: Women,
Law, and Christianity in Bavli *Shabbat* 116a–b," in Eduard Iricinschi and Holger Zellentin
(eds.), *Heresy and Identity in Late Antiquity* (Tübingen: Mohr Siebeck, 2008), 339–363.

[1] On the question of whether Christianity played a central role for the rabbis, see
note 72 in the Introduction and Chapter Five. In the following, I argue that "Christianity"
should indeed be regarded as an always already established reference in rabbinic discourse,
prone to parody or parodic allusion at any given moment. At the same time, I hold that the
rabbis had no one clear notion of Christianity, and that Christianity became troubling to

dies imitate New Testament texts in order to satirize these texts' patristic and popular interpretations. At the same time, these external parodies focus on the imminent danger from within: the "Christian" tendencies within the rabbinic communities. The first example I consider is the Babylonian story of Imma Shalom (Bavli *Shabbat* 116a–b); the Palestinian rabbis' view of Christianity will be discussed in the final chapter and in the Conclusion.

Rabbis and Christians

Suggesting that the rabbis parodied Christian texts presupposes rabbinic familiarity with them, which, as mentioned in the Introduction, remains a contentious topic. If the scholarly community is moving towards a consensus that the redactors of the Bavli were aware of Christianity and familiar with parts of the Christian corpus of literature, it is moving slowly. This reluctance, in my view, is a result of the rabbis' choice to refer to Christianity indirectly; that is, it is a reluctance based on literary analysis. Only rarely does the Bavli name Jesus, the Gospels, and Christianity explicitly. The name "Jesus," appears no more than a handful of times (in its rabbinic abbreviation *Yeshu*); the only mention of the word Gospel (i.e., "Evangel") appears in the passage discussed below, and Christianity is referred to through a number of cumbersome code words (such as *minut*, or "heresy"). These terms shift in meaning and at times may allude to Christianity, though they never shed their original meaning entirely.[2]

Despite the scarcity of explicit rabbinic references to Christianity, there is a growing body of evidence that rabbis took issue with many topoi of Christian culture. The most relevant studies (though certainly not uncontested) for my purposes are Burton Visotzky's work on the rabbinic dialogue with patristic material, Israel Yuval's argument for Jewish and Christian counter-narratives in Late Antiquity, Peter Schäfer's study of Jesus in the Talmud, and Daniel Boyarin's discussion of the mutual polarization of the two communities.[3] Moreover, there are telling indicators that the rabbis

---

them insofar as people of political power or within the rabbinic community sympathized with Christian thought.

[2] Concerning *minut*, see note 10 in Chapter Five. A discussion of the rabbinic use of code words remains a desideratum, and the issue is highly contentious.

[3] See Burton Visotzky, *Fathers of the World: Essays in Rabbinic and Patristic Literature* (Tübingen: Mohr Siebeck, 1995) and *Golden Bells and Pomegranates: Studies in Midrash Leviticus Rabbah* (Tübingen: Mohr Siebeck, 2003); Israel Yuval, *Two Nations in Your Womb: Perceptions of Jews and Christians in Late Antiquity and the Middle Ages* (Tel Aviv: Am Oved, 2000) [Hebrew]; Berkeley: University of California Press, 2006 [English]); Daniel Boyarin, *Border Lines: The Partition of Judeo-Christianity* (Philadelphia: University of Pennsylvania Press, 2004) and *Socrates and the Fat Rabbis* (Chicago:

were compelled increasingly to face Christians as Christianity proliferated in Palestine and Babylonia throughout Late Antiquity.

The political and cultural circumstances of the Babylonian rabbis may help explain their attitude towards Christianity. The Zoroastrian rulers of the Sasanian Empire accepted the Jewish community early on, and persecution was rare.[4] The Christianization of the Roman Empire actually established a natural alliance between the Sasanians and the rabbis against the common enemy. The vast and powerful Sasanian Empire proved a match for the Roman Empire already in pre-Constantinian times, and battles between the two empires were common between 240 and 390 CE.[5] The Christianization of the Roman Empire put Sasanian Christians, also a tolerated community in the Sasanian Empire, in an awkward position. Despite their Syriac background and the resulting tensions with Byzantine Christianity, these Christians now shared the religion of the Sasanian Empire's main enemy.[6] As most recently discussed by Peter Schäfer, this led the Sasanian rulers to persecute

---

University of Chicago Press, 2009); and Peter Schäfer, *Jesus in the Talmud* (Princeton: Princeton University Press, 2007). For an exhaustive (and dismissive) discussion of most of the relevant primary and secondary sources, cf. Johann Maier, *Jesus von Nazareth in der talmudischen Überlieferung* (Darmstadt: Wissenschaftliche Buchgesellschaft, 1978). For a perceptive review of Boyarin's *Border Lines*, see Ra'anan S. Boustan in *Jewish Quarterly Review* 96 (2006), 441–46; of Schäfer's *Jesus in the Talmud*, see Richard Kalmin, "Jesus in Sasanian Babylonia," *Jewish Quarterly Review* 99 (2009), 107–112 and Galit Hasan-Rokem, "Embarrassment and Riches," *Jewish Quarterly Review* 99 (2009), 113–119; on the problems of Maier's methodology, see Schäfer, *Jesus in the Talmud*, 5. See now also the important suggestion for interreligious debates in Sasanian Babylonia by Shai Secunda, "The Talmudic Bei Abedan and the Sasanian Attempt to "Recover" the Lost Avesta" (forthcoming). The institution of the *Bey Abedan* is mentioned in the immediate context of the Talmudic passage I shall discuss in this chapter.

[4] Looking back at a well-established presence of Judean settlers in Mesopotamia since at least the time of the first Exile, the Bavli famously comments on Isaiah 13:6: "*Bring my sons from far,*" R. Huna said; "These are the exiles in Babylon, whose minds are at ease like [the minds of] sons. *And My daughters from the ends of the earth*: These are the exiles in other lands, whose minds are not at ease like [the minds of] daughters" (*Menahot* 110a). Drawing on the image of gender inequality, the Bavli's parallel acknowledges the privileged status of the Babylonian rabbinic community. See Klaus Schippman, *Grundzüge der Geschichte des sasanidischen Reiches* (Darmstadt: Wissenschaftliche Buchgesellschaft, 1990); Geo Widengren, "The Status of the Jews in the Sasanian Empire," *Iranica Antiqua* (Leiden: Brill, 1961), I, 128; and Robert Brody, "Judaism in the Sasanian Empire: A Case Study in Religious Coexistence," in Shaul Shaked and Amnon Netzer (eds.), *Irano-Judaica II: Studies Relating to Jewish Contacts with Persian Culture Throughout the Ages* (Jerusalem: Ben-Zvi Institute, 1990), 52–62.

[5] See Engelbert Winter and Beate Dignas, *Rom und das Perserreich: Zwei Weltmächte zwischen Konfrontation und Koexistenz* (Berlin: Akademie Verlag, 2001).

[6] After the council of Chalcedon in 451, the cultural and linguistic differences between the Greek and Syriac churches led to an acknowledged schism. See Carl Laga, Joseph Munitiz, and Lucas van Rompay (eds.), *After Chalcedon: Studies in Theology and Church History Offered to Prof Albert Van Roey for his Seventieth Birthday* (Leuven: Departement Oriëntalistiek, 1985).

Christians throughout the fourth and early fifth centuries.[7] Only in the fifth century did the status of Christians begin to improve, and Christians were fully incorporated into the Sasanian Empire by the late sixth century.[8]

The Bavli's view of Christianity developed in this later period that began during the persecution of Christians up to the early fifth century, and continued through the Christians' rise to prominence in Sasanian Babylonia from the late fifth century onward.[9] Schäfer argues that given the often difficult situation of the Jews in Christian Palestine, Babylonia's Jewish population was not too troubled by the persecution of its Christian neighbors and at times defamed Christians publicly – perhaps as part of a general anti-Christian attitude in the Sasanian Empire.[10] Many of the Bavli's narratives about Christians likely originated in this period. We can only imagine how the growing political and intellectual influence of Christians in the Sasanian Empire in the late fifth and sixth centuries must have troubled the rabbis, likely leading to even fiercer polemics during the Bavli's redaction, the textual layer most accessible to modern readers.

Two recent studies have assembled evidence that the Bavli uses satire in its polemics against Christianity. Peter Schäfer shows that the Bavli's response to Christian Jesus narratives often contains elements of irony and parody.[11] Daniel Boyarin, moreover, discusses a lengthy rabbinic imitation and satire of the Christian Passion in the Bavli's *Avodah Zarah* 18a–b that is "close

---

[7] To quote Peter Schäfer, "The Christians became suspected of being disloyal to the [Sasanian] state and favoring the enemy, of being Rome's 'fifth column' in the midst of the Sasanian Empire. Large-scale persecutions of the Christians broke out, first under Shapur II (309–379), then under Yazdgard I (399–421), Bahram V (421–439), and Yazdgard II (439–457)" (*Jesus in the Talmud*, 117). See Sebastian Brock, "Christians in the Sasanian Empire: A Case of Divided Loyalties," *Studies in Church History* 18 (1982), 1–19, and Lucas van Rompay, "Impetuous Martyrs? The Situation of the Persian Christians in the Last Years of Yazdgard I (419–420)," in: M. Lamberigts and P. van Deun (eds.), *Martyrium in Multidisciplinary Perspective: Memorial Louis Reekmans* (Louvain: Leuven University Press, 1995), 363–375.

[8] See A. V. Williams, "Zoroastrians and Christians in Sassanian Iran," *Bulletin of the John Rylands University Library of Manchester* 78 (1996), 37–53.

[9] It is difficult to trace the development of Babylonian rabbinic culture before and during the fourth century since its entire literature was redacted in the Babylonian Talmud much later, primarily between the fifth and seventh centuries. See note 33 in the Introduction.

[10] See Schäfer's discussion of the Martyrdom of Mar Simon in *Jesus in the Talmud*, 118 ff. and Mgr. Sddai Scher and Abbé Périer, eds., *Chronique de Séert, Histoire Nestorienne Inédite* (Paris: Périer 1907), vol. I, 297.

[11] Schäfer, in *Jesus in the Talmud*, speaks about the Bavli's "parody" (23), its "wicked sense of humor" (33), and its "creative rereading" of a New Testament Passion narrative that "turns out to be a complete reversal of the New Testament's message" (74). He also states that "the rabbinic counternarrative about Jesus' punishment would then ironically invert his attack on the Pharisaic purity laws" (89).

enough to set up the parodic allusion."[12] Both studies provide enough evidence for the existence of Babylonian rabbinic parodies of Christianity, some details of which will be discussed below.

I hold that some Babylonian rabbis had first-hand or mediated familiarity with Christian foundational texts and their patristic or popular interpretations. Moreover, the keen rabbinic exegetes had an eye for tensions within Christian texts and between foundational texts and their interpretation. The Syriac church writers constantly read, translated, and edited the Gospels, turning these late first- or early second-century texts into documents of contemporary relevance for the rabbis throughout Late Antiquity; the importance of these ongoing adaptations for the purposes of the present discussion cannot be overemphasized.

The question remains: Which Christian texts, if any, were familiar to the rabbis? It is reasonable to conjecture that the rabbis were exposed at least to oral recitation and popular exegesis of the most central passages of the Christian Gospels. Oral recitation was the norm rather than the exception in Hellenistic culture, which accounts for direct or indirect rabbinic exposure to Christian preaching on the gospels both in Palestine and Babylonia. The Sermon on the Mount was one such text for the Syriac (and Greek) Christians, and its wide dissemination requires no proof beyond the exemplary patristic references discussed below.

I therefore assume that many rabbis occasionally heard snippets of the Sermon on the Mount in the marketplace, from their neighbors, or when walking by a Syriac, Aramaic, or Greek speaking church. The likelihood that the rabbis were exposed to oral versions of the gospel texts, however, does not entirely cancel the need for identifying an extant written text with which the rabbis were familiar. As the status of individual Gospels changed constantly throughout history, so did the oral recitations; in turn, the popular oral versions were then reflected in subsequent written renditions. Studying written sources is thus the closest approximation and an acceptable proxy for the Christian oral traditions with which the rabbis were surely familiar, even if generally only rudimentarily so.

Moreover, we cannot categorically exclude the possibility that some rabbis had occasional access to written Christian texts. In light of the rabbinic discussions concerning the physical handling of Gospel texts, briefly mentioned below, it in fact seems likely that some rabbis did have such access. This chapter, Chapter Five, and the Conclusion try to bridge the gap between the extant ancient Christian texts and the echoes of their oral renditions in rabbinic literature. I base my readings of the rabbinic responses to Christian texts on the most likely written Christian source to which the

---

[12] Daniel Boyarin, *Socrates and the Fat Rabbis*, 246–66.

rabbis might have had access, using it as the closest extant approximation of the oral Christian tradition.

As Peter Schäfer points out, the written collection of gospels that would have been directly or indirectly accessible to the rabbis of Babylonia (and in many cases also of Palestine) is Tatian's *Diatessaron*.[13] This gospel harmony, a pastiche of the four canonical gospels, was composed in Syriac, a dialect closely related to Babylonian Jewish Aramaic, and easily accessible to speakers of Palestinian Jewish Aramaic as well. While the Diatessaron's original Syriac is largely lost; the Syriac text is partially preserved in Ephrem's commentary on the text, and in a number of translations of various qualities. The Diatessaron, William Peterson reminds us, was for many centuries *the* Gospel for many of the Eastern Christians, while its existence is well attested in Late Antique Europe as well.[14] The Imma Shalom story in the Bavli imitates materials that originated in the Gospel of Matthew *and* the Gospel of Luke. Therefore, the Diatessaron or its popular or patristic interpretation might have been the textual sources used by the rabbinic author of the parody. Another possible source is the Peshitta, the Syriac translation of the four individual canonical Greek Gospels.[15] In many regions of the Sasanian Empire, the Peshitta began to replace the Diatessaron in the fifth century, but this process culminated in the subsequent century.[16] Given the relative textual stability of the wording of the canonical gospels throughout Late Antiquity, a degree of textual speculation and an accumulative approach in reconstructing the texts imitated by rabbinic gospel parody is warranted. Given that only quotations and translations of Tatian's Syriac Diatessaron are available to us, I quote relevant New Testament texts from the Peshitta but also refer to the structure of the Arabic translation of the Diatessaron[17] and to the original's most important commentator, Ephrem

---

[13] See *Jesus in the Talmud,* 122 f.

[14] See William L. Petersen, *Tatian's Diatessaron: Its Creation, Dissemination, Significance, & History in Scholarship,* (Leiden: Brill, 1994).

[15] All Peshitta passages are cited according to George Anton Kiraz, *Comparative Edition of the Syriac Gospels: Aligning the Sinaiticus, Curetonianus, Peshitta and Harklean Version* (Piscataway: Gorgias Press, 2004). I follow the simplified transliteration of *Hugoye: Journal of Syriac Studies*: ʾ b g d h w z ḥ t y k l m n s ʿ p ṣ q r š t.

[16] Schäfer finds that the rabbinic Jesus narratives draw on all four gospels and points to the prominence of the Gospel of John (*Jesus in the Talmud,* 123 f.). My own findings emphasize passages connected with Matthew's Sermon on the Mount and Luke's Sermon on the Plain, pointing to the Diatessaron, the one source that includes both Gospels.

[17] On the tradition of the Arabic Diatessaron see Sebastian Euringer, *Die Überlieferung der Arabischen Übersetzung des Diatessarons* (Freiburg im Breisgau; Herder, 1912); Georg Graf, *Geschichte der christlichen Arabischen Literatur,* (Vaticano: Biblioteca Apostolica Vaticana, 1944), vol. I, 150–55; and most recently John Granger Cook, "A note on Tatian's Diatessaron, Luke, and the Arabic Harmony," *Zeitschrift für antikes Christentum* 10 (2006), 462–471. Petersen points out the enduring importance of the Arabic translations as the only complete Eastern witness of the Diatessaron. While the language of many of

the Syrian (303–373), whose work dominated Syriac exegesis throughout the period during which the Bavli was produced.[18]

Corrupt Judges from Palestine to Babylonia

Like many stories in the Bavli, the story of Imma Shalom and the Philosopher, which I consider to be a gospel parody, is also based on an earlier Palestinian rabbinic narrative. The Bavli's satire of Christianity is artfully woven into its adaptation of an older rabbinic story concerning judges and bribery; the Bavli's partial (non-parodic) adaptation of the older rabbinic story guides my analysis. The discussion of the Bavli story ought to begin with a brief introduction of the Palestinian passage on which it is based, *Pesiqta de-Rav Kahana* 15.9 (*Ekha*, according to Ms. Oxford 151), which itself contemplates an even older rabbinic saying:

A story of a woman who honored the judge [with] a silver lampstand [מנורה אחת של כסף].
Her [male] adversary went and honored him with a golden foal [סייח של זהב].[19]
On the following day, she came and found her judgment reversed [הפוך].
She said to [the judge]: "Master, let my case shine forth [ינהר דיני] like that silver lamp."
He said to her: "What can I do for you since the foal overturned [וכפה] the lamp?"[20]

A woman bribes a judge with a lampstand, but her adversary bribes him with a more valuable item, a donkey. Even a bribe does not ensure a favora-

---

the Arabic readings seem to have been influenced by the Peshitta, the Arabic seems to preserve the original *sequence* of Tatian's work, which is of great value to my considerations below (see William L. Petersen, *Tatian's Diatessaron*, 133–38; and Tj. Baarda, "An Archaic Element in the Arabic Diatessaron?" *Novum Testamentum* 17 (1975), 151–55. My citation follows the *editio princeps* by P. Augustinus Ciasca, *Tatiani Evangeliorum Harmoniae Arabica* (Rome: S. C. De Propaganda Fide, 1888), and the translation by Hope W. Hogg, in Alexander Roberts and James Donaldson, *The Ante-Nicene Fathers: Translations of the Writings of the Fathers down to A.D.* 325, vol. IX (Grand Rapids: Eerdmans Publishers, 1996–2001 [1897]). The Arabic edition by A. S. Marmarji, *Diatessaron de Tatian* (Beyrouth: Imprimerie Catholique, 1935) is equally dated, as is the edition of the oldest western translation of the Diatessaron into Latin (Ernst Ranke, *Codex Fuldensis: Novum Testamentum Latine interprete Hieronymo* (Marburg; Leipzig: Sumtibus N. G. Elwerti Bibliopolae Academici, 1868), 21–165), which I both consulted.

[18] See Sebastian Brock, *The Luminous Eye: The Spiritual World Vision Of Saint Ephrem* (Kalamazoo: Cistercian Publications, 1992) and Christine Shepardson, *Anti-Judaism and Christian Orthodoxy: Ephrem's Hymns in Fourth-Century Syria* (Washington, D.C.: Catholic University of America Press, 2008).

[19] The term "סייח" can mean the foal of a donkey or of a horse. See Marcus Jastrow, *A Dictionary of the Targumim, The Talmud Babli and Yerushalmi, and the Midrashic Literature* (New York: Judaica Press, 1903), 978.

[20] Bernard Mandelbaum, *Pesikta deRab Kahana according to an Oxford Manuscript* (New York: The Jewish Theological Seminary of America, 1987), 260f. The *Pesiqta de-Rav Kahana* was edited in Palestine in the fourth- or fifth-century CE; see Günther Stemberger, *Introduction to Talmud and Midrash* (Edinburgh: T&T Clark, 1996), 316.

ble judgment because it can be surpassed by an adversary. The point is the judge's attempt to cover up his corrupt court with the help of a blatantly overt, though still cryptic, statement: "the foal overturned the lamp."

The passage's sequel in the *Pesiqta de-Rav Kahana* considers Isaiah's condemnation of bribery, and the story itself hints at the judiciary implications spelled out in Isaiah 51:3–4:

For G-d will comfort Zion; he will comfort all her ruins …
My instruction [תורתי] shall go out from me,
and I will enact my justice [משפט] as a light to the nations [לאור עמים].

Isaiah's parallel structure pairs the Torah with justice and "going out" with "light." The biblical Hebrew word משפט means both procedural and ethical justice in rabbinic Hebrew as well. Any rabbinic reader would likely recognize the woman's appeal ("let my case shine forth like that sliver lamp") as a reference to "justice" and "light" in the passage from Isaiah. The rabbinic story hence gestures at the Bible's promise of genuine justice.[21]

It should be noted that the same verse from Isaiah is alluded to in the Gospel of Matthew (5:16) where Jesus exclaims (according to the Peshitta's wording): "Let your light shine forth [*nnhr nwhrkwn*] before the people that they may see your good works and glorify your Father in heaven." The woman in the *Pesiqta de-Rav Kahana* uses the same expression to let her case, like a lamp, "shine forth." The fact that she is a corrupt plaintiff suggests that this might be a parodic allusion to the Gospel. However, as is typical of Palestinian rabbinic literature, this allusion remains far too vague and does not suffice to conclude that the *Pesiqta de-Rav Kahana*'s author intended this allusion to the Christian source. This vagueness is removed in the Bavli adaptation of the *Pesiqta de-Rav Kahana*.

Similar anecdotes appear in Greco-Roman literature as well, in which stories concerning judicial corruption are commonplace. For example, Petronius's *Satyricon* (3.14) condemns a judge, supposedly a Cynic philosopher, for considering justice to be "public merchandise," implying that the highest bidder receives a favorable judgment.[22] The *Pesiqta de-Rav Kahana*

---

[21] The anecdote in the *Pesiqta de-Rav Kahana*, in turn, adapts an even older tannaitic Palestinian saying. In *Sifre Balak* 15, an attempt to purchase the priesthood, paid in silver, is surpassed by a bid paid in gold, the ensuing moral being that "the donkey overturned the lamp." *Sifre Balak* 15 is the oldest among the story's other parallels, Yerushalmi *Yoma* 1:1.27 (38c) and *Wayiqra Rabbah* 21.9. In contrast with the *Pesiqta de-Rav Kahana*, the tannaitic saying does not include a lamp or a donkey as a bribe. The *Pesiqta de-Rav Kahana*'s incorporation of them into the plot seems like a later retelling that linked the intriguing image of the moral to the anecdote from *Sifre* itself. Wallach argues that the story developed based on a prior proverb even though he seems to have missed the only tannaitic version we have in *Sifre*; cf. Luitpold Wallach, "The Textual History of an Aramaic Proverb (Traces of the Ebionean Gospel)," *Journal of Biblical Literature* 60 (1941), 405 f.

[22] Concerning the cultural background of the Roman discourse on corruption, see

ought to be understood in the context of this cultural framework. Even if the rabbinic text is too elliptic to allow for its contextualization in the Greco-Roman tradition, we can safely assume that its audience quickly grasped the urgency of its message.

The same holds true for the story's image of the "overturned lamp." As Burton Visotzky notes, the expression was often understood as a polemical euphemism for sexual orgies in the Greco-Roman world, and perhaps the *Pesiqta de-Rav Kahana* implicitly draws a parallel between judicial and sexual corruption.[23] The story's use of the "overturned lamp" thus equates bribery with sexual debauchery and immorality in general, an exquisite realization of the metaphor, which turns the donkey into a prop and has sexual overtones given that the characters are of the opposite sex.

Visotzky shows that from the second century onwards, the euphemism of "overturning the lamp" developed into an expression specifically used by Jews and gentiles to accuse Christians of indulging in sexual orgies during worship.[24] During the *Pesiqta de-Rav Kahana*'s final redaction, there likely were Christian judges in Palestine. Still, even in light of this possible second allusion to Christianity in the *Pesiqta de-Rav Kahana*, we cannot be certain that the text parodically alludes to the Gospel or satirizes Christians. The story can be read as a composite complaint against jurisprudential and moral corruption in Roman Palestine; it would be equally effective against gentile, Christian, or Jewish judges. Nevertheless, a later Babylonian rabbinic author noted that he could effortlessly specify references to Christianity in the *Pesiqta de-Rav Kahana* story. His retelling of the story is discussed below.

Bribing a Philosopher

The Bavli (*Shabbat* 116a–b) recounts the *Pesiqta de-Rav Kahana*'s story about the corrupt judge in very similar terms, shifting the focus from corruption to Mesopotamian Christianity. The story here is part of a sugya concerning the status of the "margin" of or "blank space" (*gylywn*) in texts containing divine names. The sugya states in passing that the books of the

---

Ramsay MacMullen, *Corruption and the Decline of Rome* (New Haven: Yale University Press, 1988).

[23] See Burton L. Visotzky, "Overturning the Lamp," *Fathers of the World: Essays in Rabbinic and Patristic Literatures* (Tübingen: Mohr Siebeck, 1995), 75–84. Visotzky shows that the expression underwent several semantic shifts throughout Late Antiquity and provides overwhelming evidence that it refers to sexual and moral depravity.

[24] See Burton L. Visotzky, "Overturning the Lamp." For rabbis accusing Christians in general and Jesus in particular of sexual debauchery, see also Schäfer, *Jesus in the Talmud*, 33–40 and 97–102.

heretics are altogether like *glywnyn*, that is, like blank spaces, i.e. worthless. The discussion leads the Bavli to suggest a parodic mock etymology of the Christian gospel, spelled in Syriac the *'wnglywn*, as I shall soon argue.

The Bavli manuscripts include two versions of this story, both of which are presented in the quotation below. Version A retains more of the original plot found in the *Pesiqta de-Rav Kahana*, in which a man and a woman (the second generation tanna Rabban Gamliel II and his sister Imma Shalom) are engaged in a legal battle over their inheritance. The judge is referred to as a "philosopher," and Rabban Gamliel eventually exposes his corruption. Version B largely follows the same plot, but here the two Jewish siblings collaborate to incriminate the judge. The differences between the two versions are subtle, but they reveal a dramatic shift. The text in the left column below (Version A) is based only on the Sephardic Ms. Oxford 366 (add. Fol. 23). While Version A in its entirety is supported by only one manuscript, the most significant differences from the majority reading are supported by a crucial detail in Ms. Vatican 108 and by an addition in Ms. Munich 95, as I shall outline in detail. The majority reading (Version B) is presented in the right column, and the manuscript variants are italicized in both columns.

Version A	Version B
Rabbi Meir called it *'awen-gelayon* [און גליון]	Rabbi Meir called it *'awen-gelayon* [און גליון]
Rabbi Yohanan called it *'awon-gelayon* [עון גליון]	Rabbi Yohanan called it *'awon-gelayon* [עון גליון]
[1] Imma Shalom, Rabbi Eliezer's wife, was the sister of Rabban Gamliel.	[1] Imma Shalom, Rabbi Eliezer's wife, was the sister of Rabban Gamliel.
She had a legal dispute [דינא] *with her brother.*	*[missing]*
She went [אתאי] *to face him.*	*[missing]*
[2] And there was a certain philosopher in her neighborhood,	[2] And there was a certain philosopher in her neighborhood,
Who had the reputation of a judge who does not accept bribes.	Who had the reputation of a judge who does not accept bribes.
[3] One day, *[Rabban Gamliel]* wanted [בעי] to laugh at [the philosopher].	[3] One day, *they* wanted [בעו] to laugh at [the philosopher].
They went to [the philosopher].	They went to [the philosopher].
Imma Shalom brought [the philosopher] a golden lamp.	Imma Shalom brought [the philosopher] a golden lamp.
She said to him: "I want them to divide with me the estate of my [late] father."	She said to him: "I want them to divide with me the estate of my [late] father."[25]
[The philosopher] said: "Divide with her!"	[The philosopher] said: "Divide with her!"[26]

---

[25] Following Ms. Vatican 487.

[26] Following Ms. Vatican 487 and Ms. Munich 95. *With her* is missing in the Vilna and Soncino prints.

Version A	Version B
[4] *They* said [אמרו] to him: "It is written in the Torah that he gave us [בתורה דיהב לן]: 'If there is a son, the daughter does not inherit'"	[4] [*Rabban Gamliel,* אמר] said to him: "It is written in the Torah that he gave us [בתורה דיהב לן]: 'If there is a son, the daughter does not inherit.'
[5] [The philosopher] said: "From the day that you were exiled [גליתון] from your land, the Torah of Moses was taken away [איתנטלית] from you, and *the Torah of* the 'awon-gylayon [אוריתא דעון גיליון] was given, and it is written in it: 'Daughter and son inherit equally.'"	[5] [The philosopher] said: "From the day that you were exiled [גליתון] from your land, the Torah of Moses was taken away [איתנטלית] from you and *[missing]* the 'awon-gylayon [דעון גיליון] was given, and it is written in it: 'Daughter and son inherit equally.'"
[6] The next day [Rabban Gamliel] returned and brought him a Libyan donkey. As they came, [the Philosopher] said to them: "I went down to the end of the 'awon-gelayon, And it is written in it: 'I am the 'awon-gylayon [עון גיליון]; I did not come to reduce [למיפחת] the Torah of Moses and not to add [לאוספי] to the Torah of Moses did I come. And it is written in it: 'If there is a son, the daughter does not inherit.'"	[6] The next day [Rabban Gamliel] returned and brought him a Libyan donkey. As they came, [the Philosopher] said to them: "I went down to the end of the 'awon-gelayon, And it is written in it: 'I am the 'awon-gylayon [עון גיליון]; I did not come to reduce [למיפחת] the Torah of Moses and not to add [לאוספי] to the Torah of Moses did I come. And it is written in it: 'If there is a son, the daughter does not inherit.'"
[7] She said [to the philosopher]: "Let your light shine with the lamp [נהור נהוריך בשרגא] *Examine the judgment* [עיין בדינא]!"	[7] She said [to the philosopher]: "Let your light shine with the lamp [נהור נהוריך בשרגא] *[missing]*
[8] Rabban Gamliel said to him: "A donkey came and knocked down the lamp."	[8] Rabban Gamliel said to him: "A donkey came and knocked down the lamp."

The corrupt philosopher, like Petronius' cynic, has a good reputation, but he does not reject the bribes; he rules in favor of the highest bidder, just like in the Palestinian story retold here by the Bavli. The Bavli leaves the basic structure and message of the *Pesiqta de-Rav Kahana* story intact: two bribes (a lamp and a donkey), the woman's complaint (including the implicit reference to light and justice in Isaiah 51), and the judge's concealment of the truth with the help of the statement, "the donkey overturned the lamp," which is the punch line of the story. The Bavli, however, names the opponents, spells out the judge's reasoning, and transfers the final statement from the judge to the winning party (i.e., Rabban Gamliel), thus accusing the "philosopher" using the symbolic language from the Palestinian judge's shameless explanation of his actions.

Two Versions of Imma Shalom

There are only five differences between Versions A and B, but they are significant and relate to the Bavli's view of women and their role in religious conflicts.

– According to the Oxford manuscript alone, the story opens by stating that Imma Shalom and her brother are engaged in an actual lawsuit, and that Imma Shalom goes to face him.
– According to the second variant in Version A, it is only Rabban Gamliel alone who plans to "laugh at" the philosopher. In most other manuscripts, the two siblings plan to ridicule the philosopher together, pretending to be engaged in a legal dispute with one another.
– According to the third variant in Version A, both siblings point out to the judge that his first ruling, favoring Imma Shalom's request to receive part of the inheritance, violates Jewish law. In Version B, only Rabban Gamliel protests. The fact that in the Oxford manuscript Imma Shalom's legal meticulousness causes her to join her brother in pointing out the legal problem undermines her own case but gives her a more active role in the proceedings.[27]
– Imma Shalom's role is commensurate with the fourth variant in Version A, which depicts her as insisting on the value of her bribe once more, emphatically stating, "examine your judgment!"
– Finally, in Version A the judge calls the gospel *"the Torah of the 'awon-gylayon* (אורייתא דעון גיליון)," emphasizing more than Version B, which simply calls it *'awon-gylayon,* that his gospel replaces the Israelite Torah.

The two versions tell significantly different stories. Version A reports a legal dispute between Imma Shalom and Rabban Gamliel, who seeks to ridicule the judge, whereas Version B indicates that the two collaborate to expose the corrupt philosopher by inventing a legal dispute. It appears that the story underwent a momentous redaction, but based on the two versions themselves it cannot be determined if one constitutes an altered retelling of the other, and if so, which is which.

The evidence from the manuscripts is also not conclusive. On the one hand, the reading of Version B is the majority reading, and this might explain why Version A (based on the Oxford manuscript) has not been considered by modern scholars. On the other hand, manuscript Oxford 366, written in Sephardic square script and dating back to the thirteenth century,

---

[27] The identity of the speakers cannot be ascertained since anonymous bystanders could alternatively be the speakers at this moment; this, however, seems less likely, since the Bavli usually designates such groups (e.g. "the sages said ...").

is one of the oldest sources of tractate *Shabbat* and is generally considered to have been written with great care; errors are thus unlikely.[28]

The differences between the two versions, however, did not escape the attention of the medieval Talmudists. A note in the margin of Ms. Munich 95 is nearly identical to the language of the Oxford manuscript in indicating explicitly that the siblings indeed had a legal dispute.[29] The author of this note must have read Version A in a different manuscript. The version that includes the legal dispute, therefore, is indirectly yet indisputably attested in medieval times as well.

Finally, Ms. Vatican 108, also written in Sephardic square script and dating back to the thirteenth century, while following the majority reading otherwise, indicates that "he" (i.e., Rabban Gamliel alone) wanted to ridicule the philosopher (בעי, "he wanted") and does not follow the majority reading in which the two do so together (בעו, "they wanted").[30] The minute difference between *vav* and *yud* completely changes the narrative, and turns Imma Shalom into a corrupt and corrupting heretic. While scribal errors can never be ruled out entirely, the evidence in Ms. Vatican 108 makes clear that even in the majority reading there is only one indication that Imma Shalom was involved in her brother's scheme to ridicule the philosopher. The rest of the narrative gives no indication that an actual legal dispute did not occur, and the difference between versions A and B hinges on the length of one stroke. Hence, we cannot dismiss any of the two versions, but we can try to assess the likelihood that Version A is older, and more "original," than Version B.

If the "new" version was created by post-talmudic copyists, then Version A seems much more likely to be older than Version B for a number of reasons. The legal dispute in Version A is a sign of an intra-rabbinic struggle; eliminating the dispute and portraying the siblings as jointly confronting the (non-Jewish) judge would be desirable for any redactor striving for

---

[28] See Ad. Neubauer, *Catalogue of the Hebrew Manuscripts in the Bodleian Library and in the College Libraries of Oxford, Including Mss. in Other Languages, which Are Written with Hebrew Characters, or Relating to the Hebrew Language or Literature; and a Few Samaritan Mss.* (Oxford: Clarendon Press, 1886) and R. A. May, ed., *Catalogue of the Hebrew Manuscripts in the Bodleian Library; Supplement of Addenda and Corrigenda to Vol. I (A. Neubauer's Catalogue)*, compiled under the direction of Malachi Beit-Arié (Oxford: Clarendon Press, 1994); see also Michal Krupp, "The Manuscripts of the Babylonian Talmud," in Shmuel Safrai (ed.), *The Literature of the Sages, First Part: Oral Tora, Halakha, Mishna, Tosefta, Talmud, External Tractates* (Assen: Van Gorcum, 1987), 355.

[29] Ms. Munich 95, Folio 27, top. The addition, probably written in Paris in the fourteenth century, reads, "she had a legal dispute with Rabban Gamliel." The note does not add that "she went to face him." See William Rosenau, "Book Notices: Hermann L. Strack, *Babylonian Talmud according to the Munich Codex Hebraicus 95*," *AJSLL* 29 (1913), 304–306.

[30] Ms. Vatican 108, Folio 57, bottom. See Michael Krupp, "The Manuscripts of the Babylonian Talmud," 357.

rabbinic unity. Living during a period of profound change in the rabbinic community, under Muslim or Christian rule, could have prompted such a revision. The logical alternative (adding the legal dispute and insisting that Rabban Gamliel alone sought to ridicule the philosopher), by contrast, would undermine rabbinic unity,[31] rendering such an emendation unlikely in post-talmudic times and suggesting that the version from the Oxford manuscript is older.[32] It is just as well possible, however, that the two versions emerged from a heated discussion in the Beyt Midrash, which was the source of many variants in rabbinic narratives. I therefore discuss each version separately when appropriate.

My analysis illustrates how each version could have been understood by its rabbinic audience in Sasanian Babylonia in a time when the Byzantine Empire occupied the Land of Israel and posed both political and theological challenges to its Jewish population. It is unknown whether the story was composed in the period during which Christians were persecuted in the Sasanian Empire or afterwards, during Christians' rise to prominence in the Sasanian political system. Still, between the fourth and sixth centuries, Babylonian rabbis had ample reason to distance themselves from Christian law and theology (especially when such law and theology became attractive to Babylonian Jews).

The position of the "philosopher" concerning the implications of inheritance law for women is aligned with Christianity's view on this matter whereas Rabban Gamliel's position is representative of rabbinic Judaism. Imma Shalom stands in the middle. I conclude that in both versions the struggle between Imma Shalom and Rabban Gamliel would have led rabbinic audiences to reflect on the political realities of Sasanian Jewry and on their rulings concerning the inheritance rights of women under Jewish and Christian law. This is the case regardless of whether the story indicates that such a conflict occurred (Version A) or whether it merely invokes the possibility of such a conflict by staging it in order to mock the judge (Version B, in this latter case, the implied audience would consider the possibility of the conflict reasonable enough).

---

[31] If the story indeed was inspired by a version such as the one in the *Pesiqta de-Rav Kahana* (and the similarity between them suggests this), then a dispute between a man and a woman was part of the original story that could have been included in the Bavli's more original retelling of the Palestinian story.

[32] On the one hand, the addition in the margin of Ms. Munich 95 suggests that the siblings' lawsuit could have been added in medieval times. On the other hand, however, not all rabbinic editors amended texts according to their worldviews, and this addition probably occurred because another manuscript also included the dispute, the addition being almost identical to the language of Ms. Oxford 366 (fol. Add. 23). The manuscript evidence here is therefore inconclusive.

The main difference between the two versions ultimately lies in the portrayal of Imma Shalom. Is she advancing the position that rabbinic inheritance law is unjust? Is she seeking the help of a non-rabbinic judge, resulting in her defeat by Rabban Gamliel (A)? Or is she betraying her own financial interests in order to side with her brother (B)? In either case, her character is used to diffuse the tension caused by the Bavli's halakha concerning women, associating deviation on this matter with heresy.

The Context and the Actors

Immediately preceding the story of Imma Shalom in *Shabbat* 116a is the sugya's lively discussion of the status of books containing divine names, which leads to a consideration of the books of heretics, *minim*, and notably, of the Gospels as well and thereby to Gospel parody.[33] The discussion concludes with two pejorative puns linking the Hebrew word *gylayon*, "margin," or "blank space" with the Syriac word for "gospel." First, Rabbi Meir calls the gospel אָוֶן גִּלָּיוֹן. This corresponds directly to *'wnglywn*, the Syriac transliteration of the Greek word *euangelion*.[34] The Bavli, however, splits the Syriac word *'wnglywn* and, using the same consonants with a slight change in (implied) vocalization, reads it as *'awen gylayon*, which in mishnaic Hebrew means a margin or message of oppression, falsehood or vanity.[35] Rabbi Yohanan then distorts the name of the Gospel further, calling the text עָוֹן גִּלָּיוֹן, which should be read as *'awon gelayon*, meaning a

---

[33] The context in *Shabbat* 116a, a discussion based on Mishna *Yadayim* 3.5, Mishna *Shabbat* 16.1, and Tosefta *Yadayim* 2.13, is very ambiguous but indicates a generally negative attitude towards the heretical books. See Shamma Friedman, "The Holy Scriptures Defile the Hands – the Transformation of a Biblical Concept in Rabbinic Theology," in *Minhah le-Nahum: Biblical and other Studies Presented to Nahum M. Sarna in Honour of his 70th Birthday,* Marc Brettler and Michael Fishbane (eds.) (Sheffield: Journal for the Study of the Old Testament Press, 1993), 117–132; Sid (Shnayer) Z. Leiman, *The Canonization of Hebrew Scripture: the Talmudic and Midrashic Evidence* (New Haven: Connecticut Academy of Arts and Sciences, 1991), 102–119; Karl Georg Kuhn, "Giljonim und sifre minim," in Walther Eltester (ed.); *Judentum, Urchristentum, Kirche: Festschrift für Joachim Jeremias* (Berlin: Alfred Töpelman, 1960), 24–61. Cf. Johann Maier, *Jüdische Auseinandersetzung mit dem Christentum in der Antike* (Darmstadt: Wissenschaftliche Buchgesellschaft, 1982), 28–122.

[34] See Payne Smith, *A Compendious Syriac Dictionary* (New York: Oxford University Press, 1903), 6. This transcription appears, for example, in Mark 1:1 in the *Peshitta.* The more common Syriac word for Gospel is *sbrta* which explains why previous modern commentators on the story did not notice the Bavli's precise use of the Syriac.

[35] See Jastrow, *A Dictionary,* 27. Another possible reading of אָוֶן גִּלָּיוֹן is "margin" or "message" of "power" or "possession" (see Jastrow, ibid., 28). The reading suggested above seems more likely in the present context.

margin of perversion, wrong, or penalty.[36] The passage's trilingual pun on and satirical imitation of the Syriac word *'wnglywn* already marks this part of the sugya as a gospel parody par excellence.

The sugya provides the same distorted Aramaic spelling of "gospel" in the sequel, the Imma Shalom story. It seems likely that the story was included because it constitutes, in its entirety, a third satirical comment on the term "gospel." Since the terms de- and connotations have been clarified I will henceforth translate *'awon-gelayon* as "Gospel," the text of the heretics as the rabbis perceived it.

The Bavli's choice of rabbinic personae is not incidental. Imma Shalom was the wife of Rabbi Eliezer, a rabbi officially accused of heresy, most likely involving Christianity, according to an older rabbinic tradition hotly discussed in the Bavli.[37] (Rabbi Eliezer will be the tragic hero of a parody I discuss in the Conclusion.) She is therefore an ambiguous character from the outset, despite her playfully irenic name, "Mother of Peace." It should also be noted that Rabban Gamliel, her brother, opposed women's education elsewhere in the Bavli (see *Eruvin* 63a). Imma Shalom's knowledge of rabbinic law allows her to challenge her brother and to assume an active role in the judicial proceedings, especially so in Version A.[38] In Version B, the association of Imma Shalom's husband, Eliezer, with heresy, perhaps even with Christianity, in turn informs the insistence on her orthodoxy and willingness to ridicule Christianity. Additionally, Imma Shalom's suspiciously extensive legal knowledge might have warranted assigning her a more passive role in the court proceedings in Version B.

Rabban Gamliel (II), unlike his grandfather Gamliel (I), named explicitly in the *Acts of the Apostles* as Paul's teacher, is not associated with Christianity anywhere in rabbinic literature.[39] Rabban Gamliel and Imma Shalom's father, Shimon ben Gamliel (I), was most likely killed during the

---

[36] Jastrow, *Dictionary*, 1054.

[37] Concerning the story of Rabbi Eliezer, see most recently Schäfer, *Jesus in the Talmud*, 41–51 and Boyarin, *Border Lines*, 221 f. In the Bavli's often cited story of the Oven of Akhnai (*Baba Metsʿia* 59b), the rabbis excommunicate Rabbi Eliezer for relying on miracles and the heavenly voice rather than on the majority opinion of the sages. In the story's sequel, Imma Shalom appears faithful to both her husband and her brother, trying in vain to protect the latter from the former's curse. Concerning this story, see notes 10, 65, and 117 in Chapter Five; I discuss the Yerushalmi version of the story (in which Imma Shalom does not appear) in the Conclusion.

[38] Concerning Imma Shalom, see, for example, Tal Ilan, "The Quest for the Historical Beruriah, Rachel, and Imma Shalom," *AJS Review* 22 (1997), 1–17.

[39] See *Acts* 5:34 and 22.3. It should be noted that the *Pseudo-Clementines* indicate that Gamliel I becomes a crypto-Christian; see *Homilies* 22:3 and *Recognitions* I.65f; see also the *Gospel of Gamaliel* literature.

first-century Judean War.[40] Whether he bequeathed property worthy of litigation is unknown; the rabbis certainly do not mention it. Accordingly, his "inheritance" in the story symbolizes the communal inheritance of the Land of Israel, and ultimately, the communal inheritance of God's promises.

With each detail that it adds to the Palestinian story in the *Pesiqta de-Rav Kahana*, the Bavli comments on some aspect of the "sister religion" as part of its theological, legal, and ethical satire of Christianity. Indeed, it reinterprets most of the elements in the *Pesiqta de-Rav Kahana*'s Palestinian version in light of Christianity. My focus is on the Bavli's adaptation of previous rabbinic texts on the one hand and its dialogue with and satirical parody of Christian law, Christian doctrine, and the Gospel on the other hand as well as the ways in which both aspects are developed through references to the Pentateuch and the Prophets.

Daughters and the Law

The judge in the *Pesiqta de-Rav Kahana* becomes a "philosopher" (פילאספא) in the talmudic story. In Palestine, this figure is a stock opponent of the rabbis and Rabban Gamliel in particular.[41] The term "philosopher" appears only once more in the Bavli, also in the context of a discussion between a non-rabbinic philosopher and Rabban Gamliel.[42] The primary meaning of "philosopher" in the Bavli, hence, likely corresponds to the Greek usage of the term.[43] And while Greek philosophers continued to contribute to the intellectual landscape of Late Antiquity, some Syriac as well as Greek Church Fathers positively identified ascetic life with Christian philosophy, at times referring to each other as "philosophers."[44] Therefore, the scenario of Rabban Gamliel defeating a "philosopher" could be a stereotype familiar

---

[40] See, for example, Josephus' *War* IV.159 and *Vita* 191.

[41] See *Bereshit Rabbah* 1.9, 11.6, and 20.4, Yerushalmi *Berakhot* IX.1.34. (13b), and Burton L. Visotzky, "Goys 'Я'n't Us: Rabbinic Anti-Gentile Polemic in Yerushalmi Berachot 9:1," in Eduard Iricinschi and Holger Zellentin (eds.), *Heresy and Identity in Late Antiquity* (Tübingen: Mohr Siebeck, 2008), 304–307 and 313.

[42] The opponent is attempting to defend idol worship (*Avodah Zarah* 54b). To be precise, the term also appears in the Bavli's citation of the Mishna in *Avodah Zarah* 44b.

[43] When considering the academic implications of the term "philosopher" in our story, one may also point to the flourishing of what Adam Becker aptly calls "scholasticism" in the Christian Academies of Nisibis after 489 C.E.; see *Fear of God and the Beginnings of Wisdom: The School of Nisibis and the Development of Scholastic Culture in Late Antique Mesopotamia* (Philadelphia: University of Pennsylvania Press, 2006).

[44] See Burton L. Visotzky, "Goys 'Я'n't Us: Rabbinic Anti-Gentile Polemic in Yerushalmi Berachot 9:1," note 22 and the references provided there. It is also noteworthy that Jesus is called the true philosopher in texts such as *Pseudo-Clementines* and *Didascalia Apostolorum*, passim.

to the audience. In addition, it is possible that the story subtly identifies its enemy as one of the Greek philosophical tradition of the West. The narrative, finally, might thereby also echo the charges that Sasanian officials made against Christians.

Version A	Version B
[3] One day, *[Rabban Gamliel]* wanted to laugh at [the philosopher]. [The siblings] went to [the philosopher]. Imma Shalom brought [the philosopher] a golden lamp [שרגא דדהבא]. She said to him: "I want them to divide [דניפלגי] the estate of my [late] father with me." [The philosopher] said: "Divide [פלוגו] with her!" [4] *They* said to him: "It is written in the Torah that he gave us [בתורה דיהב לן]: 'If there is a son, the daughter does not inherit [תרות].'"	[3] One day, *they* [the siblings] wanted to laugh at [the philosopher]. [The siblings] went to [the philosopher]. Imma Shalom brought [the philosopher] a golden lamp [שרגא דדהבא]. She said to him: "I want them to divide [דניפלגי] the estate of my [late] father with me." [The philosopher] said: "Divide [פלוגו] with her!" [4] [Rabban Gamliel] said to him: "It is written in the Torah that he gave us [בתורה דיהב לן]: 'If there is a son, the daughter does not inherit [תרות].'"

Once the bribed philosopher reaches a verdict, either Rabban Gamliel (B) or the two siblings (A) confront his ignorance by paraphrasing the rabbinic objection to Imma Shalom's claim to the inheritance. Whether the conflict between the siblings is pretended or genuine, a question arises concerning its implications in the story. The lawsuit needs to be credible enough to convince the audience of its plausibility (A) or at least that a judge would have agreed to hear the case (B). In order to understand the legal reality informing the story, I suggest considering the legal autonomy in the Sasanian Empire. Since Jews and Christians typically had their own jurisdictions, we can imagine that this system led at times to legal ambiguities. And indeed, Christian jurisprudence, in contrast with its rabbinic counterpart, stipulated that a woman was entitled to inherit property even if she had brothers. In order to appreciate the precision of the parody in the Bavli, it is important to recall the precise context of the two respective legal traditions.

The rabbis held divergent opinions on the story of Zelophehad's daughters in Numbers 27:5–11, the *locus classicus* of gender differentiation in biblical inheritance law. According to the Mishna, a daughter is not entitled to inherit if there is also a son: בן קודם לבת (*Bava Batra* 8.2). Yet, the ruling led to many problems in post-mishnaic times, which are alluded to in the Bavli story of Imma Shalom, as Johann Maier points out.[45] Eventually, the

---

[45] Maier writes: "Hier liegt also auch ein in amoräischer Zeit intensiv diskutiertes rechtliches Problem vor, und die Erzählung in bSabb 116–b schließt die damals aktuelle Diskussion ein" (*Jüdische Auseinandersetzungen*, 84). See also Maier's references to further literature.

Bavli confirms the mishnaic ruling (*Ketubot* 52b), as do (post-talmudic) Gaonic *responsa*.[46] The story, however, goes beyond the rabbinic legal issues regarding inheritance mentioned by Maier. In her study on the implications of rabbinic inheritance law for women, Judith Hauptman shows the extent to which the Mishna's discriminatory inheritance laws were at odds with most surrounding cultures, particularly with the Roman legal conventions in Palestine, and considers the ample traces of heated rabbinic debates concerning this matter.[47] According to Hauptman, many strands of "feminist impulse" within both Palestinian and Babylonian rabbinic culture kept challenging the mishnaic ruling.

What was true in third-century Palestine became even more poignant with the Christianization of the Roman Empire. Byzantine rulers adopted the Roman law, while Christian bishops explicitly censured fathers for favoring sons over daughters in their wills.[48] Furthermore, in the Sasanian Empire, Zoroastrian women who had brothers were much more likely to inherit property than their Jewish counterparts, adding to the tensions created by the ruling of the rabbinic court.[49] Finally, the *Syro-Roman Law Book,* an account of traditional Christian law in the Sasanian Empire from early Islamic times and the best extant evidence of Christian customs in the Sasanian Empire in the time of the Bavli, makes it clear that there was no difference between Christian sons and daughters in this regard in cases of intestacy and that daughters were entitled to a minimum inheritance in other cases.[50] In this respect, Jewish women must have appreciated this as-

---

[46] Ibid., 85. Note the related argument between the rabbis on the one hand and Yochanan ben Zakai and "the Sadducees" on the other about whether a son's daughter is entitled to inherit before the deceased's own daughter (*Bava Batra* 115a–b). Tellingly, the rabbis' victory in this case even led to the institution of a commemorative festival.

[47] Hauptman, "Women and Inheritance in Rabbinic Texts: Identifying Elements of a Critical Feminist Impulse," in *Introducing Tosefta* (ed. Harry Fox and Tirzah Meacham; Hoboken, NJ: Ktav Publishing House, 1999), 221–240.

[48] Anttie Arjava, *Women and Law in Late Antiquity* (Oxford: Clarendon Press, 1998), 62. Johann Maier points out that the philosopher's was in accordance with Roman law. Even though he insists that the text is a "late amoraic composition," Maier does not take into account the Christianization of the Roman Empire (Maier, op. cit., 81).

[49] See B. Hjerrild, "Ayōkēn: Women between Father and Husband in the Sassanian Era," in *Medioiranica: Proceedings of the International Colloqium on Middle Iranian Studies*, Orientalia Lovaniensia 48 (ed. Wojciech Skalmowski and Alois van Tongerloo; Leuven: Peters, 1993), 79–86; on the long history of this practice see also A. Perikhanian, "Iranian Society and Law," in *The Cambridge History of Iran*, vol. 2, *The Median and Achaemenian Periods* (ed. Ilya Gershevitch; Cambridge: Cambridge University Press, 1985), vol. III, no. 2, 646.

[50] See the *Syro-Roman Law Book*, L 1 and Arjava, *Women and Law in Late Antiquity*, 65. See also Walter Selb and Hubert Kaufhold, *Das syrisch-römische Rechtsbuch* (Vienna: Verlag der Österreichischen Akademie der Wissenschaften, 2002), 22 f. and Arthur Vööbus, *The Syro-Roman Lawbook: the Syriac Text of the Recently Discovered Manuscripts Accompanied by a Facsimile Edition and Furnished with an Introduction and Translation*

pect of Christian law. The talmudic story acknowledges this and indicates rabbinic fear of the legal "emancipation" of women regardless of whether a genuine lawsuit is part of the story. In typical fashion, the Bavli stages the halakhic issue.

The "philosopher" judge is a Christian who has a perfect reputation. Imma Shalom's request to receive part of the inheritance challenges rabbinic law in Version A and pretends to do so in Version B. In Version A, as in Zoroastrian[51] and Christian heresiology[52] and in other parts of the Bavli, the figure of the woman represents the dangerous insider who challenges not only one particular ruling but orthodoxy itself.[53] In Version B, the Lady

---

(Stockholm: Papers of the Estonian Theological Society in Exile, 1982). It has been suggested that the Bavli's position on brothers and sisters inheriting "like one" (כחדא) was an application of Galatians 3.28 on the law of inheritance. If there is indeed "neither man nor women," but all are "one in Christ," as the text is traditionally understood to say, then it would also follow that everyone inherits "like one." I agree, however, with Kuhn that the reading is far-fetched (Karl Georg Kuhn, "Giljonim und sifre minim," 54), and it seems that the Syriac Christian law, and not Paul, is the focus of the story. The philosopher's ruling paraphrases the Gospel instead of quoting it directly, just as the objection to his first ruling is a paraphrase rather than a quotation of rabbinic or biblical law.

[51] The association between deviant insiders and women is suggested in a *Rivaya* (*Responsum*) based on the Pahlavi Vidēvdāt, which discusses women who mingle with outsiders in conjunction with the *ahrmōk*, a blasphemous heretic. Both, according to these accounts, potentially bring about the destruction of the world. See Kaikhusroo M. Jamaspasa, "On the Heretic and Immoral Woman in Zoroastrianism," in *Orientalia: J. Duchesne-Guillemin emerito oblata* (Leiden: E J Brill, 1984), 243–266. See also Ketayun H. Gould, "Outside the Discipline, Inside the Experience: Women in *Zoroastrianism*," in A. Sharma (ed.), *Religion and Women* (Albany: SUNY Press, 1994), 139–182, and Jamsheed K. Choksy, "Woman in the Zoroastrian Book of Primal Creation: Images and Functions within a Religious Tradition," *Mankind Quarterly* 29 (1988), 73–82.

[52] Todd Breyfogle, "Magic, Women, and Heresy in the Late Empire: the Case of the Priscillianists," in Marvin Meyer and Paul Mirecki, eds., *Ancient Magic and Ritual Power* (Leiden: Brill 1995), 435–454; and Virginia Burrus, "The Heretical Woman as Symbol in Alexander, Athanasius, Epiphanius, and Jerome," *Harvard Theological Review* 84 (1991), 229–248.

[53] The association between women and various kinds of heterodoxy is well attested; see Shulamit Valler, *Woman and Womanhood in the Talmud* (Atlanta: Scholars Press, 1999); Meir Bar-Ilan, "Witches in the Bible and in the Talmud," in J. Neusner (ed.), *Approaches to Ancient Judaism 5* (Atlanta: Scholars Press, 1993), 7–32; Simcha Fishbane, "Most Women Engage in Sorcery: an Analysis of Female Sorceresses in the Babylonian Talmud," in J. Neusner (ed.), *Approaches to Ancient Judaism 5*, 143–165; Judith Hauptman, "Images of Women in the Talmud," in Rosemary Radford Reuther (ed.), *Religion and Sexism* (; New York: Simon and Schuster, 1974), 184–212; Tal Ilan, "'Stolen Water is Sweet': Women and Their Stories between Bavli and Yerushalmi," in Peter Schäfer (ed.), *The Talmud Yerushalmi and Graeco-Roman Culture III* (Tübingen: Mohr Siebeck, 2002), 185–223; and Anne Goldfeld, "Women as Sources of Torah in the Rabbinic Tradition," Judaism 24 (1975), 245–256. See also William Horbury, "Women in the Synagogue," in William Horbury, W.D. Davies and John Sturdy (eds.), *The Cambridge History of Judaism, Volume III: The Early Roman Period* (Cambridge, UK: Cambridge University Press, 1999), 358–401.

complaineth a bit too little, and Imma Shalom's orthodox conformity to
rabbinic law and her implicit willingness to give up her part of the inheritance undermines the legal option most advantageous to Jewish women
in the talmudic period: filing a law suit at a non-rabbinic court. The text
silences the female voice at the same time that it clearly acknowledges the
tension between rabbinic law and women's concerns.

Most importantly, in both versions Imma Shalom's request has additional
Christian characteristics: her portrayal in the Bavli imitates and enacts a
scene from the Christian Gospel in order to render her appeal suitable for
consideration within the Christian legal framework. A passage from the
Gospel of Luke 12:13 f., cited according to the Peshitta (attested also in the
Arabic Diatessaron 28[54]), illustrates this point:

Somebody in the crowd said to [Jesus]: "Teacher, tell my brother [*l'hy*] to divide [*plg*]
the inheritance [*yrtwt'*] with me.

But [Jesus] said: "Man, who has set me to be a judge [*dyn'*] or a divider [*mplgn'*]
above you?"

As Moritz Guedeman already noticed, the scene in the Bavli conspicuously
resembles the Gospel: Imma Shalom addresses a Christian authority with
ly the same request: to order her brother to divide the inheritance with her.[55]
While the *Pesiqta de-Rav Kahana* story does not specify the nature of the
lawsuit, the Bavli's adaptation of the story does so with by parodying the
gospel. In Version A, the Bavli uses the same Aramaic roots for the words
that appear in the Peshitta Gospel:

Gospel of Luke	Bavli Shabbat
l'hy, "sibling"	Imma Shalom is introduced as the sister (אחתיה) of Rabban Gamliel.
plg, *mplgn'*, "divide"	She asks the philosopher to divide (דניפלגי) the inheritance, and he orders the siblings to divide (פלוגו) it.
yrtwt', "inheritance"	In their response, the siblings (or Rabban Gamliel alone) contend that a sister is not entitled to inherit (תרות) if she has a brother; the philosopher says that she is (יירתון).
dyn', "judge"	In Version A, Imma Shalom insists that the philosopher examine his judgment (בדינא).

---

[54] P. Augustinus Ciasca, *Tatiani Evangeliorum Harmoniae Arabica* (Rome: S. C. De
Propaganda Fide, 1888), 107 [Arabic text].
[55] Moritz Guedemann, *Religionsgeschichtliche Studien* (Leipzig: Leiner, 1876), 75.

While the similarities in content and language suggest that Bavli seeks to imitate the Gospel, the text itself shows that the former simultaneously distorts its source: the judge, in stark contrast to Jesus (who declines jurisdiction), does not hesitate and seizes the opportunity for profit at once. Luke's gospel, moreover, harshly criticizes the very greed that characterizes the philosopher in the Bavli and exposes his motivation for accepting the judicial role. The Bavli, therefore, parodies the Gospel in order to satirize the judge and, in Version A, Imma Shalom as well.

The sugya, in the passage immediately preceding the story, had parodied the Syriac term "gospel." By parodically reenacting the Gospel, it adopts its argument (that Jesus should decline jurisdiction) for the sake of satire. The target of the satire in this case is precisely not the Gospel, but the practices of Syriac Christians as perceived by the Bavli, and perhaps also the Gospel's Syriac interpretation. By imitating the Gospel passage, the Bavli suggests that Jesus' refusal to act as a judge was now being ignored by contemporary Christians. The most authoritative Syriac commentary of the time in effect reverses Jesus' position. The great Syriac church father Ephrem's commentary in the Diatessaron explains the Gospel passage at hand by stating that Jesus only pretends not to be a judge because the inquirers are malevolent, even though he *is* in effect the judge (3.12).[56]

The Bavli, in my view, identifies an inconsistency between the Christian Gospel and its Syriac Christian interpretation either by the Syriac church fathers, or in the popular echo of their reading. The Diatessaron is clear enough in this case, and recognizing its "original" meaning requires only superficial familiarity with the story concerning Jesus' refusal to judge. The Bavli's exegetical parody imitates the Gospel by staging it and satirizes its patristic or popular interpretation by insinuating that exegetical and judicial corruption go hand in hand.

It is impossible to determine whether the rabbinic author of the passage was familiar with this excerpt from the Christian Gospel and its interpretation through an oral or a written source. It is clear enough, however, that

---

[56] Ephrem explains that Jesus "did not reply to them as people seeking instruction, but as rebels ... Just as our Lord had said to certain people, *I am not a judge*, even though he was a judge." Carmel McCarthy, *Saint Ephrem's Commentary on Tatian's Diatessaron: an English Translation of Chester Beatty Syriac MS 709* (Oxford: Oxford University Press, 1993), 80. The story might also imitate and satirize another parable about Jesus. In Luke 18.1–8, we learn that a wicked judge (*dyn'*) finally agrees to rule in favor of a widow, lest she continue to disturb him. Ephrem emphasizes the widow's persistence (16.16, see McCarthy, ibid. 250). The story of Imma Shalom equally posits a female plaintiff against a wicked judge. Imma Shalom is equally persistent in reminding the judge about her bribe, and especially in Version A, to "examine the judgment." Her persistence, in contrast with the woman in the Gospel, does not pay off. The parodic relationship, however, is not clearly demonstrable in this case.

the author of the Imma Shalom story expected his audience to appreciate the parodic effect, which required familiarity with the Gospel passage as well. Any doubt in this regard should be dispelled by the fact that the sugya explicitly names the Gospel as the object of its inquiry, and by the precision with which the Bavli imitates the Gospel in order to satirize its patristic or popular interpretation in the present and the following cases.

Abrogation of the Torah

The philosopher responds to the rabbinic objections to his ruling in Imma Shalom's favor with a supersessionist argument. He links the exile with the abrogation of the Torah and its replacement with the Gospel, which allegedly states that sons and daughters are entitled to inherit equally:

Version A	Version B
[5] [The philosopher] said: "From the day that you were exiled [גליתון] from your land, the Torah of Moses [אוריתא דמשה] was taken away [איתנטלית] from you and *the Torah of* the Gospel [אוריתא דעון גיליון] was given, and it is written in it: 'Daughter and son inherit equally [יירתון כחדא].'"	[5] [The philosopher] said: "From the day that you were exiled [גליתון] from your land, the Torah of Moses [אוריתא דמשה] was taken away [איתנטלית] from you and [*missing*] the Gospel [דעון גיליון] was given, and it is written in it: 'Daughter and son inherit equally [יירתון כחדא].'"

The philosopher dismisses Rabban Gamliel's, or the siblings', reference to Jewish law and simply cites the abrogation of the Torah following the exile of the Jews and the giving of the Gospel, which Version A even calls "the Torah of the Gospel."[57] The philosopher invokes a sensitive issue in rabbinic identity. The validity of the Torah in exile was a major topic of contention among the rabbis, and indeed, many of the Torah's agricultural laws were never extended beyond Palestine.[58] The philosopher links the exile of the Jews with the Gospel and reinforces his bold claim with reference to the homophony of *glytwn* (you were exiled) and *gylywn* (gospel, blank space, margin, etc.), in typical rabbinic fashion. The enemy's wit, of course, heightens the glory of his impending defeat, and his own pun invokes the sugya's previous comment that the books of the heretics, the Gospels, are mere *glywnyn* ("blank spaces").

---

[57] The word can mean either the Torah as such or the Torah as the Jewish law. See Sokoloff, *A Dictionary of Jewish Babylonian Aramaic*, 95 f.

[58] See, for example, *Hagiga* 5 b on the exile and the end of the Torah's dominance.

The Bavli now reflects on longstanding Christian traditions. According to Christian lore, the exile of the Jews was a punishment for their denial of Jesus as the Messiah. This claim had already been wittily woven into Jesus' prophecy concerning the exile in Luke 21:20–24 and was exploited in great detail by Eusebius in the *Ecclesiastical History*.[59] Eusebius was translated and well received in the Syriac tradition, and the philosopher in the Bavli echoes Eusebius quite accurately by linking the exile to the introduction of the Gospel.[60]

Jesus and the Torah

The philosopher's rejection of Jewish law sets the stage for Imma Shalom's legal victory, but her brother now offers a bigger bribe:

[6] The next day Rabban Gamliel went back and brought him a Libyan donkey.
[The philosopher] said: "I went down to the end of the Gospel,
and it is written in it: 'I am the Gospel;[61] I did not come [אתיתי] to reduce the Torah of Moses, nor to add to the Torah of Moses did I come [אתיתי].'
And it is written in it: 'If there is a son, the daughter does not inherit.'"

The Libyan donkey seems to be a talmudic adaptation of the foal of a donkey, or horse, that appears in the *Pesiqta de-Rav Kahana*, the earlier rabbinic story on which the present narrative is based. The Imma Shalom story modifies the image, but the donkey's primary function in the story remains the same: it is worth more than a golden lamp. The higher bribe reverses the ruling and benefits Rabban Gamliel. On the one hand, the philosopher justifies the reversal, showing his own arbitrariness and corruption. On the other hand, he also exposes the tensions between the Syriac Church and Jesus' remarks in the Gospel, cited according to the Gospel of Matthew 5:17 in the Peshitta (attested also in the Arabic Diatessaron 8[62]):

---

[59] Eusebius links James's death to the revolt that led to the destruction of the temple (*Ecclesiastical History* 2.23). See also Luke 19:41–44 and Origen, *Against Celsus* 4.22. It is interesting that the Bavli does not note the fact that the exile in 72 only affected Jerusalem whereas the Jewish dominance in Judea came to an end only after the Bar Kokhba revolt. (See Yuval, *Two Nations in Your Womb*, 71–81.) These details, of course, were long forgotten in the time of the Bavli.

[60] Sebastian P. Brock, "The Syriac Background," in *Archbishop Theodore: Commemorative Studies on his Life and Influence* (ed. M. Lapidge; Cambridge: Cambridge University Press, 1995), 30–53.

[61] "I am the Gospel" is missing from the Vilna print but appears in all the other manuscripts.

[62] P. Augustinus Ciasca, *Tatiani Evangeliorum Harmoniae Arabica* 37.

Do not think that I have come [*d'tyt*] to abolish the law or the prophets; I have not come ['*tit*] to abolish but to fulfill. For truly I tell you, until heaven and earth pass away, not one letter of the law shall pass away until all is accomplished.

Just as in the case of the story concerning Jesus' refusal to judge (Luke 12:13f), the Bavli's adaptation of the Gospel imitates its language and structure. Additionally, it should be noted that the philosopher in the Bavli version twice repeats Jesus' remark ("I have come"), using the same verb and conjugation (אתיתי) as the Peshitta and following a similar sentence structure.

This is the most direct citation of one of the Gospels anywhere in rabbinic literature; citation is the appropriate term here since the sugya explicitly introduces the topic of the Gospel. There are, at the same time, two differences between the remarks in the Bavli and in Matthew. First, the Bavli reproduces "the law[63] and the prophets" in Matthew as "the Torah of Moses." Second, as previous commentators have noted, the Bavli's quotation of the Gospel slightly differs from its parallel in Matthew. While the general meaning and sentence structure are very similar, the Bavli suggests that the philosopher is also alluding to Deuteronomy 4:1:

So now, Israel, give heed to the statues and ordinances that I am teaching you to observe so that you may live to enter and inherit [וירשתם] the land that G-d, the God of your ancestors, is giving you. You must neither add anything to it nor take away anything from it but keep the commandments of G-d your God with which I am charging you.

The Bavli reverses the order of the sentence from Deuteronomy and replaces Matthew's "to abolish" with "to cut away" and "to fulfill" with "to add." Without definitive knowledge of the Bavli's sources, it is difficult to know whether it alludes to other Jesus traditions beyond the Gospels of the Syriac church.[64] In the context of Deuteronomy 4:1, however, the author of the Imma Shalom story would have an excellent reason to amend its rendition of the Gospel with a Deuteronomic quotation or to choose this quotation from among several versions he might have known. Namely, in Deuteronomy, the inheritance of Palestine is clearly tied to the very issue under discussion, the observance of the commandments. The talmudic story thereby associates the siblings' inheritance with the inheritance of the Land of Israel, which was at the time ruled by Christians who did not observe the Israelite law (but perhaps should have according to the Bavli's reading of Matthew). In this sense, the citation itself satirizes Christian supersessionism, even if this is evident only to a reader familiar with Deuteronomy.

---

[63] The Syriac here is *nmwsa*, the Peshitta's standard translation of Torah.

[64] It should be noted that some "Christian" texts, such as the "Two Ways" tractate in the *Didache* (4.13) and Revelation (22:18), explicitly reference Deuteronomy 4:1.

Most importantly, the Bavli regards the philosopher's revised ruling as equivalent to Matthew's view that the emergence of Jesus did not abrogate the validity of the Torah. Hence, sons still take precedence over daughters in matters of inheritance. In other words, the philosopher argues at first that the law had been abrogated, although his own tradition can easily be understood as saying that this was not the case. Then he returns to the "plain" meaning of Matthew, according to which the Torah had not been abrogated. Being able to choose among the two interpretive alternatives that are part of the Christian tradition, the judge accepts the highest bid and adjusts his ruling accordingly.

And so the Bavli parodies the Christian tradition for a third time. And just as in the case of Luke, it chooses not to satirize the passage from Matthew that it imitates but rather its Syriac patristic or popular interpretation. The exegetical parody resumes. The Bavli's imitation of Matthew strategically endorses the Christian holy text. This provisional alliance, of course, only draws attention to the shortcomings of Christianity, indicating that the Gospel is distorted by its own Christian audience.

The passage in Matthew (and in the Diatessaron) is associated with Jesus-believers who were positively inclined towards Judaism and the Israelite laws; it was also troubling for supersessionist Christian commentators.[65] Ephrem, for example, in his commentary on the Diatessaron, solves the obvious problem by qualifying "the law and the prophets." For him, the Torah is obviously obsolete; what Jesus really meant was that "the *commandments* of the New Testament" are not abrogated.[66] Ephrem's phrase, "the commandments of the New Testament," is particularly illuminating given the Bavli's phrase, "the Torah of the Gospel" in Version A, which is quite closely aligned with Ephrem's phrasing. The issue, hence, was thoroughly contemplated in Syriac communities, and the tensions concerning this matter among Christians were readily apparent.[67]

---

[65] The clearest reference to Matthew 5.17 is found in the Pseudo-Clementine Homilies 51. Intriguingly, Epiphanius seeks to use Matthew 5.17 *against* the "Nazoreans" in his *Panarion* II.29.8.1, which I will discuss in Chapter Five; see Frank Williams, *The Panarion of Epiphanius of Salamis, Book I* (Leiden: Brill, 1994), 142.

[66] VI.3; see Carmel McCarthy, *Saint Ephrem's Commentary on Tatian's Diatessaron*, 111; see also XV.4 with McCarthy, 231.

[67] An even more telling example of how Syriac Christians dealt with the conundrum posed by Matthew 5.17 can be found in the *Didascalia Apostolorum*. Here, the author uses the passage from the Gospel in order to divide biblical law into two parts: an indissoluble section and a "secondary legislation," which is temporary. See Arthur Vööbus, *The Didascalia Apostolorum in Syriac II* (Leuven: Corpus Scriptorum Christianorum Orientalium, 1979), 242; see also Charlotte Elisheva Fonrobert, "The Didascalia Apostolorum: A Mishnah for the Disciples of Jesus," *Journal of Early Christian Studies* 9 (2001), 483–511.

Let your Light Shine

Imma Shalom tries once more to salvage her case, and the Bavli again aligns her with the Gospel.

Version A	Version B
[7] She said [to the philosopher]: "Let your light shine with the lamp [נהור נהוריך בשרגא]. *Examine the judgment* [עיין בדינא]!"	[7] She said [to the philosopher]: "Let your light shine with the lamp [נהור נהוריך בשרגא] *[missing]*

Imma Shalom's statement is partially modeled on the remarks made by the woman in the *Pesiqta de-Rav Kahana* upon finding the ruling in her case reversed. There, the female plaintiff urges the judge to "let [her] case shine forth [ינהר דיני]" like the *Pesiqta de-Rav Kahana*'s silver lampstand (מנורת' דכספא), recalling the formulation of justice in Isaiah 51:4 ("light to the nations [לאור עמים]"). The Bavli, moreover, replaces the *Pesiqta de-Rav Kahana*'s Hebrew and Aramaic lampstand (מנורה and מנורתא, respectively) with a lamp (שרגא).[68] Version A, furthermore, preserves the *Pesiqta de-Rav Kahana* more fully than Version B: Imma Shalom urges the philosopher to examine the *judgment*, just as the woman in the *Pesiqta de-Rav Kahana* wishes the *judgment* to shine forth.

If the Palestinian text alludes to a Gospel passage, the allusion is too vague to be recognized, as mentioned above. The Bavli, however, adds another layer of citation, aligning Imma Shalom's language with Jesus' remark in Matthew 5.15f in the Peshitta (attested also by the Arabic Diatessaron 8[69]) and removing any ambiguity:

No one after lighting a lamp [*shrg'*] puts it under the bushel [*s't'*] but on the lampstand [*mnrt'*], and it illuminates the entire house. Thus let your light shine forth [*nnhr nwhrkwn*] before the people so that they see your good works and glorify your Father in heaven (5.15f).

This verse immediately precedes the one used by the philosopher in the Bavli to justify his new ruling. The language used by Imma Shalom to remind the judge about the bribe resumes the text's imitation of the Gospel. In the Peshitta, Jesus says, "let your light shine forth," using the word "lamp" (*shrga*) as a metaphor for good works and piety. The Syriac and Aramaic roots for "light" and "shine" are identical, and it is important to note that the Peshitta repeats this root (*nnhr nwhrkwn*). It is precisely in these two instances that the Bavli deviates from the *Pesiqta de-Rav Kahana*'s exact

---

[68] The Bavli's use of the Aramaic מנורתא is rare (see *Shabbat* 45b); the Hebrew מנורה is more common (see, e.g., *Shabbat* 46a, 47a, 90a).

[69] P. Augustinus Ciasca, *Tatiani Evangeliorum Harmoniae Arabica*, 36.

words and imitates the Peshitta: Imma Shalom says: "let your light shine with the lamp [נהור נהוריך בשרגא]." This copies the Gospel almost verbatim, but the context of her remark simultaneously deviates from the "original" or "straightforward" Christian meaning of the Gospel in order to satirize what the Bavli perceives as Christian corruption.[70]

Imma Shalom opposes her brother in Version A and sides with him in Version B. Subsequently, the Bavli depicts her imitation of the Gospel as inadvertent in Version A, and as exceedingly ironic in Version B. Both versions parody the passage from the Gospel in order to satirize the philosopher's corruption, and with him, much of Christian supercessionism. It transforms the Peshitta's "light" into the very object with which the crime is committed.

At this point, the Bavli challenges the Christian exegetes' interpretation of and adherence to their own sacred texts, meeting Ephrem and his colleagues and followers on their own terms. The Bavli's strategic adoption of the Gospel and its Christian interpretation makes its satire all the more powerful. In both versions of the sugya, of course, the rabbi prevails, and the philosopher is defeated (along with Imma Shalom, the enemy within, in Version A).

Overturning the Lamp

In the satirical climax of the story, the Bavli depicts Rabban Gamliel as combining Gospel parody with his implicit exposure of the philosopher's corruption:

[8] Rabban Gamliel said to him: "A donkey [חמרא] came and knocked down [ובטשה] the lamp."

The Bavli retains the image of the overturned lamp but adds a twist. If we assume, with Visotzky, that the talmudic author was aware of the Greco-Roman meaning of the image of the overturned lamp as a euphemism for sexual orgies, then Rabban Gamliel's closing statement regards the philosopher's judicial corruption as sexual corruption as well, invoking Jewish accusations of Christian sexual debauchery and marshalling language that has been a constant theme of religious polemics from biblical to modern times.

---

[70] Guedeman goes as far as to propose that the biblical Hebrew cognate of "bushel," חומר, is a homonym of the Aramaic חמרא, "donkey," which implies a hilarious double meaning, but at the same time he presupposes the existence of a Hebrew Matthew, for which we only have circumstantial evidence (Guedemann, *Religionsgeschichtliche Studien*, 77; see James R. Edwards, *The Hebrew Gospel and the Development of the Synoptic Tradition* (Grand Rapids: Eerdmans, 2009). The extant Syriac tradition seems much more relevant than a putative Hebrew one.

This is especially the case if the author was aware of the use of this image in anti-Christian polemics that accused Christians of mixing *agape* with *eros*. Contrasting the lamp of Christian orgies, a symbol of sexual corruption, with Jesus' and Isaiah's lamp is the Bavli's satirical way of pointing to the tensions between Jesus' teachings and post-Constantinian Christian claims to land and power.

The two versions end quite differently. In Version B, Rabban Gamliel announces that the judge is corrupt and that the rabbinic figures defeated not only the Christian philosopher but also Christian supersessionism itself. In Version A, the scenario is more complex. Rabban Gamliel of course prevails, but it cannot be determined whether his verdict is addressed to the philosopher or to Imma Shalom, or both. If the satire targets both of them, then the story amounts to a full-scale attack on Christian tendencies within rabbinic society, as epitomized by a learned rabbinical woman. The external parody, just like the inter-rabbinic parody discussed in Chapter Three, remains fully within the realm of intra-rabbinic satire. This is perhaps the most plausible scenario if the closest enemy is considered the most dangerous one. The story might be a reminder to all Israelites that the Torah regards procedural justice and halakhic observance as prerequisites for God's blessing and the inheritance of the Land of Israel.

Conclusion

We can now see why later Bavli editors would have doubted Version A, the version appearing in Ms. Oxford 366 (and supported by Ms. Vatican 108 and the addition in Ms. Munich 95). In Version A, Imma Shalom and the philosopher stand for Christianity and for the abrogation of the Torah and of rabbinic law concerning women's inheritance whereas Rabban Gamliel stands for Israel and the fulfillment of the Torah. This version features a woman who independently pursues all societal means to ensure her inheritance, including siding with a representative of the arch-enemy. Changing a yud to a vav, however, and deleting the reference to the actual lawsuit would make the story much less radical. Reading the story against the background of the *Pesiqta de-Rav Kahana* and as a parody of the Gospels, moreover, provides additional evidence that Version A may indeed be slightly older than Version B. Not only is it a *lectio difficilior* in many ways, but it also makes for a better adaptation of the *Pesiqta de-Rav Kahana* and a fuller parody of Christian texts.

While Version A portrays Imma Shalom as actively involved in her struggle for "emancipation," Version B, in the end, acknowledges the importance of at least occasional solidarity between the sexes and that a rabbi needs the help of a woman in order to defeat a Christian. Both versions link the respective Christian and rabbinic positions concerning inheritance to the inheritance of God, the Torah, and the Land of Israel itself. The author is of course aware that the historical reality of Christian rule in Palestine is not easily reconciled with his claim, but he provides ample evidence that the Christians, by his standards, do not deserve the Holy Land and are entitled to the Torah and God's favor even less. The two versions reflect extensive knowledge of several short passages from the Christian Gospel and their interpretation in the Syriac popular or patristic tradition. Most importantly, both versions expect audiences to be attuned to external parody in conjunction not only with the straight imitation of an earlier rabbinic text but also with intra-rabbinic satire.

CHAPTER FIVE

To Kill a Mockingbird:
A Palestinian Parody of the Sermon on the Mount
(Bereshit Rabbah 79.6)

"Are not two birds sold for a penny?
Yet not one of them will fall to the ground apart from your Father.
And even the hairs of your head are all counted."
– Peshitta, *Gospel of Matthew* 10:29–30

"Do not separate from the community."
– Mishna *Avot* 2.4

The preliminary survey of rabbinic parodies presented in this book features internal rabbinic parody from both the Babylonian and Palestinian traditions. The previous chapter demonstrates that Babylonian rabbis also engaged in sophisticated parodying of external texts, suggesting that the Bavli's external parody simultaneously targets internal rabbinic matters. Likewise, we saw that the Bavli's Palestinian source may already contain parodies of and other allusions to Christianity, but the brief Palestinian rabbinic passage from the *Pesiqta de-Rav Kahana* did not allow for a sufficient evaluation. This chapter discusses another Palestinian parody of the Sermon on the Mount and its patristic or popular interpretation, satirizing outsiders and insiders alike. While the Bavli focuses on the Gospel and its Syriac interpretation, I suggest that the Palestinian rabbis parodied the Gospel along with its Byzantine interpretation. Again, the Patristic readings of the Gospel will be used in lieu of the popular oral sources that might have been available to the rabbis, leaving open the question of how exactly they became familiar with the Christian exegesis echoed in the parody.

In the following, I seek to assess the rabbis' parody of a central Gospel passage in the complex cultural sphere of Greco-Roman Palestine in the fourth and fifth centuries. The parody itself is subtle and could fairly be qualified as parodic allusion instead. Yet in contrast to the elusive Palestinian example in the previous chapter, the text itself offers many opportunities to corroborate its parodic and satirical references to discourses of its time. I will therefore focus not only on the parody itself but even more so on its place in a much more complex web of textual and cultural references. (I will present another, more easily accessible Palestinian parody of a gospel passage in the Conclusion.)

To reiterate, the question concerning the extent to which rabbis were familiar with parts of the Christian gospels and their Late Antique interpretations is still hotly debated among scholars. More and more evidence of the Bavli's (often satirical) interest in Christianity has been identified over the last two decades, even though the Babylonian rabbis lived outside the Christian Roman Empire. Evidence of Palestinian rabbinic interest in Christianity is far less conclusive. The underlying difficulties include dating the different editions of Palestinian rabbinic texts, evaluating their historical context, and ultimately, assigning authorial agency to their editors.

A key issue in reading Palestinian rabbinic texts concerns their redaction history in relation to the Christianization of Jewish Palestine in Late Antiquity. The Palestinian rabbinic movement emerged in the second half of the second century CE,[1] at approximately the same time when gentile churches gained momentum, yet little is known about early interactions between the two trends. We know even less about the interactions between rabbis and followers of Jesus who sought to remain in, or to join the Jewish communities. There is little evidence concerning such Jewish following, but a number of sources throughout the classical rabbinic period show that the church fathers, and occasionally rabbis too, were concerned about by real or imagined encounters with Jewish believers in Jesus.[2] In addition, there are a small number of primary texts written by people with a dual affinity for Jesus and Judaism, but these texts do not necessarily correspond to those of the groups mentioned in rabbinic and Christian heresiology.[3]

The three "parties" – Jews, Christians, and those with a dual affinity – claimed ownership of the Torah and its heritage, and each viewed

---

[1] See Catherine Hezser, *The Social Structure of the Rabbinic Movement in Roman Palestine* (Tübingen: Mohr Siebeck, 1997).

[2] On this topic, see most recently Oskar Skarsaune and Reidar Hvalvik (eds.), *Jewish Believers in Jesus: The Early Centuries* (Peabody, MA: Hendrickson Publishers, 2007). Burton Visotzky correctly points out that this volume provides less evidence than necessary to reach its goal, and rightly emphasizes the over-readings of rabbinic references to Christianity. His review appeared in the *Catholic Biblical Quarterly* 70 (2008), 427–428. A more modest and in my view more fruitful approach is found in the volume edited by Matt Jackson-McCabe, *Jewish Christianity Reconsidered* (Minneapolis: Fortress Press, 2007); cf. Daniel Boyarin, "Rethinking Jewish Christianity: An Argument for Dismantling a Dubious Category (to which is Appended a Correction of my Border Lines)," *Jewish Quarterly Review* 99 (2009), 7–36.

[3] Many of the post-Constantinian texts with affinities for both Jesus and Judaism are discussed by Annette Reed, "Jewish-Christian Apocrypha and the History of Jewish/Christian Relations," in P. Piovanelli (ed.), *Christian Apocryphal Texts for the New Millennium: Achievements, Prospects, and Challenges* (forthcoming), a study to which I am much indebted.

itself as the recipients of God's blessing. We can safely assume that until the fourth century the relationships between the three varied markedly among their sub-groups, based on such factors as language, messianism, mystical tendencies, ritual, and law. In 313 CE, Gaius Flavius Constantinus, later known as Constantine the Great, saw it fit to secure for himself the support of the empire's Christians. He issued the Decree of Milan, granting his subjects broad freedom of religion. This period of tolerance was genuine but short lived. As Constantine and the power structures of the Roman Empire became more and more Christian, religious practices not conforming to the new imperial cult were branded as either "pagan," "heretical," or "Jewish." This ongoing development accompanied a strong effort to Christianize the territory of "Palestine," the empire's new Holy Land. The emergence of Christianity as the new ruling power in Rome and Palestine dramatically changed the existing relationships between all of the Palestinian groups. Byzantine Christianity became the new cultural and political enemy, similarly affecting Palestinian pagans, Samaritans, Christian "heretics," and Jews, be they rabbinic, Jesus-messianist, or any other sub-group.

There is no unequivocal example of a rabbinic parody of Christianity prior to the time of Constantine.[4] Even though the Yerushalmi and most of the Palestinian Midrashim were redacted during the slow Christianization of the Roman Empire, the ways in which the redactors of these texts responded to this development is not well known. Palestinian rabbinic texts continue to consider the daily reality of the traditional Greco-Roman religion as if nothing had changed. True, gentile practices of worship persisted in the Roman East for a long time after Constantine, but the archeological and historical record indicates that Christianity did play a major role in the life of Judean and Galilean Jews.[5]

---

[4] A good example of a possible parody is the image of the crucified thief in the Tosefta *Sanhedrin* 9.7. The thief's resemblance to "the king of the entire world" recalls the gospel imagery of Jesus crucified among thieves and the Christian docetic reading of this narrative, which indicate that the real Jesus was watching as someone else was crucified in his stead, but the evidence is too sparse to analyze the case. See also pages 203–5.

[5] Jerusalem, especially, became a Christian city in the fourth century. See Günther Stemberger, *Juden und Christen im Heiligen Land: Palastina unter Konstantin und Theodosius* (Munich: C.H. Beck, 1987), Robert L. Wilken, *The Land Called Holy: Palestine in Christian History and Thought* (New Haven: Yale University Press, 1992); see also the various contributions in Eric M. Meyers (ed.), *Galilee Through the Centuries: Confluence of Cultures* (Winona Lake: Eisenbrauns, 1999), Lee Levine (ed.), *The Galilee in Late Antiquity* (Cambridge: Harvard University Press, 1992), and Doron Bar, "Rural Monsticism as a Key Element in the Christianization of Byzantine Palestine," *Harvard Theological Review* 98 (2005), 49–65.

The rabbinic silence regarding Christianity can be at least partially explained by the fact that the Mishna and other tannaitic texts became the
foundation of later rabbinic literature. The tannaitic texts reflect a pagan
Rome, and rabbis under Christian rule continued to study the older texts,
and along with them the tannaitic views concerning the slowly waning cult.
At the same time, however, I suggest that the rabbinic redactors functioned
as creative authors who managed to rework traditional materials in a way
that allowed them to express polemical views, even if only implicitly.[6]
Moreover, rhetorically ignoring one's enemy may in itself be a polemical
stance, and treating New Rome as if it were Old Rome was certainly a viable
strategy for the rabbis in their attempt to discredit Christianity by regarding
it as a variation on pagan Roman practices.

In short, recent scholarship has shown that post-Constantinian rabbis
respond to many Christian narratives, without naming them explicitly, with
polemical and apologetic counter-narratives. At the same time, some scholars charge that such argumentation relies too heavily on circular readings,
finding references to Jesus because one is looking too hard. Illuminating
examples of the dispute are the two divergent readings of the tale of Titus
and the gnat (found, for example, in *Wayiqra Rabbah* 22.3 and Bavli *Gittin*
57a) by Israel Yuval and Joshua Levinson.

This case is especially relevant since both Yuval and Levinson argue that
the story constitutes what I would label an external parody. Yuval convincingly claims that the story about Titus entering the Temple and being
killed by a gnat is a "transparent parody of the Christian legend of *Vindicta
Salvatoris*."[7] The status of this legend in the fifth century, however, is unknown, making it impossible to analyze the relationship between the Christian and the rabbinic texts, as Yuval acknowledges.[8] Accordingly, Joshua

---

[6] For the argument for polemical redaction, see most recently Burton L. Visotzky,
"Goys 'Я'n't Us: Rabbinic Anti-Gentile Polemic in Yerushalmi Berachot 9:1," in Eduard
Iricinschi and Holger Zellentin (eds.), *Heresy and Identity in Late Antiquity* (Tübingen:
Mohr Siebeck, 2008), 299–313 and Israel Yuval, "The Other in Us Liturgica, Poetica,
Polemica," in ibid. 364–386. See also Peter Schäfer, *Jesus in the Talmud* (Princeton: Prin-
ceton University Press, 2007); Adam H. Becker and Annette Yoshiko Reed, eds., *The
Ways that Never Parted: Jews and Christians in Late Antiquity and the Early Middle Ages*
(Tübingen: Mohr Siebeck, 2003); Mark G. Hirshmann, *A Rivalry of Genius: Jewish and
Christian Biblical Interpretation in Late Antiquity* (Albany: SUNY Press, 1996); and E.P.
Sanders, ed., *Jewish and Christian Self-Definition* (Philadelphia: Fortress Pres, 1981); see
also note 72 in the Introduction.

[7] Yuval, *Two Nations in Your Womb: Perceptions of Jews and Christians in Late Antiquity and the Middle Ages*, 47 in the English translation; in Hebrew, it is 62 ,אירוניה שקופה.

[8] Yuval states that "most of the motifs parallel to the Christian legends are preserved
specifically in the version of the Babylonian Talmud." (44). Since the story of Titus is preserved almost entirely in *Wayiqra Rabbah*, a Palestinian text predating the Bavli by at least
a century (as discussed in Chapter Two), we should first and foremost examine the text's

Levinson considers the same story to be a parody of pre-Christian Roman imperial practices, dismissing Yuval's reading and finding his "historical reconstruction problematic."[9]

I suggest bridging Yuval's and Levinson's arguments, first, because the manifold continuities between "pagan" and "Christian" Rome would not have eluded the rabbis and second, because the rabbis might have easily exploited these continuities in order to portray the Christians as another form of Roman paganism. What would be the point of ridiculing the Roman imperial cult over a century after its demise if not in order to target the cult's Christian successors? The two interpretations should not be read competitively but complementarily: while Levinson rightly emphasizes the rabbis' Greco-Roman cultural matrix, Yuval points to one of their most urgent ideological travails – even if he relies on the manuscripts that are too late for a precise literary analysis. Neither interpretation is complete on its own, but together they strongly suggest that the Palestinian rabbis did write external anti-Christian parodies that must be understood in the entirety of their Greco-Roman context. In this chapter, I take this insight as a key to discuss an example of external parody that imitates and satirically targets accessible texts: the Christian gospels, their Greek patristic interpretations, and Christian historiography. At the same time, I argue that any cultural analysis of rabbinic culture should take into account its increasingly Christianized, yet still fully recognizable, Greco-Roman context.

The recent discussion, to reiterate, asks whether for the rabbis Christianity was an elephant in the room. I suggest asking instead whether it was perhaps a donkey in the corner of the *Beyt Midrash:* not essential for understanding most aspects of rabbinic Judaism, but always somehow present. Most importantly, I find it necessary to resist essentializing our modern scholarly concept of Christianity as a clearly defined phenomenon or suggesting that the rabbis of Late Antiquity viewed Christianity in these terms. Instead, the rabbis had the capacity subtly to allude to concrete aspects of Christian thought and practice; it would thus be a misreading to suggest that the rabbinic discussion at hand is somehow *about* (a single, unified) Christianity. Rabbis tended to busy themselves with other rabbis and to view all aspects of Christianity through the lenses of rabbinic paradigms.

Hence, in order to understand the following story as a parody engaging its contemporary environment with great nuance, we must seek to perceive "Christianity" in all of its rich and diverse cultural manifestations. Espe-

---

original relationship to Christian legends from the fifth century. On the issue of reading Palestinian vs. Babylonian texts relating to Christianity see the Conclusion.

[9] Joshua Levinson, "'Tragedies naturally performed': Fatal Charades, Parodia Sacra, and the Death of Titus," in Richard Kalmin and Seth Schwartz (eds.), *Jewish Culture and Society under the Christian Roman Empire* (Leuven: Peeters, 2003), 363.

cially, we must resist subsuming under one single category all the complexities of gentile and Jewish "Christian" asceticism, exegesis, hagiography, and heresiology and acknowledge that the Palestinian rabbis were able and willing to consider such issues individually. At the same time, these rabbis were free to discredit any objectionable rabbinic position with a mere reference to Christianity, even if the reference often proves too elusive to trace. Such are the strategies of a charged, polarized discourse, ancient as well as modern.

Hence, while the reluctance to name Christianity is shared by Palestinian and Babylonian rabbis alike, Palestinian rabbinic discourse on Christianity is even more implicit and allusive, and at times even elusive. The Bavli mentions and cites the "Evangel" once; it also names (and satirizes) Jesus, Mary, and several imaginary disciples of Jesus. The Palestinian rabbinic tradition, however, names Jesus only once, in a passage discussed below. Complicating matters even further, the Palestinian rabbis seem to have perceived gentile Christianity not only as a form of paganism, but also as an aberrant form of Judaism – as a dangerous Christian-Jewish chimera, so to speak.

While the general rabbinic tendency may have been to "Romanize" gentile Christians, the Palestinian rabbis also perceived Christianity as being very close to Judaism – perhaps through the lens of actual or remembered Palestinian Jewish followers of Jesus. "The Kingdom of star and constellation worshippers will turn to *minut*," they wrote in the Yerushalmi.[10] The kingdom, of course, is Rome, and the term *minut* refers to imperial gentile Christianity with a term previously reserved for Jewish heresy. This prime example of the rabbis' elusive language when dealing with Christianity may convey their own view of this historical irony, which brings together the rabbis' strategy of portraying Christian Rome as simultaneously gentile and Jewish. Despite of it all, the rabbis might have noticed that the Romans

---

[10] Yerushalmi *Sotah* IX.17 (24c); see also Melech Schachter, *The Babylonian and Jerusalem Mishna Textually Compared* (Jerusalem: Mosad ha-Rav Ḳuḳ, 1959), 206 [Hebrew]. The corresponding material in the Mishna (*Sotah* 9.15), in which Rabbi Eliezer predicts the kingdom's turn to heresy, is a late addition, missing from most mishnaic manuscripts. The question regarding the meaning of *minut* in fifth century Palestinian and Babylonian Aramaic (Jewish heresy, gentile Christianity, or both) remains open; see, for example, Christine E. Hayes, "Displaced Self-Perceptions: The Deployment of *Minim* and Romans in *B. Sanhedrin* 90b–91a," in Hayim Lapin (ed.), *Religious and Ethnic Communities in Later Roman Palestine* (Bethesda: University Press of Maryland, 1998), 249–89; Martin Goodman, "The Function of Minim in Early Rabbinic Judaism," in Herbert Cancik, Hermann Lichtenberger and Peter Schäfer (eds.), *Geschichte-Tradition-Reflexion. Festschrift für Martin Hengel zum 70. Geburtstag* (Tübingen: Mohr Siebeck, 1996), vol. I, 501–10; Burton Visotzky, *Fathers of the World: Essays in Rabbinic and Patristic Literature* (Tübingen: Mohr Siebeck, 1995), 144–45; and Daniel Boyarin's recent discussion in *Border Lines: The Partition of Judaeo-Christianity* (Philadelphia: University of Pennsylvania Press, 2004), 220–225. On Rabbi Eliezer's own heresy, see notes 65 and 117 below, note 37 in Chapter Four, and the Conclusion.

now believed in a heretical version of Judaism, a formerly despised eastern religion, and the vanquished party of the Judean wars finally had given some of their laws to the victors.

In turn, by portraying gentile Christianity as both Jewish and pagan, the Palestinian rabbis may also have sought to marginalize deviant Jews from their own community by insinuating that they shared a belief in Jesus with gentile Christians – that is, guilt by association. Most importantly, the following rabbinic story contains a parody of another passage from the Sermon on the Mount, which satirizes several aspects of gentile and Jewish belief in Jesus as attested by Christian writings of the fourth and fifth centuries.

Rashbi in the Cave

Bereshit Rabbah (79.5–6) is a Palestinian rabbinic text, dated by most scholars to the early fifth century.[11] The text is structured around the exegesis of Genesis 33:18 (Jacob "camped before the city" after surviving an encounter with his brother Esau). It tells the story of a rabbi and his son's sojourn in a cave, initially for unknown reasons. The protagonist of the story is Rabbi Simeon bar Yochai[12] (henceforth "Rashbi"), an important student of Rabbi Aqiva in second century Palestine.[13]

> [In Hebrew:] "Jacob came whole [שלם] to the city of Shechem [שכם]
> Complete in his body ... complete in his children ... complete in his possessions ...
> Another interpretation: "and he camped before the city."
> He started to set up shop and to sell cheaply.
> This shows that one must be grateful to a place from which one enjoys benefits.

---

[11] See the discussion in Günter Stemberger, *Introduction to Midrash and Talmud* (Edinburgh: T & T Clark, 1996), 303.

[12] Rashbi is also known as Simeon ben Yochai or, in early works, simply as Rabbi Simeon. Rashbi is quoted more than 300 times in the Mishna. See Wilhelm Bacher, *Die Agada der Tannaiten* (Strasbourg: K.J. Trübner, 1890), II 70–149; M. Beer, "Rabbi Simeon and Jerusalem," in A. Oppenheimer et al. (eds.), *Jerusalem in the Second Temple Period, Memorial Volume A. Shalit* (Jerusalem: Yad Yitshak ben Zvi, 1980), 361–75 [Hebrew]; on Rashbi more generally see Ben-Zion Rosenfeld, "R. Simeon B. Yohai – Wonder Worker and Magician Scholar, *Saddiq* and *Hasid*, *Revue des études juives* 158 (1999), 349–384; Michal Chernick, "'Turn it and Turn it Again': Culture and Talmud Interpretation," *Exemplaria* 12 (2000), 63–103; Yafa Binyamini, "עיון באגדת חז"ל, המיתוס של רבי שמעון בר יוחאי" *Mahkerei Hag* 12 (2001), 87–102; on Rashbi and his son, see Yeshayahu Ben-Pazi, "שיבוץ קובץ האגדות על רשב"י ובנו בפסיקתא דרב כהנא (פסקת 'ויהי בשלח')" *Morashtenu* 17 (2006), 137–162.

[13] The following translation is based on manuscript London, according to Theodor and Albeck, *Bereschit Rabba mit kritischem Apparat und Kommentar* (Jerusalem: Shalem Books, 1996 [1912–1927]). 940–945; for parallels of the story, see note 34.

[I]   Rabbi Simeon the Son of Yochai hid [עשה טמון][14] in a cave for thirteen years, he
       and his son.[15]
       They ate carobs from Gadara[16] until rust came up in their bodies [עד שהעלה גופן
       חלודה][17].
       [In Aramaic:] In the end, [Rashbi] came out and sat at the entrance of the cave.
       He saw a hunter hunting birds [ציפרין],
              and if [Rashbi] heard a divine voice saying from heaven "acquitted," [the
              bird] escaped;
              [If the voice said] "guilty," it was hunted down.
       He [Rashbi] said: "[if] a bird is not hunted down without [the judgment of]
       heaven,
       How much more so the soul of a man."
       He went out and saw that things had calmed down [משדכן].[18]

[II]   [Rashbi and his son] came and healed themselves [אתסון] in one of the *frigi-
       darium* baths [בית מקר].[19]
       His son said: "Father [אבא], Tiberias did us so much good,
       Shouldn't we purify it from the corpses?"
       What did he do?
       [Rashbi] took lupines [תורמוסי] and cut lupines,
              And tossed their pieces,
              And the corpses came up,
              And they purified and removed [the corpses],
              Until they purified [Tiberias] from the corpses.

[III] That night, one *am ha'aretz* [עם דארע][20] rose from the ... market[21]
       He took a corpse and hid it;
              In the morning [the am ha'aretz] said: "Didn't you say that Ben Yochai puri-
              fied Tiberias?

---

[14] See note 24 below.

[15] The Venice print adds: "in the days of the persecution;" see note 32 below.

[16] Based on the earlier appearance of "Carobs of Gadara" in rabbinic literature (see
below), I follow Levine in reading גירודא as "Gadara," inverting the consonants *d* and
r, as is common in rabbinic texts. Manuscript Oxford is the only one that offers a clear
reading in this regard; all other manuscripts can also be understood as describing "dry"
or "graded" carobs, rather than carobs from Gadara. See Lee Levine, "R. Simeon b. Yohai
and the Purification of Tiberias: History and Tradition," *Hebrew Union College Annual*,
49 (1978), 146 and 152; also see note 25 below.

[17] See pages 176 f.

[18] On this meaning of the pa'el of the verb שדך, see Sokoloff, *A Dictionary of Jewish
Palestinian Aramaic* (Ramat-Gan: Bar Ilan University Press, 2002), 538. The Venice print
and manuscript Adler add: "and the decree was nullified."

[19] This translation follows Levine, "R. Simeon b. Yohai and the Purification of Tiberias," 146. The Venice print and manuscript Adler add: "of Tiberias."

[20] The Venice print and manuscript Adler read "a Samaritan *am ha'aretz*."

[21] According to Sokoloff, the type of market, דגורה or סקאי, is not intelligible in any of
the manuscript variants and therefore needs to be bracketed (*A Dictionary of Jewish Palestinian Aramaic*, 139). Levine suggests the following: "some say from the grain-market,
some say from the sackmakers-market" ("R. Simeon b. Yohai and the Purification of
Tiberias," 146).

Come and see a corpse!"
[The am ha'aretz] went and stood next to it.
[Rashbi] said: "I decree [גזר] that the one who stands shall lie,
    And the one who lies shall stand up."
And thus it happened.
[Rashbi] went to prepare for the Sabbath at his house,
And he passed that Magdala of the Dyers.
He heard the voice of Naqai the Teacher [דנקיי ספרא].
[Naqai] said: "Didn't you say that Bar Yochai purified Tiberias?
    They say that they found a corpse."
[Rashbi] said [in Hebrew]: "May [something bad] come over me
    if I don't have rulings like the hair on my head
    that Tiberias is pure except for certain spots!
    Were you not with us in the vote [במניין]?
    You breached the fence of the sages–
    'He who breaches the fence will be bitten by a snake'" [Eccl. 10:8].
[In Aramaic] Immediately [the snake] went out, and thus it happened to him.
[Rashbi] went to a valley in Beyt Netofa.[22]
[Rashbi] saw a man pick the after-growth of the Sabbatical year.
[Rashbi] said to him: "Isn't that the after-growth of the Sabbatical year?"
[The man] said to him [in Hebrew]: "And is it not you who decreed it permissible?"
[Rashbi] said to him: "And did not my colleagues disagree with me?"
At once [Rashbi] raised his eyebrows and looked at him and turned him into
    a heap of bones.

In order to prepare my discussion of the story's parodic and satirical elements, an analysis of the story in light of both 1) its rabbinic context and 2) its self-referential elements is essential. The relationship between an individual and a community is the main theme of the story, which consists of three parts. The individual units, without being restricted to these themes, predominantly discuss [I] seclusion, asceticism, and individual divine providence, [II] purity and communal responsibility, and [III] rabbinic authority.

The first part tells of Rashbi's, and his son's, stay in a cave perhaps situated in the vicinity of Gadara in Transjordania from where they gather carobs. While the reason for Rashbi and his son's stay in the cave is at first entirely unclear, it should be noted that the length of hiding in the Rashbi story is unprecedented in rabbinic literature, and seemingly hyperbolic.[23] The verb

---

[22] Manuscript London has "Bet Tifa," which I amend, following Levine, according to the majority reading and the other references to the town in rabbinic literature (see pages 179 and 198 f. and Levine, "R. Simeon b. Yohai and the Purification of Tiberias," 147).

[23] According to a separate passage in *Bereshit Rabbah*, the number of years Rashbi spent in the cave equals the number of years he studied in *Bnei Braq*, perhaps an intentional symmetry. See *Bereshit Rabbah* 95 (possibly a later addition to the collection) and *Wayiqra Rabbah* 21.8. For other symbolic uses of the number thirteen, see Levine, "R. Simeon b. Yohai and the Purification of Tiberias," 160 f.

טמן, used to describe their sojourn, can mean "to hide," which would imply that they were forced to do so, or "to store" something, which would indicate that they deliberately chose to stay in the cave.[24] Either way, they remove themselves from the rabbinic community. The food they consume suggests that the conditions in the cave are dire. A diet of carobs signifies impoverishment in rabbinic literature, and thereby invokes ascetic practices, even if the two are merely hiding. The "Carobs of Gadara" (גירודא) specifically are known in the rabbinic tradition as poor people's food or even food "that is not eaten," perhaps the first instance of irony in the story.[25]

Moreover, the rabbis suffer from "rust" (חלודה). Elsewhere in rabbinic literature, this term is used exclusively in reference to metal, usually in conjunction with the same verb עלה "to come up".[26] The image depicts the rabbis' skin beginning to rust due to their long sojourn in the cave. The story invokes rust as a concrete metaphor, a usage found in biblical as well as Greek literatures, albeit in different contexts, and a comical metaphor still prevalent today.[27] Even though early medieval and modern commentators understood "rust" here as the name of a skin disease caused by sojourning in caves, it seems much more likely that the story uses irony to distance itself from the rabbis' seclusion.[28]

---

[24] For the latter meaning, see for example Mishna *Shabbat* 2.7, and Jastrow, *A Dictionary of Jewish Palestinian Aramaic*, 540.

[25] *Sifre* indicates that these carobs are the stereotypical food that is not eaten. The tannaitic Midrash, slightly sarcastically, states that if one is to define the Second Tithing too broadly, it "might equally include [in the category of food to be tithed] the beans of an acacia, the carobs of Zalmonah, and the carobs of Gadara, [foods] that are not eaten." (*Sifre Re'eh* 52; *Sifra Behuqotai* 12 states the same). For a later source, see Yerushalmi *Ma'asrot* 1.1 (48c). Yerushalmi *Orla* I.2.5 (61a) and *Wayiqra Rabbah* 35 represent carobs as signifying poverty, and thus edible. The attestations of "carobs of Gadara" in tannaitic literature confirm Levine's choice of "Gadara" over the variants in some manuscripts. See Levine, "R. Simeon b. Yohai and the Purification of Tiberias," 146 n. 12 and note 16 above.

[26] See, for example, Mishna *Kelim* 13.5 and *Bereshit Rabbah* 1.13.

[27] See Ezekiel 24:6–12 (חלאה); Ben Sira 29.10 ('ιόομαι); and the Letter of James 5.3 ('ιός); see also Liddell and Scott, *Greek-English Lexicon: With a Revised Supplement* (Oxford: Clarendon Press, 1996), 832 and Robert J. Edgeworth, "Terms for 'Brown' in Ancient Greek," *Glotta* 61 (1983), 34. For the modern use, see, for example, Zoltán Kövecses, *Metaphor: A Practical Introduction* (New York: Oxford University Press, 2010), 21 and 39.

[28] חלודה in this story is translated or explained as a *common* term referring to a skin disease tied to cave-dwelling. Since the tannaitic and contemporary amoraic literatures contain no support for this reading, later explanations of the Rashbi story seem to have been read into the story itself, effectively leveling the irony. (The "rust" does not appear in the Babylonian version of the Rashbi story, but it is found in all three classical Palestinian versions; see note 38 below). The earliest rabbinic text that specifies that "rust" can refer to some sort of disease caused by living in caves is *Qohelet Rabbah* (17.13), postdating *Bereshit Rabbah* considerably. *Qohelet Rabbah* also explains the Rashbi story in medical terms, perhaps the earliest historical source that read the crooked straight. (Note that some later Midrashim, namely *Tehilim Rabbah* (Warsaw 49.1) and *Midrash Tanhuma KiTavo* 2, equate "rust" with sin.) It is this later use of "rust" that the dictionaries ascribe to the

Even and especially as a metaphor, however, the image of the rabbis' "rusting" continues to imply a skin condition, and the story's irony invites scrutiny. The actual halakha concerning such ailments of course became defunct after the temple's destruction, when the story takes place.[29] Precisely the fact that the skin condition is halakhically meaningless guides the story's audience to engage with the various challenges the rabbis faced when defending their attitude towards purity. In particular, interpretation of the rabbis' rust as a grotesque metaphor links them to the real conflicts surrounding the impurity of the city of Tiberias.

By the end of the first section, Rashbi comes to believe in personal providence. His method for arriving at his conclusion, by comparing the fates of humans and animals, initially seems to be in line with similar lessons in wisdom literature.[30] In the present case, however, God judges each bird with remarkable emphasis on the individual animal. Rashbi reasons that accordingly, God judges each human individually; the fate of each individual is therefore not determined by mere chance. Accordingly, Rashbi concludes that his time in the cave was useless: hiding in a cave is not necessary.[31] Rashbi's reasoning adds a sense of absurdity to the already hyperbolical duration

---

Rashbi story when indicating that "rust" can also signify "a skin disease;" see Sokoloff, *A Dictionary of Jewish Palestinian Aramaic*, 202 and Jastrow, *A Dictionary*, 465.

[29] The respective halakha describes the ritual necessary for purification after contracting *tsaraʿat*. Many commentators have made it clear that the biblical and rabbinic word *tsaraʿat* does not mean leprosy (Hansen's disease) but rather a variety of scaly skin conditions. See J. Milgrom, *The Anchor Bible: Leviticus 1–16* (New York: Doubleday, 1991), 816–826. The rules applying to the "leper" were, of course, severely altered after the destruction of the temple (and restricted mostly to Jerusalem), but the Mishna and the Talmudim pay a great deal of attention to the issue in tractate *Negaʿim*. See Hyam Maccoby, "Corpse and Leper," *Journal of Jewish Studies*, 49 (1998), 280–285 and *Ritual and Morality: the Ritual Purity System and its Place in Judaism* (New York: Cambridge University Press, 1999), 118–130; and אנציקלופדיה תלמודית (Jerusalem: Yad haRav Hertzog, 1998), entry טהרת מצורע [Hebrew].

[30] Ecclesiastes 9:12, for example, derives a lesson about humans from birds: "For no one can anticipate the time of disaster. Like fish taken in a cruel net, and like birds caught in a snare, so mortals are snared at a time of calamity, when it suddenly falls upon them."

[31] Levine summarizes the story's message at this point: "Only Heaven decides the fate of man and beast. If God does not will capture or death, then there is nothing to fear" ("R. Simeon b. Yohai and the Purification of Tiberias," 148). While *Bereshit Rabbah* seems to dismiss the rabbis' sojourn in the cave, consider the remarkably contrasting attitude of the later Midrash *Mishle Rabbah*, whose authors derive a lesson from a biblical *statement* concerning birds when discussing the necessity of sleep-deprivation and penitential fasting in saving one's soul – which would, if anything, correspond to an ascetic return to the cave. The Midrash cites Proverbs 6:5 ("Save yourself like a deer out of the hand [of a hunter], like a bird out of the hand of the fowler [*yaqush*]"), suggesting that the fasting penitent will not be "smitten [*tinnaqesh*] by the descent into Gehenna" or that through fasting one does not "become chaff [*yaqush*] for the fire of Gehenna, seeing that the power of repentance reaches even to the Throne of Glory" (translation based on Burton L. Visotzky, *The Midrash on Proverbs* (New Haven: Yale University Press, 1992), 37).

of his stay. Only when the rabbis emerge from the cave do we learn that they were hiding in fear of some danger that had since "calmed down."[32] Rather, the author's apparent ambiguity, simultaneously invoking and dispelling the image of the Rashbi as an ascetic cave-dweller, may be deliberate. Both asceticism and flight from danger, however, are forms of withdrawal from the community that seems incompatible with personal providence as well as with rabbinic Judaism *tout court,* as the story illustrates in the sequel.

The second part of the story describes the rabbis' healing in a cold bath and the subsequent purification of Tiberias. Their healing in a bath, in conjunction with the imagery of their impure skin condition and with the subsequent purification of Tiberias from corpses, invokes the pairing of the corpse and the leper in biblical ritual law.[33] Hence, the rabbis' reintroduction into society makes them the subjects to metaphorical purification, leading to the town's actual purification. Corpse impurity in Tiberias was indeed a problem in Late Antiquity. Herod Antipas forced Jews to settle in the city although it was built on top of a former graveyard. Evidence of this stems primarily from Josephus, and Levine discusses the historical aspects of the problem.[34] The third part of the Rashbi story indicates that there had been a rabbinic vote affirming the purity of Tiberias.[35] Despite the persistent presence of one corpse in the city – the one hidden by the *am ha'aretz* who then takes its place – the Rashbi story suggests a pragmatic solution to the problem of corpse impurity. On the one hand, the story does not dismiss the necessity of such purification, and on the other hand, it solves the problem of the city's impurity with a clean-up subsequent to the vote, rendering it inhabitable for rabbinic Jews, especially priests. The central theme of the

---

[32] The story's detailed precision and the relative consistency of our textual witnesses make it unlikely that the author simply "forgot" to inform the audience of this matter earlier. Only in manuscript Adler of *Bereshit Rabbah,* the story gives away at the beginning that there was a "persecution," a passage likely to be inserted later in order to fill in the odd gap at the beginning of the story.

[33] See Maccoby, "Corpse and Leper."

[34] See Flavius Josephus, *Antiquities* XVIII 2.4 and Levine, "R. Simeon b. Yohai and the Purification of Tiberias," 167.

[35] The story indeed implies that such a vote on the status of Tiberias took place, and the respective rabbinic procedure of declaring places clean has many precedents. Levine writes: "Voting was a standard procedure in determining legal questions. According to Tosefta, the great Sanhedrin meeting in the Temple precincts would decide questions of purity by vote. Other issues such as ... the applicability of the laws of tithing ... and the Sabbatical year were all decided by a vote. In the second century, when the rabbis were particularly concerned with questions of purity, votes were taken in this regard on a whole number of occasions. Undoubtedly the radical population shift following the wars against Rome had much to do with the need to purify parts of Palestine and beyond, which had formerly not enjoyed such status. Thus we find late Second century rabbis voting on and purifying such cities as Caesarea, Ascalon, Bet Yemah and Bet Guvrin" ("R. Simeon b. Yohai and the Purification of Tiberias," 171).

second part, hence, is purity, and more specifically, the interdependence of the purity of the individual and the Jewish community.

In the third part, on his way home for Shabbat, three opponents confront Rashbi, first in Tiberias, then in Magdala of the Dyers (not the Magdala near Tiberias mentioned in the Gospels but Magdala near Gadara, also known as "Magdala Gador"),[36] and finally in Bet Netofa (known today as *Sahl al-Battuf*).[37] Rashbi leaves none of them alive. His "judgment" of them amends his previous belief in personal providence; his divinely sanctioned miracles now determine the men's fate, rather than leaving the task to God alone. Hence, the theme of the third part is rabbinic authority, calibrating the role of the deviant individual vis-à-vis the communal consensus.

This Rashbi story is included in a number of other Palestinian rabbinic compilations.[38] Lee Levine analyzes the relationship between these versions and between them and the better-known parallel in the Bavli (*Shabbat* 33b–34a).[39] He argues convincingly that the Babylonian story is an adaptation of the Palestinian version, a very reasonable claim accepted by other scholars.[40]

---

[36] Most scholars follow Graetz's identification of the place *Migdal Gadara* with "Magdala of the Dyers." See H. Graetz, "Notizen zur Topographie Palästinas," *MGWJ*, 28 (1880), 487–495. I could not locate Graetz's Greek rendition of *Migdal Gadar* as "Μάγδαλα Γαδάρων" (ibid., 490) in any extant Greek text. See also Gottfried Reeg, *Die Ortsnamen Israels nach der rabbinischen Literatur* (Wiesbaden: Dr. Ludwig Reichert Verlag, 1989), 388 f. and 393–395. On Midgal Gador, see also note 49; on the function of the different locations in the story, see page 198 f.

[37] See Reeg, *Die Ortsnamen Israels nach der rabbinischen Literatur*, 140 f.

[38] Roughly contemporary with *Bereshit Rabbah* are the parallels in *Pesiqta de-Rav Kahana* 11.15 and in the Yerushalmi *Shevi'it* IX,1, 38d. Later parallels include *Qohelet Rabbah* 10.8 and *Esther Rabbah* 3.7.

[39] Levine, "R. Simeon b. Yohai and the Purification of Tiberias," 143–85. On both the Palestinian and the Babylonian versions, see also Ben-Zion Rosenfeld, "R. Simeon B. Yohai," 364–67.

[40] Since the Bavli version appears to be an adaptation of the Palestinian story, I consider the respective Bavli author as evidence of a historical audience of the Palestinian story, an ancient witness that may give us some indication of how the Palestinian story was understood in the Babylonian rabbinic community. I will refer to this evidence where appropriate. See also Richard Kalmin, *Jewish Babylonian between Persia and Roman Palestine* (New York: Oxford University Press, 2006), 90–93; Michal Bar-Asher Siegal, *Literary Analogies in Rabbinic and Christian Monastic Sources* (PhD diss. Yale University, 2010); Ofra Meir, "The Story of R. Simeon ben Yohai and his Son in the Cave–History or Literature?" *'Alei Siah* 26 (1989), 145–60 [Hebrew]; and Jeffrey Rubenstein, *Talmudic Stories: Narrative Art, Composition, and Culture* (Baltimore: The Johns Hopkins University Press, 1999), 105–138. Rubenstein discusses in detail the Bavli's adaptations of the Palestinian versions. For another intriguing analysis of the Bavli's Rashbi story, see also Charlotte Fonrobert, "Plato in Rabbi Shimeon bar Yohai's Cave (bShabbat 33b–34a), The Talmudic Inversion of Plato's Politics of Philosophy," *AJS Review* 31 (2007), 277–296. The Neoplatonic context that Fonrobert suggests for the Bavli seems relevant to *Bereshit Rabbah* as well; the issue, however, necessitates a more thorough discussion of the rabbis' own relationship to Neoplatonism.

Several factors indicate that the story, like most rabbinic stories, was an independent text before being incorporated into rabbinic collections.[41] The relationships between the story's Palestinian versions are not clear, and their chronology cannot be accurately established.[42] I use the version from *Bereshit Rabbah* in my analysis because it allows for the fullest contextualization of its parodic elements and because of its illuminating placement in this midrashic compilation.[43]

The parody of the Gospel is fully integrated into the story's literary structure, which therefore I briefly address in order fully to assess the parody. The sequence of Rashbi's actions may at first seem random, but a closer reading reveals that the first and third parts are intrinsically linked to one another, through the narrative sequence and also through a series of lexical and conceptual repetitions:

---

[41] The most evident sign of compound composition is the switch between Hebrew and Aramaic. The appearances of Rashbi's son in *Bereshit Rabbah* and in the *Pesiqta de-Rav Kahana* also show clear traces of being a later interpolation – the details do not quite fit into the narrative. Thus, the son is mentioned in the beginning, but Rashbi observes the birds alone. After they purify Tiberias together, Rashbi travels home alone while his son disappears entirely. These and other signs of redaction show that the story uses preexisting materials, a fact that dovetails with the evidence offered by the variety of rabbinic parallels of the story. Accordingly, the son is entirely absent from the Yerushalmi's account; see the following note.

[42] In one aspect, the Yerushalmi's might be the oldest version. Here, Rashbi's son is entirely absent. The Yerushalmi, however, includes other traces of interpolation, such as an intervention of the Holy Spirit. Moreover, Rashbi's conflict with his last opponent occurs earlier in the Yerushalmi, not at the end of the Rashbi story; see note 98 below. Most importantly, Rashbi's second opponent is portrayed very differently; see note 116 below. Due to lower criticism, the chronology of the versions cannot be determined. See also Hans-Jürgen Becker, "Text and History: The Dynamic Relationship between Talmud Yerushalmi and Genesis Rabbah," in Shaye J.D. Cohen (ed.), *The Synoptic Problem in Rabbinic Literature* (Providence: Brown Judaic Studies, 2000), 145–158.

[43] First, the story is included in *Bereshit Rabbah*'s discussion of the conflict between Jacob and Esau, the latter being the rabbinic codeword for gentile, then Christian Rome. (See Friedrich Avemarie, "Esaus Hände, Jakobs Stimme. Edom als Sinnbild Roms in der frühen rabbinischen Literatur," in Reinhard Feldmeier and Ulrich Heckel (eds.), *Die Heiden: Juden, Christen und das Problem des Fremden* (Tübingen: Mohr Siebeck, 1994), 177–208). Second, *Bereshit Rabbah*'s introduction to the story also features a teaching on benefaction reciprocity, which is helpful for reading the interdependence of the individual and the community in the Rashbi story. The audience learns that one should express gratitude towards a beneficial place: just as Jacob rewarded a city for the benefits it granted him, so does Rashbi. Grateful of being healed in the baths, Rashbi purifies Tiberias. *Bereshit Rabbah* channels the audience's attention to reciprocity. Finally, the story's interpretation of Jacob's observance of the Sabbath following the story of Rashbi needs to be contextualized with the widespread antinomian patristic argument that the patriarchs did not observe many Mosaic laws. These issues, while useful for my reading of the Rashbi story, require further consideration beyond the scope of the present study.

– In part I, the rabbis hide (טמון) whereas in part III the am ha'aretz hides (טמריה) a corpse.[44]
– In part I, Rashbi "goes out" of his cave (נפק), and "goes out" again (נפק) to find that things have calmed down. The latter occurrence is paralleled and inverted in part III, where a snake "goes out" (נפק) to bite Rashbi's opponent, while the former occurrence is already paralleled in part II when the rabbis "remove" (מפקין) the corpses from the city.
– In part I, the rabbis eat the Carobs of *Gadara* (גירודא). In part III, Rashbi accuses Naqai of having breached the fence (*gader*) of the sages.
– In part I, Rashbi "hears a heavenly voice" (שמע ברת קלא). In part III, he "hears the voice" (שמע קליה) of his opponent Naqai.
– Just as God "judges" the birds in part I, Rashbi "judges" his opponents in part III. However, in contrast with God, who condemns one bird and spares another, Rashbi does not spare his opponents. The story conveys the imagery of judgment by employing "Roman" legal terminology in part I and by having Rashbi explicitly accuse his second and third opponents of Halakhic wrongdoings in part III.

The story thus links the separate parts through a system of shared motifs and verbal roots, creating a sense of cohesion and thematic interrelationship that will also guide my approach to analyze the story's references to various non-rabbinic texts. In effect, the story mirrors the personae of Rashbi as a recluse in part I and of Rashbi as a stern rabbinic leader in part III, allowing its audience to perceive the relationship between the individual and the community as one when it comes to the following topics: the problem of seclusion and individual providence in part I is linked to Rabbinic authority in part III, thereby constituting a frame around part II as the story's central sequence and emphasizing its primary topic, purity.

Purity

The structural emphasis on part II joins its thematic prominence as the axis of the story's broader parallelism; the story strengthens the cohesion of the three parts by implicitly alluding to the theme of purity and impurity in all of them:[45]

– As explained above, the image of the rabbis' "rusting" implies a skin condition, even if formerly unknown and halakhically irrelevant. The text's rabbinic audience would have perceived any skin condition, even if metaphorical and grotesque, as impure and thus in need of purification according to the now defunct biblical ritual law.

---

[44] Manuscript Rome, a Yemenite manuscript, and the Venice print have טמירין when Rashbi and his son hide as well, resulting in a complete lexical repetition.
[45] On the chiastic emphasis of central elements in Antique and Late Antique sources see John W. Welch, "Introduction," in John W. Welch (ed.), *Chiasmus in Antiquity: Structures, Analyses, Exegesis* (Hildesheim: Gerstenberg, 1981), 13.

- Accordingly, the image of the two birds is reminiscent of the biblical purification ritual of a person recovering from scale disease, in which one bird is slaughtered while another is set free, just as in Rashbi's epiphany. Even though the ritual became defunct after the destruction of the Temple, the rabbis kept it alive by reenacting it discursively.[46]
- The rabbis' "healing" from their rust in a bath also recalls the immersion in water in the biblical purification ritual, again suggesting that the story plays on the theme of physical impurity.[47] Furthermore, by presenting the rabbis' healing in the *frigidarium* and the purification of Tiberias as reciprocal, the story emphasizes that the purification of the rabbis is inherent to their healing.[48]
- An inversion and bilingual wordplay links the word "cold" with the purification of Tiberias. The expression "cold house" (בית מקר) is a *hapax legomenon* in rabbinic literature, and I follow Levine in interpreting it as *frigidarium*. Rashbi uses "lupines" to purify the city. "Lupines," in Hebrew תרמוסה, is a loanword from the Greek word for lupines, θέρμος. This same word, in turn, also means "heat" in Greek. (θερμὰ λουτρά means thermal bath; any inhabitant of the Greco-Roman world would have understood that the rabbis, in the "cold bath," were separated from such a thermal bath by a mere single wall.) Accordingly, the thermal baths of Tiberias (or of Gadara), the most likely locations of the *frigidarium*, are also known as *hammata* (thermal baths) in rabbinic literature.[49] Hence, with this lexical correspondence the story playfully links purification with lupines, the "heat plants," to cold baths, and again to thermal baths, emphasizing the theme of reciprocal purification once more.
- The *am ha'aretz* in part III, by handling a corpse, becomes impure. Moreover, any dealings of a rabbi with an *am ha'aretz* suggests impurity in the first place since the latter by definition disregards purity rules.[50] Ironically, when the *am ha'aretz* challenges Rashbi's purification, he is turned into a corpse himself. By "burying"

---

[46] See Leviticus 17:7, Mishna *Nega'im* 13.1–14.2, *Keritot* 2.3, Tosefta *Keritot* 1.14, and *Menahot* 6.11, with Hyam Maccoby, *Ritual and Morality: the Ritual Purity System and its Place in Judaism* (New York: Cambridge University Press, 1999), 130–140, and Joshua Schwartz, "On Birds, Rabbis, and Skin Disease," in M. Poorthuis and J. Schwartz, *Purity and Holiness* (Leiden: Brill, 2000), 207–222. Schwartz argues that the rabbis had sparrows in mind (צפורי דרור, literally "wild" birds) when discussing this ritual (ibid., 211 ff.).

[47] Any person recovering from scale disease needs to bathe at the beginning of his purification ritual (Leviticus 14:9, Mishna *Nega'im* 14.2–3).

[48] See Martin Jacobs, "Römische Thermenkultur im Spiegel des Yerushalmi," in Peter Schäfer, *The Talmud Yerushalmi and Graeco-Roman Culture* (Tübingen: Mohr Siebeck, 1998), vol. I, 231 f.

[49] The earliest rabbinic source that mentions the baths of Gadara, the Palestinian Tosefta, uses the term Hammata to designate both the baths of Tiberias (*Eruvin* 5.2) and those of Gadara (ibid., 4.13). In the latter passage, Rabbi Yehuda haNasi (Rashbi's teacher) rules that the inhabitants of the nearby village Migdal Gadara are allowed to visit the baths of Hammata on Shabbat. The *Yerushalmi* (*Eruvin* V.7.3 (22d) states the same and adds that not only the inhabitants of Gadar, but also those of Migdal, are allowed to visit Hammata.

[50] See Mishna *Taharot* 7.1–8.5; A'haron Oppenheimer, *The 'Am ha-Aretz:' a Study in the Social History of the Jewish People in the Hellenistic-Roman Period* (Leiden: Brill, 1977); Lee Levine, *The Rabbinic Class of Roman Palestine in Late Antiquity* (New York: The Jewish Theological Seminary of America, 1989), 112–117; and Richard Kalmin, *The Sage in Jewish Society of Late Antiquity* (London: Routledge, 1999), 27–50.

him in Tiberias, Rashbi fails to remove all corpses from the city and fails to achieve complete purity.

The pervasive presence of the purity theme links the different parts of the story through an intricate system of lexical and thematic allusions. With many variations on the themes of impurity and purification, the story manages to finely calibrate the proper rabbinic attitude: a rabbi should not dwell impurely in a cave, and a city should not be strewn with buried corpses. Yet Rashbi is also portrayed in his confrontation with Naqai ("the pure") as neither too strict nor too lenient about the requirements for declaring Tiberias pure. As I shall soon argue, the metaphorical impurity of Rashbi and his son along with the actual yet imperfect purification of Tiberias simultaneously turn the rabbinic stance against the gentile Christian disregard for matters of purity as well as against heretical inner-Jewish extremist views, such as Naqai's.

Providence

The theme of providence receives equal attention throughout the story's attempt to link the fate of the individual to that of the community. Rashbi initially perceives the epiphany as indicating that God alone judges bird and man and concludes that hiding as a hermit is not sensible. His belief in personal providence seems at first confirmed by the fact that "things have calmed down," and he returns to the community. At the behest of his son, Rashbi then interferes with the fate of Tiberias and begins to take public action, illustrating that providence plays out in public rather than in caves. After being challenged, Rashbi's belief in personal providence gives way even more to a broader sense of communal providence. He himself starts to shape the fate of others by severely judging his opponents with divine help.

It appears at first that the story does not address Christianity or belief in Jesus. It also seems, even if grotesque at times, grim rather than comical. Reading the story as a satirical forth of fifth century Palestinian Gospel parody, however, draws our attention to the fact that providence, asceticism, purity, and the authority of the sage were key issues that occupied rabbis, philosophers, and Christians alike.

The conflict between *tyche* (random fate) and *pronoia* (divine providence) had pervaded Greek philosophical and literary discourse since the Hellenistic period. To put it crudely, we find on the one extreme texts like Plutarch and some of the Greek novels that suggest the possibility of personal providence.[51] More complex were the arguments of the Stoics, who affirmed

---

[51] See Robert Lamberton, *Plutarch* (New Haven: Yale University Press, 2001), 40–58.

providence but not at the level of the individual,[52] and the Neoplatonists emphasized free will alongside providence.[53] On the other extreme, we find groups like the Epicureans, who rejected the idea of providence altogether.[54] After the time of Constantine, personal providence became a central theme also among patristic authors of the fourth and fifth centuries, who emphatically affirmed its existence.[55]

Our knowledge of Palestinian rabbinic views concerning providence is very limited, and comprehensive theories of providence are found only in the Bavli.[56] Yet Ephraim Urbach aptly notes that "belief in two principles – both in Providence and in freedom of choice – is common to [the rabbis of all generations], but they differ in fixing their boundaries and in the way of reconciling them."[57] The famous saying in Mishna *Avot* (3.13), "all is (fore)seen [צפוי], yet freedom of choice is given," seems to represent the view of most of the fourth- and fifth- century Palestinian rabbis. This very late mishnaic tractate seeks to integrate human agency and divine providence, and the rabbis here seem closest to the Greek mainstream, perhaps aligned in this respect more with the Neoplatonists than with the Stoics.[58]

Urbach has argued that the saying in *Avot* might be directed against the type of determinism prevalent in the teachings of Paul.[59] Conversely, I view predetermination and providence not so much as foci of rabbinic polemics

---

Chaereas and Callirhoe and *Leucippe and Clitophon* perhaps contain the most intense discussions on this ubiquitous topic in the Greek novels.

[52] See, for example, Dorothea Frede, "Theodicy and Providential Care in Stoicism," in idem. (ed.), *Traditions of Theology: Studies in Hellenistic Theology, its Background and Aftermath* (Leiden: Brill, 2002), 85–117.

[53] Notably, see Proclus's "On Providence," a fifth century Neoplatonic response to Stoicism.

[54] Epicurus, of course, predates the time during which "Providence" became a catchword, as already pointed out in the classic study by Norman Wentworth DeWitt, *Epicurus and his Philosophy* (Minneapolis: University of Minnesota Press, 1954), 179–182.

[55] See, for example, Theodoret of Cyrus's and of John Chrysostom's "On Providence;" hearkening back to works with the same title by Seneca or Philo. See also Silke-Petra Bergjan, *Der fürsorgende Gott: der Begriff der PRONOIA Gottes in der apologetischen Literatur der Alten Kirche* (Berlin: Walter De Gruyter, 2002).

[56] See Ephraim Urbach, *The Sages: Their Concepts and Beliefs* (Jerusalem: Magnes Press, 1975), 255–285, and Yaakov Elman, "When Permission is Given: Aspects of Divine Providence," *Tradition* 24 (1989), 24–45, and the reference provided there.

[57] Urbach, *The Sages: Their Concepts and Beliefs*, 264.

[58] For the historical precedents of the rabbis' position, see David Flusser, "The Pharisees and Stoics according to Josephus," *Iyun*, 14 (1964), 318–329; Shlomo Pines, "A Platonistic Model for two of Josephus' Accounts of the Doctrine of the Pharisees concerning Providence and Man's Freedom of Action," *Immanuel* 7 (1977), 38–43; and David Flusser, "Josephus on the Sadducees and Menander," *Immanuel* 7 (1977), 61–77. On the dating of *Pirqe Avot* see Günther Stemberger, "Mischna Avot: frühe Weisheitsschrift, pharisäisches Erbe oder spätrabbinische Bildung?," *ZNW* 96 (2005), 243–58.

[59] Urbach, *The Sages: Their Concepts and Beliefs*, 258f, referring especially to Romans 8.29f.

but rather as themes discussed both by rabbis and by Paul's heirs among orthodox Christians.[60] While Christian authors tended to consider providence in systematic treatises as well as in paranaetic homilies, Palestinian rabbis approach it through midrashic narrative that combined aspects of both genres, according to the literary preferences of each community.

Still, Rashbi's trust in God's judgment invokes a motif uncannily familiar to a Late Antique audience. Ofra Meir has already noted in passing the close resemblance between the Rashbi story and Jesus' Sermon on the Mount in the Gospel of Matthew.[61] The Rashbi story seems to parody a passage about birds and providence from the Sermon on the Mount, a part of the gospels which received constant attention (readership, translation, and preaching) throughout Late Antique Christianity. Again, in order to facilitate the comparison with the Rashbi story, I make use of the Syriac Peshitta as the version closest to the mostly lost Christian Palestinian Aramaic version.[62] Matthew quotes Jesus:

Therefore, I tell you, do not worry about your life [*nfshkwn*], what you will eat [*t'klwn*], or what you will drink, nor about your body [*pgrkwn*], what you will wear. Is not life more than food and the body more than clothing? Look at the birds of the air [*shmy'*]; they neither sow nor reap nor gather into barns, and yet your heavenly Father ['*bhwn dbshmy'*] feeds them. Are you not of more value than they? And can any of you by worrying add a single hour to your span of life? (6:25–27).

Later, Matthew has Jesus reiterate:

Do not fear those who kill the body but cannot kill the soul; rather fear him who can destroy both soul and body in hell. Are not two birds [*sfryn*] sold for a penny? Yet not one of them will fall to the ground apart [*bl'd mn*] from your Father. And even the hairs of your head [*drshkwn mn'*, old Syriac: *s'r' dryshkwn*] are all counted [*mnyn*] (10:28–30).

Matthew, in the original context, advises his audience not to worry about their earthly existence. Yet, this can easily be understood as a rejection of human agency, recalling the attempt of late ancient Christian ascetics fully to submit to divine providence, as we shall soon see. The Rashbi story, then, imitates and exaggerates Matthew's teachings by staging them as divine

---

[60] In the time of *Bereshit Rabbah*, the theme of providence occurs in rabbinic polemics against gentiles. For example, in *Bereshit Rabbah* 27.4, a gentile challenges Rabbi Joshua ben Qorha on predetermination in a way in which he could have challenged any church father, illustrating that Christian and rabbinic orthodoxy converge on this matter.

[61] Meir, "The Story of R. Simeon ben Yohai and his Son in the Cave–History or Literature?," 19.

[62] On the Peshitta citation and transliteration see Chapter Four, note 15. On the fragments of the Palestinian Aramaic version see Christa Müller-Kessler and Michael Sokoloff, *The Christian Palestinian Aramaic New Testament Version from the Early Period* (Groningen: Styx, 1998).

spectacle. Part I of the Rashbi story imitates the following thematic and lexical elements of the Sermon on the Mount, as becomes clear when aspects of Matthew and *Bereshit Rabbah* are juxtaposed:

Gospel of Matthew	Bereshit Rabbah
"do not worry about your life [*nfshkwn*]," "do not fear those who kill the body"	The rabbis are indeed concerned at first about their lives, but then Rashbi decides to stop worrying since God takes care of the "soul [נפש] of a man." He feels justified in his decision since things had indeed calmed down.
"what you will eat [*taklwn*]"	The rabbis worry about eating (אוכלים), ending up with carobs, the epitome of "food that is not eaten." Then, the rabbis emerge from the cave.
"nor about your body [*pgrkwn*]"	The rabbis worry about their sick bodies (גופן, a different root from the one in the Peshitta) but are then healed.[63]
"look at the birds of the air [*shmya*]," "are not two birds [*sfryn*] sold for a penny?"	Rashbi literally looks at the two birds (ציפרין) and learns about Heaven's (שמיא) judgment.[64]
"Yet not one of them will fall to the ground apart from [*bl'd mn*] your Father."	Rashbi sees how God judges each bird individually; one falls in the hand of the hunters, and one does not, an image not found elsewhere in rabbinic literature. Precisely like Matthew, Rashbi concludes that "[if] a bird is not hunted down without [מבלעדי] [the judgment of] heaven," personal providence prevails. Both texts reason *a minori ad majus*.

The conceptual and verbal similarities allow for a clear identification of the text being imitated. When Rashbi leaves the cave and sees the hunter, God, quite literally, judges each of the birds. Like Pasolini, whose *Uccellacci e uccellini* parodies Saint Francis's avian audience, the Midrash parodically literalizes Matthew's metonymy indicating that not even one bird "is for-

---

[63] The Peshitta's word *pgr* also appears as פגר in Jewish and Christian Palestinian Aramaic; see Sokoloff, *Dictionary of Palestinian Jewish Aramaic*, 424.

[64] Matthew 6.28 continues by stating: "And why do you worry about clothing? Consider the lilies of the desert." The version of the story in the Bavli emphasizes the rabbis' drink and clothing explicitly, adding to the imagery from Matthew. Furthermore, once the audience grasps the link to Matthew, the use of "lupines" for purification is understood anew: both texts speak about birds and flowers. However, since lupines are edible, it should not assumed that the audience would have associated the two types of flowers, lilies and lupines; I therefore bracket this question.

gotten." Here, God's concern for the birds changes from merely feeding and remembering them to an elaborate procedure conforming with the Roman imperial legal jargon well known to the rabbis.[65] The hyperbolic image of God judging birds ironizes the Sermon on the Mount without disagreeing with the Christian teaching on providence per se.[66] Just as in the previous chapter, the rabbinic author stages an exegetical and satirical gospel parody.

The gospel parody is apparent and precise, yet subtle enough to qualify only as parodic allusion. The remainder of the story contains few satirical allusions, but its subsequent parodic allusions to the Gospels are even fainter than the one just discussed. Accordingly, the object of the following is to assess the function of this gospel parody in its broader rabbinic and non-rabbinic textual milieu, and to identify its satirical target. Especially when Matthew is considered along with his fifth century interpreters and other Christian lore, it becomes clear that the parody anchors the Rashbi story deep in the enemy's foundational text, satirizing not the gospel itself but its readers. Absurdity and the grotesque may indeed mark the entire story as a burlesque that reckons with various forms of Christian teachings on asceticism, providence, purity, and finally, with forms of Jewish heresy, among them belief in Jesus. This, however, becomes clear only when we consider the respective Jewish and Christian teachings in their context of Greco-Roman philosophical discourse.

Asceticism

The Antiochian church fathers of the late fourth century – often the best source for Christian teachings in post-Constantinian Palestine as well – understood the Sermon on the Mount, along with other interpretations, as a

---

[65] As Levine points out correctly, the "legal terms – dimissio and specula – are found throughout rabbinic literature …[I]n recounting the trial of R. Eliezer before the Roman proconsul, the judge's verdict is rendered as 'dimissus' – you are released" ("R. Simeon b. Yohai and the Purification of Tiberias," 161). Intriguingly, the term "dimissus" is also used when the Roman judge dismisses the charge that Rabbi Eliezer (ben Hyrcanos) was a Christian (see most recently Schäfer, *Jesus in the Talmud*, 41–51). See also note 34 in Chapter Four and notes 10 and 117.

[66] Part three of the story contains an odd transposition of language from the same passage in the Sermon on the Mount, in the old Syriac, which I shall discuss later: "And even the hairs of your head [*s'r' dryshkwn*] are all counted" – Rashbi has as many laws as "the hair on his head (כסער ראשי)" proving that Tiberias is clean. This similarity is intriguing, but the shift from hair to laws does not readily support the assumption that the Rashbi story actually imitates the remark concerning God's counting the hair of every person's head. The shift from Matthean providence to rabbinic legal observance, however, does indeed fit the story's subsequent agenda of promoting the observance of rabbinic rulings.

promotion of ascetic practices, such as abstinence from food and bathing.[67]
A good example is found in Gregory of Nazianzus' funeral oration for his
friend Saint Basil the Great, written in 380:

Self-mastery [ἐγκράτεια] and fewness of wants [ὀλιγάρκεια] are a wondrous
thing ... Who was more free of food [ἄτροφος], without exaggerating, free of the
flesh [ἄσαρκος] [than Basil]?... He did not pay much attention to those things that
are equal to appetite and lived on the merest necessities ... His only delicacy was to
show his lack of delicacies and therefore to be free of more, but he looked at the lilies
and the birds, whose beauty is without craft and whose food is close by [σχέδιος],
according to ... Christ who impoverished his flesh for us so that we may enrich
ourselves in the divinity. Hence his coat and worn cloak and his not-washing [ἡ
ἀλουσία]... and the bread and the salt.[68]

Abstinence from washing, *alousia* (literally: "non-washing"), was a Christian way of extending asceticism, or "self-mastery."[69] Gregory equates self-
deprivation of food with abstinence from washing and invokes the Sermon
on the Mount's lilies and birds imagery. Gregory of Nazianzus was not the
only one to form this connection.[70] Non-bathing was a custom that drew
the attention of Greek contemporaries as well; it is likely that it was known
to any urban dweller of Palestine – including the author of the Rashbi story – as a Christian phenomenon.[71] The Sermon on the Mount is hence a text
of primary relevance for understanding any Palestinian text in the fourth
and fifth centuries. Its discourse on personal providence had come to stand
for Christian views of asceticism, and the author of the Rashbi story seems
to have had a good sense of this patristic or popular reading.

Intriguingly, the Rashbi story opens with an image of the two rabbis
fasting like Christian ascetics, subsisting on food "that is not eaten," and
experiencing a very Christian epiphany recalling the birds in Matthew and
paralleling the themes of Gregory's sermon.[72] I suggested that the story,

---

[67] See pages 88–94, and cf. Burton Visotzky, "Jots and Tittles: On Scriptural Interpretation in Rabbinic and Patristic Literatures," *Prooftexts* 8 (1988), 257–270.

[68] Cited according to Jean Bernardi, *Grégoire de Nazianze: Discours 42–43* (Paris: Les
Éditions du Cerf, 1992), 256.

[69] On the term "self-mastery," see note 105 in Chapter Two.

[70] For example, Gregory of Nazianzus' contemporary Gregory of Nyssa also links
the Sermon to *alousia* in his homily on the Peacemakers in *Homilies on the Beatitudes*,
Homily 7.2 (151.27), on Matthew 5.9. On the role of the Cappadocians in emphasizing
the liturgical aspects of Christian hagiographies, see Derek Krueger, *Writing and Holiness: The Practice of Authorship in the Early Christian East* (Philadelphia: University of
Pennsylvania Press, 2004), 110–132.

[71] For example, Eunapius, a sophist from Sardis who studied with a Christian sophist
in Athens and decidedly rejected the Christianization of the Empire, describes Christian
monks around the year 405 CE as "human in appeareance but swine in their way of living"
(*Lives of the Philosophers and Sophists*, 472).

[72] Interestingly, in the Bavli's version of the Rashbi story, the rabbis' diet consists of
bread and salt, stereotypically eaten by the ascetic, as explicitly mentioned in Gregory.

as a gospel parody, is ironically aligned with its Christian source. We now see that the story also may contain elements of an exegetical parody since it reenacts the Christian exegesis of the gospel passage by portraying the rabbis as ascetics. The story's satirical focus may allude to elements of the sermon's Christian exegesis or to its popular echoes, and continues with their reversal: the rabbis, in spite of Gregory's *alousia*, go on to bathe and do so ceremoniously.

The combination of gospel parody and satire of the gospel's readers recalls this strategy in the Bavli. A closer look at the story and its ascetic context indicates that this shift is part of the Rashbi story's nuanced development of a rabbi's balanced halakhic and spiritual conduct. While Gospel parody occurs primarily in the first part of the Rashbi story, parodic and satirical allusions to Christian topoi continue in the sequel. As mentioned before, I will in the remainder of this chapter continue to contextualize this parody within the story's overall message and its relationship to other rabbinic and non-rabbinic texts. I argue that Rashbi's parodic "defeat" of Christian asceticism, and his ironic appreciation of personal providence must be read in the context of the (sometimes satirical) philosopher's *Life*, and of Christian hagiography, a genre that emerged in dialogue with the same Greek philosophical genre.

Seclusion

The language of the story makes it clear from the outset that Rashbi's initial conduct is troublesome and hyperbolic. Hiding in a cave, of course, is a common motif in Jewish literature and history, starting with David's flight from Saul and Elijah's from Jezebel.[73] This motif continued to be prevalent in the time of the redaction of *Bereshit Rabbah*, when, for example, Rabbi Huna, a scholar of the fourth generation from Tiberias, flees from a mob to "a cave in Tiberias."[74] However, Rashbi and his son's extended stay in the cave is the longest one mentioned in Palestinian rabbinic sources, and there

---

[73] See I Samuel 21:1, I Kings 19:9, and *Bereshit Rabbah* 51.7. A good example of the continuing importance of caves is provided by the archeological studies of caves in the Bar Kokhba war; see Mordechai Ephraim Kislev, "Vegetal Food of Bar Kokhba Rebels at Abi'or Cave near Jericho," *Review of Palaeobotany and Palynology* 73 (1992), 153–160; Amos Kloner, "Hiding Complexes in Judaea: an Archaeological and Geographical Update on the Area of the Bar Kokhba Revolt," in Peter Schäfer (ed.), *The Bar Kokhba War Reconsidered* (Tübingen: Mohr Siebeck, 2003), 181–216.

[74] See *Bereshit Rabbah* 58.14 and Yerushalmi, *Pessachim* I:1.6 27b (2). The words for cave, בטיטא and בוטיתה respectively, are uncertain; see Sokoloff, *A Dictionary of Jewish Palestinian Aramaic*, 87 and 91. The *Yerushalmi* considered the cave to be in the great synagogue.

is no other account of anyone subsisting on so little. To the contrary, other Palestinian sources explicitly criticize such behavior. For example, we read in the Yerushalmi about a rabbi who hides (עביד טמיר) in a cave for three days in order to ponder over a problem. Subsequently, his colleagues severely admonish him for withdrawing instead of considering the quandary communally.[75] This attitude is most astutely expressed by Hillel: "do not separate from the community" (Mishna *Avot* 2.4).

As Michael Satlow and others have argued, Palestinian rabbinic literature in general is influenced as much by Stoic and Christian asceticism as by the rabbinic rejection of them.[76] The Rashbi story should thus be read in the context of a well established rabbinic discourse on asceticism, seclusion, and cave dwelling, which also informs the parody discussed in Chapter Two. Reading the rabbis' hyperbolic sojourn in the cave with similar Greek and Christian stories in mind explains why the cave episode was incorporated into the rabbinic text.

Epimenides and Rashbi in the Cave and the City

Lee Levine argues that the two rabbis' long retreat in the cave, sustained by the bare necessities, invokes the image of philosophers retreating to caves. He points to the widely circulating narrative of the pre-Socratic philosopher Epimenides as a possible inspiration for the Rashbi story. The story about Epimenides can be cobbled together from a number of sources: Epimenides subsists on appetite suppressants. He emerges from a long sojourn in a cave. He then purifies the city of Athens by exhuming corpses and puts to death two men responsible for the city's impurity. Several motifs in this story, first and foremost, the purification of a city, are of particular relevance to the present discussion.[77]

---

[75] *Nedarim* 9.1 (42c).

[76] Michael Satlow, "'And on the Earth you shall sleep': 'Talmud Torah' and Rabbinic Asceticism," *Journal of Religion* 83 (2003), 204–225; see the summary of Urbach there. Satlow emphasizes the ascetic tendencies within Palestinian rabbinic Judaism and in my view underemphasizes the strong reactions against them, which characterize the assessment of Urbach. See also Eliezer Diamond, *Holy Men and Hunger Artists: Fasting and Asceticism in Rabbinic Culture* (Oxford: Oxford University Press, 2004); and Henry A. Fischel, *Rabbinic Literature and Greco-Roman Philosophy: A Study of Epicurea and Rhetorica in early Midrashic Writings* (Leiden: Brill, 1973).

[77] See Levine, "R. Simeon b. Yohai and the Purification of Tiberias," 181 ff. The second or third century CE author Diogenes Laertius tells a version in which Epimenides, while searching for his father's sheep, falls asleep in a grotto or cave (ἄντρῳ) and reemerges 57 years later. His contemporaries interpret this miracle as a sign of divine favor and invite him to help purify plagued Athens (καθῆραι τὴν πόλιν, *Vitae Philosophorum* 1.109–10). According to a variant ending of the story in Diogenes Laertius's text, "some said that the

The importance of corpse-(im)purity in Greco-Roman culture can hardly be overemphasized. Most Greek societies in Late Antiquity carried on the classical Greek concept that considered corpses to be a source of impurity, and stories like the Epimenides tale perpetuated this notion.[78] Yet among philosophers of Late Antiquity, attitudes towards corpse impurity ranged widely. On the one extreme is the concern of Neoplatonists like Iamblichus, who, reportedly, would not walk in a street when he suspected that a corpse had been carried there before.[79] On the other extreme is the Cynics'

---

cause of the plague was the pollution contracted by the city in the matter of Cylon and that Epimenides pointed out to the Athenians how to get rid of it and that in consequence they put to death two young men, Cratinus and Ctesilius, and that thus the pestilence was brought an end to it" (C.D. Yonge, *The Lives and Opinions of Eminent Philosophers, by Diogenes Laertius* (London: Henry G. Bohn, 1853), 77). The "matter of Cylon" refers to the Athenian's betrayal of this nobleman's followers after his attempted coup in Athens. Having failed, Cylon escaped, and his followers were promised impunity if they surrendered, which they did. However, the Athenians, led by Megacles, stoned them to death. Megacles was thereupon cursed with an "impurity" and exiled with his family, the Alcmaenidae. Most noteworthy for the present inquiry is the fact that according to Thycidides (1.126) even the bodies of the clan were exhumed and removed from the city. Various philosophers of Late Antiquity retell the story; some traditions emphasize Epimenides' asceticism and add that he was able to survive on appetite suppressants; see Plutarch, *Moralia* 157d; H. Diels and W. Kranz, *Die Fragmente der Vorsokratiker* (Berlin: Wiedeman, 1952), 3; Felix Jacoby, *Die Fragmente der Griechischen Historiker*, vol. III (Leiden: Brill, 1957), F457. See also E. R. Dodds, *The Greeks and the Irrational* (Boston: Beacon Press, 1951), 207–235 and Jesper Svenbro, *Phrasikleia: An Anthropology of Reading in Ancient Greece* (Ithaca: Cornell University Press, 1993). There are, in turn, several affinities between the story of Epimenides and the "Sleeper's of Ephesus," evident from the sixth century onwards. Yet the motif of *sleeping* in a cave is absent from the Rashbi story and is found in rabbinic literature only in the narrative about Honi in the Yerushalmi 3.10 (66d) and in the Bavli (*Ta'anit* 23a).

[78] See Louis Moulinier, *Le Pur et l'impur dans la pensée des Grecs d'Homère à Aristote* (New York: Arno Books, 1952); Jean-Pierre Vernant, *Myth and Society in Ancient Greece* (New York: Zone Books, 1980); and Robert Parker, *Miasma: Pollution and Purification in early Greek Religion* (Oxford: Clarendon Press, 1983).

[79] The story of Iamblichus, according to Eunapius's *Lives of the Philosophers and Sophists*, reads as follows: Iamblichus was a native of Coelo Syria (5.1.1) who occasionally performed rites on his own and allegedly floated in the air while praying (5.1.6). One day Iamblichus returned to his home and was casually chatting when "suddenly his voice [τὴν φωνήν] was cut off. He stared at the earth [γῆν] for some time and then looked at his comrades and shouted: 'Let us take another way: a dead body [νεκρός] was carried there recently.'" Having said this, he took another road that seemed "purer" (5.1.11). Some of his companions, present at this instance, believed in the miraculous corpse-detecting powers of the philosopher while others thought he must have smelled the corpse. Even after seeing the people who had just returned from the burial, thus proving that Iamblichus was right, the doubting comrades found it necessary to inquire, and it was confirmed that the burial procession had indeed passed that way. There are a number of incidental linguistic and literary similarities between this story and the Rashbi story, such as the supernatural detection of corpse impurity, sage authority, challenge from within, piety, and miracle. These similarities do not hint at any textual relationship between the stories. Rather, they show that rabbinic and Greek authors alike drew on the ideal type of the sage , so the

complete disregard for corpse impurity: the Cynics, the rabbis knew well, slept in graveyards.[80] Here, the rabbis once more are most closely aligned with the Neoplatonists.

Levine rightfully cautions that whether the Epimenides tradition "influenced the Jews when formulating [the Rashbi story] cannot be fully answered in light of the traditions available."[81] Still, the similarities between the Epimenides and the Rashbi stories should be noted. Both sages

– Stay in a cave for a long time
– Suppress their appetites by eating food "that is not eaten"
– Emerge from the cave and find themselves favored by the divine
– Purify a major city by removing dead bodies
– Cause the death of their enemies

The fact that Diogenes Laertius and many others told this story in the third or fourth century suggests that the myth of Epimenides was still relevant in Late Antiquity. I therefore view the Rashbi story as belonging to the same genre.

Levine's question concerning "influence," however, presupposes that the rabbinic community was external to the world of Greek discourse. I would like to suggest that in the time of *Bereshit Rabbah* stories like that of Epimenides were the cultural matrix through which rabbinic as well as Christian circles expressed their similar concerns relating to asceticism, purity, and authority of the sage. The author of the Rashbi story could have indeed been "influenced" by the Epimenides story in as far as he playfully alluded to some of its elements.

It should also be noted, however, that there is no parody here: the elements that correspond to the Rashbi story are culled from different sources of the Epimenides story, and only a generic, but not a textual, relationship can be established. The imitation of the Greek cave-dwelling sage might be this rabbinic author's way of expressing his views of Rashbi. More precisely, however, it allows him to respond to the dominant Christian examples of the Greco-Roman genre of the *Life* of the sage, exemplified by the following story about the Christian holy man Porphyry.

---

story followed similar patterns in both cultures. The themes related to the representation of an ideal sage were not confined to any one group but were rather part of the general cultural discourse of the time.

[80] The rabbinic descriptions of a Cynic correspond to the popular Greek ones: a Cynic wears torn garments, destroys his property, sleeps in graveyards, and is associated with a demon cult. See the *Yerushalmi*, *Gittin* 7.1 (38b) and *Trumoth* 1.1 (2a). See also Saul Lieberman, "How much Greek in Jewish Palestine," in A. Altmann (ed.) *Biblical and other Studies* (Cambridge, Harvard University Press, 1963), 130ff; H.A. Fischel, *Rabbinic Literature and Greco-Roman Philosophy* (Leiden: Brill, 1973); and Menahem Luz, "A Description of the Greek Cynic in the Jerusalem Talmud," *JSJ* 20 (1989), 49–60.

[81] Lee Levine, "R. Simeon b. Yohai and the Purification of Tiberias," 182.

Porphyry of Gaza: Caves and Corpses in Christian Asceticism

The genre of the *Life* of the holy man was a central aspect of late ancient Christian religious activity.[82] Moreover, many Christian stories illustrate that in the time of the redaction of *Bereshit Rabbah*, cave-dwelling became a central aspect of Christian practice and discourse.[83] At the same time, however, the fact that Rashbi's stay in the cave was prolonged and that he was sustained by the bare necessities would have invoked a much more concrete contemporary practice, the Christian use of caves as a place for spiritual retreat from which the saint emerges transformed.

The most interesting context for the Rashbi narrative might be the story of Porphyry (347–407 CE), related to the Rashbi narrative both geographically and chronologically.[84] His fifth century hagiography was very popular throughout late antiquity: according to Ramsay MacMullan, it was first composed in Syriac in the fifth century, a text now lost, and subsequently translated into Greek, from which I quote, and other languages.[85] Porphyry, who later became the Bishop of Gaza, leads an ascetic life and retreats to a

---

[82] For a compelling interpretation of the genre, see Krueger, *Writing and Holiness*.

[83] A few examples of this ubiquitous motif should suffice. Thecla, the spiritual suitor of Paul in the third century *Acts of Paul and Thecla* retires to a cave for 72 years, living on herbs and water. The tradition did not disappear during the Christianization of the empire. The early sixth-century *Life* of John of Ephesus, for example, has his protagonist, blistered by the heat, sit naked in a cave full of water for a period of two years. The motif is also found in the eastern traditions. Hillaria, for example, also spent ten years in a cave, out of a thirty-year retreat in the desert; see A. J. Wensinck, *Legends Of Eastern Saints, Chiefly From Syriac Sources* (Leiden: Brill, 1913), II, 35–57. The most important literary witness is Palladius' *Lausiac History,* written around 420 CE (on caves, see 2.1, 17.10, 21.3, 23.1, 32.1, 36.1, 48.1, 51.1 and 58.1–4). See also Peter Brown, *The Body and Society: Men, Women, and Sexual Renunciation in Early Christianity* (New York: Columbia University Press, 1988), 210–388. Of equally great significance are the stories about the ascetics living in cells in the Egyptian desert, collected in the *Apophtegmata Patrum*; on the importance of this corpus for the study of the Bavli, see Michal Bar-Asher Siegal, *Literary Analogies in Rabbinic and Christian Monastic Sources*. At the same time, to a rabbinic audience, a retreat to a cave, followed by an illumination, might have recalled Plato's philosopher king's stay in a cave and his subsequent enlightenment; see Charlotte Fonrobert, "Plato in Rabbi Shimeon bar Yohai's Cave."

[84] This Porphyry, of course, is not the Neoplatonic philosopher by the same name (233–309 CE).

[85] See Ramsay MacMullen, *Christianizing the Roman Empire*, (New Haven: Yale University Press, 1984), 86. The prologue of "Life of Saint Porphyry" quotes Theodoret's *Religious History*, which was written in 444; at least the prologue, then, is a later text. The rest of the story is very difficult to date; see also J. W. Childers, "The Georgian Life of Porphyry of Gaza, in M. F. Wiles and E. J. Yarnold (eds.), *Studia Patristica XXXV: Ascetica, Gnostica, Liturgica, Orientalia* 35 (Louvain: Peeters, 2001), 374–384; Paul Peeters, "La vie géorgienne de Porphyre de Gaza", *Analecta Bollandiana* 59 (1941), 65–216; and Henri Grégoire and M.-A. Kugener, *Marc le Diacre: Vie de Porphyre, évêque de Gaza* (Paris: Société d'édition "Les Belles lettres," 1930), xxxiii.

cave (σπηλαίῳ) in the vicinity of the Jordan River (4.15–20) for five years. Due to the climate, he becomes very ill. When he reemerges from the cave, he excels in the interpretation of the Scriptures and he is able to resolve all the difficulties with which he is confronted (8.10, cf. 12.10). Shortly thereafter, the residents of Gaza accuse Porphyry of introducing a corpse into the city and thereby polluting it, but the alleged corpse, a Christian injured in a brawl with gentiles, comes back to life (8.22 f.). Porphyry thus establishes his authority and becomes a bishop.

The Porphyry narrative as well invokes the story of Epimenides in the cave and was arguably also written with the image of a cave-dwelling Greek sage in mind. The relationship between Christian sage stories and the pagan model is beyond the scope of this study. It should still be noted, however, that such an appropriation seems likely enough in light of the overwhelming evidence of Christian hagiographical sources.[86] Regardless, the specific Christian version of the Porphyry story inverts a central aspect of both the Greek and the rabbinic narratives discussed above and of Greek and rabbinic discourses and practices in general: Porphyry, like most orthodox Christians, is not concerned with the impurity of corpses.[87]

Whereas Epimenides and Rashbi had removed corpses from the two cities in order to purify them, Porphyry is accused of polluting a city by bringing a corpse into it. The Christian story needs to be understood as reflecting a fundamental cultural shift concerning corpse treatment. Unlike most of their neighbors, some Christians seem to have been, from early on, indifferent to the kind of impurity caused by the presence of corpses or even defiant of such concerns. Particularly, the Christian practice of burying corpses inside the city was starkly different from Greek and Jewish customs alike. Moreover, Christians revered the bodily remains of certain saints and attrib-

---

[86] On the interplay between Patristic and Philosophical "lives" see Laura Nasrallah, "Mapping the World: Justin, Tatian, Lucian, and the Second Sophistic," *Harvard Theological Review* 98 (2005), 283–314 and the intriguing study by Arthur Urbano, "'Read It Also to the Gentiles': The Displacement and Recasting of the Philosopher in the *Vita Antonii*," *Church History* 77 (2008), 877–914.

[87] The Christian tradition, with its emphasis on asceticism, would have had much interest in appropriating the heritages of sages such as Epimenides. Yet, in light of the Christian attitude towards corpses, it makes sense that the Porphyry story would play precisely with the aspects of purity expressed in the Epimenides stories. Porphyry technically does not pollute the city since the "corpse" he introduces is actually an almost-martyr, having been injured by brute pagans. When read in the context of the pagan reaction to the Christian indifference to corpse impurity, the story manages to deflect attention from the Christian break with this aspect of Eastern Mediterranean culture without negating it. At the same time, the many shared aspects of narratives like the Epimenides and Porphyry stories illustrate the broader complex pattern of cultural appropriation and adaptation.

uted powers of healing and resurrection to these relics.[88] Hence, even with
the most rudimentary grasp of the interplay between Christian Hagiography and philosophical *Lives*, I propose that the Rashbi story challenges the
Christian cave-dwelling sage by basing the character of Rashbi on the Greek
model. There is no traceable parody or any other direct textual relationship
here but rather a shared discursive space. In the broadest sense, the Rashbi
story is responding to the Christian appropriation of the Greek genre as a
whole. The Porphyry and the Rashbi stories share the following elements:[89]

- Retreat for a number of years to a cave in the vicinity of the Jordan River
- Sickness as a result of the retreat
- Illumination, Porphyry's in the cave and Rashbi's upon leaving it
- Introduction of a corpse into the city, the corpse comes back to life
- Accusations of endangering the purity of the city
- Establishment of authority

The resemblance between the Rashbi story and the Christian source is clear.
However, there are no linguistic similarities between the Rashbi and Porphyry stories. The Rashbi story's response to Porphyry, in my view, does
not imitate or target a specific text but rather the genre that the Porphyry
story exemplifies. The Rashbi story's use of this genre on the one hand
invokes the Greek tradition concerning cave-dwelling sages, as exemplified
by Epimenides, while on the other hand, subverts its Christian adaptations. This triangular cultural context draws particular attention to corpse
impurity.

---

[88] Cyril of Jerusalem provides a good example of this tendency in his Eighteenth Catechetical lecture (16): "Let us not be foolishly disbelieve that [the resurrections] had not
happened, for if handkerchiefs and aprons, when touching the sick body form the outside,
have raised up the ill, how much more so will the body of the prophet raise the dead?"
in W.C. Reischl and J. Rupp, *Cyrilli Hierosolymorum archiepiscopi opera quae supersunt
omnia* (Hildesheim: Olms, 1967), vol. II, 318. On relics, see most recently Joseph Patrich,
"Early Christian Churches in the Holy Land," in Ora Limor and Guy G. Stroumsa (eds.),
Christians and Christianity in the Holy Land: from the Origins to the Latin Kingdoms
(Turnhout: Brepols, 2006), 355–399; Byron McCane, "Is a Corpse Contagious? Early
Jewish and Christian Attitudes toward the Dead," *Society of Biblical Literature Seminar
Papers*, 31 (1992), 378–388; Peter Brown, *The Cult of the Saints: its Rise and Function in
Latin Christianity* (Chicago: University of Chicago Press, 1981), ch. 1; and Dennis Trout,
"Saints, Identity, and the City," in Virginia Burrus (ed.), *Late Ancient Christianity* (Min-
neapolis: Fortress Press, 2005), 165–187.

[89] Some of the parallels between Rashbi and Porphyry become even more evident in the
Bavli's version of the story, which is especially intriguing in light of the text's likely Syriac
origin. Porphyry resolves scriptural difficulties after having left the cave whereas in the
Bavli, Rashbi's attainment of the ability to resolve scriptural difficulties is the very core of
his sojourn in the cave, a period during which he studies incessantly; his refined acumen
fully emerges only after he leaves the cave (see Bavli, *Shabbat* 33b–34a). The Bavli's greater
precision in relating to the Christian text parallels the scenario depicted in Chapter Four,
in which only the Bavli fully exploits the full potential inherent to the elusive parodic allusions contained in a Palestinian rabbinic text, the *Pesiqta de-Rav Kahana*.

We now can see how broad we must cast our net to understand how the initial Gospel parody is embedded in a plethora of ways in which the rabbis situate their own views on providence, asceticism, rabbinic authority and purity vis-à-vis those of their various opponents. We also see that only an analysis that considers parody and satire along with broader intertextual and historical approaches can begin to unravel the message contained in rabbinic narrative. This approach is inherently messy, and the present analysis is certainly limited by the huge gaps in our assessment of Palestinian rabbinic culture. At the same time, my attempt in this chapter to weigh the literary against the historical evidence and vice versa in a "thick" reading of the text allows us to formulate a coherent approach to the Rashbi story.

Corpse Impurity in Rabbinic Culture

There is some indication that the issue of impurity of corpses was in flux in the time of the Rashbi story; the story thus once more addresses urgent concerns of its time. The theme is so ubiquitous in rabbinic culture that the following account is a simplified summary: The destruction of the Temple made it halakhically impossible to cleanse oneself properly from corpse impurity, and according to the rabbis, avoiding corpse impurity was also not strictly required, except for priests.[90] Yet, the rabbis sought to perpetuate the Temple cult without the Temple and in order to do so chose a combined approach. They substitute halakhic discussion for biblical rites and thereby adapt them to the new circumstances. In the case of corpse impurity, they decided to adopt a specific set of measures derived from the biblical laws, especially those concerning priests; the Mishna and the Talmudim, additionally, are replete with discussions on corpse impurity.[91]

As we have seen, the gentile Christian attitude could hardly be more different, and we may even detect some type of mutual polarization in the archeological record. According to Paul Figueras, "the start of Christian devotion for relics and the use of reliquaries concur with later [i.e., fourth century] Jewish rejection of ossilegium and secondary burial."[92] While Figueras perhaps overstates this point, this might indicate a shift in the rab-

---

[90] See Hyam Maccoby, *Ritual and Morality: the Ritual Purity System and its Place in Judaism*, 1–29.

[91] See especially tractates *Kelim*, *Oholot*, *Taharot*, *Zavim*, and *Miqvaot*.

[92] Paul Figueras, "Jewish Ossuaries and Secondary Burial: their Significance for Early Christianity," *Immanuel* 19 (1984–1985), 41. The decline of Bet Shearim in the late fourth century also supports this assessment. See also Gideon Avni and Uzi Dahari, "Christian Burial Caves from the Byzantine Period at Luzit" in Giovanni Claudio Bottini et al. (eds.), *Christian Archaeology in the Holy Land: New Discoveries: Essays in Honour of Virgilio C. Corbo* (Jerusalem: Franciscan Printing Press, 1990), 301–314.

binic attitude towards corpse impurity in the fourth century.[93] It should also be noted that the fifth (or sixth) century CE Palestinian Midrash *Pesiqta de-Rav Kahana* recounts a satirical story about Rashbi and his son, Eleazar, which links the protagonists of our story to the cult of relics, as Jeffrey Rubenstein has shown.[94] The story portrays Rashbi, his son, and the citizens of Gush Halav as utterly indifferent to the impurity caused by the contact with the corpse of Rabbi Eleazar.[95] The figure of Rashbi was thus used more than once to express such shifting rabbinic attitudes towards corpses. Finally, Levine emphasizes that both the Mishna and the Tosefta portray Rashbi as having "adopted a lenient posture on a whole range of legal discussion concerning corpse impurity."[96]

This summary provides context for the Rashbi story's concern with the impurity of corpses. Even though Rashbi and his son were not oblivious to the problem of corpse impurity, unlike the citizens of Gush Halav and even Rashbi in the *Pesiqta de-Rav Kahana* narrative, the story carefully thrusts the two rabbis into a heated debate by having them attempt to purify Tiberias and counter opposition. At stake is nothing less than rabbinic authority, and the right position concerning purity – not too little, not too much – is a key concept in the story.

---

[93] For example, the Yerushalmi permits reburial with some restrictions; see *Mo'ed Qatan* II, 2, 81b.

[94] Rubenstein is currently working on rabbinic veneration for relics of rabbis in the context of Christian practices. See his "The Burial Accounts of R. Eleazar b. R Shimon: Rabbis and the Cult of Relics in Late Antiquity," paper presented at the Association of Jewish Studies Annual Meeting, 2003; see also ibid., *Talmudic Stories*, 105–38.

[95] In the story in *Pesiqta de-Rav Kahana* 11.23, Rabbi Eleazar, Rashbi's son, says to his wife that his body will not rot and that only one worm will nibble on him since he seemed to have sinned once: he heard the voice of (ושמעת קלא) a man blaspheming in a synagogue but did not condemn ("judge") him (למעבד ביה דינא). In the sequel, Eleazar is buried in Meron, and Rashbi, who had already died, appears to the people of Gush Halav and commands them to bury his son next to him. The people of Meron fight off the people of Gush Halav with sticks, but in the end, sanctioned by a divine manifestation, the remains are transferred. As Rubenstein amply illustrates, all the motifs in the story – the body of a saint not rotting, its bestowing sanctity upon a place, and the populace engaging in violence over the ownership of the relics – are found in Greek and Syriac Christian literature. While the account, unparalleled in Palestinian rabbinic literature, probably postdates the Rashbi story in *Bereshit Rabbah*, it is an important indication that the Palestinian rabbis did associate Rashbi's son with a Christian cult of relics. The Bavli presents a similar story in *Bava Metsi'a* 84b.

[96] See Levine, "R. Simeon b. Yohai and the Purification of Tiberias," 170. Levine bases his observations on *Mishna Ohalot* 2.2, 2.9, 3.2, 18.5 and *Tosefta Ohalot* 17.9.

Rashbi's long way home

We are in better position now to read the ambiguities in the Rashbi story as precise remarks on the concerns of its time and to understand Rashbi's route to the edge of heretical territory as a homecoming, both literally and figuratively. If we posit that *Bereshit Rabbah* seeks to convey a coherent message, we should expect the story's internal structure and its literary contexts to supplement each other. Concerning the relationship between an individual and a community, however, Rashbi's initial seclusion is not in line with rabbinic norms. Hence, the unity between structure and context can only be established if we understand Rashbi as imperfect and as evolving, like one of Lucian's spoofed philosopher heroes. Rashbi's initial dwelling in the cave scandalously invokes Christian ascetic behavior, long shunned by rabbinic culture. His ascetic eating habits are just as troubling. The story's ironic enactment of the Sermon on the Mount, finally, thrusts Rashbi deep into Christian territory. The moment he adopts the belief in personal providence for birds, at the same time, constitutes the story's parodic climax and turning point.

The rabbinic audience is relieved to learn that Rashbi and his son declare that their sojourn in the cave was unnecessary. In satirical contrast to the Christian sources that link the Sermon on the Mount to asceticism, Rashbi derives the opposite lesson from the gospel. The story goes on to resolve the tension by revealing that Rashbi and his son were merely hiding rather than leading a Christian ascetic lifestyle. The rabbis return to communal practice by healing themselves in the bathhouse, leaving behind Christian *alousia*. Yet Rashbi's real enlightenment occurs not in the cave, as in the case of Christian ascetics, but in facing the public. It is the son that reminds Rashbi of his public duties, marking a clear inversion of rabbinic hierarchy and for the last time marking the inappropriateness of Rashbi's initial conduct. Rashbi adopts his son's advice and leaves behind gentile Christian indifference to corpse impurity by attempting to purify Tiberias. Only through his conflict with three Jewish opponents is he able finally to establish his authority over the community. Rashbi goes home for Shabbat, but the story does not reveal the location of his home. Tosefta *Me'ilah* (1.1) mentions that Rashbi spent one Shabbat in *Kfar Akko*, on the coast.[97] Akko

---

[97] In Mishna *Shevi'it*, Rashbi tries to allow the after-growth of all wild plants other than cabbage, but the sages oppose him (9.1). Shortly thereafter, in the same passage, he claims that all vegetables can be eaten in anticipation of the Sabbatical year "so long as סגריות are found in the Valley of Bet Netofa," that is, vegetables used for a certain sauce (Jastrow reads סגריות as an abbreviation of אכסיגרון, or ὀξύγαρον, *A Dictionary*, 64). The Rashbi story seems to combine the two passages from the Mishna (even though the second incident addresses the time before, not after, the Sabbatical year). Rashbi causes a man in

hence is a reasonable possibility: the way from Magdala of the Dyers, next to Gadara, to Akko passes through the Bet Netofa Valley near Sephoris, a fairly direct route. Accordingly, the choice of geographical locations in this story is by no means haphazard. Rather, the locations of Gadara, Tiberias, Magdala and Bet Netofa evoke existing literary material relating to Rashbi that also make sense geographically.[98] Therefore, it is especially remarkable that Rashbi, before deciding to return home for Shabbat, first goes from Tiberias back to Magdala of the Dyers, a long detour. The literary motivation behind Rashbi's detour might be associated with Magdala of the Dyers and the scribe who according to the rabbinic tradition resided there.[99] Moreover, in line with *Bereshit Rabbah*'s general emphasis on detail and locality, each scene marks an aspect of Rashbi's role in society and progressively restores his authority by depicting him upholding the rabbinic consensus. After facing (Christian) society and its practices at large, Rashbi reinforces rabbinic authority first in relation to the Jewish community in general, then within the circle of Jewish sages, and finally vis-à-vis his own individual leadership.

Rabbinic Authority

On his way home, Rashbi meets three Jewish opponents. His first opponent is an anonymous *am ha'aretz*, a Jew who blatantly disregards rabbinic notions of ritual purity. Rashbi's second opponent, Naqai, who I will claim is a heretical Jewish sage, takes purity concerns too far. The third opponent is an observant rabbinic Jew who ironically happens to side with Rashbi

---

the Bet Netofa Valley to die who cites Rashbi's own ruling concerning the after-growth, since the majority opinion had opposed him. Today's location is *Sahl al-Battuf*; see Reeg, *Die Ortsnamen Israels nach der rabbinischen Literatur*, 140 f.

[98] According to Levine, the story originally ended with the incident in Magdala (Levine, "R. Simeon b. Yohai and the Purification of Tiberias," 149). The parallel of the story in the Yerushalmi indeed recounts the incident of the man harvesting the after-growth independently, prior to telling the Rashbi story. See also Ofra Meir, "The Story of R. Simeon ben Yohai and his Son in the Cave–History or Literature?" 15.

[99] Rashbi's journey from the cave to Tiberias, through Magdala of the Dyers, and finally to Bet Netofa near Sephoris also recalls one of Rashbi's statements in Tosefta *Eruvin* 5.13 (=4.8), a tractate which the author of *Bereshit Rabbah* had in mind when writing the Rashbi story, as we have seen. After the difference between מגדל (a tower) and מערה (a cave) is explained, in the context of enlarging the inhabited area within which one is allowed to travel on Shabbat, Rashbi is quoted as saying somewhat dismissively that he likewise could permit people to "go from Tiberias to Sephoris … because of the caves and towers that are between them." I suggest that the author of *Bereshit Rabbah* adapted such an itinerary when describing Rashbi's traveling from a cave to Tiberias, through *Magdala*, a homonym of *Migdal* (tower) and finally to Bet Netofa in the vicinity of Sephoris. It does so by adapting literary units associated with Rashbi even though the "caves" and "towers" in the Tosefta are certainly different from the ones in the Rashbi story.

against the objections of the majority. All three opponents serve as foils for Rashbi's triumphant return to the rabbinic consensus, portraying his active repentance as literary polemic against all types of Jewish deviance. The story's climax is Rashbi's battle with Naqai, which I read in relation to the story's initial gospel parody.

Rashbi's punishment of his opponents invokes the principle of *measure for measure*.[100] First, the *am ha'aretz* stands (וקם) next to the corpse he had hidden and challenges Rashbi. Accordingly, Rashbi orders the standing man (דקיים) to lie down and resurrects the corpse by telling it to stand (יקום). The repetition of the verbal root emphasizes the progression from the man's offense against Rashbi's rabbinic authority to his punishment by Rashbi. Naqai's punishment also linguistically corresponds to his transgression. He simply challenges Rashbi by using his voice. Rashbi therefore kills him by citing a verse from the Torah. The third man is peacefully engaged in a halakhically dubious activity and does not challenge Rashbi at all. Rashbi, however, *sees* the man's scandalous action and kills him by merely *looking* at him.

These lexical and conceptual repetitions once more strengthen this unit's inner coherence and emphasize Rashbi's position in society. Rashbi's role as an effective judge extends to the story's parodic treatment of the Sermon on the Mount, where Matthew urges his followers not to judge,[101] but the absence of lexical imitations does not allow us to develop this idea further.[102] The themes of the story, in any case, remain in Christian territory for a while longer, and Rashbi's role surpasses that of Jesus in the gospels.

---

[100] On the principle of measure for measure, see note 21 in Chapter Two.

[101] Matthew instructs his followers: "Do not judge so that you may not be judged. For with the judgment you make, you will be judged, and the measure you give will be the measure you get (7:1 f.)." Luke incorporates this notion into the Sermon on the Plain, a parallel of the Sermon on the Mount (6:37 f.): "Be merciful, even as your Father is merciful; judge not, and you will not be judged; condemn not, and you will not be condemned; forgive, and you will be forgiven. Give, and it will be given to you; good measure, pressed down, shaken together, running over, will be put into your lap. For the measure you give will be the measure you get back."

[102] Jesus in Matthew accuses the Pharisees of being "like whitewashed tombs, which on the outside look beautiful but on the inside are full of bones of the dead and all kinds of impurity" (23:27). Interestingly, Luke's parallel suggests that the Pharisees are "like unmarked graves, and people walk over them without realizing it" (11.43 f. cf. XL.57 in the Diatessaron). The problem with such unmarked graves according to *rabbinic* halakha is that by walking over them, one becomes impure without realizing it. Hence, the Rashbi story may be an ironic response to the gospel; the story describes the situation in Tiberias prior to its purification by Rashbi (and after the *am ha'aretz* reintroduces one corpse) according to the gospel's metaphor of corpse impurity. When Naqai, in the sequel, accuses Rashbi of claiming erroneously to have removed the corpses from Tiberias, he enacts Jesus' accusation: Rashbi declares unmarked graves as pure. Once more, without lexical imitation, this matter remains inconclusive. The Bavli version of the story, however, makes explicit the halakhic ramifications of the presence of corpses in Tiberias.

For instance, Jesus is well-known in the gospels for resurrecting the dead. In Matthew 9:25, Jesus causes a dead child to stand up (*wqmh*), a characteristic as ubiquitous in fourth- and fifth-century patristic literature as Jesus' own resurrection.[103] Rashbi surpasses Jesus by making a corpse stand up (יקום) and come back to life while at the same time causing a man to die. The textual evidence of the story's imitation of Christian language is limited; the portrayal of Rashbi as resurrecting a dead man, however, is set in a well-established discursive field that leads the audience to view Rashbi as surpassing Jesus. As Levine points out, several amoraic Palestinian texts, and especially *Bereshit Rabbah*, suggestively ascribe to Rashbi "almost superhuman qualities."[104] Levine writes:

It is not the miracle working or the quality of righteousness ascribed to R. Simeon which are particularly striking. Rather it is the self-assertiveness and the pretension of being able to expiate others' sins which are bold ... One is tempted to suggest that these qualities are remarkably 'Christological' and may have been used ... with Jews to bolster them in the wake of Christian ascendancy.[105]

Levine's claim concerning these Christological qualities seems quite reasonable.[106] The rabbis' familiarity with *basic* Christology would have allowed post-Constantinian rabbinic audience to understand the remarks about

---

[103] See, for example, Gregory of Nyssa, *On the Soul and Resurrection*; John Chrysostom, *Homily 17 on First Corinthians*; *Homilies 24, 62* and *66 on the Gospel of John*, Theodoret of Cyrrhus, *Demonstrations by Syllogisms*, and Cyril of Jerusalem, *Eighteenth Catechetical lecture* (16). See also Luke 8:54 f. and the story of Lazarus in John 11:25–43.

[104] Levine, "R. Simeon b. Yohai and the Purification of Tiberias," 179.

[105] Levine, "R. Simeon b. Yohai and the Purification of Tiberias," 180.

[106] A thorough study of this technique is beyond the scope of the inquiry, but I do develop this theme further in the Conclusion. Three brief examples, building on Levine's own suggestions, illustrate how *Bereshit Rabbah* surpasses or challenges the depictions of Jesus in the Gospels: 1) In *Bereshit Rabbah* 26.5, expounding on the verse about the "Sons of God" (בני האלוהים) in Genesis 6:2, Rashbi explicitly "curses all who call themselves sons of God (בני אלהיא)." Jesus' sonship, is affirmed, for instance, in Matthew 17.6, where Jesus is visited by Elijah, confirming that the latter must arrive before the Messiah, that is, Jesus himself. In response, *Bereshit Rabbah* 35.2 reports that Elijah sat down and, in rabbinic fashion, studied the words of Rashbi. Elijah even goes to Rashbi for clarification. 2) The midrashic text continues by stating that Rashbi needed only to say: "Valley, valley, fill up with gold dinars," and it follows his command. This may be a response to Matthew's claims that commanding a tree to uproot itself or a mountain to throw itself into the sea is not be a problem for a true believer (17:20 and 21:21, a passage to which I shall return in the Conclusion). 3) Next, the Midrash quotes Rashbi: "if Abraham wishes to save judgment (מקרבה) from [his time] until [my time], I will do so from [my time] until the King Messiah." (Manuscript London has אין בעי אברהם מקרבה מגביה ועד גבי ואנא מקרב מגבי עד מלכא משיחא. Translation according to Sokoloff, who generally translates the root קרב as either "to come near" or "to sacrifice;" see *A Dictionary of Jewish Palestinian Aramaic*, 503.) Here, the Midrash responds to how the Gospel of Matthew introduces Jesus as a son of Abraham (Matthew 1:1). Indeed, *Bereshit Rabbah* presents Rashbi as an attractive alternative to the claims made by Jesus' followers concerning their Messiah. The text does not discount the Jesus-traditions in a straightforward way or attack them theologically

Rashbi's resurrection as a satirical challenge to certain qualities associated with Jesus (as I shall also argue is the case for Rabbi Eliezer in the Conclusion). This aspect of the Rashbi character is exemplified in his struggle with Naqai.

In Magdala of the Dyers, Rashbi meets Naqai Safra (נקיי ספרא). Other than Rashbi, Naquai is the only other figure in the story that is identified by name.[107] I accept Levine's claim that "Naqai ... was supposedly involved in the decision to purify Tiberias. [Rashbi's] opinion won the day, but Naqai presumably continued to oppose it."[108] This suggests that Naqai was clearly a Jew and a dignitary of the Jewish community, affiliated either with the Patriarch or the rabbis.[109] Rashbi's views on corpse impurity are relatively moderate, especially in comparison with the much stricter Naqai.

Naqai's name connotes "cleanliness" and "purity," albeit not specifically ritual purity – it seems likely that the audience would have understood his name as a pun on his strictness concerning corpse impurity.[110] The Bavli understands Naqai's name itself as an indication of belief in Jesus. In the Bavli, Naqai (נקאי) is the name of one of Jesus' executed disciples (*Sanhedrin* 43a).[111] My reading of Naqai in *Bereshit Rabbah* as a Jewish heretic whose deviance is punishable by death is here supported by the Bavli.

Naqai's title, *safra*, means "teacher," "scribe," or "barber."[112] A story about an anonymous *safra* from Magdala of the Dyers in the Second Temple period is found in the Yerushalmi:[113] he used to go up (סליק) every Friday to Jerusalem in order to expound Scripture in the Temple and then "go down" to spend the "Shabbat in his home" (שבת בבייתיה).[114] In his case, since he goes to Jerusalem to expound scripture, the title *safra* likely means teacher

---

but rather implicitly tackles and surpasses them through the narrative. The Rashbi story in *Bereshit Rabbah* fits very well into this context.

[107] Another spelling found in *Bereshit Rabbah* manuscripts is נקי or נקאי, the form that also appears in the Bavli; see below. The vocalization of the name is unclear; I follow Levine's suggestion.

[108] Levine, "R. Simeon b. Yohai and the Purification of Tiberias," 149.

[109] See also Richard Kalmin, *Jewish Babylonia*, 92.

[110] Jastrow, *A Dictionary*, 932 and Sokoloff, *A Dictionary of Jewish Palestinian Aramaic*, 360. The "purity" in question is never ritual purity. See Peter Schäfer, *Jesus in the Talmud*, 75–78. Another meaning of the root נקי is "innocence," which Schäfer connects with Jesus' innocence as declared by Pilate in Matthew 27:19; see *Jesus in the Talmud*, 78. The Peshitta here uses *sdyq*; no Palestinian Aramaic parallel is available.

[111] Peter Schäfer recently argued that Naqai stands for Jesus himself, *Jesus in the Talmud*, 75–78.

[112] Sokoloff, *A Dictionary of Jewish Palestinian Aramaic*, 386.

[113] *Ma'aser Sheni* V, 2, 2 (56a); see also Kalmin, *Jewish Babylonia*, 219 note 14, and the reference provided there.

[114] Another tradition quoted in the Yerushalmi (ad loc.) states that he used to arrange the candles, descend to Jerusalem to worship, and return in order to light the candles before Shabbat. Compare the similar tradition in *Ekha Rabbah* 3.3.

rather than scribe or barber.[115] Accordingly, the anonymous sage in the Yerushalmi's parallel to this part of the Rashbi story had nothing to do with any aspect of belief in Jesus.[116]

Naqai in the *Bereshit Rabbah* Rashbi story remains a Jewish dignitary and in no way becomes a (gentile) Christian. The story does not link him to Christian asceticism or disregard for ritual purity. The allusion and the subtext, however, remain clear. Naqai's death as the result of a snakebite recalls a rabbinic narrative concerning the death of a Jewish sage who believes in the healing power of Jesus' name.

Rashbi invokes Ecclesiastes 10:8 when telling Naqai that "he who breaches the fence will be bitten by a snake." The fact that the Rashbi story engages in dialogue with rabbinic material on Jewish believers in Jesus becomes evident in light of other early rabbinic examples in which Ecclesiastes 10:8 is linked to the "fence of the sages," the very well-known "Jesus" passage in Tosefta *Hulin* 2.22–23:

The Story of Eleazar ben Dama who was bitten by a snake.
And Jacob of the village Sama came to heal him in the name of Jesus ben Pantera
And Rabbi Ishmael did not allow him.
They said to him: "You are not permitted [ראשי], Ben Dama."
He said to him: "I will bring you proof [ראיה] that he can heal me."
And he did not manage to bring proof before he died.
Rabbi Ishmael said: "You are lucky, Ben Dama, that you left in peace,
    And did not breach the decree [גזירן] of the sages [חכמים],
    Since anyone that breaches the fence [גדירן] of the sages,
    Punishment will come upon him [בא עליו].
As it is said: 'And whoever breaks through a wall [גדר, i.e., fence] will be bitten by a snake' [Ecclesiastes 10:8].[117]

This passage from the third century Palestinian Tosefta, most recently discussed by Peter Schäfer, appears twice in the Yerushalmi as well as in other

---

[115] Rashbi's actions parallel the conduct of the teacher from the Yerushalmi. It states that Rashbi intended to go up (סלק) to spend the Shabbat in his house (ישבות בביתיה) and passes by Magdala. Compare another parallel in the later text *Qohelet Rabbah* 1.22, which treats a boisterous barber in Magdala of the Dyers. The *safra* from Magdala of the Dyers in this text promises that he is capable of curing hair disease, though he seems to be embarrassed when a rabbi wishes to use his services. Perhaps the Yerushalmi rabbinic reference to a teacher expounding Scripture in the Temple invoked the image of Jesus teaching in the Temple (as, for example, in Matthew 21:23), but such speculation begs the question. On Jesus as a Torah teacher, see Peter Schäfer, *Jesus in the Talmud*, 41–51.

[116] The same holds true for the unnamed sage in the Yerushalmi's parallel of the Rashbi story, where Rashbi also causes the death of a sage in Magdala, but the sage is not referred to as Naqai, and Rashbi kills him merely by looking at him. The uniqueness of the *Bereshit Rabbah* version presents its heresiological details even more sharply.

[117] The sequel recounts the story of Rabbi Eliezer, who was arrested and charged with being a *min* (in this case certainly a Christian) since he listened to the teaching of one Jacob of Sikhnin "in the name of Jesus," which ends with a *dimissus*, like the birds' judgment in the Rashbi story. See notes 10 and 65 above, note 37 in Chapter Four, and the Conclusion.

parallels in the Palestinian rabbinic tradition.[118] The Tosefta passage contains the first rabbinic reference to Jesus by name; together with its later
adaptations, this is the only such reference in the Palestinian rabbinic tradition.[119] It is, in a sense, all that the Palestinian rabbis felt they had to say
explicitly about belief in Jesus.

Eleazar ben Dama, presumably a (Jewish) sage, is bitten by a snake and
wishes to let Jacob of Sama heal him by invoking the name of Jesus.[120] The
text's concern is not with the efficacy of the name – the rabbis do not doubt
the (magical) power of heretics. Rather, the orthodoxy of *using* Jesus' name
is under scrutiny, and ortho*doxy* is the proper term when it comes to the
rabbis' delineating themselves from Christian creed. Rabbi Ishmael prefers
to see his nephew die rather than to accept that the name Jesus can heal by
divine authority, despite the fact that Eleazar ben Dama offers to provide
scriptural proof that his intended procedure is permissible. The passage
thereby acknowledges the possibility that the halakha pertaining to the use
of Jesus' name could be ambiguous. Still, Rabbi Ishmael applies the verse
from Ecclesiastes to Eleazar ben Dama, which threatens anyone who strays
from the rabbinic consensus because of a snakebite. Mere intention to stray
suffices in this case, and the snakebite preempts the transgression.[121]

Elsewhere in Palestinian rabbinic literature, the combination of the verse
from Ecclesiastes and the "fence of the sages" occurs almost exclusively in
the context of the usage of the name Jesus in parallels versions of the story.[122]

---

[118] See *Qohelet Rabbah* I.24 and Yerushalmi *Avodah Zarah* II.2 f. (40d–41a) and *Shabbat* 14.4 f. (14d–15a). Jesus' surname in the passage, ben Pantera, invokes a well-document-
ed slur against Jesus' Roman parentage. For a discussion of the story, see Peter Schäfer,
Jesus in the Talmud, 52–62.

[119] See also Tosefta *Shabbat* 11.15 and Yerushalmi *Shabbat* XII.4 (13d), where "Ben
Satra" is discussed; see Peter Schäfer, *Jesus in the Talmud*, 16.

[120] If the audience knew the gospels well, it might have recognized the irony in a
believer in Jesus threatening with a snake bite, for the Gospel of Luke states explicitly:
"See, I have given you authority to tread on snakes and scorpions, and over all the power
of the enemy; and nothing will hurt you" (10:19). The practice of handling snakes was
especially widespread among the Egyptian Desert Fathers, see Dom Lucien Regnault, *Les
sentences des pères du desert: troisième recueil & tables* (Sablé-sur-Sarthe: Solesme, 1976),
see index, "serpent."

[121] The irony in the fact that Eleazar ben Dama is bitten by a snake before commit-
ting the offense points to the sequel in Ecclesiastes 10:11: "if the snake bites before it is
charmed, there is no success [יתרון] for the charmer." The importance of the scriptural
context is also indicated by the Yerushalmi's rendition of the story in *Avodah Zarah*
II.2 f. (40d–41a). Here the Yerushalmi, referring to Ecclesiastes 10:5 ("a great error as if
it proceeded from the ruler"), classifies the rabbinic saying that death is preferred to a
dubious healing *post facto* as a "great error as if it proceeded from the ruler." According
to Lieberman, this is an inadvertent curse ("A Tragedy or a Comedy?" *Journal of the
American Oriental Society*, 104 [1984]: 315 f.) See also idem, *Tosefta Kifshuta* (Jerusalem:
Hotsa'at Darom 695, 1934), 187.

[122] One of the two exceptions of which I am aware, however, is the Rashbi story in the
Yerushalmi, in which the man reaping the after-growth during a Jubilee year is the one who

At the same time, the references to Jesus' name in this passage may indicate the passage's central role in rabbinic discourse, and I shall henceforth call it *the* rabbinic Jesus-passage. The fact that it is constantly repeated in Palestinian rabbinic literature supports this notion and may turn the entire passage into a lemma of "belief in Jesus" in rabbinic discourse. In other words, in the Amoraic period "breaching the fence of the sages" and getting bitten by a snake may have become a shorthand indicating a challenge to rabbinic authority by using the name of Jesus. By applying the saying to the sage from Magdala and calling him "Naqai," the Rashbi story in *Bereshit Rabbah* extends its gospel parody. Through the linkage of Naqai with a Jewish sage who believed in the power of Jesus' name, the story seems to turn the initial parody of Christian practice and preaching into a more sustained discussion of how to deal with belief in Jesus among Jews.

The Rashbi story, furthermore, has good reasons to allude to the rabbinic Jesus passage. Just like the Tosefta, it discusses a reasonable and well-founded objection to the rabbinic consensus: the purity of Tiberias and the use of Jesus' name. Just like Eleazar ben Dama's, Naqai's position is based on sound reasoning; his mistake is not his position per se but posing a challenge to Rashbi. Naqai himself was part of the vote that declared Tiberias clean and must therefore be aware of breaching the rabbinic consensus (an issue also under discussion in the Conclusion).

The Rashbi story maintains its dialogue with the rabbinic Jesus passage. It imitates and alters it in order to present a more radical message than the Tosefta: to allude to the nature of Naqai's heresy and to illustrate Rashbi's zeal. Most centrally, the Rashbi story imitates the Tosefta's image of the "fence of the sages" along with the punishment of a deviant Jewish sage, citing the same verse from Ecclesiastes. In addition, the Rashbi story appropriates several other details from the Tosefta:

- Rashbi pronounces a decree (גזר) in his first judgment, using the same word used in the Tosefta, saying that Eleazar ben Dama did *not* manage to violate the decree

---

"breaks the fence of the sages." This, once more, suggests that the parodic allusion to the Gospels in the Yerushalmi version of the Rashbi story is not a broader satire of Jewish believers in Jesus. The only other exception of which I am aware is Sifre *Ekev* 12, expounding on Ecclesiastes 10:8 without direct reference to Jesus but possibly in dialogue with the Jesus passage in the Tosefta. It is interesting to note that Yerushalmi *Sanhedrin* 11.6 (30a) applies the passage from Ecclesiastes to the "rebellious old man" (see Mishna *Sanhedrin* 11.2), suggesting that any rabbi guilty of transgressing the words of the sages is guilty of death (albeit without the wordplay on the hedge and the rabbis' "fence"). In Yerushalmi *Sanhedrin* 8.6 (26b), the "rebellious old man," even if forgiven, must not be allowed to maintain a position of public honor, so that "factions will not increase in Israel" (see also Sifre Devarim *Tetseh* 8 (218) and Bavli *Sanhedrin* 88a–b). The passage from Ecclesiastes, therefore, epitomizes the rabbinic polemic against any type of heresy among the Jewish elite, a reading also in line with the use of the verse in Mekhilta de Rabbi Ishmael, *Beshalah* 6.

despite his intentions. By contrast, it is implied that Naqai indeed violated a decree and deserves death even more than Eleazar ben Dama.

– Rashbi promises to bolster his claim that Tiberias is clean by providing "rulings" (הלכות), just as Eleazar ben Dama intended to provide "proof" (ראיה) that using Jesus' name is permitted. Both texts state that they have legal grounds supporting their claims. In both texts, the transgressors rely on facts: Eleazar ben Dama suggests that using Jesus' name is permissible; Naqai indicates that Tiberias indeed is not pure. In the Rashbi story, however, it is not the transgressor, Naqai, who proposes legal arguments but Rashbi. Rashbi defends the rabbinic position by using the language of the original transgressor, Eleazar ben Dama, against his epigone, Naqai.

– The story appropriates Eleazar ben Dama's argument a second time, exploiting a homophony of the Hebrew words for "permitted" and "my head." The word that Eleazar ben Dama uses when claiming that he is "permitted" (ראשי) to be healed by the use of Jesus' name is the same one used by Rashbi to count the number of halakhot he can offer, "like hair on my head [ראשי]." Once more, Rashbi uses the language of the rabbis' stock Jesus-believer against another.[123]

– Finally, Rashbi wishes that something "come over [him]" [ובוא עלי] if he errs, just like punishment will "come over" (בא עליו) the one that breaches the fence of the sages in the Jesus passage. Thereby, the story appropriates the language used to describe the punishment for using Jesus' name.

The manifold linguistic and thematic parallels between the Tosefta and the Rashbi story, along with the familiarity of the story's audience with the Tosefta passage or its parallels, renders the link between Naqai and Eleazar Ben Dama clearly apparent. These parallels indicate that the Rashbi story uses the Jesus passage in order to depict Naqai's challenge of Rashbi as an inversion of the conflict between Eleazar ben Dama and Rabbi Ishmael. Naqai, hence, becomes associated with belief in Jesus, and the Rashbi story ironically transposes the language from the transgressor to his rabbinic persecutor, Rashbi.

Additionally, the story continues to represent Rashbi as superior to Jesus: Jesus may be able to resurrect and his name may have healing power, but Rashbi is able simultaneously to resurrect and cause death. Rashbi even controls the snake, an ability generally reserved for God in rabbinic literature.[124]

---

[123] Rashbi's halakhot "like hair of the head" (כסער ראשי) imports Matthew's argument for personal providence into halakhic territory: in the Sermon, the "hairs of your head [s'r' dryshkwn] are all counted," and in the Rashbi story, the hair is compared to the number of rabbinic halakhot concerning the purity of Tiberias and against all challengers of the rabbinic decree. By appropriating a term from the Sermon on the Mount – and the source of the words can of course only be determined in light of the story's parody as described above – the Rashbi story posits Naqai in Jesus territory once more. At the same time, the parallel adoption of words from the gospel in this case seems to shift from the Peshitta to the Old Syriac, adding to the difficulty of assessing the case.

[124] See *Bereshit Rabbah* 10.7 and *Wayiqra Rabbah* 22.4. Rashbi shares this ability with a few other rabbis and Christian monks, see Eliezer Diamond, "Lions, Snakes and Asses: Palestinian Jewish Holy Men as Masters of the Animal Kingdom," in: Richard Kalmin and Seth Schwartz (eds.), *Jewish Culture and Society under the Christian Roman Empire* (Leuven: Peeters, 2003), 251–283 and above, note 120.

Finally, the story continues its parody of what it perceives as Matthew's teaching on personal providence. Instead of passively accepting his fate as ordained by God and not assuming the position of a judge, Rashbi becomes an agent of justice who enforces rabbinic authority. While the Jews of Palestine gradually lost their power to imperial Christian rulers in the fourth and fifth centuries, the Rashbi story describes a world in which this historical reality is reversed. Thus, the Rashbi story seeks to portray Naqai as a Jewish heretic according to the model of Eleazar ben Dama. To conclude this topic, I shall now consider a literary and heresiological parallel of the figure of Naqai. This parallel does not hint at any parodic relationship, but instead suggests a way of assessing the shared discursive space between the Christian and rabbinic orthodoxies precisely at a moment when the parallels were not subject to the critical gaze of the rabbis and of the church fathers themselves.

Rashbi as Heresiology

A link between Jewish observance of purity laws and belief in Jesus is also found in the patristic accounts concerning Ebion, a first-century arch-heretic whose historicity is highly doubtful and who was mentioned by a number of church fathers, most notably Epiphanius.[125]

In his well known account of Ebion "of the Nazoraeans' school," one of the founders of Ebionism,[126] Epiphanius uses the Septuagint rendition of Proverbs 5:14 to describe Ebion's double commitment to Jesus and purity as standing "in all evil, in the midst of the church and the synagogue."[127] Like the author of the Rashbi story, Epiphanius had previously lived in Palestine, perhaps no more than two generations separating the two authors. Epiphanius also invokes a theological duel in order to caution his audience against the dangers associated with heretics, presenting his own protagonists as victorious. Epiphanius' polemic against Ebion contains a number of thematic parallels of the representation of Naqai in the Rashbi story. I hence suggest considering the *Panarion* as an illuminating literary parallel: Epiphanius' Ebion is a Christian version of Naqai; both figures emerge ac-

---

[125] See also Hippolytus, *Contra Omnes Haereses* VII.35.1, Pseudo-Tertullian, *Contra Omnes Haereses* 3, Jerome, *Adversus Luciferum* 23 and *Doctrina Patrum* 41, and Tertullian, *De Carne Christi* 14, 18, 24. For a longer list of parallels, see Frank Williams, *The Panarion of Epiphanius of Salamis, Book I (Sects 1–46)* (Leiden: Brill, 1987), 119f.

[126] *Panarion* II.30.1.1; Williams, *The Panarion of Epiphanius of Salamis*, 120. Just as in the case of Tatian and the Encratites (see Chapter Two), Epiphanius' attempt to list a precise number of heresies is artificial. Epiphanius, indeed, seeks to simultaneously construct a taxonomy of eighty heresies and claim that on many levels, these heresies are all the offspring of the devil. See also Boyarin, *Border Lines*, 207f.

[127] *Panarion* II.30.1.4; Williams, *The Panarion of Epiphanius*, 120.

cording to the views of the respective Jewish and Christian heresiologies. This possibility allows us to view the Rashbi story as a whole in the context of anti-Christian and anti-Jesus polemics as well as contemporary heresiological discourse.

To begin with, Epiphanius alleges that the Nazoreans, and thereby Ebion, are "nothing but Jews themselves ... Yet these are the Jews' enemies ... for they harbor an extra grudge against them, if you please, because despite their Jewishness they preach that Jesus is Christ."[128] I suggested earlier that Naqai embodies the same combination of belief in Jesus and Judaism; Epiphanius' enmity parallels the Rashbi story's contempt for Naqai. The correspondence between Ebion and Naqai, moreover, extends to their strict observance of purity laws. Ebion, in Epiphanius' account, observes a number of halakhic laws more strictly than "the Jews":

"[Ebion was attached to]... Judaism's Law of the Sabbath, circumcision, and all other Jewish and Samaritan observances. But like the Samaritans, he goes still further than the Jews. He added the rule about care in [not] touching a gentile (ἀλλοεθνῶν) and that a man must immerse himself in water every day he is with a woman ... If he meets anyone while returning from his plunge and immersion in the water, he runs back for another immersion, often with his clothes on, too![129]"

Epiphanius alleges that Ebion combines the observance of Shabbat with an extreme kind of what he calls "Samaritan" observance of purity. According to Epiphanius' own testimony here as well as elsewhere in the same book, Samaritan observance also included not having contact with corpses. He emphasizes their "keeping of the Law's precepts"[130] and one in particular (which he then refutes elaborately): "They abhor the sight of a dead body."[131] Epiphanius portrays Ebion as an extreme observer of purity rules, especially those pertaining to corpses. This corresponds to Naqai's excessive concern with purity in general and with corpse impurity in particular in the Rashbi story.

Epiphanius' representation of the conflict between a beacon of Christian orthodoxy and the heretical Ebion also recalls the conflict between the rabbinic leader and the Jewish heretic in the Rashbi story. Epiphanius includes a story from Irenaeus in which the Apostle John is directed to the bathhouse, where he nearly encounters Ebion:

Though [John's] life was most admirable and appropriate for his apostolic rank, and he never bathed [μηδ᾽ ὅλως λουόμενος], he was compelled by the Holy Spirit to go to the bath ...[He went.] And the attendant stationed there to watch the clothes ... told

---

[128] *Panarion* II.29.9.1; Williams, *The Panarion of Epiphanius,* 119.
[129] *Panarion* II.30.2.1–5; Williams, *The Panarion of Epiphanius,* 120.
[130] *Panarion* I.9.1.5; Williams, *The Panarion of Epiphanius,* 30.
[131] *Panarion* I.9.4.1; Williams, *The Panarion of Epiphanius,* 32.

Saint John that Ebion was inside ... John immediately became disturbed and cried out in anguish, and as a testimony of uncontaminated teaching, he said, in an aside audible to all, "Brothers, let us get away from here quickly! Or the bath may fall and bury us with Ebion, in the bathing-room inside, because of his impiety."[132]

Epiphanius associates Ebion with the bathhouse. The Apostle John, as a good orthodox churchman adhering to Epiphanius' ideals, practices *alousia*. The text is a valuable and illuminating parallel of the Rashbi story in a number of ways.

First, it contrasts (gentile) Christian alousia with bathing, mirroring in a way how the Rashbi story leads the rabbis from the impure cave to the bathhouse. Each text celebrates precisely what is rejected in the other. Second, the battle between orthodoxy and heresy is reflected in a encounter between Saint John and Ebion, which recalls Rashbi's conflict with Naqai. And third, regardless of their diverging views on bathing, Epiphanius and the Rashbi story agree on the danger associated with this kind of marginal and hybrid characters. The polarization of Judaism and Christianity produced different practices, but at the same time, the two orthodoxies shared hermeneutical methods and heresiological stereotypes.

Epiphanius emphasizes that the Ebionites "accept the Gospel according to Matthew [and]... use it alone [i.e., as their only gospel]."[133] In turn, the Rashbi story's parody focuses on a version of the Sermon on the Mount comparable to the one in Matthew, another thematic, albeit indirect, parallel between Epiphanius and the Rashbi story. Epiphanius writes that the Gospel of Matthew was originally written in Hebrew; he then alleges that other New Testament texts are "in the Jewish treasuries; I mean the treasuries at Tiberias."[134] Tiberias must have acted as a trigger for Epiphanius, for he incorporates a narrative concerning Joseph of Tiberias, the Jewish convert to orthodox Christianity, into his description of the Ebionites.[135]

Epiphanius' diatribe against Ebion seems at first unrelated to the story of Joseph, and Epiphanius returns to the Ebionites later in his discussion. Yet the apparently idiosyncratic presence of the Joseph of Tiberias story within Epiphanius' heresiology paradoxically yields another parallel with the Rashbi story. Both texts combine a discussion of the heresy of Jewish believers in Jesus with an account of two orthodoxies, rabbinic and Christian and both texts despise the hybrid model, as Daniel Boyarin illustrates.[136]

---

[132] Ibid., 24.1–5. The story is not unique to Epiphanius. Rather, he adopts it from Irenaeus, in which John the Apostle encounters Cerinthus, another stock Jesus-believer who observes purity rules in a bathhouse. Epiphanius replaces Cerinthus with Ebion. Compare Irenaeus, *Against Heresies* II.3.4.

[133] *Panarion* II.30.3.7; Williams, *The Panarion of Epiphanius*, 122.

[134] *Panarion* II.30.3.8; Williams, *The Panarion of Epiphanius*, 122.

[135] *Panarion* II.30.4.1–12.9; Williams, *The Panarion of Epiphanius*, 122–29.

[136] See Boyarin, *Border Lines*, 211–14.

It should be noted that Epiphanius describes another group of Jews with dual affinities for Judaism and for Jesus. He alleges that Jewish dignitaries of Tiberias of his own time secretly believed in Jesus and eventually converted from "one orthodoxy to another," unlike Ebion, who scandalously opted for the middle ground.[137] Epiphanius portrays Joseph of Tiberias himself as a Jewish dignitary who secretly believed in Jesus. Joseph witnesses a "miracle" in the hot baths in Gadara, which he took as proof of the power of "Christ's name."[138] His conversion to orthodox Christianity occurs only a while after he witnesses the power of "the name of Jesus of Nazareth."[139] Finally, Epiphanius concludes his Joseph narrative with a battle between Jews and Christians in Tiberias, who are assisted by magic and the Holy Spirit respectively. The Jews seek to convert an ancient building into a public bath, whereas Joseph wishes to turn it into a church. The battle, tellingly, ends in a draw.[140]

These parallels are palpable: The potency of the name Jesus is of course the theme of the rabbinic Jesus passage, which is central to my reading of Naqai. Rashbi, also in a bathhouse, moves from Gadara to Tiberias and engages in an inter-religious battle, just like Joseph. Yet Epiphanius and the Rashbi story share more than common themes and a common enemy. They also play out their own victory over this enemy in the same locales and with comparable strategies. Trying to determine whether the Rashbi story makes Naqai a sort of "Ebionite" or a secret orthodox Christian or both misses the polemical force of the story. Rather, discussions of Jews who observed Jewish purity laws while also believing in Jesus and of the secrecy of belief in Jesus among Jewish dignitaries are found in both rabbinic and Christian literatures. The Rashbi story, then, seeks to discredit Naqai through guilt by association. Invoking Christianity – Jewish or gentile – discredits Naqai's insistence on purity and establishes the rabbinic consensus.

In other words, neither Naqai's historical status nor the nature of the factions of the Jewish elite in the time of *Bereshit Rabbah* can be determined. Epiphanius' testimony, however, contextualizes the interaction between the Rashbi story and rabbinic polemics in relation to the story's parody of the gospel and its satirical allusions to Christian hagiography. The resemblance between Ebion and Naqai indicates the resemblance between the heresi-

---

[137] For example, the Jewish patriarch *Ellel* and Joseph of Tiberias himself; see Panarion II.30.4.5; Williams, *The Panarion of Epiphanius of Salamis*, 122 and Boyarin, *Borderlines*, 214.

[138] An "unusually beautiful free [i.e., unmarried] woman" who happens to be Christian manages to break the love spell of a young Jew; breaking the spell is proof of the power of Jesus' name. *Panarion* II.30.7.5–8.10; Williams, *The Panarion of Epiphanius*, 125 f.

[139] *Panarion* II.30.10.4; Williams, *The Panarion of Epiphanius*, 127.

[140] Panarion II.29.9.4; Williams, *The Panarion of Epiphanius of Salamis*, 119.

ologies that engendered them. Epiphanius shares with the Rashbi story not only the desire for the destruction of the Ebion/Naqai type but also a discussion of corpse impurity, bathhouses and (abstinence from) bathing, heretics, religious conversion, secretive belief in Jesus among Jews, battles with supernatural assistance, the power of Jesus' name, and the Sermon on the Mount (and thereby Matthew).

The parallels between the stories are not surprising given the historical and geographical proximity of the two writers. The parallels and differences that emerge from reading the Rashbi story in conjunction with Epiphanius, however, strengthen my reading of Naqai as the product of fifth century Christian and Jewish heresiological discourse. The villains in both stories, Ebion and Naqai, remain in the liminal space between the two groups whereas the protagonists, Joseph of Tiberias and Rashbi, move toward their respective orthodoxies – this seems obvious in Epiphanius's case and corresponds to my conclusion concerning Rashbi and his transition from cave-dwelling asceticism to observing Shabbat in his own home.

Rashbi between Heresy and Orthodoxy

At the beginning of the story, Rashbi is characterized as a figure leading a "Christian" ascetic and solitary lifestyle. He retreats to a cave, fasts, never washes, and is impervious to the impurity that results from his skin condition. He adopts a belief in personal providence based on an avian epiphany modeled on the Sermon on the Mount. Eventually, Rashbi admits that his retreat to the cave had been superfluous.

As Rashbi emerges from the cave, he leaves behind his Christian characteristics; it turns out that he was hiding in the cave, not practicing asceticism. Even after his healing and "purification," it is his son who initiates Rashbi's full return to the rabbinic community by urging him to purify Tiberias. Even now, however, opposition and heresy loom large as Rashbi heads home for Shabbat, and he needs to defend the purification of the city from three opponents. Having left behind gentile Christianity, Rashbi must now face three Jewish opponents, who represent three degrees of Jewish deviations from the consensus of rabbinic Judaism. Ironically, the degree of their offense diminishes as the danger inherent to their respective heresies seems to grow.

The first opponent is a non-rabbinic Jew, an *am ha'aretz*, with his disregard for purity laws. The *am ha'aretz*'s departure from the rabbinic way of life, while still remaining within the bounds of Judaism, challenges Rashbi in the most blatant way: the *am ha'aretz* buries a corpse in Tiberias and causes the city to become impure again, seeking to ridicule Rashbi publicly.

The second Jewish opponent does observe purity laws. Naqai's uncompromising insistence on the complete purification of Tiberias is also at odds with the rabbinic consensus, as is his implied belief in Jesus. In accordance with his proximity to rabbinic Judaism, Naqai's offense is also less severe than the *am ha'aretz*'s: he merely reports what he had heard about Tiberias, challenging Rashbi publicly without attempting to contaminate the city anew.

The third opponent, finally, is a rabbinic Jew, who observes rabbinic halakha, even Rashbi's ruling concerning reaping the after-growth during a Jubilee year. This last detail gets a little too close to the center of rabbinic identity, especially since the rabbinic majority had voted against Rashbi in this regard. Fiercely defending the rabbinic consensus from his own previous halakhic position, Rashbi punishes the man even though he is a rabbinic Jew and his offense relatively insignificant. The hyperbole evident elsewhere in the story (the long stay in the cave, the rabbis' "rust," God's judgment of birds), never fully vanishes.

The few lines in *Bereshit Rabbah* that recount the Rashbi story are a treasure of fourth or fifth century rabbinic discourse; my first step was to contextualize the narrative in relation to contemporary Jewish, Greek, and Christian cultural traditions. Briefly and elliptically, as is typical of Palestinian rabbinic literature especially, the story manages to position itself against several of the era's most intensely discussed topics: cave-dwelling asceticism and *alousia*, corpse impurity and purification procedures, providence and human agency. The story's turning point is a parody of a passage from the Sermon on the Mount. I sought to illustrate how the story places the second-century figure of Rabbi Simeon bar Yochai in the fifth century in order to stage the period's theological, philosophical, and social concerns, polemically alluding to Christian hagiography. Rashbi, however, is not an idealized hero. True, he prevails over his opponents, but the story simultaneously exposes his weaknesses and incongruity, in the best manner of late ancient philosophical *Lives*.

While references to Christianity pervade nearly the entire story, it would be dangerous to regard it as an anti-Christian parody *tout court*. This, in my view, would disregard the story's nuanced engagement with many aspects of society, and its refusal to essentialize Christianity. Instead, the story offers an insider's view of a province of a Christianizing empire. The rabbis, once more, responded with witty parody, satire, and polemics, all without removing either themselves or their opponents from their daily lives; instead, they are trying to understand the Torah as well as their surroundings.

Incline After the Majority:
Rabbinic Parody and Rabbinic Literature
(Yerushalmi Mo'ed Qatan 3.1, 81c–d)

"He who Sits in the Heavens Laughs"
– Psalms 2:4

quod licet bovi, non licet jovi
– Hannah Arendt,
Reflections on Literature and Culture

I have discussed three modes of rabbinic parody: intra-rabbinic parody (an internal parody within the Babylonian and within the Palestinian rabbinic community, in the Bavli and in *Wayiqra Rabbah* respectively); inter-rabbinic parody (a parody of the Palestinian tradition in the Bavli and another, which inverts the scenario in the Yerushalmi); and external parody of non-rabbinic texts in Babylonia and in Palestine (in the Bavli and in *Bereshit Rabbah*).[1] The examples here along with those discussed by Dov Noy, Joshua Levinson, Israel Yuval, Burton Visotzky, Peter Schäfer, and Daniel Boyarin, are few, and the following assessment of the ubiquity and the general nature of parody in rabbinic literature remains preliminary.

Textual imitation and alteration are basic modes of rabbinic literature, and irony is prevalent as well. This, however, does not mean that we can regard all rabbinic texts as parodic simply because they repeat traditional Jewish (or Christian) texts and play with the difference between the source and its repackaged version. Such an approach would merely circumvent the question of parody and make us return instead to what I see as one of the core questions in the study of rabbinic literature: to what extent, and how exactly, did the rabbis express (or ironize) any cognizance of their own inventiveness?[2] Satirical parody, in my view, allows us to address this ques-

---

[1] See pages 25 f. for a discussion of the modes of rabbinic parody.

[2] As I argued in the Introduction and throughout this book, the rabbis often repeat the teachings of the Torah and of their rabbinic ancestors with hints of ironical distance. If this fact were to lead us to consider reclassifying most of the Midrash and the Talmud as parodic, we would have to deal with two unwelcome results. First, since there are many indications of such distance between traditional texts and their rabbinic repetition, we would potentially have to expand the notion of parody radically, to include much of

tion in a preliminary way. Hence, while I hope that future studies will focus on ironic parodies, this conclusion is dedicated to satirical ones, parodies that humorously criticize the Jewish and Christian texts they imitate, or much more commonly, these texts' previous *rabbinic* audiences.

While elements of humor and irony are prevalent in rabbinic literature, I suspect that only a fraction of rabbinic stories contain elements of satirical parody. I conclude by reflecting on the usefulness and limitations of viewing rabbinic literature through the lens of satirical parody and by discussing a final example from the Palestinian tradition that leads to a revaluation of the relationship between internal to external parodies, and between Palestinian and Babylonian ones.

Parody, as I have argued, is not a genre of rabbinic literature but rather a literary technique employed in all of the Amoraic rabbinic genres: exegetical Midrash, homiletic Midrash, and the talmudic sugya. There are some recurrent patterns in the ways the rabbis use parody. For example, *voiced parody*, in which a character voices the imitated text, occurs in intra-rabbinic, inter-rabbinic, and external parodies. I argued that the intra-rabbinic parodies in the Palestinian and Babylonian traditions are redactional; that is, the parodic effect is achieved by the redactor's deliberate placement of the parody near the imitated text. Redactional parody thus only occurs in intra-rabbinic parody. (Inter-rabbinic parody, as discussed in Chapter Three, is of course also the product of redaction, but the imitated text in its recognizable "original" form is not found near the text that parodies it.) *Halakhic parody*, in which a character attempts to undermine the foundation of rabbinic legal discourse, also occurs only in intra- and inter-rabbinic parodies since it presupposes a shared halakhic framework. At the same time, the two examples of external parody incorporate halakhic elements into their broader discussions, or are structured around halakhic discussions.

---

rabbinic literature. This would evacuate our notion of parody of much of its analytical edge and bring us back to the starting point of our discussion, merely using new terms. Second, the rabbis are not only cognizant of the difference between the original text and its repetition and not only exploit the resulting ironies, but also inscribe the ironic difference into the authorial intent of the divine author of the written and the oral Torah. The rabbis thereby confound any attempt easily to apply modern concepts of irony to these texts. The locus classicus of rabbinic reflection on the difference between the Bible and its interpretation is the Bavli's depiction of Moses's incomprehension of the laws Aqiva that his students derive from the Torah in *Menahot* 29b. For a recent consideration of this passage in relation to Greek satire, see Boyarin, *Socrates and the Fat Rabbis* (Chicago: Chicago University Press, 2009), 232–42. Yet, already the tannaitic exploitations of the difference between biblical and rabbinic Hebrew prepared the ground for such irony. See Howard Eilberg-Schwartz's perceptive study of this matter, focusing on tannaitic literature, in "Who's Kidding Whom?: A Serious Reading of Rabbinic Word Plays," *Journal of the American Academy of Religion* 55 (2004), 765–88. On rabbinic irony see also note 47 below and note 24 in the Introduction.

Most importantly, all of my examples of rabbinic parodies contain elements of *exegetical parody*, imitating a foundational texts and targeting its interpretation by an opponent. Here, the continuities between intra-rabbinic, inter-rabbinic, and external parodies are most fruitful and allow us to evaluate external parody in light of rabbinic self-criticism and vice versa. The external parodies discussed in this book relate the non-rabbinic texts they imitate to tendencies within the rabbinic movements, and thereby offer clear moments of rabbinic self-criticism. Recognizing external parodies, therefore, allows us to analyze the critical aspects of inner- and inter-rabbinic parodies from an established basis. Studying the imitative technique of intra- and inner rabbinic parodies, in turn, provides the foundation for the study of the ways in which external parody imitates non-rabinnic texts.

All of the parodies discussed in this book reflect the Hellenistic cultural contexts in which they were produced. The combination of the serious and the comic, which Boyarin associates with the Bakhtinian notion of "Menippean satire," is particularly relevant, as I explain in the Introduction. Moreover, the parodies I discuss fall well within Boyarin's categories: they "call into question" or put "limits on the efficacy of intellectuals' practice," as Boyarin puts it, when Rava for example does not live up to his own standards, or falls prey to Bar Hedya, or when Rashbi dwells in a cave like an ascetic or believes in a "Christian" epiphany. Similarly, the parodies do "not involve an abandonment of the authority" of these intellectuals' practices, and Rava and Rashbi ultimately prevail on behalf of the rabbinic majority. Like other forms of narrativized Hellenistic philosophical discourse, the parodies all play out their comical criticism in very concrete and physical terms. A cat and mice, a drunkard in a graveyard, a book lost on a boat, beatings in front of a synagogue, bribes, family strife, and the buried bones in Tiberias produce the decorum typical of what Boyarin calls "slum naturalism."[3] While it may be too early to determine whether Boyarin's terms will remain useful in the long run, I hold that his cultural contextualization of the rabbis within the broader realm of the Second Sophistic is already fruitful.[4] Boyarin has rightly emphasized the rabbis' penchant for

---

[3] Boyarin, *Socrates and the Fat Rabbis*, 21, 209, 250–51.

[4] Recent scholarship emphasizes that the cultural sphere of the Second Sophistic continued well into the fourth and fifth centuries CE, see Tim Whitmarsh, *The Second Sophistic* (New York: Oxford University Press, 2005), Simon Swain, *Hellenism and Empire. Language, Classicism and Power in the Greek World, AD 50–250* (New York: Oxford University Press, 1996), Graham Anderson, *The Second Sophistic: a Cultural Phenomenon in the Roman Empire* (New York: Routledge, 1993) and Glenn W. Bowersock, *Greek Sophists in the Roman Empire* (New York: Oxford University Press, 1969). For an attempt at considering rabbinic thought in dialogue with the Second Sophistic, cf. Amram Tropper, *Wisdom, Politics, and Historiography: Tractate Avot in the Context of the Graeco-Roman Near East* (New York: Oxford University Press, 2004). Tropper's work

the serio-comic, obviating or at least complicating the question of whether or not the Bavli is serious at any given point. It is often both serious and comic, and uses irony and comedy at least occasionally to heighten the drama of serious halakhic discourse.

Boyarin's argument for the serio-comic, of course, focuses on the Bavli, effectively sidelining the greatest part of late antique rabbinic literature, and the part which originated in the same milieu as the authors and epigones of the Second Sophistic – the Palestinian Midrashim and the Yerushalmi. I would like to conclude by considering another parody from the Yerushalmi and the historical development of the serio-comic from Palestine to Babylonia.

The following Yerushalmi story describes the banning of Rabbi Eliezer, perhaps the best-known narrative in Talmudic literature. Whereas interpretations of the Bavli version of the "Oven of Akhnai" (in *Bava Metsi'a* 59b) abound, few analyses consider the Bavli's Palestinian source, let alone its literary sophistication.[5] Yet in my view, it is precisely in the Yerushalmi that we find another external satirical parody, subsequently adapted and watered down by the Bavli. The following story about the excommunication and reinstatement of Rabbi Eliezer, like the one discussed in Chapter Five, recognizes the dangers associated with departing from the view of the rabbinic majority. In this case, the majority holds that an oven whose segments are detachable is susceptible to uncleanness ("unclean" in rabbinic parlance) whereas Rabbi Eliezer disagrees with great perseverance and heavenly support, arguing that this "Oven of Hakhina" is always to be considered unsusceptible to uncleanness ("pure"):

[The rabbis] wished to ban Rabbi Eliezer.
They said, "Who will go and let him know?"
Rabbi Akiba said, "I shall go and let him know."
He went to him and said to him, "Rabbi, Rabbi, your colleagues are banning you."
[Eliezer] took [Aqiva] and went outside
　　and said, "Carob, O Carob, if the law is according to the words [of the rabbinic majority], uproot yourself [איתעוקרין],"
　　But it did not uproot itself.

---

precedes Stemberger's dating of Mishna *Avot* to a later period, and does not consider the enduring relevance of the Second Sophistic in Early Byzantium; Tropper's contributions thereby remain valid. On the dating of *Pirqe Avot* see Günther Stemberger, "Mischna Avot: frühe Weisheitsschrift, pharisäisches Erbe oder spätrabbinische Bildung?," *ZNW* 96 (2005), 243–58.

[5] For a list of recent work on the story, see Jeffrey Rubenstein, *Talmudic Stories: Narrative Art, Composition, and Culture* (Baltimore: The Johns Hopkins University Press, 1999), 314f. note 1; on the story itself, see ibid., 34–63. Rubenstein discusses the Yerushalmi version in order to highlight aspects of the Bavli's compositional technique and comments that the Yerushalmi version is "less developed literarily" (ibid., 49). While this holds true in some ways, the opposite applies as well in the case of parody.

"If the law is according to my words, uproot yourself,"
And it uprooted itself.
"If the law is according to them, return,"
And it did not return.
"If the law is according to my words, return,"
And it returned.
All this [divine] praise [שבחא, is bestowed upon him] and [still] the law is not accord-
ing to Rabbi Eliezer?
Rabbi Hananya said, "When [the Torah] was given, it was given only [within the pa-
rameters that one must] *incline after the majority* [אחרי רבים להטות, Exodus 23:2]."
But did not Rabbi Eliezer know [to] *incline after the majority* [Exodus 23:2]?
He became angry only because they burned his purities in front of him.
We learned [in the Mishna]: *If he cut* [an oven] *into segments and placed sand in*
between the segments, Rabbi Eliezer rules that it is pure and the sages rule that
it is impure. This is the oven of Hakhinai. [Mishna *Kelim* 5:10, see also Tosefta
Eduyot 2.1]
Rabbi Yirmiah said, "A great tribulation occurred on that day.
Every place on which Rabbi Eliezer cast his eyes burned."
Not only that but even one grain of wheat, half of it was burned [after Rabbi Eliezer
looks at it] and [the other] half [not looked at by the rabbi] was not burned.
And the columns of the assembly house were trembling.
Rabbi Yehoshua said to them, "If the sages are fighting, what care is it of yours?"
A heavenly voice [בת קול] came forth and said, "The law accords with Eliezer my
son (בני)."
Rabbi Yehoshua said, "*It is not in heaven* [Deuteronomy 30:12]."
Rabbi Qerispa, Rabbi Yohanan in the name of Rabbi [Yehuda haNasi] said, "If some-
one says to me, 'Thus teaches Rabbi Eliezer,' then I teach according to his words.
But the Tannaim change [the names and attribute Eliezer's teachings to others]."
Once [Rabbi Eliezer] was walking through a market, and he saw a woman cleaning
her house, and she threw it out and [the refuse] fell on his head.
He said, "It seems that today my colleagues will bring me near [i.e., lift the ban],
as it is written, '*He that lifts up the needy* [אביון] *from the heap of refuse* [מאשפות,
Psalms 113:7]."[6]

Rabbi Eliezer's halakhic opinion concerning the susceptibility of this oven
to impurity is supported by miracles, a local earthquake and a voice from
heaven that supports his interpretation of the Torah. Despite this, however,
the majority of rabbis disagrees with him and even bans him for being obstinate, attributing his own (acceptable) legal opinions to others – the ultimate
damnatio memoriae, perhaps much worse for the rabbis than the fate of
Rashbi's opponents discussed in the previous chapter.[7]

---

[6] Yerushalmi *Moʿed Qatan* 3,1/10–12 (81c–d) according to Ms. Leiden; translation
based on Jeffrey Rubenstein, *Talmudic Stories*, 48f., modified.

[7] For an exemplary discussion of passages on the topic of the rule of the majority and
the value of the minority report see most recently Günter Stemberger, " Mehrheitsbeschlüsse oder Recht auf eigene Meinung? Zur Entscheidungsfindung im rabbinischen

As is well known, the Torah itself states that it is "not in heaven," as the rabbis ironically repeat this Scriptural saying at the expense of the biblical context. In Deuteronomy 30:12, this remark emphasizes the ubiquity of the Torah on earth rather than its absence from heaven. At the same time, the rabbis' interpretation of "not in heaven," does not lead to interpretative anarchy among its rabbinic readers, even though it does limit the relevance of the intent of Scripture's divine author. Rather, one ought to "incline after the majority," another biblical saying that the rabbis repeat once more with great irony, as stating, to use Boyarin's words, that "the majority of the community which holds cultural hegemony controls interpretation."[8] The passage in Exodus 23:2, of course, condemns precisely such "inclination after the majority" to such an extent that the rabbis take the repetitive insistence as an invitation to derive the opposite lesson from the text. The subtle self-ironizing of rabbinic hermeneutics is apparent but is very difficult to analyze.[9] The satirical target of the story, however, can be discussed in terms of external parody: Rabbi Eliezer's illicit halakhic discourse and his *imitatio Christi*. I will not analyze this marvelous story here since the extensive treatment of the story's parallel in the Bavli pertains to the Yerushalmi's version as well.[10] Instead, I seek to focus on external parody and satire in the Yerushalmi story.

One major difference between the story in the Yerushalmi and its imitation in the Bavli, however, deserves our attention. In the Yerushalmi, Eliezer only performs two miracles, that of moving a carob tree in order to prove his view, and of burning the wheat in order to express his anger. The other two "miracles," the near-collapse of the assembly house and the heavenly voice, are unmediated divine interventions. In the Bavli, while the destruction of the wheat occurs in a way that is roughly similar, Rabbi Eliezer's grief also causes the death of Rabban Gamliel, and he performs *four* miracles in order to prove his point. The rabbis, in turn, neutralize each of Eliezer's

---

Judentum," in Susanne Plietzsch (ed.), *Literatur im Dialog: die Faszination von Talmud und Midrasch*, (Zürich: Theologischer Verlag Zürich, 2007), 19–39.

[8] Daniel Boyarin, *Intertextuality and the Reading of Midrash* (Bloomington: Indiana University Press, 1990), 35. Boyarin considers the Bavli, but his analysis is pertinent to the Yerushalmi's use of the same scriptural passage as well.

[9] A study of ironic parody in rabbinic literature may include the ways in which the rabbis engage in or reflect on their repetition of the Bible with a difference. Such a study, as I mentioned above, is beyond the score of the present inquiry, which focuses on satirical parodies, see e.g. Introduction, note 39.

[10] According to Rubenstein, "even a cursory glance at the [Yerushalmi] reveals stunning parallels: the same characters, the ban, the miracle with the carob, the burning of crops, the heavenly voice, the quotation of Exod. 23:2 and Deut 30:12." *Talmudic Stories: Narrative Art, Composition, and Culture* (Baltimore: The Johns Hopkins University Press, 1999), 49. We can add to this the near-collapse of the house.

miracles.[11] According to Schäfer's persuasive reading of this Bavli passage and other talmudic passages concerning Rabbi Eliezer, the story's four miracles are regarded by the rabbis as magic even though they are divinely sanctioned. The Bavli's rabbis, so Schäfer, portrays Rabbi Eliezer "as the dangerous arch-magician, [and] model Rabbi Eliezer along the lines of the other arch-magician, who threatened their authority – Jesus."[12] Christianity or Jesus are of course not mentioned in either the Yerushalmi or the Bavli versions of the story. Schäfer rightly emphasizes that the story's portrayal of Eliezer as an alter ego of Jesus "is more indirect and becomes obvious only when we have a closer look at the rabbinic persona of Rabbi Eliezer," a look which Schäfer duly provides.[13]

A reading of the story as a parody confirms Schäfer's suggestion that the story indirectly addresses Christianity. A closer look at the two *specific* miracles in the Yerushalmi version in the context of late antique Christian literature reveals that each of the miracles indeed ironically repeats a particular "Christian" miracle and, most importantly, that using miracles in doctrinal arguments itself is a characteristic of late antique Christianity which the Yerushalmi ironizes. In particular, the specific miracle of the uprooted tree is more hermeneutically significant in the Yerushalmi than in the Bavli. Only the Yerushalmi, in my view, allows for a full contextualization of the

---

[11] Eliezer causes 1) the uprooting of a tree, 2) the near-collapse of a house, and 3) the voice from heaven; the Bavli also has him perform 4) the reversal of the direction of a stream. At the command of the rabbis, the tree returns to its place and the stream reverses to its original course. On the significance of these miracles and rabbinic miracles in general, see Alexander Guttman, "The Significance of Miracles for Talmudic Judaism," *HUCA* 20 (1947), 347–81. See also Rubenstein, *Talmudic Stories*, 50 for further discussion and references.

[12] Peter Schäfer, *Jesus in the Talmud* (Princeton: Princeton University Press, 2007), 51. On the rabbis' diverse views of magic in general, see Judah Goldin, "The Magic of Magic and Superstition," in Elisabeth Schuessler Fiorenza (ed.), *Aspects of Religious Propaganda in Judaism and Early Christianity* (Notre Dame; London: University of Notre Dame Press, 1976) 115–147 [= ibid., *Studies in Midrash and Related Literature* (Philadelphia; New York; Jerusalem: The Jewish Publication Society, 1988) 337–357] and Peter Schäfer, "Magic and Religion in Ancient Judaism," in Peter Schäfer and Hans G. Kippenberg (eds.), *Envisioning Magic: A Princeton Seminar and Symposium* (Leiden; New York: Brill, 1997), 19–44. On Palestinian Magic, see Gideon Bohak, *Ancient Jewish Magic* (Cambridge, UK: Cambridge University Press, 2008), and Guiseppe Veltri, *Magie und Halakha: Ansätze zu einem empirischen Wissenschaftsbegriff im spätantiken und frühmittelalterlichen Judentum* (Tübingen: Mohr Siebeck, 1997). Apotropaic magic, as well as magic in general, is even more commonly accepted in the Bavli than in Palestine; see Michael G. Morony, "Magic and Society in Late Sasanian Iraq," in Scott B. Noegel, Joel T. Walker and Brannon M. Wheeler (eds.), *Prayer, Magic, and the Stars in the Ancient and Late Antique World* (University Park, PA: The Pennsylvania State University Press, 2003), 83–110.

[13] Peter Schäfer, *Jesus in the Talmud*, 49. The importance of Rabbi Eliezer for understanding the rabbis' view of Christianity has been a prominent aspect of my study as well; see note 37 in Chapter Four and notes 10, 65, and 117 in Chapter Five.

story, and a comparison with patristic exegesis of the New Testament reveals that the story contains a Gospel parody and satire of rabbinic followers of Christian hermeneutics.

Both in the Greek and Syriac Christian traditions one finds treatises dealing with the topic of doctrinal proof with the help of miracles. Rabbi Eliezer's confirmation of halakha with the help of miracles imitates the Christian topos of faith in Jesus confirmed by miracles. The Yerushalmi thereby invokes one of the central topics of Christian discourse. This theme is so dominant in ancient Christian documents from the New Testament to Byzantine and Sasanian Syriac literatures that one can easily lose sight of the precise language in the Yerushalmi. Two examples from the Christian tradition, one Greek and the other Syriac, shall suffice to illuminate the parody in the Yerushalmi. Cyril of Jerusalem (313–386 CE) argues the following in his lecture *On Faith*:

> But there is a second type of faith, which is given by Christ as a gift of grace [ἐν χάριτος]. 'For to one is given the word [λόγος] of wisdom through the spirit, to another the word of knowledge according to the same spirit, to a different one faith in the same spirit, and to another gifts of healing [1 Corinthians 12:8–9].' Now this faith, given as a gift of grace by the Spirit, is not only doctrinal [δογματική] but also works supernatural things [τῶν ὑπὲρ ἄνθρωπον ἐνεργητική]. For one who has this faith will say to this mountain: 'Move yourself there!' and it will move [Mark 11:23]. For he who will say this in faith, believing that it will happen without doubt in his heart, will then receive the grace [τὴν χάριν].[14]

Cyril's reading of the New Testament explicitly indicates that faith can indeed move mountains and that the miracle is proof of true faith; Eliezer, likewise, moves trees, thereby providing proof of the true halakha. Both Cyril's Gospel citation and the Yerushalmi employ the same formula: say to x to move to y, and x shall move to y. Rabbi Eliezer does not doubt and thus receives God's "grace" in the form of divine justification of his halakhic ruling – Cyril's divine "grace" (τὴν χάριν) and the Yerushalmi's divine "praise" (שבחא) are not dissimilar.

The same moving a mountain theme is also found in Syriac literature of the period from the Sasanian Empire. Aphrahat, a prominent Syriac church father (~270––345 CE) also wrote a *Demonstration of Faith* and cites the same Gospel passage concerning moving mountains (1.17). Intriguingly, elsewhere in Aphrahat, a Jewish sage mobilizes the same Gospel passage against the church father, reasoning that if faith can move mountains, the Christians should not be persecuted so harshly:

---

[14] Cyril of Jerusalem, Fifth Catechetical Lecture ("On Faith," 11), in W.C. Reischl and J. Rupp, *Cyrilli Hierosolymorum archiepiscopi opera quae supersunt omnia* (Hildesheim: Olms, 1967), vol. I, 146–8; see also note 88 in Chapter Five. On the broader context of Cyril's catechetical lectures, see Jan Willem Drijvers, *Cyril of Jerusalem: Bishop and City* (Leiden: Brill, 2004), 53–62.

I have heard a reproach, which has greatly troubled me ... Darkness still more thickens upon me when even the Jews reproach us and magnify themselves over the children of our [Christian] people ['*mn*]. It happened that one day a man who is called "the sage [*hkym'*] of the Jews" met me and asked, saying Jesus, who is called your teacher, has written to you, "If there shall be in you faith like one seed of mustard, you will say to this mountain, 'move,' and it will move from before you; and [you may say] even, 'be lifted up and fall into the sea,' and it shall obey you (Matthew 17:19).' Thus [he continued] there is not [to be found] among your entire people not one sage [*hkym'*], whose prayer is listened to, who seeks from God that your persecutions should cease from you. Thus it is written to you in the word, "There is nothing which you will be unable to do [Matthew 21:22]."[15]

According to Aphrahat, the Jewish sage was able to marshal the Gospel passage against Christians, but there is no way to verify neither the accuracy of the statement nor the relationship between the Jewish sage and a talmudic rabbi (even though the Syriac term *hkyma* which Aphrahat uses for Jewish and Christian sages is commensurate with the rabbinic self-designation חכם). Still, a closer look at the Gospel passage itself reveals that the author of the Yerushalmi was familiar with and parodied the Christian tradition with far more playfulness than Aphrahat might have imagined.

Eliezer's miracles indeed align him with Christian hermeneutics, thereby setting him apart from his rabbinic colleagues. The idea that faith moves mountains and trees is indeed central to the Gospels and patristic literature and the rabbis were thus likely exposed to it or its oral formulation.[16] It is expressed in the gospels of Mark (11:23), Matthew (21:22) and Luke (17:3–6), cited here based on the Syriac *Peshitta*:

Mind your souls! If your brother sins, you must rebuke the offender, and if there is repentance, forgive him. And if the same person sins against you seven times a day, and turns back to you seven times and says, "I repent", forgive him. The apostles said to the Lord, 'Increase our faith!' He said to them, 'If you had faith of a mustard seed, you could say to this mulberry tree [*twt'*], "Be uprooted [*d't'qr*] and planted in the sea", and it would obey you.[17]

---

[15] Aphrahat, Demonstration 21, *On Persecution* (1), translation based on Jacob Neusner, *Aphrahat and Judaism: the Christian-Jewish Argument in Fourth-Century Iran* (Leiden: Brill, 1971), 97; for the Syriac, see R. Graffin, *Patrologia Syriaca* (Paris: Didot et Socii, 1894), I, 933–4. For the historical background of Demonstration 20 and 21 during the Sasanian persecution of Christians, see Adam Becker, "Anti-Judaism and Care for the Poor in Aphrahat's *Demonstration* 20," *Journal of Early Christian Studies* 10 (2002), 305–327. For an extensive summary of studies on Aphrahat and the Jews, see Christine Shepardson, *Anti-Judaism and Christian Orthodoxy: Ephrem's Hymns in Fourth-Century Syria*, (Washington: Catholic University of America Press, 2008), 23 f. note 7. On the transliteration of Syriac see Chapter Four, note 15.

[16] See Chapter Four, pages 141–43.

[17] On the Peshitta citation see Chapter Four, note 15.

The Syriac Gospel here uses exactly the same reflexive verbal form (*d't'qr*) that we find in the Yerushalmi (איתעוקרין, the Palestinian Aramaic Gospel is sadly lost). Rabbi Eliezer's repetition of Jesus' remark hence seems to express the Yerushalmi's critical stance toward him as enacting Christian teachings. Given the Yerushalmi's precise parodic imitation of the passage's language and message, we can therefore confirm Schäfer's reading of the rabbis' banning of Eliezer as a banning of his Christian hermeneutics, especially in the Yerushalmi, but also, in a more complex way, in the Bavli's expansion of the story.

The fact that the tree in the Gospel is mulberry rather than carob, moreover, underscores the dynamic oral context of the rabbis' familiarity with the gospel. The Arabic version of the remark in the *Diatessaron* (32–33), clarifies this matter:

And [Jesus] saw one fig tree [*wr'y tynh w'hdh*] at a distance on the beaten highway, bearing leaves. And he came unto it, expecting to find something on it; and when he came, he found nothing on it but the leaves – and it was not the season of figs – and he said unto it, Henceforward for ever let no man eat fruit of you. And his disciples understood … And when evening came, Jesus went forth outside of the city, he and his disciples. And as they passed in the morning, the disciples saw that fig tree withered away from its root. And they passed by, and said, How did the fig tree dry up immediately? And Simon remembered, and said unto him, My Master, behold, that fig tree which you cursed has dried up. And Jesus answered and said unto them, "Let there be in you the faith of God. Verily I say unto you, if you believe, and doubt not in your hearts, and assure yourselves that that will be which ye say, you shall have what ye say. And if you say to this mountain, 'Remove, and fall into the sea,' it shall be. And all that you ask God in prayer, and believe, he will give you." And the apostles said unto our Lord, "Increase us in faith." He said unto them, "If there be in you faith like a grain of mustard, you shall say to this fig tree ['*l-tyn'h*], 'Be torn up, and be planted in the sea,' and it will obey you."[18]

Jesus sees a fig tree, curses it, and it dries about miraculously. After the disciples inquire about the fate of the tree, the Diatessaron and its Syriac commentary teaches that one can command a fig tree to be torn up and transplanted in the sea, and it will obey. The Diatessaron's rendition of various Gospel passages combines the miraculous destruction of a plant with Jesus' teaching. Yet another variant of the passage is implied by Ephrem's

---

[18] Translation by Hope W. Hogg, in Alexander Roberts and James Donaldson, *The Ante-Nicene Fathers: Translations of the Writings of the Fathers down to A.D. 325* (Grand Rapids: Eerdmans Publishers, 1996–2001 [1897]), IX, 94; for the Arabic, see P. Augustinus Ciasca, *Tatiani Evangeliorum Harmoniae Arabica* (Rome: S. C. De Propaganda Fide, 1888) 123–5; Arabic cited according to the Buckwalter transliteration. On the importance of the Arabic Diatessaron and Ephrem's commentary for understanding the rabbis' exposure to the gospel see note 17 in Chapter Four.

commentary on the Diatessaron: here, the mountain *along with* its trees is removed, allowing us to see the parody more clearly.[19]

First, we can now understand Eliezer's anger, which leads him to burn wheat merely by looking at it, as a playful imitation of Jesus' destruction of the fig tree. We are not dealing here with precise imitation; rather, Eliezer's destructive anger over the halakha is a parodic allusion to Jesus' paraenetic anger.

Second, the shift from a mulberry to a fig tree helps us recognize the significance of the Yerushalmi's use of carob. There are variations in the Christian source, and the rabbinic parodist would not have been interested in preserving the integrity of a passage he might have heard only in passing. The Diatessaron refers to a fig tree only because such a tree is already under discussion in the same passage. The Yerushalmi, in turn, changes the tree to a carob in accordance with his audience's familiarity with it.[20]

God's addressing Eliezer as "my son" is a more precise imitation of another central gospel passage: "a voice [*ql'*] from heaven said, 'this is my Son [*bry*], the beloved, with whom I am well pleased,'" found in the Gospels' Syriac description of Jesus' baptism.[21] Similarly, when Jesus reappears next to Moses and Elijah, a heavenly voice (*ql'*) is heard, saying, "this is my son (*bry*), the beloved, with whom I am well pleased, *listen to him*.[22] The Yerushalmi precisely imitates God's command to Jesus' disciples in this

---

[19] See Carmel McCarthy, *Saint Ephrem's Commentary on Tatian's Diatessaron: an English Translation of Chester Beatty Syriac MS 709* (Oxford: Oxford University Press, 1993), 244–7. Mark 11:12–25 and Matthew 21:18–21 link the withering of a fig tree to the saying on the ability of faith to move mountains, but not to trees. The passage from Luke 17:6 cited above also features faith that is able to move trees but without the miracle of the withering fig tree. Only the Arabic Diatessaron and Ephrem's commentary combine the destruction of a plant with the moving of a tree in a way that recalls the Yerushalmi version. Note that the Latin Diatessaron preserves Luke's text structure of relating the cursed dried fig tree (*ecce ficus cui maledixit aruit*) to the mountain that casts itself in the sea (*monte huic dixeritis: tolle te et iacta te in mare fiet*) without including the miracle of the moving fig tree at all, see Ernst Ranke, *Codex Fuldensis: Novum Testamentum Latine interprete Hieronymo* (Marburg; Leipzig: Sumtibus N. G. Elwerti Bibliopolae Academici, 1868), 107.

[20] The carob tree is ubiquitous in rabbinic narrative and halakha whereas the mulberry tree (תות or תותא) is rare. The carob tree, moreover, features prominently in the Babylonian miracle stories associated with Rashbi's stay in the cave (Bavli *Shabbat* 33b; see Chapter Five) and with Honi the circle-maker (*Ta'anit* 23a), providing a helpful parallel of the Diatessaron's adaptation of the tree in the Gospel.

[21] Matthew 3:17; see also Mark 1:11, Luke 3:22, and Tatian's Diatessaron (IV) in Roberts and Donaldson, *The Ante-Nicene Fathers*, 49–50 and P. Augustins Ciasca, *Tatiani Evangeliorum Harmoniae Arabica*, 16–17.

[22] Matthew 17:3–5; see also Mark 9:7 and Luke 9:35, and cf. Acts of the Apostles 13:33, Hebrews 1:5 and 5:5, 2 Peter 1:17, and Tatian's Diatessaron (XXIV) in Roberts and Donaldson, *The Ante-Nicene Fathers*, 80; also see P. Augustinus Ciasca, *Tatiani Evangeliorum Harmoniae Arabica*, 16–17 and Carmel McCarthy, *Saint Ephrem's Commentary on Tatian's Diatessaron*, 93.

second passage. The *voice* in the gospel says: this is *my son*, listen to him, while the *voice* (בת קול) in the Yerushalmi states that "the halakha accords with Eliezer *my son* (בני)," granting the same authority to Rabbi Eliezer that the gospel grants Jesus and rendering the heavenly voice from the Gospel's Syriac Aramaic in the more suitable Hebrew.[23]

Rabbi Yehoshua's shocking and hilarious exclamation that the Torah *is not in heaven* seeks to reject a central presupposition of Christian herme-neutics that justifies Jesus' sonship as well as to undermine Eliezer's ha-lakha. Divine voices are found throughout rabbinic literature, and in the Bavli, God on numerous occasions even refers to a rabbi as "my son." Yet as far as I know language of *singular* divine sonship is absent from the Yerushalmi and is even directly rejected elsewhere in Palestinian rabbinic literature.[24] This indicates that the Yerushalmi's parody of Christian texts is more pointed than the Bavli's.

What is at stake in the Yerushalmi is not belief in Jesus as the Messiah, let alone Christological speculation. Rabbi Eliezer may be Jesus' alter ego, but the Yerushalmi's portrayal of the dispute as an internal rabbinic mat-ter can hardly be overemphasized. The Yerushalmi disembeds Christian hermeneutics and recontextualizes it within talmudic halakhic discourse, once again linking external parody to internal discussion, as we have seen in Chapters Four and Five as well.

To conclude my discussion of the story, a look at its satirical context in Graeco-Roman literature seems helpful. In his most recent publication, just as in earlier ones, Boyarin focuses on the Bavli's version of the story of Rabbi Eliezer and the Oven of Akhnai, seeking to contextualize the Bavli within Hellenistic genres such as the Menippean Satire, Lucian's writings, and the Greek Novels, as outlined in my Introduction. He writes that the story's notion of

"trees ... being conduits for the word of God is finally, or so it seems to me, as fan-tastical as the notion of Menippus tying an eagle to one arm and a vulture wing to the other and flying to heaven. It is difficult to imagine the Rabbis believing in such a story ... The form of the text certainly fits, as well, into the Menippean mode of conversation between heaven and earth and fantastical occurrences."[25]

I certainly agree with Boyarin's reading, and his invaluable emphasis on the Talmud's ability "to be both serious in one register and satirical in another

---

[23] See Joseph Yahalom, "Angels do not Understand Aramaic: On the Literary Use of Jewish Palestinian Aramaic in Late Antiquity," *Journal of Jewish Studies* 47 (1996), 33–44.

[24] In the Bavli version of the story, God calls "the rabbis," not Rabbi Eliezer, "my sons", thereby softening the Yerushalmi's anti-Christian attack on Rabbi Eliezer, a difference that only readers of both texts can, and perhaps are meant to, discern. On the opposition to the so called "sons of God" in Palestinian rabbinic literature, see note 106 in Chapter Five.

[25] Boyarin, *Socrates and the Fat Rabbis*, 224.

at the same time."[26] This helps us recognize the coexistence in the Rabbi Eliezer story of the serious and the humorous criticism of Christian tendencies among the rabbis. And again, Boyarin's insights, like Schäfer's, are just as relevant to the Yerushalmi as they are to the Bavli, if not more so.

To reiterate, Boyarin's argument views Babylonian Hellenism as the cultural context of the Bavli's use of the serio-comic. Babylonia certainly absorbed Hellenistic traditions for hundreds of years before the Bavli was composed. Yet Greek novels, Menippean Satire, and even Lucian's texts were scarce among the residents of the Sasanian Empire.[27] Boyarin is aware of this problem and suggests that motifs from these literatures were "transmitted to the Babylonian Rabbis through the medium of oral transcultural transmission."[28]

My above reading of the Yerushalmi extends Boyarin's insight and illustrates my discussion in the Introduction of a specific cultural milieu of such transmission.[29] The type of Neoplatonic Greek learning that reached the Christian schools in Babylonian in the late fifth century, for one, was not particularly interested in satirical works, and I am not aware of comical Zoroastrian texts.[30] Hence, I would like to suggest that the one evident medium of "transcultural transmission" that channeled Menippean, novelistic, and Lucian-style motifs to the Bavli was the writings of the rabbis themselves, whose role as active agents of intense literary and cultural exchange between the Roman and Sasanian empires is amply illustrated.[31]

---

[26] Boyarin, *Socrates and the Fat Rabbis*, 224.

[27] While Syriac was Lucian's mother tongue, he seems to have composed the entirety of his work in Greek. The only preserved translation of Lucian into Syriac, to the best of my knowledge, is the early sixth-century rendition of Lucian's work *On Calumnies* by Sargis of Theodosiopolis (died 536 CE) in Eastern Asia Minor, well within the cultural sphere of the Sasanian Empire. Sargis's Syriac text, however, is much more a "'lay' homily based upon the writing by Lucian" than a translation, as Rothstein suggested in 1888 and Macleod and Wickham later confirmed, and does not preserve Lucian's playful spirit (M. D. Macleod and L. R. Wickham, "The Syriac Version of Lucian's De Calumnia, " *The Classical Quarterly* 20 (1970), 297–99).

[28] Boyarin, *Socrates and the Fat Rabbis*, 138.

[29] See pages 16–21.

[30] See note 53 in the Introduction. On the limited playfulness of the Christian writings of the Sassanian Empire, see note 59 in the Introduction.

[31] On the rabbinic transmission of Hellenistic culture see note 64 in the Introduction. One concrete example of how novelistic material found its way into the Bavli is evident in its adaptation of a text from *Ekha Rabbah*. Levinson has shown that the story of the two children of the High Priest in *Ekha Rabbah* 1.46 ought to be understood against the background of the Greco-Roman erotic novel; see, "The Tragedy of Romance: a Case of literary Exile," *Harvard Theological Review* 89 (1996), 227–244. The story appears with minor differences in *Gittin* 58a, importing the novelistic motifs without necessarily participating in the same discursive milieu as the Palestinian rabbinic authors who first told it. The issue demands further consideration.

Palestinian rabbinic literature, and not the Bavli, was in my view first responsible for incorporating the serio-comic into rabbinic discourse. If the Bavli's retelling of the Oven of Akhnai story was at all satirical, then the Yerushalmi's original was at least as much so, and the most obvious path of the serio-comic to Babylonia passed through Jewish Palestine.

The Palestinian satirical parodies discussed in this book are all I can offer here in lieu of a sustained argument for such a broad claim of how parody and satire reached Babylonia. In the context of the example just discussed, a close reading of its ending may be suggestive as well. Trash is thrown at Rabbi Eliezer as he walks through the market. Imagining the scene as enacted slapstick reveals the literary potential of the story. Far from being upset, Eliezer cites Psalms 113:7 "He that lifts up the needy [אביון] from the refuse heap [מאשפות]," concluding that his colleagues are about to lift the ban since he is covered in trash.[32]

The comedy hardly requires explanation; but there is an element here of external parody. First, it should be noted that Eliezer refers to himself with the Hebrew word *Ebion* (needy), the same word used by orthodox Christian heresiologies to refer to Jews who believe in Jesus. Eliezer's evocation himself of *Ebion*, involuntarily invoking the common enemy of the Jewish and Christian orthodoxies, satirically associates Eliezer with Jewish believers in Jesus. This association becomes especially suggestive in light of my analysis in Chapter Five of the cultural proximity between rabbinic and Christian heresiologies that concern the alleged group of "Ebionites"; the questionable historicity of Ebionism does not affect the powerful reality of the Christian and possibly Jewish heresiological discourses.[33] Again, the text is not so much portraying an actual rabbi who believes in one Messiah or another but rather insinuating Eliezer's hermeneutical guilt by association. Vagueness has always been an effective weapon of polemics.

Comparison of the use of Psalm 113:7 with Christian uses of the same verse allows us to fully appreciate the Yerushalmi's satire.[34] For example, Maria alludes to the same psalmic verse (Luke 1:52, a text that became part

---

[32] Note the comical and positive ending of the Oven of Akhnai story in the Yerushalmi, which concludes with hope that Eliezer will rejoin his colleagues. In contrast, the Bavli version leads to the tragic demise of Rabban Gamliel, and metonymically of rabbinic orthodoxy, despite the efforts of Imma Shalom to save him.

[33] See pages 207–11.

[34] On the topic of comparative exegesis see the important recent volume by Emmanouela Grypeou and Helen Spurling, *The Exegetical Encounter between Jews and Christians in Late Antiquity* (Leiden: Brill, 2009), Burton Visotzky, *Fathers of the World: Essays in Rabbinic and Patristic Literature* (Tübingen: Mohr Siebeck, 1995) and *Golden Bells and Pomegranates: Studies in Midrash Leviticus Rabbah* (Tübingen: Mohr Siebeck, 2003); and the other volumes discussed by Judith Baskin, "Rabbinic-Patristic Exegetical Contacts: Some New Perspectives," *Religious Studies Review* 24 (1998), 171–173.

of the *Magnificat* of the later Latin tradition). Other Latin church fathers, such as Augustine and Ambrose, cited the verse regularly in Christological contexts.[35] Most interesting, however, is the Palestinian Greek tradition illustrated by Basil of Caesarea (330–379 CE). In a letter to an unknown supporter, Basil describes his fears of being denounced as a heretic:

I make my usual request that you do not stop to pray for my miserable life, lest I, sunk in the unreal appearances [τῇ φαντασίᾳ] of this life, forget God, "who lifts the poor from the ground" [τοῦ ἐγείροντος ἀπὸ γῆς πτωχόν, Psalms 112:7]; and because of any sensation of elation [ἔπαρσιν], [or that I] "become subject to the court of the devil" [1 Timothy 3:6]... or [lest I] even through evil deeds also hurt the conscience of my fellow servants ... But know that I expect, according to the threat of the heretics, to be summoned to court, professedly for the sake of peace!"[36]

Basil, in the context of Psalms 113.7, explores self-elation as well as injury of the conscience of other ecclesiastical servants. These themes are also found in the Yerushalmi, which describes the consequences of an overly confident rabbi who begins to burn crops in response to being attacked by his colleagues. Most interesting, in light of Eliezer's heretical behavior, are the "unreal appearances of life" described by Basil; around 375 CE, he expects to be summoned to court by a group he calls "the heretics," a fate very similar, mutatis mutandis, to the one that Rabbi Eliezer faces.[37]

Without any linguistic similarities, it seems unlikely that the thematic affinities between the Yerushalmi and Basil are the result of the former's imitation of some specific patristic text.[38] To a degree, the affinities certainly reflect a shared discursive milieu concerning heresy and orthodoxy. Still, the example from Basil amply illustrates how precisely the Yerushalmi Gospel parody satirizes Christian discourse, targeting a heretical rabbi who begins by behaving very much like the church fathers of his time, and, as he returns to orthodoxy, begins behaving very much unlike them. Furthermore, precisely in light of this proximity, we can also point to the differences between Christian and Jewish discourses in this regard, noting for example, the contrast between Basil's somber tone and the Yerushalmi's literary artistry, playfulness, and absorption of Hellenistic serio-comic

---

[35] See, for example, Augustine, *Exposition on Psalm 113*; Ambrose, *Letter 22* and *Concerning Virginity*, 3.

[36] Basil of Caesarea, Letter 213.1–2, cited according to Yves Courtonne, *Saint Basile: Lettres* (Paris: Les Belles Lettres, 1961), II, 200–1; see also Philip Rousseau, *Basil of Caesarea* (Berkeley: University of California Press, 1994), esp. 190–232.

[37] Basil addresses this episode as well in Letters 120 and 129; see Wolf-Dieter Hauschild, *Basilius von Caesarea: Briefe* (Stuttgart: Anton Hiersemann, 1973), vol. II, 164 note 98 and 183 note 332.

[38] The Yerushalmi's play with "trash" is not evident in the Greek translation of the psalm which the church fathers used, in which "earth" is used instead of "trash."

genres.[39] The authors of the Bavli, in turn, were eager students of the Yerushalmi, and Jewish Hellenism prevailed in rabbinic Babylonia.

At least in the case of the Oven of Akhnai story, it seems that parody and the serio-comic reached the Bavli through inner-rabbinic transmission. While this seems typical, we also should note that the Bavli occasionally waters down different elements of particular parodies like this one, since the imitation of the Gospel and the satirical allusion to Greek patristic discourse had become obscured in its new context. Still, as Schäfer's analysis of the story and circumstantial evidence provided by Ephrem, the Diatessaron, and others suggests, the figure of Rabbi Eliezer in the Bavli maintains the prominent theme in the Yerushalmi of contemplating how far a rabbi can go in exploring Christian hermeneutics. The Bavli's examination of the value of miracles for halakhic discourse in even greater detail, then, should equally be viewed as a further and more daring exploration of the Yerushalmi's main theme. The gospel parody in the Bavli, even if less clearly recognizable as such, may turn out to be more, not less, engaged in the consequences of Christian hermeneutics. Moreover, even if elements of particular parodies were compromised during their journey east, the rabbinic heyday of the serio-comic in general and parody in particular was not in Palestine but in Babylonia, where the rabbis further developed Palestinian styles and techniques.

Parodies between the Yerushalmi and the Bavli

In order to explore how rabbinic parodic techniques evolved upon reaching the Babylonian rabbis, I first tentatively seek to differentiate between Palestinian and Babylonian parodies, while of course taking into account the generic qualities of the two corpora as a whole. The two most obvious differences between Babylonian and Palestinian parodies concern the imitation of texts and the laying bare of inconsistencies in the views of the rabbis' opponents – whether the rabbis shared these opponents' views or not.

Criticizing an opponent using his own logic and terminology, to begin with, is perhaps the most sophisticated aspect of late ancient satire, and among the examples in this book it is most clearly evident in the Babylonian parodies.[40] The technique of exposing internal tensions in the targeted

---

[39] On the role of humor in the Greek and Syriac patristic tradition see Introduction, notes 60 and 61.

[40] This becomes already clear in the intra-rabbinic example in Chapter One, where Rava's students use his own legal category against him; the case of the cat also employs Rava's own language against him. Defeats against an opponent in his own territory become even more pronounced in the Babylonian examples of inter-rabbinic and external parody.

text is less developed in Palestinian parodies.[41] The Babylonian parodies, in contrast, seem to be more focused on textual imitation than the Palestinian ones.[42] The Palestinian parodies imitate texts in a most understated way, showing less interest in analyzing the inner logic of the imitated texts. These differences between Babylonian and Palestinian rabbinic parody, based on the dozen or so examples discussed here and elsewhere, reveal the status of parody in rabbinic literature in general in two ways.

While textual play and irony may abound, satire and parody are indeed rare in Babylonian as well as Palestinian rabbinic literature, and the absence of a formal rabbinic notion of parody also points to their exceptional character. At the same time, the satirical sophistication and imitative intensity of Babylonian parody in comparison with its Palestinian precursor may indicate two apparently contradictory possibilities: either the Babylonian rabbinic authors were *more* aware of the parodic effect they created and hence dedicated more effort to it, while the Palestinian rabbis employed parody as "natural" and self-evident part of their discursive tradition; or, the Babylonian rabbinic audience was *less* attuned to the understated Hellenistic parodic allusion, and therefore needed clearer guidance, whereas the Palestinian audience had greater mastery of parodic conventions. Seeking to reconcile this contradiction of greater Babylonian parodic sophistication outside of the context of Graeco-Roman literary traditions might thus tell us something about the history of the pan-rabbinic textual community, a history that contains elements of continuity and evolution as much as partial brakes and new beginnings.[43]

The story of Bar Hedya in Chapter Two constructs a logical conundrum by linking the Palestinian rabbinic doctrine of dream interpretation to the Palestinian rabbinic insistence on the dream-interpreter's remuneration. The parody thereby evaluates the Palestinian rabbinic system on its own terms. Similarly, the story of Imma Shalom in Chapter Four identifies a tension between the Gospel text that exhorts followers of Jesus to abstain from adjudication and the Christian claim to political power. The Bavli in this instance adopts the Gospel's "true" meaning and turns it against the Christian "philosopher," and most pointedly against the Syriac interpretation of the gospel passage.

[41] Rabbi Hananya, discussed in the Introduction, simply violates the halakha, as do the sons of the drunken father discussed in Chapter Two and Rashbi's opponents in Chapter Five. Even in the more forgiving parody of Rabbi Eliezer's Christian inclination, satirical vagueness seems to govern Palestinian parody, whereas analytical rigor, and strategic charity for one's opponents distinguishes those of Babylonia.

[42] The sugya on the rebellion of Rava's students, for example, contains three instances of parody; the Bar Hedya story attacks all of the aspects of Rabbi Ishmael's dream interpretation reported in the Yerushalmi; and the story of Imma Shalom engages in a very "thick" reading of several Gospel passages and their Syriac patristic interpretations.

[43] On the concept of a textual community, see Brian Stock, *Listening for the Text: on the Uses of the Past* (Baltimore: Johns Hopkins University Press, 1990), 37. On rabbinic textual communities, see, for example, Michael Walzer et al. (eds.), *The Jewish Political Tradition* (New Haven: Yale University Press, 2000).

Rabbinic parody might have been one such new beginning. The textual community of the Hebrew Bible at some point made use of parody, but these parodies seem all but forgotten in the late ancient readings of the Bible.[44] While the reasons for this break are beyond the scope of this study, it is important to note that the rupture caused by the slow linguistic shift from Hebrew to Aramaic and Greek during the Second Temple period would have limited the possibility of a nuanced literary reading of biblical Hebrew texts.[45] The canonization of the Bible in many ways homogenized the biblical corpus, a development that might have overshadowed the satirical elements contained in it.[46] The destruction of the Second Temple and its aftermath and the growing distance from the cultural context of the Bible might have rendered the biblical parodies imperceptible to late ancient rabbis.

Comical reflection on the Israelite tradition in general, as well as reflection on comical aspects of the Israelite tradition in particular, became a mostly dispensable commodity for the rabbinic guardians and interpreters of Scripture. Accordingly, we have little evidence of parody in early, tannaitic rabbinic literature, even though textual imitation, irony, and criticism are present.[47] We do find satirical parodies in Palestinian rabbinic literature, but its imitative technique is limited and allusive and presupposes the familiarity of its audience with imitative criticism. Finally, we find obvious parodies and parodic virtuosity and rather well-marked parodies in the Bavli.

Though evidence is scarce, it remains tempting to point to a chronological trajectory from the virtual nonexistence of parody in the tannaitic period, through the recognizable parodies in the Palestinian Amoraic texts, and to the well-substantiated and sophisticated parodies in the Bavli. If the overwhelmingly parodic orientation of some post-talmudic rabbinic texts, such as *Alpha Beta de-Ben Sira* and late versions of *Toldoth Yeshu*, are also considered, the literary evolution of parody becomes more evident. This evolution began in the Graeco-Roman milieu of serio-comic philosophical discourse but, continuing past the prime of the Second Sophistic, relied on

---

[44] See note 56 in the Introduction.

[45] On this rupture, see most recently Seth Schwartz, "Hebrew and Imperialism in Jewish Palestine," in *Ancient Judaism in its Hellenistic Context*, edited by Carol Bakhos (Leiden: Brill, 2005), 53–82.

[46] On the rabbinic canonization of the Hebrew Bible, see, for example, Sid (Shnayer) Z. Leiman, *The Canonization of Hebrew Scripture: the Talmudic and Midrashic Evidence* (New Haven: Connecticut Academy of Arts and Sciences, 1991).

[47] I discuss irony in the Rabbi Eleazar ben Dama story in Tosefta *Hulin* 2.22–23; see note 121 in Chapter Five. Schäfer provided a counterexample in which the rabbis ironize the Bible's view regarding priests. On irony in the tannaitic literature, see note 2 above and note 24 in the Introduction.

an increasing awareness among rabbinic authors of the techniques and potential of parodic criticism (long before the invention of the term).[48]

As a corollary to such broad speculations, it should be noted that the development of rabbinic literature itself over time became more conducive to providing the prerequisite of parody I discussed throughout this book: a parody imitates texts that it expects its audience to know. In the tannaitic period, the rabbis constituted themselves as a movement and aside from the Bible did not have a clear body of Jewish texts that could be imitated.[49] Parodic allusion and understated parody became a part of the Palestinian Amoraic literature along with the literary sensitivity of Greco-Roman Hellenism, and the parodies of the Amoraic rabbis could imitate a much larger number of rabbinic and non-rabbinic texts. We find fully-developed and clearly apparent parodies in the Bavli and in the early post-talmudic period (though in this post-talmudic stage they were not so much part of halakhic discourse). The second break in the history of Jewish parody occurred in the Middle Age, when, to the best of my knowledge, parody was largely absent from halakhic discourse. Still, parody continued to be appreciated in medieval gospel parodies, and a sense of the parodic effect remained a part of the Jewish tradition, as evidenced, for example, by the late medieval and early modern Purim-spiel.

To reiterate, our limited understanding of many aspects of rabbinic culture and the transmission history of rabbinic texts skews our perception of rabbinic parody. On the one hand, many of the parodied texts are now lost, and many parodies were subsequently altered to such an extent that the relationship between the parody and the imitated text became obfuscated. This diminishes our ability to recognize a potentially greater prominence of rabbinic parody. More troubling, on the other hand, is the fact that due to a series of textual alterations, determined by factors fully or partially

---

[48] See note 41 in the Introduction. On the age of the Toldoth Yeshu tradition, see note 58 in the Introduction.

[49] One example of a possible parody in tannaitic literature is the ironic story of Honi the circle-maker in Mishna *Ta'anit* 3.8. The Rabbinic Honi is portrayed as a miracle-worker in conflict with the rabbis, suggesting parody of a preexisting literary figure. The story, moreover, imitates earlier materials, as evidenced by Josephus (*Antiquities* 14.2.1–21). It is difficult, however, to determine whether the Mishna imitates Josephus, retells his materials non-parodically, or reflects yet another putative shared tradition between Josephus, the Mishna, and the Tosefta. The topic deserves further consideration; see William Scott Green, "Palestinian Holy Men: Charismatic Leadership and Rabbinic Tradition," in Wolfgang Haase (ed.), *Aufstieg und Niedergang der Römischen Welt* 19/2 (Berlin: Walter de Gruyter, 1979), 619–647. For another possible tannaitic parody and a similar difficulty in identifying the imitated text, see note 4 in Chapter Five.

unknown to us, late versions of an earlier text may seem parodic to us even though the rabbinic author never intended this.[50]

This insight, however, is not the end but the beginning of a critical examination of rabbinic parody. As I pointed out in the Introduction and have attempted to illustrate throughout the book, there are many ways to evaluate the intention of a satirical parodist. Moreover, the efficient application of the concept of parody generates cumulative evidence for assessing the relationship between the parody and the imitated text. Parodies combine straightforward imitation with alterations at the expense of the imitated text, and an analysis of this relationship between the two texts can confirm or refute our suspicion of a rabbinic author's parodic intention. Among our inroads into rabbinic critical thought, parody enjoys a special privilege of internal verifiability.

My findings have the potential to affect the way we read broader aspects of rabbinic literature. Perhaps the most important suggestion in this book concerns the continuity between intra-, inter-, and external rabbinic parody. Parody may be a modern concept, but it is a concept that allows us to reassess two important aspects of rabbinic literature about which a scholarly consensus has not yet been reached: rabbinic self-criticism and rabbinic familiarity with non-rabbinic literature. If parody is not a peculiar and isolated phenomenon but a constant, albeit infrequent, presence in all amoraic texts, then it may be possible to generalize our findings concerning parody and apply them to these two controversial issues in rabbinic scholarship.

As indicated in the Introduction and throughout this book, rabbinic self-criticism is the subject of important recent studies. Boyarin has argued that the Bavli stages the figure of the rabbinic sage both in tragedy and in comedy; Wimpfheimer has pointed to the self-criticism that constitutes rabbinic legal narratives; Vidas illustrates the Bavli's ability to examine the human motivations behind the making of rabbinic Judaism; Kalmin and Rubenstein focus on the Bavli's distance from and criticism of the Palestinian rabbinic community, and Schäfer considers the ironic early rabbinic reckonings with the Israelite past. This book builds on and seeks to develop these findings, which collectively amount to our beginning understanding of a limited, but real rabbinic sense of critical self-assessment. These scholarly treatments are

---

[50] One such case is the Palestinian adaptation of Hellenistic Osiris myths in the rabbinic stories about Joseph's bones. The rabbis' "imitation" of the Hellenistic story has long been recognized, and thinking about Joseph in relation to Osiris is certainly incongruous. Yet after defining more clearly the textual relationship between the Greek base texts (as for example in Plutarch) and the rabbinic adaptations, it became clear that the original adaptation of the Hellenistic myths into late ancient Palestinian literature took place in Samaritan exegesis, as evidenced by the *Tibat Marqe*. I argued for a non-parodic adaptation of the myth in "How Plutarch Gained his Place in the Tosefta," in *Zutot: Perspectives on Jewish Culture*, volume 4 (Boston: Kluwer Academic Publishers, 2004), 19–28.

concerned primarily with the Bavli (and with the tannaitic tradition); I have explored the implications of these findings for Amoraic Palestinian rabbinic Judaism as well. The concept of parody helps us recognize in Palestinian texts aspects of rabbinic self-criticism comparable to those in the Bavli; perhaps fully understanding the parodies in the Bavli necessitates examining comparable elements in the Yerushalmi first.

Parody also sheds light on rabbinic criticism of non-rabbinic texts. Parody may, in due time, teach us more about the rabbis' views of many non-rabbinic texts: Jewish and gentile magical and mystical narratives, Greek Novels, and Manichean, Mandean and Zoroastrian texts. In as far as such texts have been preserved, I would not be surprised to find rabbinic parodies of those aspects of these texts that would have been appealing to the rabbis. I did, however, begin my inquiry with the most obvious non-rabbinic group, "Christians" of all sorts, especially because they produced a large amount of literature in close geographical, temporal, and especially cultural proximity to the Palestinian and the Babylonian authors of rabbinic parodies. Christians, moreover, competed with the rabbis for a monopoly on the Hebrew Bible and challenged the Jewish claim to Jerusalem and Palestine. Such cultural proximity made them a prime target of rabbinic satirical parody, which builds on shared exegetical traditions, disputed religious territory, and rabbinic attraction to and bewilderment by many aspects of Christianity. If the rabbis had not parodied Christians, they probably would not have parodied any other extra-rabbinical group as well.

Since Christians in many ways played a prominent role in the lives of all Palestinian Amoraim and likely in the lives of many Babylonian Amoraim as well, the absence of a term translatable as "Christian" may also reflect the rabbinic perception of "Christianity" as many things and many groups. If so, it may well be that aspects of what we today call "Christian" simply do not correspond to a single word or concept that refers to the vast array of characteristics and groups, such as the orthodox Greek and Syriac Christians, Valentinian and Sethian Gnostics, Tatianist ascetics, Mandeans, Montanists, Manicheans, and other loosely associated factions that might have included believers in Jesus who considered themselves Jewish.

Hence, the problem with the rabbinic view of Christians is two-sided. On the one hand, the rabbis might have had a very fragmented, localized, and idiosyncratic understanding of Christianity combined with genuine or strategic lack of interest. On the other hand, our historical perspective might lead us astray: examining *the* rabbis' view of *Christianity* might be historically objectionable not only because there were many rabbinic views but also because the question itself is misleading. The terms "Christian" and "Christianity" evoke, even in the mind of a critical scholar, associations that have little to do with the phenomena experienced by the late ancient rabbis.

"Christianity," just like "parody," is in this sense a modern phenomenon that should be applied to rabbinic times only with utmost care. Identifying certain rabbinic texts as parodies helps us recognize the non-rabbinic texts imitated by the rabbis and the specific "Christian" aspects with which they were concerned.

A good example is the Encratite background of the sermon against wine in *Wayiqra Rabbah* discussed in Chapter Two. The simultaneously essential and tangential relevance of "Christianity" for this parody, furthermore, illustrates the importance of distinguishing between a Christian background of rabbinic parody and a rabbinic parody of Christianity. The story about the drunken father is a parody of the temperance sermon's Encratite exegesis. Calling these tendencies "Christian" would obliterate not only the Encratites' historical status as outlawed heretics but would also hint at theological issues ranging from the Nicene creed through the abrogation of the Torah and finally to Christian anti-Judaism and its historical consequences. The temperance sermon, or at least its parody, has no interest in such issues. Calling the Encratite tendencies of the sermon against wine "Gnostic" (as Epiphanius implies in his version of Tatian's cosmology) may be slightly more relevant to the parody of the sermon – the story of the drunken father focuses, among other things, on the nature of evil. The central concern of the story of the drunkard, however, is simply the status of wine and the evil nature of the sons, and the Gnostic context distracts from the most important intra-rabbinic focus of the parody. In this sense, Christianity or Gnosticism are not immediately relevant to the parody itself.

Hence, even if the rabbinic sermon against wine, the imitated text, has very strong affinities with non-rabbinic texts, we must carefully distinguish between this background and the parody's limited interest in it. Here the "Christian" background is peripheral. At the same time, the Encratite background proves essential in contextualizing the intellectual climate of the fourth and fifth centuries, allowing us to evaluate and illustrate the possibility of a rift between the story of the drunkard on the one hand and the sermon against wine on the other and the odd nature, by rabbinic standards, of the sermon against wine itself. In this sense, "Christian" "Gnostic" "asceticism" is central for understanding the parody.[51]

---

[51] Aspects of what we call Christianity are indeed central or peripheral in the three external parodies as well. The Rashbi story, to give just one example, treats a plethora of hotly disputed topics of its time and engages in dialogue with various literary genres. The life of the Christian saint (itself a likely adaptation of the Greek "Life of the Philosopher") is as much a model of and a parodic foil for the Rashbi figure. The story imitates teachings from the Sermon on the Mount and depicts Naqai, one of Rashbi's enemies, with language that marks him as a believer in Jesus. Christianity as a religious movement, however, is never one single issue for the parody, and calling the Rashbi story a parody "of" Christianity would render a nuanced analysis impossible. Rather, the Rashbi story treats topics such

Hence, "Christianity," in the totalizing sense in which it is often understood, as a religion, a tradition, in fact, as anything associated with belief in Jesus, might not have preoccupied the rabbis all that much. There is no word for Christians in rabbinic literature, just as there is no word for parody, if such nominalist speculations are admissible. In Palestine, under Christian rule, the rabbis' "natural" notion of parody might explain the absence of the word in rabbinic literature, just as "Christianity," might have been too ubiquitous for the rabbis, and at the same time too fragmented, to necessitate a word.[52] The rabbis refer to things "Christian" only obliquely and ambiguously and mostly abstain from doing so at all – at least partially as a polemical gesture of seeking to condemn them to oblivion.

Unsurprisingly, the notion of "Christianity" is more relevant in the Bavli, which was written at a time during which there were fewer and more easily defined Christian movements. And just as we saw a clearer notion of parody in the Bavli precisely because it does not operate in the discursive realm of Greco-Roman satire, we also see a much clearer notion of Christianity in the Bavli, outside of Byzantium. As the story of Imma Shalom illustrates, the Bavli stands on much firmer ground when it comes to confronting Christianity.[53] The story corroborates my reluctant nominalism by naming the "evangel." If "the gospel" exists as a term for the rabbis, albeit merely as a foil for a parodic etymology as a "margin of falsehood," Christianity may exist as well for the Bavli's authors.[54]

---

as asceticism, personal providence, and Jewish belief in Jesus in both interconnected and differentiated ways. It is a story about a rabbi at the limits of orthodoxy, and one of the heresies with which he toys happens to have some affinities with Christianity. Christianity is central to the story because the story is partially set in a Christian environment. At the same time, Rashbi's long way home is a greater concern of the story, as we have also seen in the case of Rabbi Eliezer's questionable hermeneutics.

[52] I suggest that the word "Christianity" shares the status of words such as "Magic," "Gnosticism," "Judaism," or even "Jewish Christianity." While dispensing with these categories altogether seems unhelpful, the weight that they bear often obfuscates any attempt to study them in detail. Concerning the term "magic," see note 12 above; on "Gnosticism," see Michael Williams, *Rethinking "Gnosticism": An Argument for Dismantling a Dubious Category* (Princeton: Princeton University Press, 1996), and Karen King, *What Is Gnosticism?* (Cambridge: Belknap Press of Harvard University Press, 2003); on "Jewish Christianity," see Daniel Boyarin, "Rethinking Jewish Christianity: An Argument for Dismantling a Dubious Category (to which is Appended a Correction of my Border Lines)," *Jewish Quarterly Review* 99 (2009) 7–36 and Chapter Five, note 2.

[53] I argued that the Bavli even seeks to construct a difference between "what Jesus really said" and what the Christians of its time did in order to ridicule both the object and subject of veneration. The story, moreover, invokes distinctly Christian issues like the imperial claims to Palestine, the Christian holy land, and supersessionism. Also, see Boyarin's *Border Lines: The Partition of Judeo-Christianity*, 151–226 and Schäfer, *Jesus in the Talmud*, 202–226.

[54] Yet again, referring to "Christianity" as the target of the story threatens to foreclose the possibility of a more nuanced reading, according to which Imma Shalom herself falls

Parody, in short, can be a useful approach for assessing rabbinic views of Christianity. No rabbinic text, however, focuses on Christianity exclusively. Rabbinic parodies and the rabbinic concerns they negotiate emerge as most poignant if we view the rabbis as capable of simultaneously reflecting on internal and external matters. Here, in my view, resides the central lesson to be learned from this study. When reading rabbinic texts, we should expect a conservative outlook that allows for self-criticism of the rabbinic endeavor. Simultaneously, we should always consider the possibilities of rabbinic dialogue with outsiders as well as constant presence of non-rabbinic voices. Sometimes, other cultures are the focus of criticism; other times, these cultures, be they Greco-Roman, Christian, or Zoroastrian, manifest themselves within the text, hidden even from the rabbinic author himself – heresiology itself may be a prime example of this phenomenon. Sometimes we can tell the difference, and sometimes we cannot. Sometimes non-rabbinic voices are welcome, and sometimes they are parodied. Parody helps us better understand the rabbis' critical views of themselves and their opponents and allows us to relate conflicts within rabbinic circles to the rabbis' conflicts with those beyond, and vice versa.

---

prey to the lure of the legal philosophy of the Christian Other. "Christianity" at this moment does not have much to do with belief in Jesus or other cultural differences. The issue, plain and simple, is inheritance law, and the challenge (at least according to one version) comes from a prominent Jewish woman. In this sense, the story employs the language of the Christian Other strategically in order to rebuke Imma Shalom's demand; it depicts her legal challenge of the halakha as religious treason, heresy. This strategy, of course, would not work at all if Imma Shalom "were" Christian: the heretic is not an apostate, and the apostate is not nearly of the same parodic appeal as the heretic. I discuss this difference, together with Eduard Iricinschi, in "Introduction. From Heresy to Heresiology: Recent Trends in Scholarship and the Contribution of This Volume," in Eduard Iricinschi and Holger Zellentin (eds.), *Heresy and Identity in Late Antiquity* (Tübingen: Mohr Siebeck, 2008), 1–27.

Bibliography

Abouzayd, Shafiq, "The Prohibition and the Use of Alcohol in the Syrian Ascetic Tradition and its Biblical and Spiritual Origins." *Aram* 17 (2005), 135–156.

Adler, Yonathan, "Identifying Sectarian Characteristics in the Phylacteries from Qumran," *Revue de Qumran* 23 (2007), 79–92.

Afik (Abecassis), Isaac, *Hazal's Perception of the Dream* (PhD diss., Bar Ilan University, 1991 [Hebrew]).

Alexander, Elizabeth Shanks, *Transmitting Mishnah: The Shaping Influence of Oral Tradition* (Cambridge: Cambridge University Press, 2006).

Alexander, Philip S., "*Bavli Berakhot* 55a–57b: the Talmudic Dreambook in Context." *JJS* 46 (1995), 230–248.

–, "Quid Athenis et Hierosolymis? Rabbinic Midrash and Hermeneutics in the Graeco-Roman World," in: Philip Davies and Richard White (eds.), *A Tribute to Géza Vermès: Essays on Jewish and Christian Literature and History* (Sheffield: Sheffield Academic Press, 1990), 101–124.

–, "Yeshu/Yeshua ben Yosef of Nazareth: Discerning the Jewish Face of Jesus," in: George J. Brooke (ed.), *The Birth of Jesus: Biblical and Theological Reflections* (Edinburgh: T & T Clark, 2000), 9–21.

Anderson, Graham, *The Second Sophistic: a Cultural Phenomenon in the Roman Empire* (London; New York: Routledge, 1993).

Anklesaria, Behramgore Tehmuras, *Zand-Ākāsīh: Iranian or Greater Bundahišn/ transliteration and translation in English by Behramgore Tehmuras Anklesaria* (Bombay: Dastur Framroze A. Bode, 1956).

Ararat, Nissan, "מעשה דור הפלגה כדרמה סאטירית," in: *Beyt Mikra*, 39 (1994), 224–231.

Arjava, Anttie, *Women and Law in Late Antiquity* (Oxford: Clarendon Press, 1998).

Arzi, Avraham, "איכא דאמרי" *Sinai* 89 (1981), 151–56.

Avni, Gideon and Uzi Dahari, "Christian Burial Caves from the Byzantine Period at Luzit," in: Giovanni Claudio Bottini et al. (eds.), *Christian Archaeology in the Holy Land: New Discoveries: Essays in Honour of Virgilio C. Corbo* (Jerusalem: Franciscan Printing Press, 1990), 301–314.

Ax, Wolfram, *Literaturparodie in Antike und Mittelalter* (Trier: Wissenschaftlicher Verlag, 1993).

Baarda, Tj., "An Archaic Element in the Arabic Diatessaron?" *Novum Testamentum* 17 (1975), 151–55.

Bacher, Wilhelm, *Die Agada der Palästinensischen Amoräer* (Strasbourg: K.J. Trübner, 1892–99).

–, *Die Agada der Tannaiten* (Strasbourg: K.J. Trübner, 1890).

–, *Die exegetische Terminologie der jüdischen Traditionsliteratur* (Leipzig: J.C. Hinrichs, 1899).

Bakhtin, Mikhail M., *The Dialogic Imagination* (Austin: University of Texas Press, 1981).

–, *Problems of Dostoevsky's Poetics* (Minneapolis: University of Minnesota Press, 1984).

Baldick, Chris, "Pastiche," in: idem., *The Concise Oxford Dictionary of Literary Terms* (Oxford: Oxford University Press, 2001), 183–185.

Bar, Doron, "Rural Monsticism as a Key Element in the Christianization of Byzantine Palestine," *Harvard Theological Review* 98 (2005), 49–65.

Bar-Ilan, Meir, "Witches in the Bible and in the Talmud," in: Jacob Neusner (ed.), *Approaches to Ancient Judaism* 5 (Atlanta: Scholars Press, 1993), 7–32.

Barthes, Roland, *The Pleasure of the Text* (New York: Hill and Wang, 1975).

Bartsch, Shadi, *Decoding the Ancient Novel: the Reader and the Role of Description in Heliodorus and Achilles Tatius* (Princeton: Princeton University Press, 1989).

Baskin, Judith, "Rabbinic-Patristic Exegetical Contacts: Some New Perspectives," *Religious Studies Review* 24 (1998), 171–173.

Becker, Adam, "Anti-Judaism and Care for the Poor in Aphrahat's *Demonstration* 20," *Journal of Early Christian Studies* 10 (2002), 305–327.

–, *Fear of God and the Beginnings of Wisdom: The School of Nisibis and the Development of Scholastic Culture in Late Antique Mesopotamia* (Philadelphia: University of Pennsylvania Press, 2006).

– and Annette Yoshiko Reed (eds.), *The Ways that Never Parted: Jews and Christians in Late Antiquity and the Early Middle Ages* (Tübingen: Mohr Siebeck, 2003).

Becker, Hans-Jürgen, *Avot de-Rabbi Natan: Synoptische Edition beider Versionen* (Tübingen: Mohr Siebeck, 2006).

–, "Text and History: The Dynamic Relationship between Talmud Yerushalmi and Genesis Rabbah," in Shaye J.D. Cohen (ed.), *The Synoptic Problem in Rabbinic Literature* (Providence: Brown Judaic Studies, 2000), 145–158.

Beer, M., "Rabbi Simeon and Jerusalem," in: A. Oppenheimer et al. (eds.), *Jerusalem in the Second Temple Period, Memorial Volume A. Shalit* (Jerusalem: Yad Yitshak ben Zvi, 1980), 361–75 [Hebrew].

Ben-Amos, Dan, "Lamentations Rabbah: Trauma, Dreams, and Riddles," *Prooftexts* 21 (2001), 399–409.

Ben-Porat, Ziva, "Method in *Mad*ness: Notes on the Structure of Parody, Based on the MAD TV Series," *Poetics Today* 1 (1979), 245–272.

Bergian, Silke-Petra, *Der fürsorgende Gott: der Begriff der PRONOIA Gottes in der apologetischen Literatur der Alten Kirche* (Berlin: Walter De Gruyter, 2002).

Bernardi, Jean, *Grégoire de Nazianze: Discours 42–43* (Paris: Les Éditions du Cerf, 1992).

Bibb, Bryan D., "Nadab and Abihu Attempt to Fill a Gap: Law and Narrative in Leviticus 10.1–7," *Journal for the Study of the Old Testament* 96 (2001), 83–99.

Billaut, A. "Le comique d'Achille Tatius et les réalités de l'époque impériale," in: Monique Trédé and Philippe Hoffmann (eds.), *Le Rire des Anciens: Actes du colloque international* (Presses de l'École Normale Supérieure: Paris, 1998), 143–160.

Billerbeck, Margarethe (ed.), *Die Kyniker in der modernen Forschung: Aufsätze mit Einführung und Bibliographie* (Amsterdam: B.R. Grüner, 1991).

Binyamini, Yafa, "המיתוס של רבי שמעון בר יוחאי – עיון באגדת חז"ל," *Mahkerei Hag* 12 (2001), 87–102.

Blumenthal H. (ed.), *The Divine Iamblichus: Philosopher and Man of Gods* (London: Bristol Classical Press, 1993).

Boertien, Maas, *Nazir* (Berlin: Walter de Gruyter, 1971).

Bohak, Gideon, *Ancient Jewish Magic* (Cambridge, UK: Cambridge University Press, 2008).

–, "New Trends in the Study of Greco-Roman Jews" *Classical Journal* 99 (2003), 195–202.

Boustan, Ra'anan S. "Review of Boyarin, *Border Lines*". *Jewish Quarterly Review* 96 (2006), 441–46.

Bowersock, Glenn W., *Greek Sophists in the Roman Empire* (New York: Oxford University Press, 1969).

Boyarin, Daniel, *Border Lines: The Partition of Judaeo-Christianity* (Philadelphia: University of Pennsylvania Press, 2004).

–, *Carnal Israel: Reading Sex in Talmudic Culture* (Berkeley: University of California Press, 1995).

–, "De/re/constructing Midrash," in: Carol Bakhos (ed.), *Current Trends in the Study of Midrash* (Leiden: Brill 2006), 299–322.

–, *Intertextuality and the Reading of Midrash* (Bloomington: Indiana University Press, 1990).

–, "Literary Fat Rabbis: On the Historical Origins of the Grotesque Body," *Journal of the History of Sexuality* 1 (1991), 551–584.

–, "Patron Saint of the Incongruous: Rabbi Meir, the Talmud, and Menippen Satire," *Critical Inquiry*, 33 (2007).

–, "Rethinking Jewish Christianity: An Argument for Dismantling a Dubious Category (to which is Appended a Correction of my Border Lines)," *Jewish Quarterly Review* 99 (2009) 7–36.

–, *Socrates and the Fat Rabbis* (Chicago: University of Chicago Press, 2009)

–, "Why is Rabbi Yohanan a Woman? Or, A Queer Marriage Gone Bad: 'Platonic Love' in the Talmud," in: Mark D. Jordan (ed.), *Authorizing Marriage?: Canon, Tradition, and Critique in the Blessing of Same-Sex Unions* (Princeton: Princeton University Press, 2006), 52–67 and 178–184.

Boyce, Mary, *A History of Zoroastrianism* (Leiden: Brill, 1989).

Branham, Robert B., *Unruly Eloquence: Lucian and the Comedy of Traditions* (Cambridge: Harvard University Press, 1989).

Breyfogle, Todd, "Magic, Women, and Heresy in the Late Empire: the Case of the Priscillianists," in: Marvin Meyer and Paul Mirecki (eds.), *Ancient Magic and Ritual Power* (Leiden: Brill 1995), 435–454.

Brock, Sebastian P., "Christians in the Sasanian Empire: A Case of Divided Loyalties," *Studies in Church History* 18 (1982), 1–19.

–, *The Luminous Eye: The Spiritual World Vision Of Saint Ephrem* (Kalamazoo: Cistercian Publications, 1992).

–, "Sobria Ebrieteas according to some Syriac Texts," *Aram* 17 (2005), 185–191.

–, "The Syriac Background," in: M. Lapidge (ed.), *Archbishop Theodore: Commemorative Studies on his Life and Influence* (Cambridge, New York: Cambridge University Press, 1995), 30–53.

Brody, Robert, "Judaism in the Sasanian Empire: A Case Study in Religious Coexistence," in: Shaul Shaked and Amnon Netzer (eds.), *Irano-Judaica II: Studies*

Relating to Jewish Contacts with Persian Culture Throughout the Ages (Jerusalem: Ben-Zvi Institute, 1990), 52–62.

Brown, Peter, *The Body and Society: Men, Women, and Sexual Renunciation in Early Christianity* (New York: Columbia University Press, 1988).

–, *The Cult of the Saints: its Rise and Function in Latin Christianity* (Chicago: University of Chicago Press, 1981).

Brunner-Traut, Emma. "Der Katzenmäusekrieg im Alten und Neuen Orient," *Zeitschrift der Deutschen Morgenländischen Gesellschaft* 54 (1954), 347–51.

Burrus, Virginia, "The Heretical Woman as Symbol in Alexander, Athanasius, Epiphanius, and Jerome," *Harvard Theological Review* 84 (1991), 229–248.

Burstein, Abraham, "לבעית עיבורי השנה בחוץ-לארץ," *Sinai* 19 (38) (1955), 32–46.

–, "עיבורי השנה בנהרדעא ובעסיא," *Sinai* 20 (41) (1957), 387–99.

Cacciari, Antonio, "Philo and the Nazirite," in: Francesca Calabi (ed.), *Italian Studies on Philo of Alexandria* (Leiden: Brill, 2003), 147–166.

Caillois, Roger, *Man, Play, and Games* (New York: Free Press of Glencoe, 1961).

Cèbe, Jean-Pierre, *La Caricature et la parodie dans le monde romain antique des origines à Juvenal* (Paris: E. de Boccard, 1966).

Chadwick, H., "Enkrateia", in: Theodor Klauser (ed.), *Reallexikon für Antike und Christentum, Sachwörterbuch zur Auseinandersetzung des Christentums mit der antiken Welt* (Stuttgart: Hiersemann, 1950), vol. V, 343–365.

Chamgry, Émile, *Ésope, Fables* (Paris: Les Belles Lettres, 2002).

Chernick, Michal, "'Turn it and Turn it Again': Culture and Talmud Interpretation," *Exemplaria* 12 (2000), 63–103.

Chew, Kathryn, "Achilles Tatius and Parody," *Classical Journal*, 96 (2000), 57–70.

Childers, J. W., "The Georgian Life of Porphyry of Gaza, in M. F. Wiles and E. J. Yarnold (eds.), *Studia Patristica XXXV: Ascetica, Gnostica, Liturgica, Orientalia* 35 (Louvain: Peeters, 2001), 374–384

Choksy, Jamsheed K., "Woman in the Zoroastrian Book of Primal Creation: Images and Functions within a Religious Tradition," *Mankind Quarterly* 29 (1988), 73–82.

Ciasca, P. Augustinus, *Tatiani Evangeliorum Harmoniae Arabica* (Rome: S. C. De Propaganda Fide, 1888).

Clark, Elizabeth, *History, Theory, Text: Historians and the Linguistic Turn* (Cambridge, MA: Harvard University Press, 2004).

Cohen, Aryeh. *Rereading Talmud: Gender, Law and the Poetics of Sugyot* (Atlanta: Scholars Press, 1998).

Cohn, Yehudah, *Tangled up in Text: Tefillin and the Ancient World* (Providence, RI: Center for Judaic Studies, 2008).

Colebrook, Claire, *Irony* (London: Routledge, 2004).

Courtonne, Yves, *Saint Basile: Lettres* (Paris: Les Belles Lettres, 1961), vol. II.

Culler, Jonathan, *The Pursuit of Signs: Semiotics, Literature, Deconstruction* (Ithaca: Cornell University Press, 1981).

Cutter, William. "Citing and Translating a Context: the Talmud in its 'Post Modern' Setting," *Judaism* 39 (1990), 104–111.

Dalman, Gustaf, *Jesus Christ in the Talmud, Midrash, Zohar, and the Liturgy of the Synagogue* (New York: Arno Press, 1973 [1893]).

Dane, Joseph A. *Parody: Critical Concepts Versus Literary Practice, Aristophanes to Sterne* (Norman: University of Oklahoma Press, 1988).

Daniélou, Jean, *The Theology of Jewish Christianity* (London: Darton, 1964).

Davidson, Israel, *Parody in Jewish Literature* (New York: AMS Press, 1966 [1907]).

Dean, William, "The Dehellenization of the Religious Imagination," *Word & World* 5 (1985), 269–278.

Dentith, Simon, *Parody: The New Critical Idiom* (London: Routledge, 2000).

Diamond, Eliezer, "An Israelite self-Offering in the Priestly Code; a new Perspective on the Nazirite," *Jewish Quarterly Review* 88 (1997), 1–18.

Diamond, James A., "King David of the Sages: Rabbinic Rehabilitation or Ironic Parody?" *Prooftexts* 27 (2007), 373–426.

Diels, H. and Kranz, W., *Die Fragmente der Vorsokratiker* (Berlin: Wiedeman, 1952).

Dodds, E. R., *The Greeks and the Irrational* (Boston: Beacon Press, 1951).

Dolezalova, Lucie, "The Cena Cypriani, or the Game of Endless Possibilities," in: Wilhelm Geerlings and Christian Schulze (eds.), *Der Kommentar in Antike und Mittelalter: Beiträge zu seiner Erforschung* (Leiden, Boston: Brill, 2002).

Dor, Zvi Moshe, תורת ארץ-ישראל בבבל (Tel Aviv: Devir, 1971).

Downing, Francis Gerald, *Cynics and Christian Origins* (Edinburgh: T & T Clark, 1992).

Drexl, Franz, "Achmet und das syrische Traumbuch des cod. syr. or. 4434 des Brit. Mus.," *Byzantinische Zeitschrift* 30 (1929–30), 110–113.

Edgeworth, Robert J., "Terms for 'Brown' in Ancient Greek," *Glotta* 61 (1983), 31–40.

Edwards, James R., *The Hebrew Gospel and the Development of the Synoptic Tradition* (Grand Rapids: Eerdmans, 2009).

Eilberg-Schwartz, Howard, "Who's Kidding Whom?: A Serious Reading of Rabbinic Word Plays," *Journal of the American Academy of Religion* 55 (2004), 765–88.

Elbaum, Jacob, "מעשים בשכור ומכוער באגדתנו ובאגדת יון," *Mahanayim* 112 (1967), 122–29.

Elman, Yaakov, "Acculturation to Elite Persian Norms and Modes of Thought in the Babylonian Jewish Community of Late Antiquity," in: idem, Ephraim Bezalel Halivni, and Zvi Arie Steinfeld (eds.), *Neti'ot Ledavid: Jubilee Volume for David Weiss Halivni* (Jerusalem: Orhot, 2004), 31–56.

–, "Marriage and Marital Property in Rabbinic and Sasanian Law," in: Catherine Hezser (ed.), *Rabbinic Law in Its Roman and Near Eastern Context* (Tübingen: Mohr Siebeck, 2003), 227–276.

–, "Orality and the Redaction of the Babylonian Talmud," *Oral Tradition* 14 (1999), 52–99.

–, "When Permission is Given: Aspects of Divine Providence," *Tradition* 24 (1989), 24–45.

–, "Who are the kings of east and west in Ber 7a? Roman Religion, Syrian Gods and Zoroastrianism in the *Bavli*," in: Shaye J.D. Cohen and Joshua J. Schwartz (eds.), *Studies in Josephus and the Varieties of Ancient Judaism; Louis H. Feldman Jubilee Volume* (Leiden: Brill, 2007), 43–80.

–, "The World of the 'Sabboraim': Cultural Aspects of Post-Redactional Additions to the Bavli," in: Jeffrey Rubenstein (ed.), *Creation and Composition: The Contribution of the Bavli Redactors (Stammaim) to the Aggada*, (Tübingen: Mohr Siebeck, 2005), 383–415.

Engelman, Benyamin, "הומור מוצהר, גלוי וסמוי בתלמוד בבלי," in: *Be-khol derakhekha da'ehu: ketav-et le-inyane Torah u-madah* 8 (1990), 5–28.

Emmerson, Grace I., "The Song of Songs, Mystification, Ambiguity and Humour", in: Stanley E. Porter et al. (eds.), *Crossing the Boundaries, Essays in Biblical Interpretation in Honour of Michael D. Goulder* (Leiden: Brill, 1994), 97–111.

Ervad Tahmuras Dinshaji Anklesaria, *Bûndahishn, being a facsimile of the TD manuscript no. 2 brought from Persia by Dastur Tîrandâz and now preserved in the late Ervad Tahmuras' library* (Byculla: British India Press, 1908).

Euringer, Sebastian, *Die Überlieferung der Arabischen Übersetzung des Diatessarons* (Freiburg im Breisgau; Herder, 1912).

Figueras, Paul, "Jewish Ossuaries and Secondary Burial: their Significance for Early Christianity," *Immanuel* 19 (1984–1985), 41–57.

Fischel, Henry A., *Rabbinic Literature and Greco-Roman Philosophy: A Study of Epicurea and Rhetorica in early Midrashic Writings* (Leiden: Brill, 1973).

Fishbane, Simcha, "Most Women Engage in Sorcery: an Analysis of Female Sorceresses in the *Bavli*," in: Jacob Neusner (ed.), *Approaches to Ancient Judaism 5* (Atlanta: Scholars Press, 1993), 143–165.

Fiss, Owen, "Objectivity and Interpretation," in Sanford Levinson and Steven Mailloux (eds.), *Interpreting Law and Literature* (Evanston: Northwestern University Press, 1988 [1982]), 229–318.

Flannery-Dailey, Frances, *Dreamers, Scribes, and Priests: Jewish Dreams in the Hellenistic and Roman Eras* (Leiden: Brill, 2004).

Flusser, David, "Josephus on the Sadducees and Menander," *Immanuel* 7 (1977), 61–77.

–, "The Pharisees and Stoics according to Josephus," *Iyun* 14 (1964), 318–329.

Fonrobert, Charlotte, "On *Carnal Israel* and the Consequences: Talmudic Studies since Foucault," *The Jewish Quarterly Review* 95 (2005), 462–269.

–, "The Didascalia Apostolorum: A Mishnah for the Disciples of Jesus," *Journal of Early Christian Studies* 9 (2001), 483–511.

–, "Plato in Rabbi Shimeon bar Yohai's Cave (bShabbat 33b–34a): The Talmudic Inversion of Plato's Politics of Philosophy," *AJS Review* 31 (2007), 277–296.

Frazer, James George, *The Golden Bough: A Study in Magic And Religion* (New York: Macmillan, 1890).

Frenkel, Yonah, דרכי האגדה והמדרש (Massada: Yad la-Talmud, 1991).

–, "שאלות הרמנוטיות בחקר סיפור האגדה," *Tarbiz* 47 (1977/78), 139–72 [reprinted in: idem, *The Aggadic Narrative: Harmony in Content and Form* (Tel Aviv: Hakibbutz Hameuchad Publishing House, 2001), 11–50].

Friedman, Shamma, "כתיב השמות "רבה" ו"רבא" בתלמוד הבבלי," *Sinai* 110 (1992), 140–64.

–, "The Holy Scriptures Defile the Hands – the Transformation of a Biblical Concept in Rabbinic Theology," in Marc Brettler and Michael Fishbane (eds.), *Minhah le-Nahum: Biblical and other Studies Presented to Nahum M. Sarna in Honour of his 70th Birthday* (Sheffield: Journal for the Study of the Old Testament Press, 1993), 117–132.

–, "Uncovering Literary Dependencies in the Talmudic Corpus," in: Shaye J.D. Cohen (ed.), *The Synoptic Problem in Rabbinic Literature* (Providence, RI: Brown Judaic Studies, 2000), 119–144.

Frede, Dorothea, "Theodicy and Providential Care in Stoicism," in: ibid. (ed.), *Traditions of Theology: Studies in Hellenistic Theology, its Background and Aftermath* (Leiden: Brill, 2002), 85–117.

Freund, Winfried, *Die Literarische Parodie* (Stuttgart: Metzler, 1981).

Frye, Northrop, *Anatomy of Criticism: Four Essays* (New York: Athenaeum, 1957).

Furlani, G., "Une clef des songes en syriaque," *Revue de l'Orient Chrétien* 21 (1918–19), 119–44 and 224–248.

Gaca, Kathy L., "Driving Aphrodite from the World: Tatian's Encratite Principles of Sexual Renunciation," *Journal of Theological Studies* 53 (2002), 28–52.

Gafni, Isaiah M., "היישיבה הבבלית לאור סוגיית ב"ק קיז ע"א," *Tarbiz* 49 (1980), 292–301.

–, *The Jews of Babylonia in the Talmudic Era*. (Jerusalem: Merkaz Zalman Shazar, 1990) [Hebrew].

–, *Land, Center and Diaspora: Jewish Constructs in Late Antiquity* (Sheffield: Sheffield Academic Press, 1997)

–, "Nestorian Literature as a Source for the History of the Babylonian *Yeshivot*," *Tarbits* 51 (1981), 567–576 [Hebrew].

Gauville, Jean-Luc, "La conception du contrôle de soi dans le récit de l'«Épitomé des Césars»," *Cahiers des études anciennes* 37 (2001), 83–87.

Genette, Gérard, *Palmipsestes. La littérature au second degré* (Paris: Seuil, 1982).

Goldberg, Abraham, "על כמה מעקרונות העריכה של ויקרא רבה," in: Joshua Levinson, Jacob Elbaum, and Galit Hasan-Rokem (eds.), *Higayon L'Yona* (Jerusalem: Magnes Press, 2007), 333–344.

–, "The Term *gufa* in Midrash Leviticus Rabba", *Leshonenu* 38 (1973–74), 163–169 [Hebrew].

Goldberg, Arnold, "Entwurf einer formanalytischen Methode für die Exegese der rabbinischen Traditionsliteratur," *Frankfurter Judaistische Beiträge* 5 (1977), 1–41.

Goldfeld, Anne, "Women as Sources of Torah in the Rabbinic Tradition," *Judaism* 24 (1975), 245–256.

Goldhill, Simon, *The Poet's Voice: Essays on Poetics and Greek Literature* (Cambridge: Cambridge University Press, 1991).

Goldin, Judah, "The Magic of Magic and Superstition," in Elisabeth Schuessler Fiorenza (ed.), *Aspects of Religious Propaganda in Judaism and Early Christianity* (Notre Dame; London: University of Notre Dame Press, 1976) 115–147 [reprinted in idem, *Studies in Midrash and Related Literature* (Philadelphia; New York; Jerusalem: The Jewish Publication Society, 1988) 337–357].

Goldziher, Ignaz, *Muslim Studies* (Oxford: Oxford University Press, 1971).

Goodenough, Erwin R., *Jewish Symbols in the Greco–Roman Period*, v. 5–6: *Bread, Fish, and Wine* (New York: Pantheon Books, 1956).

Goodman, Martin, "The Function of Minim in Early Rabbinic Judaism," in Herbert Cancik, Hermann Lichtenberger and Peter Schäfer (eds.), *Geschichte-Tradition-Reflexion. Festschrift für Martin Hengel zum 70. Geburtstag* (Tübingen: Mohr Siebeck, 1996), vol. I, 501–10.

Gould, Ketayun H., "Outside the Discipline, Inside the Experience: Women in Zoroastrianism," in: Aryind Sharma (ed.), *Religion and Women* (Albany: State University of New York Press, 1994), 139–182.

Goulet–Cazé, Marie–Odile et al. (eds.), *L'Ascèse cynique: un commentaire de Diogène Laërce VI 70–71* (Paris: J. Vrin, 1986).

–, *Le Cynisme ancien et ses prolongements: actes du colloque international du CNRS, Paris, 22–25 juillet 1991* (Paris: Presses Universitaires de Frances, 1993).

Gordon, Dane R., and Suits, David B. (eds.), *Epicurus: His Continuing Influence and Contemporary Relevance* (Rochester: RIT Cary Graphic Arts Press, 2003).

Graetz, H., "Notizen zur Topographie Palästinas," *MGWJ* 28 (1880), 487–495.

Graf, Georg, *Geschichte der christlichen Arabischen Literatur* (Vaticano: Biblioteca Apostolica Vaticana, 1944), vol. I.

Grégoire, Henri and Kugener., M.-A., *Marc le Diacre: Vie de Porphyre, évêque de Gaza* (Paris: Belles lettres, 1930).

Green, William Scott, "Palestinian Holy Men: Charismatic Leadership and Rabbinic Tradition," in Wolfgang Haase (ed.), *Auftstieg und Niedergang der Römischen Welt* 19/2 (Berlin: Walter de Gruyter, 1979), 619–647.

–, "Romancing the Tome: Rabbinic Hermeneutics and the Theory of Literature," *Semeia* 40 (1987), 147–168.

Greenberg, Martin A., "The True Sin of Nadab and Abihu," *Jewish Bible Quarterly* 26 (1998), 263–267.

Greenstein, Edward, "An Inner-Biblical Midrash of the Nadab and Abihu Episode," in: *Proceedings of the Eleventh World Congress of Jewish Studies* (Jerusalem: World Union of Jewish Studies, 1994), A*71–*78 [Hebrew].

Greenstein, Eliezer, "חכמים גם בלילה: הדו-שיח הבבלי בין האדון ועבדו וספר קהלת," in: *Beyt Mikra* 44 (1998), 97–106.

Gruen, Erich, *Diaspora: Jews amidst Greeks and Romans* (Cambridge: Harvard University Press, 2002).

–, *Heritage and Hellenism: the Reinvention of Jewish Tradition* (Berkeley: University of California Press, 1998).

Guedemann, Moritz, *Religionsgeschichtliche Studien* (Leipzig: Oskar Leiner, 1876).

Guinot, Jean-Noël, "La Christologie de Théodoret de Cyr," *Vigilae Christianae* 39 (1985), 256–272.

Guttman, Alexander, "The Significance of Miracles for Talmudic Judaism," *HUCA* 20 (1947), 347–81.

Hägg, Tomas, *Narrative Technique in Ancient Greek Romances: Studies of Chariton, Xenophon, Ephesius, and Achilles Tatius* (Stockholm: Svenska institutet i Athen, 1971).

Halbertal, Moshe and Shlomo Naeh, "מעייני הישועה: סטירה פרשנית ותשובת המינים," in: Joshua Levinson, Jacob Elbaum, and Galit Hasan-Rokem (eds.), *Higayon L'Yona: New Aspects in the Study of Midrash Aggadah, and Piyut in Honor of Professor Yona Frenkel* (Jerusalem: The Hebrew University Magnes Press, 2006), 179–98.

Halevi, Elimelekh Epshtain, *ערכי האגדה וההלכה לאור מקורות יוונים ולאטיניים* (Tel Aviv: Devir, 1980).

–, *שערי האגדה: על מהות האגדה, סוגיה, דרכיה, מטרותיה וזיקתה לתרבות זמנה* (Tel Aviv: Levinsky, 1982).

Halivni (Weiss), David, "On the Supposed Anti-Asceticism or Anti-Nazritism of Simon the Just," *Jewish Quarterly Review* 58 (1967–69), 243–252.

Hanschke, D., "Abbaye and Rava: Two Approaches to the Mishna of the Tannaim," *Tarbits* 49 (1979f), 187–193 [Hebrew].

Harle, Paul, "Un 'Private-Joke' de Paul dans le livre des Actes (26:28–29)," *New Testament Studies* 24 (1978), 527–533.

Hasan-Rokem, Galit, "Embarrassment and Riches" [review of Schäfer, *Jesus in the Talmud*], *Jewish Quarterly Review* 99 (2009), 113–119.

–, *Web of Life: Folklore and Midrash in Rabbinic Literature* (Stanford: Stanford University Press, 2000).

Hauptman, Judith, "Images of Women in the Talmud," in: Rosemary Radford Ruether (ed.), *Religion and Sexism* (New York: Simon and Schuster, 1974), 184–212.

–, "Women and Inheritance in Rabbinic Texts: Identifying Elements of a Critical Feminist Impulse," in: Harry Fox and Tirzah Meacham (eds.), *Introducing Tosefta* (Hoboken: Ktav Publishing House, 1999), 221–240.

Hausrath, A. and Hunger, H., *Corpus Fabularum Aesopicarum* (Leipzig: Teubner 1970).

Hauschild, Wolf-Dieter, *Basilius von Caesarea: Briefe* (Stuttgart: Anton Hiersemann, 1973), vol. II.

Hayes, Christine E., "Displaced Self-Perceptions: The Deployment of *Minim* and Romans in *B. Sanhedrin* 90b–91a," in Hayim Lapin, (ed.), *Religious and Ethnic Communities in Later Roman Palestine* (Bethesda: University Press of Maryland, 1998), 249–89.

Heffening, W., "Die griechische Ephraem-Paraenesis gegen das Lachen in arabischer Übersetzung," *Oriens Christianus* vol. III no. 2 [21] (1927), 94–119.

Heineman, Yitzhak, דרכי האגדה (Jerusalem: Magnes Press, 1954).

Heinemann, Joseph, אגדות ותולדותיהן: עיונים בהשתלשלותן של מסורות (Jerusalem: Keter, 1978).

–, "The Art of the Sermon of Palestinian Amora'im: Analysis of two Proems," *HaSifrut/Literature* 25 (1977), 69–79 [Hebrew].

Hennecke, Edgar (ed.), *Handbuch zu den Neutestamentlichen Apokryphen* (Tübingen: Mohr/Siebeck 1904).

Herford, Robert Travers, *Christianity in Talmud and Midrash* (London: Williams and Norgate, 1903).

Hezser, Catherine, *The Social Structure of the Rabbinic Movement in Roman Palestine* (Tübingen: Mohr Siebeck, 1997).

Himmelfarb, Martha, *Tours of Hell: an Apocalyptic Form in Jewish and Christian Literature* (Philadelphia: University of Pennsylvania Press, 1983).

Hirshmann, Mark G., *A Rivalry of Genius: Jewish and Christian Biblical Interpretation in Late Antiquity* (Albany: Sate University of New York Press, 1996).

Hjerrild, B., "Ayōkēn: Women between Father and Husband in the Sassanian Era," in: Wojciech Skalmowski and Alois van Tongerloo (eds.), *Medioiranica: Proceedings of the International Colloqium on Middle Iranian Studies*, (Leuven: Peters, 1993), 79–86.

Hogg, Hope W. Translation of *The Diatessaron of Tatian*, in Alexander Roberts and James Donaldson (eds.), *The Ante-Nicene Fathers: Translations of the Writings of the Fathers down to A.D. 325*, vol. IX (Grand Rapids: Eerdmans Publishers, 1996–2001 [1897]).

Holowchak, Mark, *Ancient Science and Dreams: Oneirology in Greco-Roman Antiquity* (Lanham: University Press of America, 2002).

Houston, Walter J., "Tragedy in the Courts of the Lord: a Socio-Literary Reading of the Death of Nadab and Abihu," *Journal for the Study of the Old Testament* 90 (2000), 31–39.

Huizinga, Johan, *Homo Ludens: a Study of the Play-Element in Culture* (London: Routledge & K. Paul, 1949).

Husser, Jean-Marie, *Dreams and Dream Narratives in the Biblical World* (Sheffield: Sheffield Academic Press, 1999).

Hyman, Aaron, *Toldot Tannaim ve-Amoraim* (Jerusalem: Makhon Pri ha'aretz, 1981).

Ilan, Tal, "'Stolen Water is Sweet': Women and Their Stories between Bavli and Yerushalmi," in: Peter Schäfer (ed.), *The Talmud Yerushalmi and Graeco-Roman Culture* (Tübingen: Mohr Siebeck, 2002), vol. III, 185–223.

–, "The Quest for the Historical Beruriah, Rachel, and Imma Shalom," *AJS Review* 22 (1997), 1–17.

Iricinschi, Edward and Holger Zellentin, "Introduction. From Heresy to Heresiology: Recent Trends in Scholarship and the Contribution of This Volume," in idem., (eds.), *Heresy and Identity in Late Antiquity* (Tübingen: Mohr Siebeck, 2008), 1–27.

Jackson-McCabe, Matt (ed.), *Jewish Christianity Reconsidered* (Minneapolis: Fortress Press, 2007).

Jacobs, Martin, "Römische Thermenkultur im Spiegel des Yerushalmi," in Peter Schäfer (ed.), *The Talmud Yerushalmi and Graeco-Roman Culture* (Tübingen: Mohr Siebeck, 1998), vol. I, 219–311.

Jacoby, Felix, *Die Fragmente der Griechischen Historiker*, vol. III (Leiden: Brill, 1957).

Jaffee, Martin, "Oral Tradition and Rabbinic Studies" *Oral Tradition* 18 (2003), 37–39.

–, "Oral Tradition in the Writings of Rabbinic Oral Torah: On Theorizing Rabbinic Orality," *Oral Tradition* 14 (1999), 3–32.

–, *Torah in the Mouth: Writing and Oral Tradition in Palestinian Judaism, 200 BCE–400 CE* (Oxford: Oxford University Press, 2001).

–, "What Difference Does the 'Orality' of Rabbinic Writing Make for the Interpretation of Rabbinic Writings?" in: Matthew Kraus (ed.), *How Should Rabbinic Literature Be Read in the Modern World?* (Piscataway, NJ: Gorgias Press, 2006).

Jakob, Jonsson, *Humour and Irony in the New Testament: Illuminated by Parallels in Talmud and Midrash* (Reykjavik: Bókaútgáfa Menningarsjóds, 1965).

Jamaspasa, Kaikhusroo M., "On the Heretic and Immoral Woman in Zoroastrianism," in *Orientalia: J. Duchesne-Guillemin emerito oblata* (Leiden: E J Brill, 1984, 243–266.

Jastrow, Marcus, *A Dictionary of the Targumim, the Talmud Bavli and Yerushalmi, and the Midrashic Literature* (New York: The Judaica Press, 1996 [1903]).

Jones, C. P., *Culture and Society in Lucian* (Cambridge: Harvard University Press, 1986).

Jonnson, Jakob, *Humour and Irony in the New Testament: Illuminated by Parallels in Talmud and Midrash* (Reykjavik: Bókaútgáfa Menningarsjóds, 1965).

Junod, Eric and Jean Daniel Kaestli, "L'histoire des Actes Apocryphes des Apôtres du 3e au 9e siècle: le cas des Actes de Jean," *Cahiers de la Revue de Théologie et de Philosophie* 7 (1982), 1–152.

Kalmin, Richard, "Jesus in Sasanian Babylonia" [review of Schäfer, *Jesus in the Talmud*], *Jewish Quarterly Review* 99 (2009), 107–112.

–, *Jewish Babylonia between Persia and Roman Palestine* (Oxford: Oxford University Press, 2006).

–, "'Manasseh Sawed Isaiah with a Saw of Wood:' An Ancient Legend in Jewish, Christian, Persian, and Arabic Sources," in: Mark Geller (ed.), *Talmudic Archaeology* (Leiden: Brill, forthcoming).

–, "The Miracle of the Septuagint in the Babylonian Talmud," in: Oded Irshai, Jodi Magness, Seth Schwartz, and Zeev Weiss (eds.), (Festschrift for Lee I. Levine (Winona Lake, IN: Eisenbraun's, forthcoming).

–, *The Redaction of the Babylonian Talmud: Amoraic or Saboraic?* (Cincinnati: Hebrew Union College Press, 1989).

–, *The Sage in Jewish Society of Late Antiquity* (London: Routledge, 1999).

–, *Sages, Stories, Authors, and Editors in Rabbinic Babylonia* (Atlanta: Scholars Press, 1994).

Karff, Samuel Egal, "Laughter and Merriment in rabbinic Literature," in: Abraham J. Karp (ed.), *Threescore and Ten: Essays in Honor of Rabbi Seymour J. Cohen on the Occasion of his Seventieth Birthday* (Hoboken: Ktav 1991), 75–85.

Karrer, Wolfgang, *Parodie, Travestie, Pastiche* (Munich: W. Fink, 1977).

Katsh, Abraham, *Ginzei Talmud Bavli: The Antonin Genizah in the Saltykov-Schedrin Public Library in Leningrad* (Jerusalem: Rubin Mass, 1979), vol. I.

King, Karen, *What Is Gnosticism?* (Cambridge: Belknap Press of Harvard University Press, 2003).

Kiraz, George Anton, *Comparative Edition of the Syriac Gospels: Aligning the Sinaiticus, Curetonianus, Peshitta and Harklean Version* (Piscataway: Gorgias Press, 2004).

Kirschner, Robert, "The Rabbinic and Philonic Exegeses of the Nadab and Abihu Incident (Lev 10:1–6)," *Jewish Quarterly Review* 73 (1983), 375–393.

Kislev, Mordechai Ephraim, "Vegetal Food of Bar Kokhba Rebels at Abi'or Cave near Jericho," *Review of Palaeobotany and Palynology* 73 (1992), 153–160.

Kitchen, R.A., and Parmentier, M.F.G. (trs.), *The Book of Steps: The Syriac Liber Graduum,* Cistercian Studies Series 196 (Kalamazoo, Michigan: Cistercian Publications, 2004).

Kloner, Amos, "Hiding Complexes in Judaea: an Archaeological and Geographical Update on the Area of the Bar Kokhba Revolt," in Peter Schäfer (ed.), *The Bar Kokhba War Reconsidered* (Tübingen: Mohr Siebeck, 2003), 181–216.

Koet, Bart J., *Dreams and Scripture in Luke-Acts: Collected Essays* (Leuven: Peeters, 2006).

Kohut, Alexander, "Wit, Humor and Anecdote in the Talmud and Midrash," *The American Hebrew* (May 7th– June 11th 1886), nos. 2–3 (6 issues).

Konstan, David, *Sexual Symmetry: Love in the Ancient Novel and Related Genres* (Princeton: Princeton University Press, 1994).

Koonammakkal, T., "Ephrem's Theology of Humour," *Studia Patristica* 41 (2006), 51–56.

Koslofsky, Rela, "הומור ותפקודיו בגירסאות הסיפור 'ר' יהושע בן לוי ומלאך-המוות," *Mehqere Yerushalayim befolklor yehudi* 19/20 (1998), 329–344.

Kovelman, Arkady, "Farce in the Talmud," *Review of Rabbinic Judaism* 5 (2002), 86–92.

Kövecses, Zoltán, *Metaphor: A Practical Introduction* (New York: Oxford University Press, 2010).

Kraemer, David, *Reading the Rabbis: The Talmud as Literature* (New York: Oxford University Press, 1996).

Krauss, Samuel, *Das Leben Jesu nach jüdischen Quellen* (Berlin: Calvary, 1902).

Krueger, Derek, *Symeon, the Holy Fool: Leontius' Life and the Late Antique City* (Berkeley: University of California Press, 1996).

–, *Writing and Holiness: The Practice of Authorship in the Early Christian East* (Philadelphia: University of Pennsylvania Press, 2004).

Kruger, Steven F., *Dreaming in the Middle Ages* (Cambridge; New York: Cambridge University Press, 1992).

Krupp, Michael, "Manuscripts of the Babylonian Talmud," in Shmuel Safrai (ed.), *The Literature of the Sages, First Part: Oral Tora, Halakha, Mishna, Tosefta, Talmud, External Tractates* (Assen: Van Gorcum 1987), 346–66.

Künstlinger, David, *Die Petichot des Midrasch rabba zu Leviticus* (Krakow: Verlag des Verfassers, 1913).

Kugel, James L., "Two Introductions to Midrash," in: Geoffrey H. Hartman and Sanford Budick (eds.), *Midrash and Literature* (Evanston: Northwestern University Press, 1996), 77–103.

Kuhn, Karl Georg, "Giljonim und sifre minim," in: Walther Eltester (ed.), *Judentum, Urchristentum, Kirche: Festschrift für Joachim Jeremias* (Berlin: Alfred Töpelman, 1960), 24–61.

LaCapra, Dominick, *Rethinking Intellectual History: Texts, Contexts, Language* (Ithaca: Cornell University Press, 1983).

Laga, Carl, Joseph Munitiz, and Lucas van Rompay (eds.), *After Chalcedon: Studies in Theology and Church History Offered to Prof Albert Van Roey for his Seventieth Birthday* (Leuven: Departement Oriëntalistiek, 1985).

Lamberton, Robert, *Plutarch* (New Haven: Yale University Press, 2001).

Lamoreaux, John, *The Early Muslim Tradition of Dream Interpretation* (Stony Brook: SUNY Press, 2002).

–, "The Sources of Ibn Bahlul's Chapter on Dream Divination," *Studia Patristica* 33 (1997), 553–557.

Lampe, G. W. H., *A Patristic Greek Lexicon* (Oxford: Clarendon Press, 1961).

de Lange, Nicholas, *Origen and the Jews: Studies in Jewish-Christian Relations in Third-Century Palestine* (Cambridge: Cambridge University Press, 1976).

Larsen, B., *Jamblique de Chalcis* (PhD Diss., Aarhus University, 1972).

Lawrence, Stuart E., "Self-Control in Homeric Deliberations," *Prudentia* 34 (2002), 1–15.

Lauterbach, Jacob Zallal, "Jesus in the Talmud," in: idem., *Rabbinic Essays* (Cincinnati: Hebrew Union College Press, 1951), 473–570.

Leiman, Sid (Shnayer) Z. *The Canonization of Hebrew Scripture: the Talmudic and Midrashic Evidence* (New Haven: Connecticut Academy of Arts and Sciences, 1991), 102–119.

Lelièvre, F. J., "The Basis of Ancient Parody," *Greece & Rome* 1 (1954), 66–81.

Leloir, Louis, "L'humeur au service d'un message spirituel: les Pères du Désert," in: A. Theodoridis, P. Noster and J. Ries (eds), *Humeur, travail et science en Orient* (Louvain: Peeters, 1988), 83–91.

Levine, Lee I. (ed.), *The Galilee in Late Antiquity* (Cambridge: Harvard University Press, 1992).

–, *The Rabbinic Class of Roman Palestine in Late Antiquity* (New York: Jewish Theological Seminary of America, 1989).

–, "R. Simeon b. Yohai and the Purification of Tiberias: History and Tradition," *Hebrew Union College Annual*, 49 (1978), 143–85.

Levinson, Joshua, "אחת דיבר אלהים שתים זו שמעתי: קריאה דיאלוגית בסיפור הדרשני", in idem, Jacob Elbaum, and Galit Hasan-Rokem (eds.), *Higayon L'Yona: New Aspects in the Study of Midrash Aggadah and Piyut in Honor of Professor Yona Frenkel* (Jerusalem: The Hebrew University Magnes Press, 2006), 405–432.

–, הסיפור שלא סופר: אמנות הסיפור המקראי המורחב במדרשי חז"ל (Jerusalem: Magnes Press, 2005).

–, "עולם הפוך ראיתי': עיון בסיפור השיכור ובניו," *Jerusalem Studies in Hebrew Literature* XIV (1993), 7–23.

–, "Literary approaches to Midrash," in: Carol Bakhos (ed.), *Current Trends in the Study of Midrash* (Leiden: Brill, 2006), 189–226.

–, "'Tragedies naturally performed': Fatal Charades, Parodia Sacra, and the Death of Titus," in: Richard Kalmin and Seth Schwartz (eds.), *Jewish Culture and Society under the Christian Roman Empire* (Leuven: Peters, 2003), 349–382.

–, "The Tragedy of Romance: a Case of Literary Exile," *Harvard Theological Review* 89 (1996), 227–244.

–, *The Twice-Told Tale: A Poetics of the Exegetical Narrative in Rabbinic Midrash* (Jerusalem: Magnes Press, 2005) [Hebrew].

Liddell, H. G., and Scott, R., *Greek-English Lexicon: With a Revised Supplement* (Oxford, Clarendon Press, 1996).

Lieberman, Saul, *Hellenism in Jewish Palestine: Studies in the Literary Transmission, Beliefs and Manners of Palestine in the I century B.C.E. – IV century C.E.* (New York: Jewish Theological Seminary of America, 1950).

–, "How much Greek in Jewish Palestine?," in: A. Altmann (ed.), *Biblical and other Studies* (Cambridge, Harvard University Press, 1963), 123–141.

–, *Tosefta Kifshuta* (Jerusalem: Hotsa'at Darom, 5695 [1934]).

–, "A Tragedy or a Comedy?," *Journal of the American Oriental Society* 104 (1984), 315–319.

Lifshitz, David, "שמות וכינויים בתלמוד באספקלריה ההומוריסטית," *Ve-Eleh Shemot*, 3 (2002), 95–109.

–, "Humor as a Device for Solving Problems," *Justice* 15 (1997), 38–42.

Löw, Leopold, *Die Lebensalter in der Jüdischen Literatur* (Szegdin: Sigmund Burger's Wwe, 1875).

Lorand, Sandor, "L'interprétation des rêves selon le Talmud," *Revue d'histoire de la médecine hébraïque* 9 (1957), 69–71 and 101–102.

Louth, Andrew, "Palestine: Cyril of Jerusalem and Epiphanius," *Cambridge History of Early Christian Literature* (Cambridge: Cambridge University Press, 2004), 283–288.

Luz, Menahem, "A Description of the Greek Cynic in the Jerusalem Talmud," *JSJ* 20 (1989), 49–60.

–, "Oenomaus and Talmudic Anecdote," *Journal for the Study of Judaism* 23 (1992), 42–80.

Maccoby, Hyam, "Corpse and Leper," *Journal of Jewish Studies* 49 (1998), 280–285.

–, *Ritual and Morality: the Ritual Purity System and its Place in Judaism* (New York: Cambridge University Press, 1999).

Macleod, M. D., and L. R. Wickham, "The Syriac Version of Lucian's De Calumnia," *The Classical Quarterly* 20 (1970), 297–99.

MacMullen, Ramsay, *Corruption and the Decline of Rome* (New Haven: Yale University Press, 1988).

Maier, Johann, *Jesus von Nazareth in der talmudischen Überlieferung* (Darmstadt: Wissenschaftliche Buchgesellschaft, 1978).

–, *Jüdische Auseinandersetzungen mit dem Christentum in der Antike* (Darmstadt: Wissenschaftliche Buchgesellschaft, 1982).

de Man, Paul, *Aesthetic Ideology* (Minneapolis: University of Minnesota Press, 1996).

Mandel, Pinhas, מדרש איכה רבתי: מבוא, ומהדורה ביקורתית לפרשה השלישית (PhD diss. The Hebrew University of Jerusalem, 1997).

–, "על 'פתח' ועל פתיחתה: עיון חדש," in: Joshua Levinson, Jacob Elbaum, and Galit Hasan-Rokem (eds.), *Higayon L'Yona: New Aspects in the Study of Midrash Aggadah, and Piyut in Honor of Professor Yona Frenkel* (Jerusalem: The Hebrew University Magnes Press, 2006), 49–82.

Mandelbaum, Bernard, *Pesikta de-Rab Kahana according to an Oxford Manuscript* (New York: Jewish Theological Seminary of America, 1987).

Marcus, David, *From Balaam to Jonah: Anti-Prophetic Satire in the Hebrew Bible* (Atlanta: Scholars Press, 1995).

Margulies, Mordecai, *Midrash Wayyikra Rabbah* (New York: The Jewish Theological Seminary of America, 1993).

Martin, Dale B., and Patricia Cox Miller (eds.) *The Cultural Turn in Late Ancient Studies: Gender, Asceticism, and Historiography* (Durham, NC: Duke University Press, 2005).

Marmarji, A. S., *Diatessaron de Tatian* (Beyrouth: Imprimerie Catholique, 1935).

Mavroudi, Maria, *A Byzantine Book on Dream Interpretation: The Oneirocriticon of Achmet and Its Arabic Sources* (Leiden: Brill, 2002).

May, R. A. (ed.), *Catalogue of the Hebrew Manuscripts in the Bodleian Library; Supplement of Addenda and Corrigenda to Vol. I (A. Neubauer's Catalogue), compiled under the direction of Malachi Beit-Arié* (Oxford: Clarendon Press 1994).

McCane, Byron, "Is a Corpse Contagious? Early Jewish and Christian Attitudes toward the Dead," *Society of Biblical Literature Seminar Papers* 31 (1992), 378–388.

McCarthy, Carmel, *Saint Ephrem's Commentary on Tatian's Diatessaron: an English Translation of Chester Beatty Syriac MS 709* (Oxford: Oxford University Press, 1993).

McMahon, John M., "A Petronian Parody at *Sat.* 14.2–14.3," *Mnemosyne* 50 (1997), 77–81.

McWilson, Robert, "Alimentary and Sexual Encratism in the Nag Hammadi Texts," in: Ugo Bianchi (ed.), *La tradizione dell'enkrateia: motivazioni ontologiche e protologiche* (Rome: Edizioni dell'Ateneo, 1985), 317–322.

Meir, Ofra, "The Story of R. Simeon ben Yohai and his Son in the Cave – History or Literature?," *'Alei Siah*, 26 (1989), 145–60 [Hebrew].

Meyers, Eric M. (ed.), *Galilee Through the Centuries: Confluence of Cultures* (Winona Lake: Eisenbrauns, 1999).

Milgrom, J., *The Anchor Bible: Leviticus 1–16* (New York: Doubleday, 1991).

Moore, George Foot, "The Definition of the Jewish Canon and the Repudiation of Jewish Scriptures," in: Ch. A. Briggs, ed., *Essays in Modern Theology and Related Subjects* (New York: Scribner's Sons, 1911), 99–125.

Morgenstern, M. and M. Segal, "XHev/SePhylactery," *Discoveries in the Judaean Desert* 38 (Oxford: Oxford University Press, 2000), 183–91.

Morony, Michael G., "Magic and Society in Late Sasanian Iraq," in: Scott B. Noegel, Joel T. Walker and Brannon M. Wheeler (eds.), *Prayer, Magic, and the Stars in the Ancient and Late Antique World* (University Park, PA: The Pennsylvania State University Press, 2003), 83–110.

Moscovitz, Leib, *Talmudic Reasoning: From Casuistics to Conceptualization* (Tübingen: Mohr Siebeck, 2002).

Moulinier, Louis, *Le Pur et l'impur dans la pensée des Grecs d'Homère à Aristote* (New York: Arno Books, 1952).

Muecke, D. C. *Irony and the Ironic* (London: Methuen, 1970).

–, *Irony: The Critical Idiom* (Fakenham: Methuen, 1970).

Müller-Kessler, Christa, and Sokoloff, Michael, *The Christian Palestinian Aramaic New Testament Version from the early Period* (Groningen: Styx, 1998).

Münz-Manor, Ophir, "Carnivalesque Ambivalence and the Christian *Other* in Aramaic Poems from Byzantine Palestine," (forthcoming).

–, "Other Voices: Haman, Jesus, and the Representation of the Other in Purim Poems from Byzantine Palestine," in: Yael Shapira, Omri Herzog and Tamar S. Hess (eds.) *Popular and Canonical: Literary Dialogues* (Tel Aviv: Resling, 2007), 69–79 and 211–217 [Hebrew].

Murray, Donald, "Humour in the Bible?," in: Keith Cameron (ed.), *Humour and History* (Oxford: Intellect, 1993), 21–40.

Nanos, Mark, *The Irony of Galatians: Paul's Letter in first-century Context* (Minneapolis: Fortress Press, 2002).

Neubauer, A., *Catalogue of the Hebrew Manuscripts in the Bodleian Library and in the College Libraries of Oxford, Including Mss. in Other Languages, which Are Written with Hebrew Characters, or Relating to the Hebrew Language or Literature; and a Few Samaritan Mss.* (Oxford: Clarendon Press, 1886 [repr. 1994]).

Newby, Gordon Darnell, "Tafsir Isra'iliyyat," in: Alford T. Welch (ed.), *Studies in Qur'an and Tafsir* (*Journal of the American Academy of Religion Thematic Studies* 57 no. 4, 1979), 685–97.

Newman, Hillel I., "The Death of Jesus in the Toledot Yeshu Literature," *Journal of Theological Studies* 50 (1999), 59–79.

Neusner, Jacob, *Aphrahat and Judaism: the Christian-Jewish Argument in Fourth-Century Iran* (Leiden: Brill, 1971).

–, *The Integrity of Leviticus Rabbah: The Problem of the Autonomy of a Rabbinic Document* (Chico: Scholars Press, 1985).

Niehoff, Maren, "A Dream which is Not Interpreted is like a Letter which is Not Read," *JJS* 43 (1992), 58–84.

Nieting, Lorenz, "Humor in the New Testament," *Dialog* 22 (1983), 168–170.

Noy, Dov, מבוא לספרות האגדה (Jerusalem: Hebrew University of Jerusalem, 1966).

–, "הפאורודיה בספרות ישראל הקדומה," *Mahanayim* 54 (1961–62), 92–99.

Oberhelman, Steven M., *The Oneirocriticon of Achmet: A Medieval Greek and Arabic Treatise on the Interpretation of Dreams* (Lubbock: Texas Tech University Press, 1991).

–, *Dreambooks in Byzantium: Six Oneirocritica in Translation, with Commentary and Introduction* (Surrey: Ashgate, 2008).

Omidsalar, Mahmud, "Cat," in: Ehsan Yar-Shater (ed.), *Encyclopaedia Iranica* (London: Routledge, 1982), s.v. "Cat.".

O'Neill, Patrick. *The Comedy of Entropy: Humour, Narrative, Reading* (Toronto: University of Toronto Press, 1990).

Orbe, A., "El pecado original y el matrimonio en la teologia del s. II," *Gregorianum*, 45 (1964), 449–50.

Oppenheim, A. Leo, *The Interpretation of Dreams in the Ancient Near East* (Philadelphia: American Philosophical Society, 1956).

Oppenheimer, Aharon, *The 'Am ha-Aretz:' a Study in the Social History of the Jewish People in the Hellenistic-Roman Period* (Leiden: Brill 1977).

Pagels, Elaine, *Adam, Eve, and the Serpent* (New York: Random House, 1988).

Parker, Robert, *Miasma: Pollution and Purification in early Greek Religion* (Oxford: Clarendon Press, 1983).

Patrich, Joseph, "Early Christian Churches in the Holy Land," in: Ora Limor and Guy G. Stroumsa (eds.), *Christians and Christianity in the Holy Land: from the Origins to the Latin Kingdoms* (Turnhout: Brepols, 2006), 355–399.

Paul, Shlomo M., "Classifications of Wine in Mesopotamian and Rabbinic Sources," *Israel Exploration Journal*, 25 (1975), 42–44.

Paquet, Léonce, *Les cyniques grecs: fragments et témoignages* (Ottawa: Éditions de l'Université d'Ottawa, 1988).

Patrich, Joseph, "Early Christian Churches in the Holy Land," in Ora Limor and Guy G. Stroumsa (eds.), *Christians and Christianity in the Holy Land: from the Origins to the Latin Kingdoms* (Turnhout: Brepols, 2006), 355–399.

Peeters, Paul, "La vie géorgienne de Porphyre de Gaza," *Analecta Bollandiana* 59 (1941), 65–216

Perikhanian, A., "Iranian Society and Law," in: Ilya Gershevitch (ed.), *The Cambridge History of Iran*, Volume 2: *The Median and Achaemenian Periods* (Cambridge: Cambridge University Press, 1985) vol. III, no. 2, 646.

Perrot, Charles, "The Reading of the Bible in the Ancient Synagogue," in Martin Jan Mulder (ed.), *Mikra: Text, Translation, Reading, and Interpretation of the Hebrew Bible in Ancient Judaism and Early Christianity* (Assen: Van Gorcum; Philadelphia: Fortress Press, 1988), 137–159.

Petersen, William, *Tatian's Diatessaron: Its Creation, Dissemination, Significance, and History in Scholarship* (Leiden: Brill, 1994).

Pines, Shlomo, "A Platonistic Model for two of Josephus' Accounts of the Doctrine of the Pharisees concerning Providence and Man's Freedom of Action," *Immanuel* 7 (1977), 38–43.

Poinsotte, Jean-Michel, "Fin de l'Antiquité, mort du comique antique," in: Monique Trédé and Philippe Hoffmann (eds.), *Le Rire des Anciens: Actes du colloque international* (Presses de l'École Normale Supérieure: Paris, 1998), 315–26.

Radday, Yehuda T. and Brenner, Athalya, *On Humour and the Comic in the Hebrew Bible* (Sheffield: The Almond Press, 1990).

Ranke, Ernst, *Codex Fuldensis: Novum Testamentum Latine interprete Hieronymo* (Marburg; Leipzig: Sumtibus N. G. Elwerti Bibliopolae Academici, 1868).

Reardon, B.P. (ed.), *Collected Ancient Greek Novels* (Berkeley: University of California Press, 2008).

Reed, Annette Yoshiko, "Jewish-Christian Apocrypha and the History of Jewish/Christian Relations," in: P. Piovanelli (ed.), *Christian Apocryphal Texts for the New Millennium: Achievements, Prospects, and Challenges* (forthcoming).

Reeg, Gottfried, *Die Ortsnamen Israels nach der rabbinischen Literatur* (Wiesbaden: Dr. Ludwig Reichert Verlag, 1989).

Reischl, W.C. and J. Rupp, *Cyrilli Hierosolymorum archiepiscopi opera quae supersunt omnia* (Hildesheim: Olms, 1967), vol. II.

Relihan, Joel C., *Ancient Menippean Satire* (Baltimore: Johns Hopkins University Press, 1993).

Richard, Marcel, "L'activité littéraire de Théodoret avant le concil d'Éphèse," in: *RSPT* 24 (1935), 82–106.

–, "Notes sur l'évolution doctrinale de Théodortet de Cyr," *RSPT* 25 (1936), 459–481.

Riikonen, H. K., *Menippean Satire as a Literary Genre: with Special Reference to Seneca's Apocolocyntosis* (Helsinki: Societas Scientiarum Fennica, 1987).

van Rompay, Lucas, "Impetuous Martyrs? The Situation of the Persian Christians in the Last Years of Yazdgard I (419–420)," in: M. Lamberigts and P. van Deun (eds.), *Martyrium in Multidisciplinary Perspective: Memorial Louis Reekmans* (Louvain: Leuven University Press, 1995), 363–375.

van Rooy, C. A., *Studies in Classical Satire and Related Literary Theory* (Leiden: Brill, 1965).

Rose, Margaret A., *Parody: Ancient Modern, and Post-Modern* (Cambridge: Cambridge University Press, 1993).

–, *Parody/Meta-Fiction: An Analysis of Parody as a Critical Mirror to the Writing and Reception of Fiction* (London: Croom Helm, 1979).

Rosenau, William, "Book Notices: Hermann L. Strack, *Bavli according to the Munich Codex Hebraicus, 95,*" *The American Journal of Semitic Languages and Literatures* 29 (1913), 304–306.

Rosenfeld, Ben-Zion, "R. Simeon B. Yohai – Wonder Worker and Magician Scholar, *Saddiq* and *Hasid, Revue des études juives* 158 (1999), 349–384.

Rousseau, Philip, *Basil of Caesarea* (Berkeley: University of California Press, 1994).

Rubenstein, Jeffrey, "The Bavli's Ethic of Shame," *Conservative Judaism* 53 (2001), 27–39.

–. "The Burial Accounts of R. Eleazar b. R Shimon: Rabbis and the Cult of Relics in Late Antiquity," paper presented at the Association of Jewish Studies Annual Meeting, 2003.

–, *The Culture of the Babylonian Talmud* (Baltimore: Johns Hopkins University Press, 2003).

–, "The Exegetical Narrative: New Directions," review of Joshua Levinson, *The Twice-Told Tale: A Poetics of the Exegetical Narrative in Rabbinic Midrash*, in *The Jewish Quarterly Review* 99 (2009), 88–106.

–, "Introduction," in: ibid (ed.), *Creation and Composition: The Contribution of the Bavli Redactors (Stammaim) to the Aggada* (Tübingen: Mohr Siebeck, 2005), 1–20.

–, *Talmudic Stories: Narrative Art, Composition, and Culture* (Baltimore: The Johns Hopkins University Press, 1999).

–, "The Thematization of Dialectics in Bavli Aggada." *Journal of Jewish Studies* 54 (2003), 71–84.

Safrai, Shmuel, *The Literature of the Sages. First Part: Oral Tora, Halakha, Mishna, Toefta, Talmud, External Tractates* (Assen: Van Gorcum 1987).

Salmanowitsch, H., *Das Naziräat nach Bibel und Talmud* (PhD diss. Giessen University, 1931).

Samely, Alexander, "Scripture's Implicature: the Midrashic Assumptions of Relevance and Consistency," *Journal of Semitic Studies* 37 (1992), 167–205.

Sanders, E. P. (ed.), *Jewish and Christian Self-Definition* (Philadelphia: Fortress Press, 1981).

Sandt, Huub van de (ed.), *Matthew and the Didache: Two Documents from the Same Jewish-Christian Milieu?* (Assen: Royal Van Gorcum Press, 2005).

Sarason, R. S., "The Petihtot in Leviticus Rabbah: 'Oral Homilies' or Redactional Constructions?," *JJS* 33 (1983), 557–67.

Satlow, Michael, "'And on the Earth You Shall Sleep': 'Talmud Torah' and Rabbinic Asceticism," *Journal of Religion* 83 (2003), 204–225.

–, "Beyond Influence: Towards a New Historiographic Paradigm," in: Anita Norich and Yaron Z. Eliav (eds.), *Jewish Literatures and Cultures: Context and Intertext* (Providence: Brown Judaic Studies, 2008), 37–53.

–, "'They Abused Him like a Woman': Homoeroticism, Gender Blurring, and the Rabbis in Late Antiquity," *Journal of the History of Sexuality* 5 (1994), 1–15.

Schachter, Melech, *The Babylonian and Jerusalem Mishna Textually Compared* (Jerusalem: Mosad ha-Rav kuk, 1959), 206 [Hebrew].

Schäfer, Peter, "Introduction", in: idem. (ed.), *The Talmud Yerushalmi and Graeco-Roman Culture* Tübingen: Mohr Siebeck, 1998), vol. I, 1–17.

–, *Jesus in the Talmud* (Princeton: Princeton University Press, 2007).

–, "Magic and Religion in Ancient Judaism," in idem and Hans G. Kippenberg (eds.), *Envisioning Magic: A Princeton Seminar and Symposium* (Leiden; New York: Brill, 1997), 19–44.

–, "Rabbis and Priests, or: How to Do Away with the Glorious Past of the Sons of Aaron," in: Gregg Gardner and Kevin Osterloh (eds.), *Antiquity in Antiquity: Jewish and Christian Pasts in the Greco-Roman World* (Tübingen: Mohr Siebeck, 2008), 155–172.

–, "Research into Rabbinic Literature: An Attempt to Define the Status Quaestionis." *Journal of Jewish Studies* 37 (1986), 139–152.

–, *Synopse zum Talmud Yerushalmi I/6–11* (Tübingen: Mohr Siebeck 2001).

Schaff, Philip (ed.), *Select Library of the Nicene and post-Nicene Fathers of the Church* (New York: Christian Literature Publishing Company, 1893).

Scher, Mgr. Sddai and Périer, Abbé (eds.), *Chronique de Séert, Histoire Nestorienne Inédite* (Paris: Périer, 1907), vol. I.

Schippman, Klaus, *Grundzüge der Geschichte des sassanidischen Reiches* (Darmstadt: Wissenschaftliche Buchgesellschaft, 1990).

Schwartz, Joshua, "Cats in Ancient Jewish Society," *Journal of Jewish Studies* 52 (2001), 211–234.

–, "On Birds, Rabbis, and Skin Disease," in: M. Poorthuis and J. Schwartz (eds.), *Purity and Holiness* (Leiden: Brill, 2000), 207–222.

–, "Treading the Grapes of Wrath: The Wine Press in Ancient Jewish and Christian Tradition," *Theologische Zeitschrift* 49 (1993), 215–228 and 311–324.

Schwartz, Seth, "Hebrew and Imperialism in Jewish Palestine," in: Carol Bakhos (ed.) *Ancient Judaism in its Hellenistic Context* (Leiden: Brill, 2005), 53–82.

Segal, J.B. *Edessa, 'the Blessed City'* (Oxford: Oxford University Press, 1970).

Seely, Jo Ann H., "The Fruit of the Vine: Wine at Masada and in the New Testament," *BYU Studies* 36 (1996–1997), 207–227.

Selb, Walter and Hubert Kaufhold, *Das syrisch-römische Rechtsbuch* (Vienna: Verlag der Österreichischen Akademie der Wissenschaften, 2002).

Sharp, Carolyn J., *Irony and Meaning in the Hebrew Bible* (Bloomington: Indiana University Press, 2009).

Shemesh, Aaron, *Punishment and Sins from Scripture to the Rabbis* (Jerusalem: The Magnes Press, 2003) [Hebrew].

Shepardson, Christine, *Anti-Judaism and Christian Orthodoxy: Ephrem's Hymns in Fourth-Century Syria*, (Washington: Catholic University of America Press, 2008).

Shinan, Avigdor, "The Sins of Nadav and Avihu in Rabbinic Aggadah", *Tarbits*, 48 (1979), 201–214 [Hebrew].

Shklovsky, Victor, "'Sterne's *Tristram Shandy*: Stylistic Commentary," in: Lee T. Lemon and Marion Reis (eds.), *Russian Formalist Criticism: Four Essays* (Lincoln: University of Nebraska Press, 1965), 27–57.

Siegal, Michal Bar-Asher, *Analogies in Rabbinic and Christian Monastic Sources* (PhD diss. Yale University, 2010).

Skarsaune, Oskar and Reidar Hvalvik (eds.), *Jewish Believers in Jesus: The Early Centuries* (Peabody, MA: Hendrickson Publishers, 2007).

Stökl-Ben Ezra, Daniel, "Parody and Polemics on Pentecost: Talmud Yerushalmi Pesahim on Acts 2?," in Alberg Gerhards and Clemens Leonhard (eds.), *Jewish and Christian Liturgy and Worship: New Insights into its History and Interaction* (Leiden: Brill, 2007), 279–294.

Slater, Richard N., "An Inquiry into the Relationship between Community and Text: The Apocryphical Acts of Philip 1 and the Encratites of Asia Minor," in: F. Bovon, A. Brock, and C. Matthews (eds.), *The Apocryphal Acts of the Apostles: Harvard Divinity School Studies* (Cambridge: Harvard University Center for the Study of World Religions, 1999), 281–306.

Smith, Dennis E., *From Symposium to Eucharist: The Banquet in the Early Christian World* (Minneapolis: Fortress Press, 2003).

Smith, Margaret deMaria, "Enkrateia: Plutarch on Self-Control and the Politics of Excess," *Ploutarchos* 1 (2003–2004), 79–88.

Smith, Payne, *A Compendious Syriac Dictionary* (Oxford: Oxford University Press, 1903).

Sokoloff, Michael, *The Christian Palestinian Aramaic New Testament Version from the Early Period* (Groningen: Styx, 1998).

–, *A Dictionary of Jewish Babylonian Aramaic* (Ramat–Gan: Bar Ilan University Press, 2002).

–, *A Dictionary of Jewish Palestinian Aramaic* (Ramat-Gan: Bar Ilan University Press, 2002).

Sperber, Daniel, "On Pubs and Policemen in Roman Palestine," *Zeitschrift der Deutschen Morgenländischen Gesellschaft* 120 (1970), 257–263.

Spurling, Helen, *The Exegetical Encounter between Jews and Christians in Late Antiquity* (Leiden: Brill, 2009).

Stein, Dina, מגיה מיתוס: פרקי דרבי אליעזר לאור מחקר הספרות העממית (Jersualem: Magnes Press, 2004).

–, "On the Unfortunate Adventures of Rav Kahana," in Shaul Shaked (ed.), *Irano-Judaica: Studies Relating to Jewish Contacts with Persian Culture throughout the Ages* (Jerusalem: Ben-Zvi Institute for the Study of Jewish Communities in the East, 1982), 88–100.

Stemberger, Brigitte, "Der Traum in der Rabbinischen Literatur," *Kairos; Zeitschrift für Religionswissenschaft und Theologie* 18 (1976), 1–42.

Stemberger, Günter, "The Derasha in Rabbinic Times," in: Alexander Deek, Walter Homolka, and Heinz-Günther Schöttler (eds.), *Preaching in Judaism and Chris-*

tianity: Encounters and Developments from Biblical Times to Modernity (Berlin, New York: Walter de Gruyter, 2008), 7–21.

–, *Introduction to Talmud and Midrash* (Edinburgh: T & T Clark, 1996).

–, *Juden und Christen im Heiligen Land: Palastina unter Konstantin und Theodosius* (Munich: C.H. Beck, 1987).

–, " Mehrheitsbeschlüsse oder Recht auf eigene Meinung? Zur Entscheidungsfindung im rabbinischen Judentum," in Susanne Plietzsch (ed.), *Literatur im Dialog: die Faszination von Talmud und Midrasch*, (Zürich: Theologischer Verlag Zürich, 2007), 19–39.

–, "Mischna Avot: Frühe Weisheitsschrift, Pharisäisches Erbe oder spätrabbinische Bildung?" *ZNW* 96 (2005), 243–258.

Stern, David, "The Alphabet of Ben Sira" and the early History of Parody in Jewish Literature," in: Hindy Najman and Judith H. Newman (eds.), *The Idea of Biblical Interpretation: Essays in Honor of James L. Kugel* (Leiden: Brill, 2004), 423–448.

–, "Midrash and Indeterminacy," *Critical Inquiry* 5 (1988), 132–161.

–, "Midrash and the Language of Exegesis: a Study of Vayikra Rabbah Chapter 1," in: Geoffrey H. Hartman and Sanford Budick (eds.), *Midrash and Literature* (Evanston: Northwestern University Press, 1996), 105–124.

–, *Midrash and Theory: Ancient Jewish Exegesis and contemporary Literary Studies.* (Evanston, IL: Northwestern University Press, 1996).

Stern, Sacha, *Calendar and Community: A History of the Jewish Calendar, 2nd Century BCE–10th Century CE* (Oxford: Oxford University Press, 2001).

Steudel, Marion, *Die Literaturparodie in Ovids Ars Amatoria* (Hildesheim: Olms-Weidmann, 1992).

Stock, Brian, *Listening for the Text: on the Uses of the Past* (Baltimore: Johns Hopkins University Press, 1990).

Sussman, Yaakov, "תורה שבעל פה' פשוטה כמשמעה: כוחו של קוצו של יו'ד," in: *Mehkere talmud: Kovets mehkarim be-talmud uvi-tehumim govlim* (Jerusalem, The Hebrew University Magnes Press, 2005), vol. III, 209–384.

Svenbro, Jesper, *Phrasikleia: An Anthropology of Reading in Ancient Greece* (Ithaca: Cornell University Press, 1993).

Swain, Simon, *Hellenism and Empire. Language, Classicism and Power in the Greek World, AD 50–250* (New York: Oxford University Press, 1996).

Swanson, Scott A., *Fifth Century Patristic and Rabbinic Ethical Interpretation of Cult and Ritual in Leviticus* (PhD diss. Hebrew Union College, 2004).

Tanenbaum, M., "Humour in the Talmud" *Concilium* 5 (1974), 141–150.

Thatcher, Tom, "The Sabbath Trick: Unstable Irony in the Fourth Gospel," *Journal for the Study of the New Testament* 76 (1999), 53–77.

Theodor, Yehudah and Albeck, Hanokh, *Bereschit Rabba mit kritischem Apparat und Kommentar* (Jerusalem: Shalem Books, 1996 [1912–1927]).

Thompson, Stith, *Motif-Index of Folk-Literature: a Classification of Narrative Elements in Folktales, Ballads, Myths, Fables, Mediaeval Romances, Exempla, Fabliaux, Jest-Books, and Local Legends* (Bloomington and Indianapolis: Indiana University Press, 1955–1958).

Tissot, Yves, "L'Encratisme des Actes de Thomas," in: Hildegard Temporini et al. (eds.), *Aufstieg und Niedergang der römischen Welt: Geschichte und Kultur Roms im Spiegel der neueren Forschung* II vol. 25 no. 6 (Berlin: Walter de Gruyter, 1988), 4415–4430.

Tropper, Amran, *Wisdom, Politics, and Historiography: Tractate Avot in the Context of the Graeco-Roman Near East* (New York: Oxford University Press, 2004).

Trout, Dennis, "Saints, Identity, and the City," in: Virginia Burrus (ed.), *Late Ancient Christianity* (Minneapolis: Fortress Press, 2005), 165–187.

Trueblood, David Elton, *The Humor of Christ* (Harper, San Francisco, 1964).

Tsananas, Georgios, "Humor bei Basilius dem Grossen," in: Anastasius Kallis (ed.), *Philoxenia: Festschrift B. Kötting* (Münster: Aschendorff, 1980), 259–279.

Ulmer, Rivka, "The Semiotics of the Dream Sequence in Talmud Yerushalmi Maʿaser Sheni," *Henoch* 23 (2001), 305–323.

Urbach, Ephraim, *The Sages: Their Concepts and Beliefs* (Jerusalem: Magnes Press, 1975).

Urbano, Arthur, "'Read It Also to the Gentiles': The Displacement and Recasting of the Philosopher in the *Vita Antonii*," *Church History* 77 (2008), 877–914.

Valler, Shulamit, *Woman and Womanhood in the Talmud* (Atlanta: Scholars Press, 1999).

Veltri, Giuseppe, *Magie und Halakha: Ansätze zu einem empirischen Wissenschafts-begriff im spätantiken und frühmittelalterlichen Judentum* (Tübingen: Mohr Siebeck, 1997).

Vernant, Jean-Pierre, *Myth and Society in Ancient Greece* (New York: Zone Books, 1980).

Vidas, Moulie, "The Bavli's Discussion of Genealogy in *Qiddushin* IV," in: Gregg Gardner and Kevin Osterloh (eds.), *Antiquity in Antiquity: Jewish and Christian Pasts in the Greco-Roman World*, (Tübingen: Mohr Siebeck, 2008), 285–326.

Visotzky, Burton L., "Anti-Christian Polemic in Leviticus Rabbah," *American Academy for Jewish Research Proceedings*, LVI (1990), 83–100. [Reprinted in: idem, *Fathers of the World: Essays in Rabbinic and Patristic Literature* (Tübingen: Mohr Siebeck, 1995), 93–105.]

–, *Fathers of the World: Essays in Rabbinic and Patristic Literature* (Tübingen: Mohr Siebeck, 1995).

–, *Golden Bells and Pomegranates: Studies in Midrash Leviticus Rabbah* (Tübingen: Mohr Siebeck, 2003).

–, "Goys 'Я'n't Us: Rabbinic Anti-Gentile Polemic in Yerushalmi Berachot 9:1," in: Holger Zellentin and Eduard Iricinschi (eds.), *Heresy and Identity in Late Antiquity*, (Tübingen: Mohr Siebeck, 2008), 299–313.

–, "Jots and Tittles: On Scriptural Interpretation in Rabbinic and Patristic Litera-tures," *Prooftexts* 8 (1988), 257–270.

–, *The Midrash on Proverbs* (New Haven: Yale University Press, 1992).

–, "The Misnomers '*Petihah*' and 'Homiletic Midrash' as Descriptions for Leviticus Rabbah and Pesikta DRav Kahana," *Jewish Studies Quarterly*, forthcoming.

–, "Overturning the Lamp," in: idem, *Fathers of the World: Essays in Rabbinic and Patristic Literatures* (Tübingen: Mohr Siebeck, 1995), 75–84.

–, "Review of Skarsaune and Hvalvik (eds.), *Jewish Believers in Jesus: The Early Centuries, Catholic Biblical Quarterly* 70 (2008).

Vööbus, Arthur, *The Didascalia Apostolorum in Syriac II* (Leuven: Corpus Scripto-rum Christianorum Orientalium, 1979).

–, *The Syro-Roman Lawbook: the Syriac Text of the Recently Discovered Manu-scripts Accompanied by a Facsimile Edition and Furnished with an Introduction and Translation* (Stockholm: Papers of the Estonian Theological Society in Exile, 1982).

Wallach, Luitpold, "The Textual History of an Aramaic Proverb (Traces of the Ebionean Gospel)," *Journal of Biblical Literature* 60 (1941), 403–415.

Wallis, Richard T., *Neoplatonism* (London: Duckworth, 1972).

Walzer, Michael et al. (eds.), *The Jewish Political Tradition* (New Haven: Yale University Press, 2000).

Weinbrot, Howard, *Menippean Satire Reconsidered: From Antiquity to the Eighteenth Century* (Baltimore: Johns Hopkins University Press, 2005).

Weiss, Avraham, *The Talmud in its Development I* (New York: Philipp Feldheim,
1954) [Hebrew].

Weiss, David Halivni, "On the Supposed Anti-Asceticism or Anti-Nazritism of
Simon the Just," in *JQR* 58 (1967–69), 243–252.

Weiss, Haim, *מעמדו ותפקידו של החלום בספרות חז"ל - היבטים תרבותיים: קריאה ספרותית ב'מסכת
החלומות' שבתלמוד הבבלי (מסכת ברכות, נ"ה ע"א-נ"ז ע"ב)* (PhD diss. The Hebrew University of Jerusalem, 2006).

Welch, John W., "Introduction," in idem (ed.), *Chiasmus in Antiquity: Structures,
Analyses, Exegesis* (Hildesheim: Gerstenberg, 1981).

Wensinck, A. J., *Legends Of Eastern Saints, Chiefly From Syriac Sources* (Leiden:
Brill, 1913), vol. II.

West, Edward William, *Pahlavi Texts II*. (Sacred Books of the East 18, Oxford:
Clarendon Press, 1882).

Whitmarsh, Tim, *The Second Sophistic* (New York: Oxford University Press, 2005)

Widengren, Geo, "The Status of the Jews in the Sassanian Empire," *Iranica Antiqua*
1 (1961), 117–162.

Widenmann, R., "Christian Earnestness (Seriousness)," in: Marie Mikulová Thul-
strup (ed.), *Sources and Depths of Faith in Kierkegaard* (Copenhagen: A Reitzels
Boghandel, 1978), 83–99.

Wilken, Robert L., *The Land Called Holy: Palestine in Christian History and
Thought* (New Haven: Yale University Press, 1992).

Williams, A. V., "Zoroastrians and Christians in Sassanian Iran," *Bulletin of the John
Rylands University Library of Manchester* 78 (1996), 37–53.

Williams, Frank, *The Panarion of Epiphanius of Salamis* (Leiden: Brill, 1994).

Williams, Michael, *Rethinking "Gnosticism": An Argument for Dismantling a Dubious Category* (Princeton: Princeton University Press, 1996).

Wimpfheimer, Barry, "*Ashgera Delishna*: A Case Study in List Transmission," paper
presented at the annual meeting of the Association for Jewish Studies (AJS), Los
Angeles, December 16, 2002.

–, "'But it is not so': Toward a Poetics of Legal Narrative in the Talmud," *Prooftexts* 24 (2004), 51–86.

–, *Telling Tales out of Court: Literary Ambivalence in Talmudic Legal Narratives*
(Philadelphia: University of Pennsylvania Press, forthcoming).

Winkler, John, "The Mendacity of Kalasiris and the Narrative Strategy of Heliodoros' Aithiopika," *Yale Classical Studies* 27 (1982), 93–158.

Winter, Engelbert, and Dignas, Beate, *Rom und das Perserreich: Zwei Weltmächte
zwischen Konfrontation und Koexistenz* (Berlin: Akademie Verlag, 2001).

Yadin, Azzan, *Scripture as Logos: Rabbi Ishmael and the Origins of Midrash* (Pennsylvania: University of Pennsylvania Press, 2004).

Yahalom, Joseph, "Angels do not Understand Aramaic: On the Literary Use of Jewish Palestinian Aramaic in Late Antiquity," *Journal of Jewish Studies* 47 (1996), 33–44.

Yar-Shater, Ehsan (ed.), *Encyclopaedia Iranica* (London: Routledge, 1982).

Yassif, Eli, "סיפורי הומור באגדה: טיפולוגיה, נושא, משמעות," *Mehqere Talmud* 3 (2005), 403–430.

–, *The Tales of Ben Sira in the Middle Ages: A Critical Text and Literary Studies* (Jerusalem: Magnes Press, 1984).

Yonge, C.D., *The Lives and Opinions of Eminent Philosophers, by Diogenes Laertius* (London: Henry G. Bohn, 1853).

Yuval, Israel, "The Other in Us Liturgica, Poetica, Polemica," in: Holger Zellentin and Eduard Iricinschi (eds.), *Heresy and Identity in Late Antiquity* (Tübingen: Mohr Siebeck, 2008), 364–386.

–, *Two Nations in Your Womb: Perceptions of Jews and Christians in Late Antiquity and the Middle Ages* (Tel Aviv: Am Oved, 2000) [Hebrew]; Berkeley: University of California Press, 2006) [English]).

Zellentin, Holger, "The End of Jewish Egypt: Artapanus and the Second Exodus," in: Gregg Gardner and Kevin Osterloh (eds.), *Antiquity in Antiquity: Jewish and Christian Pasts in the Greco-Roman World* (Tübingen: Mohr Siebeck, 2008), 27–73.

–, "How Plutarch Gained his Place in the Tosefta," in *Zutot: Perspectives on Jewish Culture*, volume 4 (Boston: Kluwer Academic Publishers, 2004), 19–28.

Zeitlin, S., "Jesus in Early Tannaitic Literature," in: *Abhandlungen zur Erinnerung an Hirsch Peres Chajes* (Vienna: The Alexander Kohut Memorial Foundation, 1933), 304–307.

Zevin, Shlomoh Yosef and Berlin, Meir (eds.), אנציקלופדיה תלמודית (Jerusalem: Yad haRav Hertzog, 1998).

Zuckschwerd, Ernst, "Das Naziräat des Herrenbruders Jakobus nach Hegesipp (Euseb, H E II 23:5–6)," *Zeitschrift für die Neutestamentliche Wissenschaft und die Kunde der älteren Kirche* 68 (1977), 276–287.

–, "Nazōraîos in Matth 2, 23," *Theologische Zeitschrift* 31 (1975), 65–77.

Index Scripture

Hebrew Bible

New Testament

Mishna

Tosefta

Halakhic Midrashim

Talmud Yerushalmi

Aggadic Midrashim

Talmud Bavli

Index of Modern Authors

General Index

Texts and Studies in Ancient Judaism
Alphabetical Index

Hauptman, Judith: Rereading the Mishnah. 2005. *Vol. 109.*

Hayman, A. Peter: Sefer Yesira. 2004. *Vol. 104.*

Herrmann, Klaus (Ed.): Massekhet Hekhalot. 1994. *Vol. 39.*
– see *Schäfer, Peter*

Herzer, Jens: Die Paralipomena Jeremiae. 1994. *Vol. 43.*

Hezser, Catherine: Form, Function, and Historical Significance of the Rabbinic Story in Yerushalmi Neziqin. 1993. *Vol. 37.*
– Jewish Literacy in Roman Palestine. 2001. *Vol. 81.*
– see *Schäfer, Peter*
– The Social Structure of the Rabbinic Movement in Roman Palestine. 1997. *Vol. 66.*

Hezser, Catherine (Ed.): Rabbinic Law in its Roman and Near Eastern Context. 2003. *Vol. 97.*

Hirschfelder, Ulrike: see *Schäfer, Peter*

Horbury, W.: see *Krauss, Samuel*

Houtman, Alberdina: Mishnah und Tosefta. 1996. *Vol. 59.*

Ilan, Tal: Jewish Women in Greco-Roman Palestine. 1995. *Vol. 44.*
– Integrating Woman into Second Temple History. 1999. *Vol. 76.*
– Lexicon of Jewish Names in Late Antiquity.
Part I: Palestine 330 BCE – 200 CE. 2002. *Vol. 91.*
Part III: The Western Diaspora, 330 BCE – 650 CE. 2009. *Vol. 126.*
– Silencing the Queen. 2006. *Vol. 115.*

Instone Brewer, David: Techniques and Assumptions in Jewish Exegesis before 70 CE. 1992. *Vol. 30.*

Ipta, Kerstin: see *Schäfer, Peter*

Iricinschi, Eduard and Holger M. Zellentin (Ed.): Heresy and Identity in Late Antiquity. 2008. *Vol. 119.*

Jacobs, Martin: Die Institution des jüdischen Patriarchen. 1995. *Vol. 52.*

Kasher, Aryeh: The Jews in Hellenistic and Roman Egypt. 1985. *Vol. 7.*
– Jews, Idumaeans, and Ancient Arabs. 1988. *Vol. 18.*

– Jews and Hellenistic Cities in Eretz-Israel. 1990. *Vol. 21.*

Knittel, Thomas: Das griechische ‚Leben Adams und Evas‘. 2002. *Vol. 88.*

Krauss, Samuel: The Jewish-Christian Controversy from the earliest times to 1789. Vol. I. Ed. by W. Horbury. 1996. *Vol. 56.*

Kuhn, Peter: Offenbarungsstimmen im Antiken Judentum. 1989. *Vol. 20.*

Kuyt, Annelies: The ‚Descent‘ to the Chariot. 1995. *Vol. 45.*

Lange, A.: see *Albani, M.*

Lange, Nicholas de: Greek Jewish Texts from the Cairo Genizah. 1996. *Vol. 51.*

Lapin, Hayim: Economy, Geography, and Provincial History in Later Roman Galilee. 2001. *Vol. 85.*

Lehnardt, Andreas: Qaddish. 2002. *Vol. 87.*

Leibner, Uzi: Settlement and History in Hellenistic, Roman, and Byzantine Galilee. 2009. *Vol. 127.*

Leonhardt, Jutta: Jewish Worship in Philo of Alexandria. 2001. *Vol. 84.*

Levine, Lee I. and Daniel R. Schwartz (Ed.): Jewish Identities in Antiquity. 2009. *Vol. 130.*

Lohmann, Uta: see *Schäfer, Peter*

Loopik, M. van (Transl. a. comm.): The Ways of the Sages and the Way of the World. 1991. *Vol. 26.*

Luttikhuizen, Gerard P.: The Revelation of Elchasai. 1985. *Vol. 8.*

Mach, Michael: Entwicklungsstadien des jüdischen Engelglaubens in vor-rabbinischer Zeit. 1992. *Vol. 34.*

Mendels, Doron: The Land of Israel as a Political Concept in Hasmonean Literature. 1987. *Vol. 15.*

Miller, Stuart S.: Sages and Commoners in Late Antique ᾿Erez Israel. 2006. *Vol. 111.*

Moscovitz, Leib: Talmudic Reasoning. 2002. *Vol. 89.*

Mutius, Georg von: see *Schäfer, Peter*

Necker, Gerold: see *Schäfer, Peter*

Netzer, Ehud: The Architecture of Herod, the Great Builder. 2006. *Vol. 117.*

Niehoff, Maren: Philo on Jewish Identity and Culture. 2001. *Vol. 86.*

Noy, David, Alexander Panayotov, and *Hanswulf Bloedhorn* (Ed.): Inscriptiones Judaicae Orientis. Vol. 1: Eastern Europe. 2004. *Vol. 101.*

–, and *Hanswulf Bloedhorn* (Ed.): Inscriptiones Judaicae Orientis. Vol. 3: Syria and Cyprus. 2004. *Vol. 102.*

Olyan, Saul M.: A Thousand Thousands Served Him. 1993. *Vol. 36.*

Oppenheimer, Aharon: Between Rome and Babylon. 2005. *Vol. 108.*

Orlov, Andrei A.: The Enoch-Metatron Tradition. 2005. *Vol. 107.*

Osterloh, Kevin L.: see *Gardner, Gregg*

Otterbach, Rina: see *Schäfer, Peter*

Panayotov, Alexander: see *Noy, David*

Prigent, Pierre: Le Judaisme et l'image. 1990. *Vol. 24.*

Pucci Ben Zeev, Miriam: Jewish Rights in the Roman World. 1998. *Vol. 74.*

Pummer, Reinhard: Early Christian Authors on Samaritans and Samaritanism. 2002. *Vol. 92.*

– The Samaritans in Flavius Josephus. 2009. *Vol. 129.*

Rebiger, Bill / Schäfer, Peter (Ed.): Sefer ha-Razim – Das Buch der Geheimnisse.
Vol. I: Edition. 2009. *Vol. 125.*
Vol. II: Einleitung, Übersetzung und Kommentar. 2010. *Vol. 132.*

Reed, A. Y.: see *Becker, A. H.*

Reeg, Gottfried (Ed.): Die Geschichte von den Zehn Märtyrern. 1985. *Vol. 10.*

– see *Schäfer, Peter*

Reichman, Ronen: Abduktives Denken und talmudische Argumentation. 2005. *Vol. 113.*

–: Sifra und Mishna. 1998. *Vol. 68.*

Renner, Lucie: see *Schäfer, Peter*

Rocca, Samuel: Herod's Judaea. 2008. *Vol. 122.*

Rohrbacher-Sticker, Claudia: see *Schäfer, Peter*

Rubenstein, Jeffrey L. (Ed.): Creation and Composition. 2005. *Vol. 114.*

Salvesen, A. (Ed.): Origen's Hexapla and Fragments.1998. *Vol. 58.*

Salzer, Dorothea M.: Die Magie der Anspielung. 2010. *Vol. 134.*

Samely, Alexander: The Interpretation of Speech in the Pentateuch Targums. 1992. *Vol. 27.*

Schäfer, Peter: Der Bar-Kokhba-Aufstand. 1981. *Vol. 1.*

– Hekhalot-Studien. 1988. *Vol. 19.*

Schäfer, Peter (Ed.): Geniza-Fragmente zur Hekhalot-Literatur. 1984. *Vol. 6.*

– The Bar Kokhba War Reconsidered. 2003. *Vol. 100.*

– see *Goldberg, Arnold*

– in cooperation with *Klaus Herrmann, Rina Otterbach, Gottfried Reeg, Claudia Rohrbacher-Sticker, Guido Weyer:* Konkordanz zur Hekhalot-Literatur. Band 1: 1986. *Vol. 12.*

– Band 2: 1988. *Vol. 13.*

Schäfer, Peter, Margarete Schlüter, and *Hans Georg von Mutius* (Ed.): Synopse zur Hekhalot-Literatur. 1981. *Vol. 2.*

Schäfer, Peter (Ed.) in cooperation with *Hans-Jürgen Becker, Klaus Herrmann, Ulrike Hirschfelder, Gerold Necker, Lucie Renner, Claudia Rohrbacher-Sticker, Stefan Siebers:* Übersetzung der Hekhalot-Literatur. Band 1: §§ 1–80. 1995. *Vol. 46.*

– Band 2: §§ 81–334. 1987. *Vol. 17.*

– Band 3: §§ 335–597. 1989. *Vol. 22.*

– Band 4: §§ 598–985. 1991. *Vol. 29.*

Schäfer, Peter, and *Hans-Jürgen Becker* (Ed.) in cooperation with *Anja Engel, Kerstin Ipta, Gerold Necker, Uta Lohmann, Martina Urban, Gert Wildensee:* Synopse zum Talmud Yerushalmi. Band I/1–2: 1991. *Vol. 31.*

– Band I/3–5: 1992. *Vol. 33.*

– Band I/6–11: 1992. *Vol. 35.*

– Band II/1–4: 2001. *Vol. 82.*

- Band II/5–12: 2001. *Vol. 83.*
- Band III: 1998. *Vol. 67.*
- Band IV: 1995. *Vol. 47.*

Schäfer, Peter, and *Shaul Shaked* (Ed.): Magische Texte aus der Kairoer Geniza. Band 1: 1994. *Vol. 42*
- Band 2: 1997. *Vol. 64.*
- Band 3: 1999. *Vol. 72.*

Schäfer, Peter (Ed.): The Talmud Yerushalmi and Graeco-Roman Culture I. 1998. *Vol. 71.*

Schäfer, Peter, and *Catherine Hezser* (Ed.): The Talmud Yerushalmi and Graeco-Roman Culture II. 2000. *Vol. 79.*

Schäfer, Peter (Ed.): The Talmud Yerushalmi and Graeco-Roman Culture III. 2003. *Vol. 93.*
- see *Rebiger, Bill*

Schlüter, Margarete: see *Goldberg, Arnold*
- see *Schäfer, Peter*

Schmidt, Francis: Le Testament Grec d'Abraham. 1986. *Vol. 11.*

Schröder, Bernd: Die ‚väterlichen Gesetze'. 1996. *Vol. 53.*

Schwartz, Daniel R.: Agrippa I. 1990. *Vol. 23.*

Schwartz, Daniel R. (Ed.): see *Levine, Lee I.*

Schwemer, Anna Maria: Studien zu den frühjüdischen Prophetenlegenden. Vitae Prophetarum. Band I: 1995. *Vol. 49.*
- Band II (mit Beiheft: Synopse zu den Vitae Prophetarum): 1996. *Vol. 50.*

Shahar, Yuval: Josephus Geographicus. 2004. *Vol. 98.*

Shaked, Shaul: see *Gruenwald, I.*
- see *Schäfer, Peter*

Shatzman, Israel: The Armies of the Hasmonaeans and Herod. 1991. *Vol. 25.*

Shayegan, Rahim: see *Bakhos, Carol*

Siebers, Stefan: see *Schäfer, Peter*

Sivertsev, Alexei: Private Households and Public Politics in 3rd – 5th Century Jewish Palestine. 2002. *Vol. 90.*

Spilsbury, Paul: The Image of the Jew in Flavius Josephus' Paraphrase of the Bible. 1998. *Vol. 69.*

Stemberger, Günter: Judaica Minora I. 2010. *Vol. 133.*
- Judaica Minora II. 2010. *Vol. 138.*

Stroumsa, G.G.: see *Gruenwald, I.*

Stuckenbruck, Loren T.: The Book of Giants from Qumran. 1997. *Vol. 63.*

Swartz, Michael D.: Mystical Prayer in Ancient Judaism. 1992. *Vol. 28.*

Sysling, Harry: Tehiyyat Ha-Metim. 1996. *Vol. 57.*

Teppler, Yaakov Y.: Birkat haMinim. 2007. *Vol. 120.*

Tov, Emanuel: Hebrew Bible, Greek Bible, and Qumran. 2008. *Vol. 121.*

Urban, Martina: see *Schäfer, Peter*

Veltri, Giuseppe: Eine Tora für den König Talmai. 1994. *Vol. 41.*
- Magie und Halakha. 1997. *Vol. 62.*

Visotzky, Burton L.: Golden Bells and Pomegranates. 2003. *Vol. 94.*

Wandrey, Irina: „Das Buch des Gewandes" und „Das Buch des Aufrechten". 2004. *Vol. 96.*

Weyer, Guido: see *Schäfer, Peter*

Wewers, Gerd A.: Probleme der Bavot-Traktate. 1984. *Vol. 5.*

Wildensee, Gert: see *Schäfer, Peter*

Wilson, Walter T.: The Mysteries of Rigtheousness. 1994. *Vol. 40.*

Zellentin, Holger Michael: Rabbinic Parodies of Jewish and Christian Literature. 2011. *Vol. 139.*
- see *Iricinschi, Eduard*

For a complete catalogue please write to the publisher
Mohr Siebeck • P.O. Box 2030 • D-72010 Tübingen/Germany
Up-to-date information on the internet at www.mohr.de